ROBERT L. SMITH

Treatment Strategies for Substance and Process ADDICTIONS

AMERICAN COUNSELING
ASSOCIATION
6101 Stevenson Avenue, Suite 600 ■ Alexandria, VA 22304
www.counseling.org

Treatment
Strategies
for Substance
and Process
ADDICTIONS

Copyright © 2015 by the American Counseling Association. All rights reserved. Printed in the United States of America. Except as permitted under the United States Copyright Act of 1976, no part of this publication may be reproduced or distributed in any form or by any means, or stored in a database or retrieval system, without the written permission of the publisher.

AMERICAN COUNSELING ASSOCIATION
6101 Stevenson Avenue, Suite 600
Alexandria, VA 22304

ASSOCIATE PUBLISHER   Carolyn C. Baker

DIGITAL AND PRINT DEVELOPMENT EDITOR   Nancy Driver

PRODUCTION MANAGER   Bonny E. Gaston

COPY EDITOR   Beth Ciha

Cover and text design by Bonny E. Gaston.

LIBRARY OF CONGRESS CATALOGING-IN-PUBLICATION DATA
Treatment strategies for substance and process addictions/[edited by] Robert L. Smith.
  p.; cm.
  Includes bibliographical references and index.
  ISBN 978-1-55620-353-4 (pbk.: alk. paper)
  I. Smith, Robert L. (Robert Leonard), 1943– , editor.   II. American Counseling Association, issuing body.
  [DNLM: 1. Substance-Related Disorders—therapy.   2. Behavior, Addictive—therapy.   3. Evidence-Based Practice—methods. WM 270]
  RC564
  362.29—dc23   2015002551

This text is dedicated to the individuals and families who have experienced substance and process addictions and to the courageous mental health professionals devoted to working and conducting research in treating addictions.

—Robert L. Smith

TABLE OF CONTENTS

TABLE OF CONTENTS

PREFACE

This text describes treatment strategies for working with substance and process addictions. The content of this text goes beyond an introduction to the field of addictions by examining treatment approaches, many of which are evidence based. The contributors, each of whom has clinical experience working with addictions, have thoroughly researched the most current treatment strategies. Readers will find this text a viable option for introductory courses on addictions or for the second course in a sequence of classes in addictions counseling. Students and practitioners will find this book useful in understanding the link between substance and process addictions as well as identifying recommended evidence-based treatment practices.

This book addresses strategies and treatment programs often used with addictions to alcohol, tobacco, cannabis, amphetamines, and prescription drugs. Although a large number of substances are misused, these five represent some of the most prevalent substance addictions. Yet many of the interventions covered in this text can also be successfully applied to other substance addictions. An overview of additional drug addictions treatments is available in a number of textbooks (Capuzzi & Stauffer, 2008; Doweiko, 2012; Stevens & Smith, 2013).

A unique and significant feature of this book is its inclusion of full chapters devoted to the major process addictions, often referred to as *behavioral addictions.* The process addictions covered include gambling, sex, food, work, exercise, shopping, and Internet use. Strategies and treatment programs used with these process addictions are emphasized. This focus on process addictions is timely, as recently researchers, professional groups, and government agencies (e.g., the American Society of Addiction Medicine, National Institute on Drug Abuse, American Psychiatric Association, and Substance Abuse and Mental Health Services Administration) have recognized similarities between process addictions and substance addictions, especially as related to mechanisms in the brain. This recognition has led experts to consider both substance and process addictions as a type of brain disease. This text aims to provide clinicians at all skill levels with a reference for understanding the evolving field of substance and process addictions. In addition, the contributors provide readers with links to supplemental Web-based materials to further enhance comprehension of substance and process treatment, addiction, and supports.

REFERENCES

Capuzzi, D., & Stauffer, M. D. (Eds.). (2008). *Foundations of addictions counseling*. Boston, MA: Allyn & Bacon.

Doweiko, H. (2012). *Concepts of chemical dependency* (8th ed.). Belmont, CA: Brooks/Cole.

Stevens, P., & Smith, R. (2013). *Substance abuse counseling: Theories and techniques* (5th ed). New York, NY: Prentice Hall.

ABOUT THE AUTHOR/EDITOR

Robert L. Smith, PhD, NCC, FPPR, author and editor, is the department chair and professor in the Counseling and Educational Psychology Department at Texas A&M University–Corpus Christi. He is the 63rd president of the American Counseling Association (2014–2015). He serves as the executive director and cofounder of the International Association of Marriage and Family Counselors. He is also a founder of the National Credentialing Academy for Family Therapists. He completed his doctorate at the University of Michigan. As a nationally certified counselor and licensed psychologist, he has worked as a private practitioner in addition to serving as the department chair in three university settings. He has worked with a variety of addiction cases in private practice, consulted with the U.S. Navy in the area of substance abuse, and authored several books and close to 100 professional articles. He is the coeditor of the text *Substance Abuse Counseling: Theory and Practice,* which is in its sixth edition. He is a counseling fellow of the American Counseling Association, a diplomat-fellow in psychopharmacology with the International College of Prescribing Psychologists, and a consultant with the Substance Abuse Program in the U.S. Navy. As an international lecturer, Dr. Smith is currently involved in the development and implementation of graduate programs in counseling and psychology in Latin America.

ABOUT THE CONTRIBUTORS

Richard S. Balkin, PhD, LPC, is professor and coordinator of the Doctoral Program in Counseling at the University of Louisville. He completed his doctorate at the University of Arkansas. He has worked in private clinics and hospital settings with a number of clients diagnosed with an addiction.

Fredericka DeLee, PhD, LPC, is a professional counselor in private practice working with a wide range of client problems, including eating disorders. She resides in San Antonio, Texas.

Tamara Duarte, MS, is a professional counselor in private practice with a specialty in food addictions. She resides in Seattle, Washington.

Dawn Ellison, PhD, is a clinical professor in the Doctor of Professional Counseling program at Mississippi College. She works as a clinician treating a variety of mental health problems.

Kimberly Frazier, PhD, NCC, is an assistant professor in the Counseling and Educational Psychology Department at Texas A&M University–Corpus Christi. In addition to having clinical experience, she has authored a number of professional articles and textbook chapters.

Mark Hagwood, PhD, is a graduate of the Psychology and Counseling Department at Mississippi College. He is in private practice at Turning Point Counseling Services in Ridgeland, Mississippi, specializing in addiction treatment.

Katherine Hilton, PhD, DPC, LPC, is a clinical professor in the Doctor of Professional Counseling program at Mississippi College.

Michele Kerulis, PhD, LPC, CC-AASP, is the director of the Sport and Health Psychology Program at the Adler School of Professional Psychology in Chicago. She has extensive clinical and teaching experience in the area of sport and health psychology.

Todd F. Lewis, PhD, LPC, NCC, is an associate professor of counselor education at North Dakota State University. He also served in this capacity in the Counseling and Educational Development Department at the University of North Carolina at Greensboro. In addition to having clinical experience, he has taught and authored articles in the area of drug addictions.

Summer M. Reiner, PhD, LMHC, NCC, is an associate professor in the Department of Counselor Education at The College at Brockport, State University of New York. In addition to having clinical experience in counseling, she is the author of numerous articles and textbook chapters.

Helena G. Rindone, MS, is a faculty member in the Counseling Department at the University of Wisconsin–River Falls and a doctoral candidate at Texas A&M University–Corpus Christi. She has an extensive history of working with clients with drug addictions.

Stephen Southern, EdD, LPC, is professor and chair in the Department of Psychology and Counseling at Mississippi College. Over close to 35 years he has integrated the roles of clinician, supervisor, consultant, administrator, and educator. He has also served as a clinical consultant to several hospitals and residential treatment centers in the United States and China.

Joshua C. Watson, PhD, LPC, is an associate professor in the Counseling and Educational Psychology Department at Texas A&M University–Corpus Christi. In addition to having clinical experience, he is a prolific author of professional articles, book chapters, and textbooks.

ACKNOWLEDGMENTS

I wish to thank the professors and practitioners who will be using this text along with those who provided feedback during its publication process. Without the insight and wisdom of professionals in the field of addictions, this text would not have been possible.

Thanks to Carolyn Baker and the publications team at the American Counseling Association for pressing to keep timelines and for carefully editing this text. Their support and encouragement are very much appreciated. In addition to the staff of the American Counseling Association, I would also like to thank two doctoral students, Shanice Armstrong and Rachel Henesy, for their assistance with this text.

Special thanks go out to the contributors for their expertise and patience. Their clinical experience, research savvy, and writing skills are what make this a state-of-the-art text that emphasizes treatment strategies for both substance and process addictions.

CHAPTER 1

ADDICTIONS: AN OVERVIEW

Robert L. Smith

STUDENT LEARNING OUTCOMES

At the conclusion of this chapter students will

1. Be able to define addictions
2. Identify the criteria used when defining addictions
3. Distinguish between substance and process addictions
4. Identify the etiology and prevalence of addictions
5. Identify addiction treatment strategies, interventions, and programs
6. Identify practitioner characteristics considered essential when working with addictions

CASE AND CASE DISCUSSION

Individuals who directly or indirectly experience the chaos associated with addictions come from all sectors of society. The case of Angie, a 34-year-old Caucasian woman, represents the vast number of individuals who have struggled with and lost their lives to co-occurring addictions. The particulars of this case resemble those of family members, friends, neighbors, colleagues, supervisors, doctors, homeless individuals, and others across the globe who have been, or currently are, severely impacted by multiple addictions.

Angie, a 34-year-old Caucasian woman, experienced a high-risk lifestyle. As a bright, attractive, and entertaining young person she enjoyed the attention of others, and as an impulsive risk taker she exhibited minimal restraint in satisfying her personal needs. Angie had been a popular and smart, capricious adolescent. Her energy and athleticism were assets that had helped her gain recognition as a cheerleader and member of the debate team. She craved the attention of others and took pleasure in being recognized. She also enjoyed the excitement and the high from using alcohol, marijuana, cocaine,

1

and mixed drugs. Her obsession with weight and her personal appearance led to bulimic episodes that were preceded by negative self-talk. Body image and weight were life-long concerns.

Family stressors existed throughout Angie's adolescent years that had affected her development. Angie's father, a gifted athlete, introduced her to golf when she was 12 years old. Angie initially enjoyed the attention provided by her father and her success as a young golfer. She enjoyed the high of being recognized as an up-and-coming athlete within her age group. She was victorious in several tournaments. She worked hard and participated in several golf seminars and intense practice sessions. However, the attention given to Angie by her father and family expectations led her to withdraw from both her family and golf.

The stress placed on Angie by her family and the competition was overwhelming. An additional family stressor, however, was more significant. After practice sessions, Angie would sit with her father, often on his lap, discussing golf and how she was growing up so fast. This time together led to fondling and inappropriate touching by her father. Angie at first was confused but soon realized that something was wrong. She eventually quit golf and distanced herself from her father. She soon withdrew from all of her family members, including her mother, who she felt was aware of but did nothing to stop her husband's behavior.

With excellent grades and a record of leadership, Angie was offered several college scholarships. She selected a university known for its communications department, theatrical productions, and social life. Both students and professors immediately noticed Angie as an attractive, radiant, and fun individual. During her first semester, she was invited to audition for acting roles in the department's theatrical productions. For Angie, it was exciting to be viewed on campus and within the community as a future entertainer.

While in college, Angie misused substances, mainly alcohol and marijuana. Her exposure in local productions, along with some nude modeling, attracted Hollywood associates. These contacts led to auditions for television commercials. Angie's new lifestyle provided access to cocaine, methamphetamines, and designer drugs. Angie also frequently mixed alcohol with other drugs that had initially been prescribed to relieve anxiety.

Angie was popular and met influential executives in the entertainment field. Her contacts led to additional commercials and minor roles in television. She craved recognition and imagined herself in movies.

After years of drug abuse and violent relationships, Angie experienced health issues, career disappointment, and financial problems. Following the stress of an abortion, she became depressed and viewed herself as a failure. Angie lost hope for the future she once imagined. Her severed relationships from family and friends further contributed to her depression. Feelings of being used by others led to distrust and withdrawal from society. Angie continued abusing alcohol and prescription medications, even when receiving help from psychiatrists, psychologists, substance abuse counselors, and family therapists. Angie was hospitalized following a suicide attempt. She attended, but was reluctant to participate in, a mandated inpatient program for substance dependence. Resenting these treatment attempts, Angie with-

VMarvel95@gmail.com

P@ssword 1

continued to self-medicate with alcohol and
alone and craving drugs. Her health deterio-
ite, weight loss, muscle loss, loss of strength,
and kidney failure. The 15-plus years of drug
gie's body and hijacked her brain. While in
and out of consciousness. Angie died at the

look at someone whose life ended as the result
ody broke down because of her habitual abuse
cked by the pleasure she craved as the result of
substance and process addictions. The continuous mixing of drugs caused permanent harm to her brain and body. She craved substances and the high obtained from a repeated behavior pattern. Angie's drug addiction and the behavior pattern used to gain personal recognition became her top priority, despite physical, psychological, career, and social consequences.

Both substance and process addictions are presented in the case of Angie. Co-occurring addictions are frequent, as process and substance addictions work together, influencing the continuation of the self-defeating behavior and substance misuse. Treatment therefore takes more time and is complex.

After reviewing this case, one might conclude that the professionals and treatment programs failed Angie. Treatment attempts, whether individual, group, or multidimensional, seemed to have little or no effect on her misuse of drugs or her self-defeating behaviors. Interventions also failed to provide Angie with a sense of hope or relief from her depression. Coping strategies, if learned, were not enacted. This case thus emphasizes the complex nature of addictions.

In this chapter, I first review genetic influences, environmental influences, family factors, stress/trauma factors, and other factors that play a role in the addictions process, with a focus on the brain. Then I address the practitioner characteristics considered necessary when working with clients who have addictions. I conclude the chapter by discussing evidence-based practices and treatment strategies/interventions.

ADDICTION DEFINED

The term *addiction* is derived from the Latin *addīcō* meaning "enslaved by" or "bound to," and for many individuals like Angie, this derivative has meaning. The term *addiction* is frequently attached to a substance and viewed as dependence. Opium and morphine were two of the first addictive substances identified because of misuse of prescriptions. Society today often also characterizes individuals who participate in repetitive behaviors as being addicted. Thus, the term *addiction* currently applies to the misuse of alcohol, other drugs, and substances and to a large number of behavior patterns. It is safe to say that a large number of individuals can be viewed as being addicted to something. Perhaps someone you know has been accused of having a food addiction, such as to chocolate, ice cream, coffee, or a certain brand of soda. Maybe you know someone who is addicted to golf or to a special series on television. The conversational use of the term *addiction* has convoluted its meaning and definition.

Scientifically speaking, individuals are considered addicted when they relentlessly pursue a sensation or activity, whether it is a substance such as alcohol or a behavior like gambling, despite consequences to their health or well-being (W. R. Miller, Forcehimes, & Zweben, 2011). Similarly, *addiction* has been defined as the condition of being habitually or compulsively occupied with or involved in something. W. R. Miller et al. (2011) identified three kinds of actions that define an addiction: (a) an action that is habitual, done regularly, and repeated; (b) an action that appears to be compulsive in nature and at least partially outside of one's conscious control; and (c) an action that does not necessarily involve a drug.

The American Society of Addiction Medicine (ASAM; 2011) refers to addiction as follows:

> Addiction is a primary, chronic disease involving brain reward, motivation, memory and related circuitry; it can lead to relapse, progressive development, and the potential for fatality if not treated. While pathological use of alcohol and, more recently, psychoactive substances have been accepted as addictive diseases, developing brain science has set the stage for inclusion of the process addictions, including food, sex, shopping and gambling problems, in a broader definition of addiction as set forth by the American Society of Addiction Medicine in 2011. (D. E. Smith, 2012, p. 1)

ASAM credits several years of research for providing the foundation for its definition of addictions, stating that brain damage is caused by the long-term abuse of a substance.

The National Institute on Drug Abuse (NIDA; 2012b) has put forth the following definition of *addiction:*

> Addiction is a chronic, often relapsing brain disease that causes compulsive drug seeking and use, despite harmful consequences to the addicted individual and to those around him or her. Although the initial decision to take drugs is voluntary for most people, the brain changes that occur over time challenge an addicted person's self control and hamper his or her ability to resist intense impulses to take drugs.
>
> Fortunately, treatments are available to help people counter addiction's powerful disruptive effects. Research shows that combining addiction treatment medications with behavioral therapy is the best way to ensure success for most patients. Treatment approaches that are tailored to each patient's drug abuse patterns and any co-occurring medical, psychiatric, and social problems can lead to sustained recovery and a life without drug abuse.
>
> Similar to other chronic, relapsing diseases, such as diabetes, asthma, or heart disease, drug addiction can be managed successfully. And as with other chronic diseases, it is not uncommon for a person to relapse and begin abusing drugs again. Relapse, however, does not signal treatment failure—rather, it indicates that treatment should be reinstated or adjusted or that an alternative treatment is needed to help the individual regain control and recover. (NIDA, 2012b, "What Is Drug Addiction," paras. 1–3)

When referring to drugs, NIDA (2012d) also has defined addiction as a brain disease:

> Addiction is defined as a chronic, relapsing brain disease that is characterized by compulsive drug seeking and use, despite harmful consequences. It is considered

a brain disease because drugs change the brain; they change its structure and how it works. These brain changes can be long lasting and can lead to many harmful, often self-destructive, behaviors. (NIDA, 2012d, "What Is Drug Addiction," para. 1)

The *Diagnostic and Statistical Manual of Mental Disorders, Fifth Edition* (*DSM–5;* American Psychiatric Association [APA], 2013) does not define addiction, nor does it advocate using the term as a diagnosis. In fact, the *DSM–5* states that use of the term *addiction* in diagnosis could potentially create a negative connotation (APA, 2013, p. 485). Under the category of "Substance-Related and Addictive Disorders" in the *DSM–5,* however, one finds addiction to 10 separate classes of drugs along with the process addiction of gambling cited as disorders. Gambling is also referred to as a behavioral addiction in the *DSM–5,* in the same vein as Internet gaming, sex, exercise, and shopping. Because it has been researched more extensively than other behavioral addictions, gambling is the only process addiction covered in detail in the *DSM–5* under the heading "Non-Substance-Related Disorders." A diagnostic criterion is provided to help assess the severity level of gambling as a disorder.

Research indicates that addictive behaviors occur in part as the result of a neurotransmission process involving interactions within the reward circuitry system of the brain (ASAM, 2011). Changes in brain chemistry and the memory system seem to evolve from one's addiction, whether it is to a behavior or a substance. The reward center in the addicted brain is stimulated and overtaxed, often by the release of dopamine. The addict keeps chasing the high, whether it be the up-and-down rollercoaster of gambling or the highs and lows of cocaine ("What Is a Process Addiction?" 2012).

According to the *DSM–5,* all drugs taken in excess have in common the direct activation of the brain reward system, which is involved in the reinforcement of behaviors and the production of memories, producing a pleasure referred to as a *high* (APA, 2013, p. 481). Moreover, gambling behaviors activate reward systems similar to the effects of a drug. The implication is that behavioral (process) addictions, such as addictions to sex, the Internet, shopping, exercise, and work, operate within the brain in a manner similar to addictions to alcohol and other drugs. Indeed, findings have shown that these repetitive behaviors produce similar chemical changes in the brain to those associated with the use of drugs. And like a drug, the continued use of a behavior can get out of control, and attempts to stop can result in withdrawal symptoms, including anxiety, worry, and irritation. Supporting the idea that substance and process addictions are brain diseases are findings that changes in brain circuits are induced by thoughts and behavior patterns long before a behavior or drug becomes addictive. However, further research is needed before experts can validate the notion of process addictions as a brain disease.

Individuals addicted to the excitement of viewing pornography on the Internet, gambling, shopping, or exercise, for example, are believed to be at risk for developing a tolerance that manifests itself by taking greater risks in order to reach a high similar to or greater than what has previously been experienced. Perhaps the neurological reward and memory system of the brain changes, and becomes highjacked, by repetitious thoughts and behavior patterns, similar to what takes place when using a drug. The craving experienced by someone who is addicted to a behavior becomes prominent, similar to the craving for a drug. Thus, both substance and process addictions involve a loss of control and dysfunctional decision making. The behavior or substance becomes the individual's lifeline for survival. In both cases, use of the behavior or drug continues despite consequences.

CRITERIA FOR ADDICTION

Not everyone who experiments with drugs, gambles, or spends time on the Internet becomes addicted. In fact, only a small percentage actually become addicted. Several groups of scientists have studied the addiction process, attempting to identify at what point one actually becomes addicted. Professionals, including medical doctors, psychiatrists, psychologists, counselors, and social workers, have suggested criteria to use to identify when an individual has become addicted. One marker of an addiction involves the excessive use of a substance or behavior despite consequences related to work, home, finances, health, the legal system, relationships, or one's general well-being. Consequences related to aspects of everyday life play a major role in criteria used to assess addictions. However, caution is suggested when diagnosing and labeling individuals who are misusing drugs or using repetitious behaviors. In addition, one should consider that few individuals prefer the label of *addict* or being categorized as dependent.

The *DSM–5* suggests a cautionary stance when using the term *addiction*, realizing its potential for having a negative connotation. The *DSM–5* discusses substance use disorders as consisting of a cluster of cognitive, behavioral, and physiological symptoms affecting individuals who continue using a substance (APA, 2013, p. 483). The diagnostic criteria for alcohol use disorders in the *DSM–5* include loss of control, unsuccessful attempts to stop or cut down, tolerance, excessive use of time and behaviors to obtain the substance, strong urges or cravings, withdrawal when quitting the use of the substance, and continued use despite consequences (APA, 2013, pp. 490–491). When six or more of the 11 symptoms are present, the person's condition is considered severe. At this point perhaps one could say that the individual meets the standard for a substance addiction.

The category "Non-Substance-Related Disorders" in the *DSM–5* includes gambling. Gambling is the sole process addiction included in the *DSM–5*, as it is more widely researched than addictions to Internet use, exercise, work, and other behaviors. Nine symptoms are used as the diagnostic criteria for assessing a gambling disorder (APA, 2013, p. 585). A gambling disorder is considered severe if eight or nine of the criteria are met. At this point perhaps the individual meets the standard for a gambling addiction.

Table 1.1 provides a generic listing of symptoms for assessing process addictions. Criteria were adapted from a template used to identify a gambling disorder. It is suggested that the diagnostic criteria in Table 1.1 be revised in accordance with each behavioral addiction.

A number of well-trained health care professionals make decisions to assess whether an individual has reached a threshold of being addicted, whether it is to a substance or behavior. Addiction counselors, physicians, psychologists, nurses, social workers, and therapists are some of the clinicians trained to make these assessments. Most professionals will refer to the *DSM–5* or the *International Classification of Diseases* (*ICD*) when making their assessments. Like the

TABLE 1.1   DIAGNOSTIC CRITERIA FOR ASSESSING PROCESS DISORDERS

A persistent and recurrent problematic behavior leading to clinically significant impairment or distress, as indicated by the individual exhibiting four (or more) of the following in a 12-month period:

1. Needs to increase the frequency of the behavior in order to achieve the desired excitement.
2. Is restless or irritable when attempting to cut down on the behavior.
3. Has made repeated unsuccessful efforts to control, cut back, or stop the behavior.
4. Is often preoccupied with the behavior (e.g., has persistent thoughts of reliving past experiences, handicapping or planning the next venture, thinking of a way to partake in the behavior).
5. Often engages in the behavior when feeling distressed (e.g., helpless, guilty, anxious, depressed).
6. After unsuccessfully reaching an anticipated high when participating in the behavior, tries riskier scenarios when using the behavior.
7. Lies to conceal the extent of involvement with the behavior.
8. Has jeopardized or lost a significant relationship, job, or educational or career opportunities by repeating the behavior.
9. Relies on others to minimize the consequences of the repeated behavior.

Note. Adapted from *Diagnostic and Statistical Manual of Mental Disorders, Fifth Edition* (p. 585), by American Psychiatric Association, 2013, Arlington, VA: American Psychiatric Association. Copyright 2013 by the American Psychiatric Association. Reprinted with permission. All rights reserved.

DSM–5, the *ICD-10* and previous manuals by the World Health Organization have not consistently used the word *addiction* in their diagnoses. However, terminology and categories differ between the *ICD* and the *DSM*. For instance, the *DSM* includes seven criteria for substance dependence and the *ICD* six. Furthermore, in the area of substance abuse the *ICD* has used the concept of "harmful," which focuses on damage caused by a substance to one's physical and mental health. Yet despite these differences, both manuals are helpful in the diagnosis process.

Professionals are also guided by research and documents provided by organizations such as ASAM and NIDA, as well as a number of other professional publications and organizations (see "Resources" at the conclusion of this chapter).

ASAM (2011) identified several behaviors and subsequent consequences that are associated with an addiction:

- Excessive use of and/or engagement in addictive behaviors, at higher frequencies and/or quantities than the person intended, often associated with a persistent desire for and unsuccessful attempts at behavioral control
- Excessive time lost in substance use or recovering from the effects of substance use and/or engagement in addictive behaviors, with significant adverse impact on social and occupational functioning (e.g., the development of interpersonal relationship problems or the neglect of responsibilities at home, school, or work)

- Continued use and/or engagement in addictive behaviors despite the presence of persistent or recurrent physical or psychological problems that may have been caused or exacerbated by substance use and/or related addictive behaviors
- A narrowing of the behavioral repertoire focusing on rewards that are part of addiction
- An apparent lack of ability and/or readiness to take consistent, ameliorative action despite the recognition of problems

ASAM (2011) further identified the following cognitive and emotional changes one should consider during the assessment process.

Cognitive Changes
- Preoccupation with substance use
- Altered evaluations of the relative benefits and detriments associated with drugs or rewarding behaviors
- The inaccurate belief that problems experienced in one's life are attributable to other causes rather than being a predictable consequence of addiction

Emotional Changes
- Increased anxiety, dysphoria, and emotional pain
- Increased sensitivity to stressors associated with the recruitment of brain stress systems, such that things seem more stressful as a result
- Difficulty identifying feelings, distinguishing between feelings and the bodily sensations of emotional arousal, and describing feelings to other people (sometimes referred to as *alexithymia*)

Findings by ASAM can be helpful when assessing patients and can serve as a much needed guide throughout the diagnosis process. Hartney (2011a) identified the following common symptoms and signs associated with addictions:

- Extreme mood changes (happy, sad, excited, anxious, etc.)
- Sleeping a lot more or less than usual or at different times of the day or night
- Changes in energy (e.g., unexpectedly and extremely tired or energetic)
- Weight loss or weight gain
- Unexpected and persistent coughs or sniffles
- Seeming unwell at certain times and better at other times
- Pupils of the eyes seeming smaller or larger than usual
- Secretiveness
- Lying
- Stealing
- Financial unpredictability, perhaps having large amounts of cash at times but no money at all at other times
- Changes in social groups, new and unusual friends, odd cell phone conversations
- Repeated unexplained outings, often with a sense of urgency
- The presence of drug paraphernalia, such as unusual pipes, cigarette papers, small weighing scales, and so on
- Stashes of drugs, often in small plastic, paper, or foil packages

Engs (2012) noted the following common characteristics of an addict:

1. The person becomes *obsessed* with (constantly thinks of) the object, activity, or substance.
2. The person will seek it out or *engage in the behavior even though it is causing harm* (physical problems; poor work or study performance; problems with friends, family, fellow workers).
3. The person will *compulsively engage* in the activity, that is, do the activity over and over even if he or she does not want to, and finds it difficult to stop.
4. On cessation of the activity, the person often experiences *withdrawal* symptoms. These can include irritability, craving, restlessness, or depression.
5. The person does not appear to have control over when, how long, or how much he or she will continue the behavior (*loss of control*; e.g., he drinks six beers when he only wanted one, she buys eight pairs of shoes when she only needed a belt, he ate the whole box of cookies, etc.).
6. The person often *denies problems* resulting from his or her engagement in the behavior, even though others can see the negative effects.
7. The person *hides the behavior* after family or close friends have mentioned their concern (e.g., hides food under the bed, hides alcohol bottles in the closet, does not show his or her spouse the credit card bill, etc.).
8. The person reports a *blackout* for the time he or she was engaging in the behavior (e.g., doesn't remember how much or what was bought, how much was lost gambling, how many miles were run on a sore foot, what was done at the party while drinking).
9. The person experiences *depression*. Because depression is common in individuals with addictive behaviors, it is important to make an appointment with a physician to find out what is going on.
10. The person has *low self-esteem*, feels anxious if he or she *does not have control over the environment*, and comes from a *psychologically or physically abusive family*.

It is suggested that in addition to using the *DSM–5*, clinicians refer to listings as those from Engs (2012) and Hartney (2011a) during the assessment process.

In *Treating Addiction: A Guide for Professionals*, W. R. Miller et al. (2011) suggested a set of guidelines for assessing addictions (see Exhibit 1.1). The first dimension provides a baseline by identifying the number of occasions on which one engages in the addiction. Information on variability and other specifics related to drug use can be further queried. Under the category "Problems," one obtains information about the consequences resulting from the addiction. Specificity is emphasized. Tolerance, or the body's adjustment to a drug or activity, is examined under the category "Physical Adaptation." Questions such as the following are asked: Does the patient require more of the drug in order to receive the same reward? Does the patient need to take more risks in order to obtain the same high?

Under the category "Behavioral Dependence," the clinician focuses on the role of the drug or behavior. For example, does the patient depend on the drug for his or her very existence, or is it used as a way of coping? Is use of the drug or behavior becoming detrimental to other activities? Under "Medical Harm," physiological and psychological changes are examined. "Cognitive Impairment" involves as-

```
                          EXHIBIT 1.1
                             Use
Low------------------------------------------------------------High
                           Problems
Low------------------------------------------------------------High
                      Physical Adaptation
Low------------------------------------------------------------High
                    Behavioral Dependence
Low------------------------------------------------------------High
                         Medical Harm
Low------------------------------------------------------------High
                    Cognitive Impairment
Low------------------------------------------------------------High
                    Motivation for Change
Low------------------------------------------------------------High
```

sessing changes in brain chemistry, frequently affecting one's memory, decision making, and reward seeking. The final dimension, "Motivation for Change," assesses whether the person recognizes a problem or a potential problem related to the continued use of the drug or behavior.

In applying the dimensions of addictions, W. R. Miller et al. (2011) believe that it is possible to view addiction on a continuum. However, this view, supported by the World Health Organization and the National Institute on Alcohol Abuse and Alcoholism (NIAAA), remains controversial.

Table 1.1 and Exhibit 1.1 provide clinicians with tools to assess addictions. A wide range of theories and hypotheses regarding addictions and methods of assessment are available in the literature. For example, *Theories on Drug Abuse: Selected Contemporary Perspectives* (Lettieri, Sayers, & Pearson, 1980) identified 43 theories of chemical addiction and 15 methods of treatment. What is interesting is that most of the theories include similar characteristics that are associated with the process of becoming addicted. This process includes the following:

1. Trying a behavior, such as gambling, or a drug, such as alcohol, for the first time, often voluntarily
2. Expecting to obtain a reward or some pleasure from the activity pursued or substance ingested
3. Being reinforced, or rewarded, with a sense of satisfaction
4. Enjoying a pleasurable feeling as a result of an increase in the neurotransmitter dopamine (dopamine floods the brain faster and with greater potentiality than what can occur as the result of everyday activities)
5. Creating a memory of the pleasurable process and remembering the resultant reward produced by the activity or drug
6. Wanting to experience more of the pleasurable event, obsessively recalling the behavior or substance that created the sought-after high

7. Minimizing the natural production of dopamine in the brain as it waits, and craves, for the real thing, which is the behavior or drug that produced the pleasurable response
8. Losing control as the activity or drug takes over
9. Allowing the activity or drug to become the highest priority in one's life
10. Viewing the activity or drug as necessary for survival
11. Becoming desperate and taking greater risks in order to continue the behavior or ingest the drug
12. Experiencing the loss of family, friends, one's health, and one's career
13. Altering the mechanisms of the brain, including disruption of decision making, memory, and judgment

SUBSTANCE AND PROCESS ADDICTIONS

The concept of addiction has most often been associated with the continued misuse of a substance. *Addiction* has also been used synonymously with *dependence*, typically involving drugs such as alcohol, heroin, cocaine, marijuana, or prescription medications. Substances of addiction have increased over time and now include an array of designer drugs, paint, kerosene, glue, gasoline, funeral balm, food products, feces, wood, chalk, cat hair, dirt, paste, drywall board, toilet paper, and so on. There is an unlimited number of substances to which an individual can be addicted. This includes anything one can ingest, sniff, snort, or place in the body. Experimentation with these substances is often not consequential, particularly when tried over a brief period of time. However, the consistent misuse of any substance over a long period of time can lead to an addiction.

The etiology, prevalence, treatment, and consequences of substance addictions have been given significant attention during the past several decades. Yet process addictions, also referred to as *behavioral addictions*, have only recently gained attention within the public and scientific community. The distinguishing feature of process addictions is that they do not typically involve a substance. Process addictions often co-occur with a drug addiction. It is the high produced by a continued activity or behavior, not a drug, that identifies a process addiction. Gambling is the most studied of the process addictions. An individual addicted to gambling is addicted to the pleasure, excitement, or high that takes place when participating in this activity. When natural everyday activities are unable to compete with the high (mainly the rush of dopamine) produced by gambling, the individual is on the road to becoming addicted. The individual begins to crave the high that only gambling can produce. When he or she continues to participate in the act of gambling, including the anticipation of gambling, the addict experiences changes in brain functioning. At this point, despite the consequences, the individual continues the behavior.

Process addictions frequently mentioned include exercise, hand washing, Internet use, love, money, relationships, self-injurious behaviors, sex, shopping, sleep, spending, stealing, television, trichotillomania, video games, and work. Participation in these behaviors does not mean that one is, or will become, addicted. Individuals who maturely enjoy these activities in ways that have not produced negative consequences should not be referred to as addicts. "Addictions List" (n.d.) shows the scope of potential addictions, both substance and process.

THE PREVALENCE OF ADDICTIONS

Prevalence is the epidemiological term for the percentage of a population identified as having a specific problem or addiction. Prevalence rates for process addictions have been infrequently reported because of a lack of research, whereas prevalence rates for drug abuse in the United States and across the globe have been widely reported.

Drug Addictions: Alcohol and Nicotine

Substance use and misuse is costly. NIDA (2012b) estimates the cost of drug addiction in the United States to be more than $600 billion yearly in health care, law enforcement, subsidized treatment, and prevention efforts. Additional costs to individual patients and their families are significant but difficult to calculate.

The National Survey on Drug Use and Health (Substance Abuse and Mental Health Services Administration, 2012) reported an increase in the use of illicit drugs from 2009 to 2010, with 2010 having the highest reported drug use since 2002. The survey, released in September 2011, indicated that marijuana use was the reason for the overall increase in drug use, with about 17.4 million Americans using marijuana in 2010.

Alcohol remains one of the most prevalent drugs used and abused in the United States. Results of the Monitoring the Future survey revealed that 25% of 18-year-olds, 42% of 20-year-olds, and 20% of 50-year-olds reported engaging in alcohol use (five or more drinks at least once in the past 2 weeks; Johnston, O'Malley, Bachman, & Schulenberg, 2011). These findings cite the use of alcohol but fail to identify problem drinking. It has been estimated that approximately 10% of the adult population in the United States abused or was dependent on alcohol in the past 12 months (Pirkola, Poikolainen, & Lonnqvist, 2006; Teesson, Baillie, Lynskey, Manor, & Degenhardt, 2006). Alcohol use (binge and heavy drinking) was the same in 2010 as in 2009 but with a decline in drinking among adolescents ages 12 to 17.

The prevalence of tobacco use and other drug use has also been studied by the Monitoring the Future research group (Johnston et al., 2011). Daily cigarette smoking (20 or more days in the past 30 days) was reported by 11.4% of 18-year-olds and 17% of 50-year-olds (Johnston et al., 2011). Daily cigarette smoking, considered tobacco addiction (dependence) among older teenagers, has been reported among 6% to 8% of the U.S. population (Chen, Sheth, Elliott, & Yeager, 2004; Young et al., 2002). Studies have found prevalence rates for tobacco addiction of 9.6% among college students and 4.4% among incoming college students (Cook, 1987; Dierker et al., 2007). Other studies have reported a prevalence rate of 12.8% for tobacco addiction among a national sample of U.S. adults (Grant, Hasin, Chou, Stinson, & Dawson, 2004). Goodwin, Keyes, and Hasin (2009) reported prevalence rates of 21.6% and 17.8% for tobacco addiction among male and female adults in the general U.S. population. Tobacco dependence among adults in the United States has been estimated at 15% (Sussman, Lisha, & Griffiths, 2011).

Process Addictions

There are limited research findings on the prevalence of process addictions, which are more difficult than substance addictions to define and measure (Gambino,

2006). Of the process addictions, gambling is the most widely researched (Griffiths, 2009). As a disorder, gambling had a prevalence rate in 2012 of 0.2% to 0.3% in the general population and a rate of 0.4% to 1.0% over a lifetime (APA, 2013, p. 587). A gambling addiction has been reported among 1% to 3% of adults in the United States (Bondolfi, Osiek, & Ferrero, 2000; Griffiths, 2009; Volberg, Gupta, Griffiths, Olason, & Delfabbro, 2010). Males have a higher prevalence of gambling addiction than females, and African Americans are believed to have a higher rate of gambling addiction than Whites, who are estimated to have a higher rate than Hispanics. Note, however, that any study or estimate related to gambling or any other process addiction needs to be critically examined, keeping the following in mind: origin of the study, date of the investigation, sample size, sample demographics, geography, and culture. Estimates of the prevalence of the process addictions covered in this text vary based on the year of the study and the sample.

A limited amount of data have been reported for sexual addictions and food disorders. Kaplan and Krueger (2010) estimated that approximately 3% to 6% of adults in the United States have a sexual addiction. Anorexia nervosa, a food disorder, is believed to have had a prevalence rate in 2012 of approximately 4%, with most of those affected being female (APA, 2013, p. 341). Prevalence rates for bulimia nervosa in 2012 were approximately 1% to 1.5%, again with most of those affected being female (APA, 2013, p. 347). Earlier studies on food disorders among older teens and adults reported prevalence rates between 1% and 2% (Allison, Grilo, Masheb, & Stunkard, 2005; Gadalla & Piran, 2007; Gleaves & Carter, 2008).

Early studies on video gaming found that 10.3% of students in Grades 7–12 in Ontario, Canada, reported having a video gaming problem (Keowan, 2007). Additional studies reported that 6% to 10% of university students had an Internet addiction (Grüsser, Thalemann, & Griffiths, 2007; Kubey, Lavin, & Barrows, 2001; Morahan-Martin & Schumacher, 2000).

Sussman et al. (2011) reported a study by Keowan (2007) that found that 31% of working Canadians between the ages of 19 and 64 viewed themselves as workaholics. This percentage is one of the highest recorded in studies of self-identified workaholics. The prevalence rate of workaholism among college graduates has been reported at 8% to 17.5% (Burke, 2000; MacLaren & Best, 2010). An estimated prevalence rate for workaholism in the U.S. adult population is 10% (Sussman et al., 2011).

Previous studies have estimated that exercise addiction affects 3% to 5% of college students (Allegre, Souville, Therme, & Griffiths, 2006; D. Downs, Hausenblas, & Nigg, 2004; Terry, Szabo, & Griffiths, 2004). However, one study of college students reported prevalence rates at 21.8 to 25.6% (MacLaren & Best, 2010).

Estimates of shopping addictions have ranged from 1% to 6% among adults (Freimuth et al., 2008; Koran, Faber, Aboujaoude, Large, & Serpe, 2006). Koran et al. (2006) estimated the prevalence rate of shopping addiction in the United States at 6%.

Gambling, work, sex, video games, and exercise have been ranked as the top five process addictions according to prevalence (Griffiths, 2009). Further studies will reveal changes in ranking among process addictions, with Internet and gaming addictions becoming more prevalent. Additional information on prevalence estimates for process addictions is available in subsequent chapters of this text.

In summary, a greater number of studies have focused on substance addictions compared to process addictions. Individual researchers have reported prevalence rates of process addictions, but large-scale studies by government agencies such as NIDA and the Substance Abuse and Mental Health Services Administration are lacking. Current data on prevalence rates of process addictions need to be reviewed with care, considering the following:

1. Process addictions lack agreed-on, identifiable criteria.
2. Process addictions are more difficult to identify than drug addictions.
3. Consequences of process addictions are more subtle than those of drug addictions.
4. Studies examining the cost and prevalence of process addictions are not government funded.
5. The impact of process addictions, or repeated behaviors, on brain functioning requires further research to be convincingly viewed as a disease.
6. Process addictions are less likely than substance addictions to cause a breakdown of bodily organs, leading to death.

Many of the same indicators are present with behavioral addictions as with drug addictions. In both cases, loved ones, friends, and families suffer the emotional pain caused by the addiction, as well as a loss of resources. Individuals' jobs, careers, reputations, social lives, marriages, and relationships with children and others are severely affected or destroyed. Despite these consequences, individuals continue to repeat the behavior to the point that little else matters in their life. The repeated behavior (process addiction) becomes a top priority. As with a drug addiction, individuals are convinced of the need to continue the behavior in order to survive. Similar chemical and biological changes seem to occur with both types of addictions, taking it out of the individual's control ("What Is a Process Addiction?" 2012).

Treatment is necessary for both substance and process addictions. Yet the results of a 2010 study of 67,500 civilians revealed that only 11.2% of individuals who needed treatment for a substance addiction actually received help at a specialty facility (Substance Abuse and Mental Health Services Administration, 2011). Research studies on treatment provided for those suffering from process addictions are unavailable. There is reason to believe that the percentage of individuals who receive help for process addictions from a specialty facility is less than the 11.2% currently reported for substance addictions.

THE ETIOLOGY OF ADDICTIONS

Addictions, including the road to an addiction, vary widely. The addictive process is complex, including several influencing factors. An individual's mental state, genetics, social status, and experiences influence the addict and the timeline the addiction takes. Despite several theories on the causes of addiction, definitive reasons for why and how one becomes addicted remain a mystery. Several research questions beg investigation: Why is one individual able to drink in moderation whereas another needs to remain abstinent? Why are addictions intergenerational in nature, but only with certain members of a family? To what degree does the specific substance or behavior play a role in determining whether one will become addicted? Longitudinal studies will eventually answer these questions. Some factors currently identified as potential causes of addictions include genetic factors, brain structure and function, environmental factors, and individual development.

NIDA (2010) provided a basic explanation for why people take drugs or become addicted to a particular behavior:

- *To feel good.* Drugs and certain activities produce intense feelings of pleasure. Many individuals want to revisit the pleasurable situation caused by taking a drug or continued involvement in an exciting activity such as gambling or sex. Other effects follow the initial sensation of euphoria, a dopamine rush with drugs. With stimulants such as cocaine, the high is followed by feelings of power, self-confidence, and increased energy, whereas the euphoria caused by opiates such as heroin is followed by feelings of relaxation and satisfaction. In both situations the individual experiences pleasurable feelings. With a process addiction such as gambling, a high is obtained with the thought of winning and the risk involved. With many process addictions, such as gambling, sex, and exercise, the greater the risk, the greater the high produced.
- *To feel better.* Stressful situations occur in the lives of all individuals. The kind and degree of stress plays a role in whether one begins to use drugs or engage in stress-relieving behavior. To relieve stress or to feel better, individuals return to the behavior, such as sex, or the drug, such as marijuana. Soon the behavior or drug is viewed as the only thing that can alleviate their stress.
- *To do better.* Individuals can be drawn to drugs, such as steroids, or behaviors, such as exercise, to enhance their performance. Competition is a driving force to do better. Using chemicals or high-stress exercise programs to enhance or improve athletic or cognitive performance is tempting.
- *To satisfy curiosity.* Statements such as "I'd like to try it just once" or "I wonder what that feeling is like" involve one's curiosity. Unfortunately, the innocent trial of a drug or high-risk behavior can lead to its repeated use and possibly become an addiction. Adolescents are particularly vulnerable because of the strong influence of peer pressure and therefore are more likely to satisfy their curiosity and engage in thrilling and daring behaviors (NIDA, 2008).

Genetic Factors

Genetic factors are believed to account for 50% of an individual's vulnerability to an addiction (Volkow, 2011). DNA is made up of genes that are nearly identical for 99.9% of individuals. However, it is believed that the 0.1% variation contributes to a person's vulnerability to an addiction, as well as to other diseases such as diabetes, heart problems, and stroke (NIDA, 2008). Studies of identical twins have supported the role of genetic properties in vulnerability to addiction. Using a sample of 861 identical twin pairs and 653 fraternal twin pairs, researchers found that when one identical twin was addicted to alcohol, the other twin had a high probability of having the same addiction, although this was not true for nonidentical (fraternal) twins (Enoch & Goldman, 2001; Prescott & Kendler, 1999). Other studies (Enoch & Goldman, 2001; Prescott & Kendler, 1999) have found that children of addicts (to alcohol or other drugs) are 8 times more likely to develop an addiction, supporting the premise that substance addictions seem to run in families as the result of a genetic predisposition. There is speculation that genetics also plays a role in behavioral addictions, despite insufficient research tracing gambling, sex, work, exercise, shopping, and other process addictions to one's genetic makeup.

Addiction as a Brain Disease: Brain Structure and Function

Closely aligned with genetic research are studies related to the brain and its importance in addictions. The brain, weighing approximately 3 pounds, controls and directs just about everything people do, including how they respond to the intake of substances, other people, stress, work, pleasure, loss, disease, and so on. It is therefore understandable that the brain plays a major role in addictions, leading to the identification of addiction as a brain disease. The functioning of the brain as it relates to addictions is demonstrated in Figure 1.1.

Neuroscience research provides evidence that the long-term use of drugs can change brain structure and functioning (NIAAA, 2009; Smith 2013). Changes in brain structure and functioning are also believed to take place with process addictions. Addiction is therefore viewed as a brain disease, as it plays a major role in the disease model of addiction that includes biological, neurological, genetic, and environmental factors (NIDA, 2012d). The definition of disease provides the possible inclusion of both substance and process addictions. Components of the brain, brain functioning, and related concepts are central to the consideration of addiction as a brain disease. Several parts of the brain have been identified as playing a role in the addiction process. However, the midbrain and the frontal cortex (refer to Figure 1.1) have been given the most attention, particularly as related

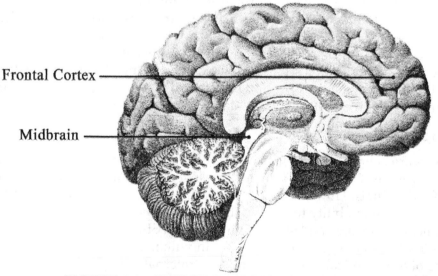

Frontal Cortex

Midbrain

FIGURE 1.1   THE HUMAN BRAIN AND ADDICTION

Note. Two central components of the human brain, the frontal cortex and the midbrain, relate to addiction. Image from http://commons.wikimedia.org/wiki/File:PSM_V46_D168_Mesial_view_of_the_human_brain.jpg

to substance addictions. The midbrain, often referred to as the *lower brain* or *old brain*, is viewed as the area where drugs began. The midbrain does not think and is believed to handle things only in the next 15 seconds in order to survive (Institute for Addiction Studies, 2009). The midbrain tells people to eat and drink, and it is the pleasure system of the brain (Olds & Milner, 1954). The midbrain releases dopamine, a neurotransmitter, a pleasurable reward, induced by drugs as well as other activities and experiences. The excessive flow of dopamine generated by drugs is known as the *dopamine hypothesis.* Dopamine is also released as a reward in process addictions. When a behavior or drug is used over and over again, it is the midbrain's survival characteristic that helps create the craving, placing the drug or activity at the highest priority level for everyday functioning.

The frontal cortex is the most evolved part of the brain. Because it continues to develop throughout adolescence, it is negatively affected by early and continued use of drugs. The frontal cortex makes decisions, serves as the moral compass and conscience, and keeps the midbrain in control (Institute for Addiction Studies, 2009). The frontal cortex is the thinking center of the brain involved with planning, problem solving, and decision making. Imaging research has provided information on the role played by the prefrontal cortex in the regulation of the midbrain reward regions. Neuroimaging has revealed that drug addiction affects the prefrontal cortex as related to self-control, salience attribution, awareness, as well as the erosion of free will (Goldstein & Volkow, 2011). Goldstein and Volkow (2011) emphasized the importance of the prefrontal cortex in drug addiction, postulating that drug-addicted individuals attribute excessive salience to the drug and drug-related cues and insignificant salience to non-drug-related stimuli such as food or social relationships. This change of impaired behavioral control and movement toward impulsivity is hypothesized to take place in the prefrontal cortical brain regions (Patoine, 2007). Addiction, as related to these findings, supports the disease concept and includes disorders of neural pathways. Disorders in neural pathways result in hypofrontality leading to performance decline in the prefrontal cortex and loss of executive functioning (Institute for Addiction Studies, 2009). Evidence suggests that these changes in the brain are the origin of the cognitive and emotional problems of individuals who have an addiction.

Environmental Factors

A wide range of environmental factors, many of which are social, play a role in the addiction process. These include family, friends (peers), socioeconomic status, cultural norms, career, job, stressors, and so on. For an adolescent, social factors involving family, peers, school, and community are of major importance (Lundberg, 2013). A parent's attitude toward drugs is also significant. However, drug use by peers places adolescents at the greatest risk for becoming addicted. Student performance and participation in school are mitigating factors related to drug use, as is the community's overall attitude toward the use of drugs.

Additional factors contributing to an addiction include early substance use. For example, if one tries drugs or participates in a repeated behavior at an early age, there is a greater risk of becoming addicted as an adult. If a young person becomes accustomed to a substance or behavior early in his or her development, it can lead to a habit and eventually to an addiction.

With drugs, the method used to take the drug is often relevant. Injecting, snorting, or smoking drugs tends to facilitate the addiction process. These methods quickly introduce drugs to the brain. But the effect is often short lived, leading the individual to want to use again.

Stress in one's life, early physical or sexual abuse, witnessing violence, and the availability of drugs are additional environmental factors contributing to an addiction (NIDA, 2008). Research with nonhuman primates has demonstrated that levels of dopamine receptors in the brain are influenced by the environment, particularly social factors that lead to the propensity to self-administer drugs (NIDA, 2008).

Individual Development

In the early 1970s, researchers believed that having an addictive personality was responsible for the development of addictive behavior. Then Alan R. Lang (1983) researched personality traits as they related to addiction. Lang concluded that no single set of traits was definitive of an addictive personality. However, he did cite several traits thought to be common among individuals who are addicted, including impulsivity, nonconformity, lower achievement goals, social alienation, stress, deviance, and poor coping skills. Most of the traits attributed to addicts were negative. The negativity of these traits was believed to have affected treatment and disposition by individuals who administered treatment to those suffering from an addiction, particularly an addiction to alcohol. Today, however, most professionals view these character traits as occurring because of the addiction rather than as part of an individual's basic personality.

TREATMENT STRATEGIES

The treatment of substance and process addictions is a global concern. Interventions and complete treatment programs concerning addictions continue to increase in complexity as more drugs are developed and as experts learn more about co-occurring process addictions. Ongoing research, particularly technology used to study brain functioning, perhaps can provide avenues for designing effective treatment programs that include medications and interventions for drug and process addictions. Findings identifying changes in brain makeup and functioning resulting from addictions hold promise for the discovery of medications that, combined with behavioral interventions, will provide more expedient and effective interventions.

Several substance and process addiction treatment programs have been subjected to efficacy research that has led to their identification as evidence-based programs. However, the administration of an addiction treatment program, mainly the relationship between the clinician and the patient, is as important as the intervention itself. All addiction treatment programs require that clinicians possess superb relationship skills. Professionals working with clients who are challenged by an addiction need to possess and demonstrate the necessary and essential conditions for change as identified by Rogers (1957). Research supports the importance of the relationship in counseling and psychotherapy (Lambert, 1991; S. D. Miller, Duncan, & Hubble, 2005). Research findings have shown that the relationship between the counselor and client accounts for no less than 30% of any change in therapy with individuals suffering from a wide range of problems, including addictions. An effective relationship is critical in work with clients with drug and process addictions (W. R. Miller et al., 2011). Relationship skills are often referred to as *core dimensions* or *core conditions* of counseling. These dimensions include empathy, congruence, genuineness, positive regard, immediacy, and concreteness.

In an attempt to provide proven treatment interventions for clients experiencing addictions, the scientific community has targeted the use of evidence-based treatment programs. Evidence-based programs have been submitted to rigorously controlled research studies and consistently emphasize positive outcomes. To be considered evidence based, programs must meet standards similar to the following:

1. *Randomized clinical trials of the practice or intervention.* Randomized clinical trials demonstrate the effectiveness of the programs.
2. *Demonstrated effectiveness using different samples.* Programs have been effective in a variety of settings with diverse samples, such as hospitals, clinics, business settings, and universities.
3. *Clear definition of dependent and independent variables.* Dependent, outcome variables are clearly defined, as are predictor variables.
4. *Feasibility of the practice or program.* Programs have been implemented in a wide range of settings with clarity of practices and procedures.
5. *Grounded in theory.* Programs are grounded in and supported by theory.
6. *Assurances of fidelity.* Programs are consistent in infusing concepts with clear, ethically based procedures.
7. *The practice addresses diversity.* Programs have been used in a variety of settings with diverse populations (R. L. Smith, 2011).

Over the past decade, NIDA has identified a number of evidence-based programs considered effective for working with addictions. These include treatment with medication and behavioral treatment programs.

Medication

It is recommended that treatment with medication concurrently include behavioral interventions. Treatment with medication most frequently occurs in a hospital setting, involving withdrawal from a drug. For example, methadone and naltrexone are two anti-addiction medications used to suppress withdrawal symptoms during detoxification. However, heroin addiction can also be treated by a physician in his or her office with buprenorphine (Suboxone). Since 2004, clinical trials have investigated whether drugs currently used to treat other diseases can also be used to treat addictions. Supported by the dopamine hypothesis, Ritalin, which is used to treat attention-deficit/hyperactivity disorder, produces dopamine at a lesser level than cocaine; therefore, it is used to provide a more gradual withdrawal from cocaine.

Goals of treatment with medication include the extinction of craving, the prevention of relapse, and the establishment of normal brain functioning. NIDA has identified medications for the treatment of addictions to opioids (heroin and morphine), tobacco (nicotine), and alcohol.

Opioids

Methadone, buprenorphine, and naltrexone are medications used to treat an opiate addiction. These medications act on the same regions of the brain as heroin and morphine (Goldstein & Volkow, 2011) but suppress withdrawal symptoms and relieve cravings. Naltrexone works by blocking the effects of opioids at their receptor sites and is administered following detoxification. The goal of administering these medications is to eliminate drug seeking and dysfunctional behavior while receiving behavioral treatment.

Tobacco

A large number of nicotine replacement therapies (the patch, gum, nasal spray, oral inhalers, and lozenges) have been used. These interventions have few side effects and are available over the counter. Bupropion SR tablets and varenicline tablets, two prescription medications, have been approved by the U.S. Food and Drug Administration (FDA) for treating tobacco addiction. They act on the brain through different mechanisms, but both help prevent relapse. These medications are usually used in combination with behavioral treatment (e.g., educational groups, group therapy, group counseling).

Alcohol

The medications naltrexone, acamprosate, and disulfiram have been approved by the FDA to treat alcohol dependence. Naltrexone blocks the opioid receptors affecting the reward system and the craving for alcohol. Studies have indicated that naltrexone has a greater effect on drinking when craving is high (Richardson et al., 2008). Acamprosate is thought to reduce symptoms of protracted withdrawal, such as insomnia, anxiety, restlessness, and dysphoria (an unpleasant or uncomfortable emotional state, such as depression, anxiety, or irritability). It may be more effective in patients with severe dependence. Acamprosate appears to be an effective and safe treatment for alcohol-dependent patients as a support for continued abstinence after detoxification (Rösner et al., 2011). Disulfiram works by blocking the processing of alcohol in the body. It causes one to have an unpleasant reaction when drinking alcohol, including flushing, nausea, and palpitations. Compliance is a problem, despite the effectiveness of disulfiram. Topiramate, approved to treat certain types of seizures and migraine headaches, has been successfully used to treat individuals who are still drinking. However, because of its severe side effects, Topiramate does not have FDA approval (Hanson, 2007).

Behavioral Strategies

According to NIDA (1999), several behavioral treatment programs are evidence based. These programs, many of which are described in greater detail later in this chapter, include outpatient and residential programs:

- *Cognitive behavior therapy (CBT)*. CBT works with cognitive processes, helping clients to recognize prevailing thoughts, disrupt and change self-defeating thinking, and develop effective coping strategies.
- *Multidimensional family therapy*. Multidimensional family therapy is primarily used with adolescents who have drug abuse problems. Family participation is necessary in order to address systemic influences on drug abuse patterns while improving family functioning.
- *Motivational interviewing*. Motivational interviewing approaches clients from a humanistic perspective, facilitating change and bringing out ambiguity related to continued drug use.

- *Motivational incentives/contingency management.* Contingency management programs focus on incentives and positive reinforcement to move toward abstaining from drug use.
- *Therapeutic communities.* Therapeutic communities are residential programs 3 to 12 months in duration that focus on changing one's lifestyle and becoming drug free. These structured programs utilize the community and include the treatment staff and individuals in recovery. Therapeutic communities accommodate women who are pregnant or have children.

Several other treatment strategies and programs warrant further examination of their content before they can be characterized as evidence based.

12-Step Programs

Twelve-step programs are frequently recommended as outpatient treatment for various types of addiction. It is commonly acknowledged that anyone, regardless of his or her religious beliefs or lack thereof, can benefit from participation in 12-step programs such as Alcoholics Anonymous or Narcotics Anonymous. The number of visits to 12-step self-help groups exceeds the number of visits to all mental health professionals combined. There are 12-step groups for all major substance and process addictions.

The 12 steps, paraphrased, are as follows:

- Admit powerlessness over the addiction.
- Believe that a Power greater than yourself can restore sanity.
- Make a decision to turn your will and your life over to the care of God as you understand him.
- Make a searching and fearless moral inventory of self.
- Admit to God, yourself, and another human being the exact nature of your wrongs.
- Become willing to have God remove all of these defects from your character.
- Humbly ask God to remove your shortcomings.
- Make a list of all persons harmed by your wrongs and be willing to make amends to them all.
- Make direct amends to such people, whenever possible, except when to do so would injure them or others.
- Continue to take personal inventory and promptly admit any future wrongdoings.
- Seek to improve contact with the God of your understanding through meditation and prayer.
- Carry the message of spiritual awakening to others and practice these principles in all your affairs. (Alcoholics Anonymous, n.d.)

CBT

CBT was first used as a method to prevent relapse when treating problem drinking. It has since been adapted for use in treating most drug addictions, including addictions to cocaine, marijuana, and methamphetamines. Cognitive–behavioral programs utilize an approach that focuses on self-defeating thoughts that lead to maladaptive behavior patterns. CBT helps clients identify problematic thinking sequences and behaviors.

CBT focuses on helping clients develop effective coping strategies rather than depend on past behaviors, including drug abuse or involvement in process addictions as gambling or spending. Greater self-control is emphasized. Individuals are taught how to recognize cravings, including the thought processes associated with the cravings. Techniques are used to disrupt the thinking and the craving. New thought processes are introduced and developed with clients that can lead to new behavior patterns. As part of a CBT program, clients explore both positive and negative consequences of continuing an addiction. They also are taught to become cognizant of their surroundings, including peers who could influence drug use.

Contingency Management

Contingency management involves the use of tangible rewards to reinforce positive behaviors such as abstinence. Such incentive-based interventions are believed to be highly effective in increasing treatment retention and promoting abstinence from drugs. *Voucher-based reinforcement* treatments are used with adults who have abused drugs, including heroin and cocaine. For example, patients might receive a voucher for every drug-free urine sample. Vouchers have a monetary value and can be used to purchase groceries and entertainment, such as movie passes. The rewards available increase gradually the longer one is drug free. Additional reward systems, as drawings and lottery-type systems, are used in contingency management. Opportunities for additional rewards are provided to individuals who remain drug free and participate in programs such as individual and group counseling. The goal is to create a healthy lifestyle that does not depend on drugs or include self-defeating behaviors. By being rewarded for positive behavior patterns rather than ingestion of a drug, the individual develops a lifestyle that is free of drugs.

Motivational Enhancement Therapy (MET)

MET focuses on the ambivalence one has about changing his or her use of a drug or a self-defeating behavior. MET can be used with substance and process addictions. The emphasis of MET is to facilitate change through one's internal motivation. A series of initial assessments are used to begin therapy, followed by several individual counseling sessions. Relationship building is important in the initial sessions. A trusting relationship needs to be built in order for the client to discuss his or her problems and any ambiguity about changing drug use or a behavior. Motivational interviewing principles guide the sessions and create an atmosphere in which change can take place. The counselor does not judge or evaluate the client but rather rolls with the conversation. Effective coping strategies are often part of the counselor–client interaction. The sessions focus on change, including just examining the possibilities of change. Once changes are made, the client is reinforced and encouraged to continue progress.

MET has been used successfully with individuals addicted to alcohol as related to participation in treatment and reduction in drinking. MET has also been used with marijuana-dependent adults. MET has been successful when combined with CBT.

Community Reinforcement Approach

NIDA (2012a) describes Community Reinforcement Approach Plus Vouchers:

Community Reinforcement Approach (CRA) Plus Vouchers is an intensive 24-week outpatient therapy for treating people addicted to cocaine and alcohol. It uses a range of recreational, familial, social, and vocational reinforcers, along with material incentives, to make a non-drug-using lifestyle more rewarding than substance use. The treatment goals are twofold:

- To maintain abstinence long enough for patients to learn new life skills to help sustain it; and
- To reduce alcohol consumption for patients whose drinking is associated with cocaine use

Patients attend one or two individual counseling sessions each week, where they focus on improving family relations, learn a variety of skills to minimize drug use, receive vocational counseling, and develop new recreational activities and social networks. Those who also abuse alcohol receive clinic-monitored disulfiram (Antabuse) therapy. Patients submit urine samples two or three times each week and receive vouchers for cocaine-negative samples. As in [voucher-based reinforcement], the value of the vouchers increases with consecutive clean samples, and the vouchers may be exchanged for retail goods that are consistent with a drug-free lifestyle. Studies in both urban and rural areas have found that this approach facilitates patients' engagement in treatment and successfully aids them in gaining substantial periods of cocaine abstinence.

A computer-based version of CRA Plus Vouchers called the Therapeutic Education System (TES) was found to be nearly as effective as treatment administered by a therapist in promoting abstinence from opioids and cocaine among opioid-dependent individuals in outpatient treatment. A version of CRA for adolescents addresses problem-solving, coping, and communication skills and encourages active participation in positive social and recreational activities.

The Matrix Model

The Matrix Model has been used as a framework for working with individuals who abuse stimulants (methamphetamine and cocaine). The treatment goal is abstinence. Education sessions involve learning about addictions and relapse. Professionals trained in addictions counseling work with patients. Self-help programs are used as an adjunct to therapy. Patients are monitored for drug use through urine testing. The relationship between the therapist and patient is critical to eventual change. The therapist provides a support system for patients and often functions as a teacher and coach. The building of the patient's self-esteem, dignity, and self-worth is emphasized. The overall treatment program includes relapse prevention, family and group therapies, drug education, and self-help activities. Treatment manuals are utilized. Patients often utilize worksheets found within the treatment manuals. In addition, patients participate in 12-step programs and social support groups. Patients are monitored through urine tests. According to NIDA (2012a), the Matrix Model has shown statistically significant reductions in drug and alcohol use, improvements in psychological indicators, and reduced risky sexual behaviors associated with HIV transmission.

Family Behavior Therapy

Family behavior therapy, utilized with both adults and adolescents, focuses on substance abuse and other co-occurring issues. A wide range of family-related concerns are often covered, including family violence, child abuse, depression, family communication, family finances, and unemployment. Behavioral contracting is used, along with contingency management. Behavioral goals are reviewed at the beginning of each session. Goal accomplishments are rewarded.

When possible, the entire family is involved in treatment. However, many sessions might involve an adolescent and one family caregiver. Behavior therapy is emphasized with psychoeducational activities that teach family members new skills. A cohesive and adaptable home environment is emphasized. Behavioral goals to stop or prevent substance misuse are utilized. Positive communication skills are taught along with effective parenting skills. The participatory treatment allows patients to choose interventions. Family behavior therapy has been found to be effective, particularly along with other approaches (NIDA, 2012c).

Dialectical Behavior Therapy (DBT)

DBT is an evidence-based therapy for individuals with co-occurring disorders. Evidence supporting the use of DBT with substance dependence issues is being recognized. For example, the Substance Abuse and Mental Health Services Administration presented a 2008 Science and Service Award to a DBT program based in Portland, Oregon. In addition, NIDA published a paper recommending the use of DBT with co-occurring disorders (A. Downs, 2010). DBT emphasizes quality-of-life issues when working with substance abuse problems. Behavioral targets in a DBT substance-abuse treatment program include

- decreasing the abuse of substances, including illicit drugs and legally prescribed drugs taken in a manner not prescribed
- alleviating physical discomfort associated with abstinence and/or withdrawal
- diminishing urges, cravings, and temptations to abuse
- avoiding opportunities and cues to abuse, for example, by burning bridges to persons, places, and things associated with drug abuse and by destroying the telephone numbers of drug contacts, getting a new telephone number, and throwing away drug paraphernalia
- reducing behaviors conducive to drug abuse, such as momentarily giving up the goal to get off drugs and instead functioning as if the use of drugs cannot be avoided
- increasing community reinforcement of healthy behaviors, such as fostering the development of new friends, rekindling old friendships, pursuing social/vocational activities, and seeking environments that support abstinence and punish behaviors related to drug abuse (Dimeff & Linehan, 2008)

Aversive Behavior Therapy Programs: Counterconditioning

The physical and psychological aspects of drug addiction are the focuses of the drug treatment program at Schick Shadel Hospital in Santa Barbara, California. Abstinence is emphasized. An aversive behavior therapy approach is utilized that involves mild counterconditioning and sedation-assisted therapy to relieve the desire for the addictive substance. Alcohol or drug use is associated with discomfort, and the craving to use a substance is eliminated.

The Schick Shadel treatment program also focuses on relationships, involving positive sessions with the professional staff and other patients. Nutrition, exercise, and rest are emphasized as a lifestyle change. The goal is to have individuals obtain pleasure from natural, healthy activities rather than drugs. Research findings for this aversive behavior therapy program are promising (J. W. Smith & Frawley, 1993). A sample of 600 patients treated in a multimodal treatment program using aversion therapy and narcotherapy was studied at three freestanding Schick addiction treatment hospitals and one Schick unit in a general hospital. Telephone contact was made by an independent research organization with 427 of the patients (71.2%) 12 to 20 months after completion of treatment. Of these, 65.1% were totally abstinent for 1 year after treatment, and 60.2% were abstinent until follow-up ($M = 14.7$ months; J. W. Smith & Frawley, 1993).

CONCLUSIONS

Addiction is a complex term, often difficult to define. However, in recent years, *drug addiction* has been defined as a chronic, relapsing brain disease characterized by compulsive drug seeking and use despite harmful consequences. It is considered a brain disease because drugs change the structure of the brain and how it works. These changes in the brain can be long lasting and can lead to the harmful behaviors seen in people who abuse drugs (NIDA, 2010). Process addictions, such as addictions to gambling, sex, the Internet, food, work, exercise, and shopping, are believed to involve similar pleasure-seeking principles, with the brain rewarding a behavior that is exciting and high risk. Many view addiction as similar to other diseases, such as heart problems, diabetes, and cancer, as it disrupts the normal, healthy functioning of an individual; has serious harmful consequences; is preventable and treatable; and, if left untreated, can last a lifetime (NIDA, 2010).

Certain criteria can help clinicians in assessing whether a person has an addiction. Criteria found within the *DSM–5* are recommended for assessing substance and process addictions, as is information on assessing addictions found in the literature (Engs, 2012; Hartney, 2011a; W. R. Miller et al., 2011). These criteria include several common factors: increased tolerance, decreased willpower, continued use, lack of control, withdrawal, and consequences. Generic criteria for assessing process addictions (see Table 1.1) have been offered with the hope this will lead to more clearly identifying process addictions. In addition to defining addiction and examining the criteria used in determining an addiction, this chapter has discussed the etiology of addictions, concluding that there are multiple reasons why individuals become addicted.

As experts learn more about addictions, human behavior, and the mechanisms of the brain, they perhaps can further understand addictions, their etiology, and the best methods for addressing both substance and process addictions. It is reasonable to believe that no single factor determines whether a person will become addicted to a substance or behavior. Research has indicated that the overall risk of developing a substance or process addiction is affected by one's biological makeup, gender, ethnicity, developmental stage, and surrounding environment (family, friends, peers, school, and neighborhood). Scientists have estimated that genetic factors account for between 40% and 60% of a person's vulnerability to addiction. Adolescents and individuals with mental disorders are at greater risk for drug abuse and addictive behaviors than the general population.

After genetics, environmental factors play a major role in addictions. The influence of one's home environment is important in childhood, as are a child's earliest interactions within the family. Having family members, particularly parents, who abuse alcohol or drugs or who engage in criminal behavior is believed to increase a child's risk of developing his or her own drug problems or addictive behavior patterns. Peers, one's school, and friends are highly influential during the adolescent years. Peers in particular can be very influential in persuading an adolescent to try a drug or participate in a high-risk behavior. Peer influence can mitigate protective factors provided by the family or school. Lack of success in academics and ineffective social skills place one at risk for engaging in destructive behaviors or abusing drugs.

Although taking drugs at any age can lead to addiction, research shows that the earlier a person begins to use drugs, the more likely he or she is to progress to more serious abuse. This may reflect the harmful effect that drugs can have on the developing brain; it also may result from a constellation of early biological and social vulnerability factors, such as genetic susceptibility, mental illness, unstable family relationships, and exposure to physical or sexual abuse. The fact remains that early use is a strong indicator of problems ahead with substance abuse and addiction. The initial decision to take drugs is often voluntary. At first, people may perceive what seem to be positive effects of drug use. They also may believe that they can control their use. However, drugs can quickly take over their lives. Consider how a social drinker can become intoxicated, put himself behind a wheel, and quickly turn a pleasurable activity into a tragedy for himself and others. Over time, if drug use continues, pleasurable activities become less pleasurable, and drug abuse becomes necessary for abusers to feel normal. Drug abusers reach a point where they seek and take drugs despite the tremendous problems for themselves and their loved ones. Some individuals may develop a tolerance and start to feel the need to take higher or more frequent doses, even in the early stages of their drug use.

After continued use of a substance or process, a person's ability to exert self-control can become seriously impaired. Brain-imaging studies from addicted individuals show physical changes in areas of the brain that are critical to judgment, decision making, learning and memory, and behavior control. Scientists believe that these changes alter the way the brain works and may explain the compulsive and destructive behaviors of addiction. The prefrontal cortex, the part of the brain that enables people to assess situations, make sound decisions, and keep their emotions and desires under control, changes as the result of continued addiction. This part of the brain is still developing throughout adolescence and therefore places one at increased risk for poor decision making and judgment.

Several treatment strategies and programs addressing substance and behavioral addictions have been studied. Evidence-based treatment strategies included in this chapter and examined further in this text included CBT, MET, contingency management, community reinforcement, DBT, 12-step programs, medication, the Matrix Model, family behavior therapy, and counterconditioning. The research on many of these strategies and treatment programs has focused on substance addictions. Efficacy research on interventions that address process addictions is currently lacking. It is hypothesized that the dearth of efficacy studies involving process addictions is the result of a gap in the literature related to process addictions as well as limited skills training in treating behavioral addictions (Wilson & Johnson, 2013). Perhaps this text and others like it that address the exponential growth of process addictions, along with continued crises surrounding substance misuse, will encourage further research on and direct greater attention toward treatment strategies addressing these co-occurring disorders.

RESOURCES

Resources for Treatment

Addiction Treatment Forum
   http://atforum.com/

Initiatives Designed to Move Treatment Research Into Practice

Blending Teams
   www.drugabuse.gov/nidasamhsa-blending-initiative
Criminal Justice-Drug Abuse Treatment Studies
   http://tpj.sagepub.com/content/87/1/9.short
NIDA's National Drug Abuse Treatment Clinical Trials Network
   www.drugabuse.gov/CTN/Index.htm

National Agencies

Center for Substance Abuse Treatment
   www.samhsa.gov/about-us/who-we-are/offices-centers/csat
National Institute of Mental Health
   www.nimh.nih.gov
National Institute on Alcohol Abuse and Alcoholism
   www.niaaa.nih.gov
National Institute on Drug Abuse
   www.drugabuse.gov

Selected NIDA and Other Educational Resources on Drug Addiction Treatment

Alcohol Alert (published by NIAAA)
   www.niaaa.nih.gov/publications/journals-and-reports/alcohol-alert
Addiction Severity Index
   http://www.tresearch.org/tools/download-asi-instruments-manuals/
Drugs, Brains, and Behavior: The Science of Addiction
   www.drugabuse.gov/publications/science-addiction
Helping Patients Who Drink Too Much: A Clinician's Guide (published by NIAAA)
   http://pubs.niaaa.nih.gov/publications/Practitioner/CliniciansGuide2005/clinicians_
   guide.htm
NIDA DrugFacts: Treatment Approaches for Drug Addiction
   www.drugabuse.gov/publications/drugfacts/treatment-approaches-drug-addiction

Principles of Drug Abuse Treatment for Criminal Justice Populations: A Research-Based Guide
    www.drugabuse.gov/publications/principles-drug-abuse-treatment-criminal-justice-
    populations/principles
Research Report Series: Therapeutic Community
    http://archives.drugabuse.gov/researchreports/Therapeutic/
Seeking Drug Abuse Treatment: Know What to Ask
    www.drugabuse.gov/publications/seeking-drug-abuse-treatment

Other Federal Resources

ClinicalTrials.gov
    http://clinicaltrials.gov
NIDA DrugPubs Research Dissemination Center
    http://drugpubs.drugabuse.gov
National Institute of Justice
    http://nij.gov
National Registry of Evidence-Based Programs and Practices
    http://nrepp.samhsa.gov
Substance Abuse and Mental Health Services Administration
    www.samhsa.gov/

REFERENCES

Addictions list. (n.d.). Retrieved from http://www.addictionz.com/addictions.htm
Alcoholics Anonymous (n.d.). Twelve steps of Alcoholics Anonymous. Retrived from http://www.aa.org/assets/en_US/smf-121_en.pdf
Allegre, B., Souville, M., Therme, P., & Griffiths, M. (2006). Definitions and measures of exercise dependence. *Addiction Research and Theory, 14,* 631–646.
Allison, K. C., Grilo, C. M., Masheb, R. M., & Stunkard, A. J. (2005). Binge eating disorder and night eating syndrome: A comparative study of disordered eating. *Journal of Consulting and Clinical Psychology, 73,* 1107–1115.
American Psychiatric Association. (2013). *Diagnostic and statistical manual of mental disorders* (5th ed.). Arlington, VA: Author.
American Society of Addiction Medicine. (2011). *Definition of addiction.* Retrieved from http://www.asam.org/research-treatment/definition-of-addiction
Bondolfi, G., Osiek, C., & Ferrero, F. (2000). Prevalence estimates of pathological gambling in Switzerland. *Acta Psychiatrica Scandinavica, 101,* 473–475.
Burke, R. J. (2000). Workaholism in organizations: Concepts, results and future directions. *International Journal of Management Reviews, 2,* 1–16.
Chen, K., Sheth, A. J., Elliott, D. K., & Yeager, A. (2004). Prevalence and correlates of past-year substance use, abuse and dependence in a suburban community sample of high school students. *Addictive Behaviors, 29,* 413–423.
Cook, D. R. (1987). Self-identified addictions and emotional disturbances in a sample of college students. *Psychology of Addictive Behaviors, 1,* 55–61.
Dierker, L. C., Donny, E., Tiffany, S., Colby, S. M., Perrine, N., & Clayton, R. R. (2007). The association between cigarette smoking and *DSM–IV* nicotine dependence among first year college students. *Drug and Alcohol Dependence, 86,* 106–114.
Dimeff, L. A., & Linehan, M. M. (2008). Dialectical behavior therapy for substance abusers. *Addiction Science & Clinical Practice, 4*(2), 39–47.
Downs, A. (2010). *Dialectical behavior therapy (DBT) and substance abuse treatment.* Retrieved from the RecoveryView website: http://www.recoveryview.com/Articles/TabId/107/ArtMID/657/ArticleID/1156/Dialectical-Behavior-Therapy-DBT-and-Substance-Abuse-Treatment.aspx

Downs, D., Hausenblas, H. A., & Nigg, C. A. (2004). Factorial validity and psychometric examination of the Exercise Dependence Scale–Revised. *Measurement in Physical Education and Exercise Science, 8,* 183–201.

Engs, R. C. (2012). *What are addictive behaviors?* Bloomington, IN: Tichenor.

Enoch, M. A., & Goldman, D. (2001). The genetics of alcoholism and alcohol abuse. *Current Psychiatry Reports, 3*(2), 144–151.

Freimuth, M., Waddell, M., Stannard, J., Kelley, S., Kipper, A., Richardson, A., & Szuromi, I. (2008). Expanding the scope of dual diagnosis and co-addictions: Behavioral addictions. *Journal of Groups in Addiction & Recovery, 3,* 137–160.

Gadalla, T., & Piran, N. (2007). Eating disorders and substance abuse in Canadian men and women: A national study. *Eating Disorders, 15,* 189–203.

Gambino, B. (2006). A comment on the utility of prevalence estimates of pathological gambling. *Journal of Gambling Studies, 22,* 321–328.

Gleaves, D. H., & Carter, J. D. (2008). Eating addiction. In C. A. Essau (Ed.), *Adolescent addiction: Epidemiology, assessment and treatment* (pp. 179–203). New York, NY: Academic Press.

Goldstein, R. Z., & Volkow, N. D. (2011). Dysfunction of the prefrontal cortex in addiction: Neuroimaging findings and clinical implications. *Nature Reviews Neuroscience, 12,* 652–669.

Goodwin, R. D., Keyes, K. M., & Hasin, D. S. (2009). Changes in cigarette use and nicotine dependence in the United States. *American Journal of Public Health, 99,* 1471–1477.

Grant, B. F., Hasin, D. S., Chou, S. P., Stinson, F. S., & Dawson, D. A. (2004). Nicotine dependence and psychiatric disorders in the United States: Results from the National Epidemiologic Survey on Alcohol and Related Conditions. *Archives of General Psychiatry, 61,* 1107–1115.

Griffiths, M. D. (2009). *Problem gambling in Europe: An overview.* Nottingham, England: Nottingham Trent University, International Gaming Research Unit and Apex Communications.

Grüsser, S. M., Thalemann, R., & Griffiths, M. D. (2007). Excessive computer game playing: Evidence for addiction and aggression? *Cyberpsychology, Behavior, and Social Networking, 10,* 290–292.

Hanson, D. (2007). *Topamax for alcoholism: A closer look.* Retrieved from http://addiction-dirkh.blogspot.com/2007/10/topamax-for-alcoholism-closer-look.html

Hartney, E. (2011a). *Symptoms of addiction: Signs and symptoms of addiction to look out for.* Retrieved from http://addictions.about.com/od/howaddictionhappens/a/symptomslist.htm

Hartney, E. (2011b). *What is addiction? A broad definition of addiction.* Retrieved from http://addictions.about.com/od/howaddictionhappens/a/defaddiction.htm

Institute for Addiction Studies. (2009). *Pleasure unwoven: A personal journey about addiction* [DVD]. United States: Author.

Johnston, L. D., O'Malley, P. M., Bachman, J. G., & Schulenberg, J. E. (2011). *Monitoring the Future national results on adolescent drug use: Overview of key findings in 2010.* Ann Arbor: University of Michigan, Institute for Social Research.

Kaplan, M. S., & Krueger, R. B. (2010). Diagnosis, assessment, and treatment of hypersexuality. *Journal of Sex Research, 47,* 181–198.

Keowan, L. A. (2007). *Time escapes me: Workaholics and time perception* (Canadian Social Trends Catalogue No. 11-008). Retrieved from http://www.statcan.gc.ca/pub/11-008-x/2007001/pdf/9629-eng.pdf

Koran, L. M., Faber, R. J., Aboujaoude, E., Large, M. D., & Serpe, R. T. (2006). Estimated prevalence of compulsive buying behavior in the United States. *American Journal of Psychiatry, 163,* 1806–1812.

Kubey, R. W., Lavin, M. J., & Barrows, J. R. (2001). Internet use and collegiate academic performance decrements: Early findings. *Journal of Communication, 51,* 366–382.

Lambert, M. J. (1991). Introduction to psychotherapy research. In L. E. Beutler & M. Crago (Eds.), *Psychotherapy research: An international review of programmatic studies* (pp. 1–23). Washington, DC: American Psychological Association.

Lang, A. R. (1983). Addictive personality: A viable construct? In P. K. Levison, D. R. Gerstein, & D. R. Maloff (Eds.), *Commonalities in substance abuse and habitual behavior* (pp. 157–236). New York, NY: Lexington Books.

Lettieri, D. J., Sayers, M., & Pearson, H. W. (Eds.). (1980). *Theories on drug abuse: Selected contemporary perspectives.* Rockville, MD: U.S. Department of Health and Human Services.

Lundberg, K. (2013). *Environmental risk factors for addiction.* Retrieved from http://learn.genetics.utah.edu/content/addiction/environment

MacLaren, V. V., & Best, L. A. (2010). Multiple addictive behaviors in young adults: Student norms for the shorter PROMIS Questionnaire. *Addictive Behaviors, 35,* 252–255.

Miller, S. D., Duncan, B. L., & Hubble, M. A. (2005). Outcome-informed clinical work. In J. C. Norcross & M. R. Goldfried (Eds.), *Handbook of psychotherapy integration* (2nd ed., pp. 84–102). New York, NY: Oxford University Press.

Miller, W. R., Forcehimes, A. A., & Zweben, A. (2011). *Treating addiction: A guide for professionals.* New York, NY: Guilford Press.

Morahan-Martin, J., & Schumacher, P. (2000). Incidence and correlates of pathological Internet use among college students. *Computers in Human Behavior, 16,* 13–29.

National Institute on Alcohol Abuse and Alcoholism. (2009). The past and future of research on treatment of alcohol dependence. *Alcohol Alert, 77,* 1–6.

National Institute on Drug Abuse. (1999). *Principles of drug addiction treatment: A research based guide.* Bethesda, MD: Author.

National Institute on Drug Abuse. (2008). *Addiction science: From molecules to managed care.* Bethesda, MD: Author.

National Institute on Drug Abuse. (2010). *Drugs, brains, and behavior: The science of addiction.* Retrieved from http://www.drugabuse.gov/sites/default/files/soa_2014.pdf

National Institute on Drug Abuse. (2012a). *Community Reinforcement Approach Plus Vouchers (alcohol, cocaine, opioids).* Retrieved from http://www.drugabuse.gov/publications/principles-drug-addiction-treatment-research-based-guide-third-edition/evidence-based-approaches-to-drug-addiction-treatment/behavioral-1

National Institute on Drug Abuse. (2012b). *DrugFacts: Understanding drug abuse and addiction.* Retrieved from http://www.drugabuse.gov/publications/drugfacts/understanding-drug-abuse-addiction

National Institute on Drug Abuse. (2012c). *Principles of drug addiction treatment: A research-based guide* (3rd ed.). Retrieved from http://www.drugabuse.gov/publications/principles-drug-addiction-treatment/resources

National Institute on Drug Abuse. (2012d). *The science of drug abuse and addiction: The basics.* Retrieved from http://www.drugabuse.gov/publications/media-guide/science-drug-abuse-addiction

Olds, J., & Milner, P. (1954). Positive reinforcement produced by electrical stimulation of septal area and other regions of rat brain. *Journal of Comparative and Physiological Psychology, 47,* 419–427.

Patoine, B. (2007). *Addiction and the prefrontal cortex: An interview with Rita Z. Goldstein, Ph.D.* Retrieved from http://www.dana.org/news/publications/detail.aspx?id=6470

Pirkola, S. P., Poikolainen, K., & Lonnqvist, J. K. (2006). Currently active and remitted alcohol dependence in a nationwide adult general population: Results from the Finnish Health 2000 Study. *Alcohol & Alcoholism, 41,* 315–320.

Prescott, C. A., & Kendler, K. S. (1999). Genetic and environmental contributions to alcohol abuse and dependence in a population-based sample of male twins. *American Journal Psychiatry, 156,* 34–40.

Richardson, K., Baillie, A., Reid, S., Morley, K., Teesson, M., Sannibale, C., . . . Haber, P. (2008). Do acamprosate or naltrexone have an effect on daily drinking by reducing craving for alcohol? *Addiction, 103,* 953–959. doi:10.1111/j.1360-0443.2008.02215.x

Rogers, C. R. (1957). The necessary and sufficient conditions of therapeutic personality change. *Journal of Counseling Psychology, 21,* 95–103.

Rösner, S., Hackl-Herrwerth, A., Leucht, S., Lehert, P., Vecchi, S., & Soyka, M. (2011). Acamprosate for alcohol dependent patients. *Cochrane Database of Systematic Reviews, 2010*(9), CD004332. doi:10.1002/14651858.CD004332.pub2

Smith, D. E. (2012). Editor's note: The process addictions and the new ASAM definition of addiction. *Journal of Psychoactive Drugs, 44*(1), 1–4.

Smith, J. W., & Frawley, P. J. (1993). Treatment outcome of 600 chemically dependent patients treated in a multimodal inpatient program including aversion therapy and pentothal interviews. *Journal of Substance Abuse & Treatment, 10,* 359–369.

Smith, R. L. (2011). *Achievement motivation training: An evidence-based approach to enhancing performance.* Retrieved from http://counselingoutfitters.com/vistas/vistas11/Article_56.pdf

Smith, R. L. (2013). Major substances of abuse and the body. In P. Stevens & R. L. Smith (Eds.), *Substance abuse counseling: Theory and practice* (5th ed., pp. 51–97). Upper Saddle River,NJ: Merrill/Pearson.

Substance Abuse and Mental Health Services Administration. (2011). *Results from the 2010 National Survey on Drug Use and Health: Summary of national findings* (NSDUH Series H-41, HHS Publication No. [SMA] 11-4658). Rockville, MD: Author.

Substance Abuse and Mental Health Services Administration. (2012). *Results from the 2011 National Survey on Drug Use and Health: Summary of national findings* (NSDUH Series H-44, HHS Publication No. [SMA] 12-4713). Rockville, MD: Author.

Sussman, S., Lisha, N., & Griffiths, M. (2011). Prevalence of the addictions: A problem of the majority or the minority? *Evaluation and the Health Professions, 34,* 3–56. doi:10.1177/0163278710380124

Teesson, M., Baillie, A., Lynskey, M., Manor, B., & Degenhardt, L. (2006). Substance use, dependence and treatment seeking in the United States and Australia: A cross-national comparison. *Drug and Alcohol Dependence, 81,* 149–155.

Terry, A., Szabo, A., & Griffiths, M. (2004). The Exercise Addiction Inventory: A new brief screening tool. *Addiction Research and Theory, 12,* 489–499.

Volberg, R. A., Gupta, R., Griffiths, M. D., Olason, D. T., & Delfabbro, P. (2010). An international perspective on youth gambling prevalence studies. *International Journal of Adolescent Medicine and Health, 22,* 3–38.

Volkow, N. (2011). *The essence of drug addiction.* Retrieved from http://science.education.nih.gov/supplements/nih2/addiction/guide/essence.htm

What is a process addiction? (2012). Retrieved from http://www.processaddictions.com/

Wilson, A. D., & Johnson, P. (2013). Counselors understanding of process addiction: A blind spot in the counseling field. *The Professional Counselor, 3,* 16–22.

Young, S. E., Corley, R. P., Stallings, M. C., Rhee, S. H., Crowley, T. J., & Hewitt, J. K. (2002). Substance use, abuse and dependence in adolescence: Prevalence, symptom profiles and correlates. *Drug and Alcohol Dependence, 68,* 309–322.

CHAPTER 2

ALCOHOL ADDICTION

Todd F. Lewis

STUDENT LEARNING OUTCOMES

At the conclusion of this chapter students will

1. Identify key terms and definitions related to alcohol addiction and treatment
2. Identify criteria used to define alcohol addiction
3. Understand costs of alcohol abuse and addiction in the United States and key sociodemographics often associated with alcohol use
4. Identify screening and diagnostic procedures related to alcohol abuse and addiction
5. Be able to summarize the literature on alcohol treatment

CASE AND CASE DISCUSSION

Sam, a 42-year-old African American man, enters counseling under his own volition. Tall and domineering, Sam has a deep voice and commands attention when he speaks. "I take pride in working hard and providing for my family, but this alcohol thing has kicked me hard!" Sam works in real estate as a mid-level manager and makes a good salary. He and his wife, Meredith, have a 6-year-old girl and 3-year-old boy. Upon inquiry, Sam reveals that his drinking dates back to his days in college when he would binge drink frequently as part of being in a fraternity.

Unlike many of his fraternity brothers, Sam continued to drink heavily on and off after college. It wasn't until the past few years, however, that Meredith began to see changes in Sam's behavior and appearance; she was worried about his health. "I have been late to work, I get angry often, and I yell at my kids. I've gained about 50 pounds. My wife is very concerned about me. She knew I drank a lot, but I don't think she knows the extent of it. I feel like I can't relate to my kids." It was an ultimatum from his boss, and his increasing problems at home, that propelled Sam to seek help.

Sam reports that on a typical day of drinking he consumes up to 16 beers. He notes that he has tried to stop or at least cut down before, but to no avail. "My tolerance must be through the roof!" He also reports experiencing withdrawal symptoms when he tries to stop drinking. Sam reports feeling strong urges to drink, even when he is not particularly busy or stressed out. "It's like a compelling drive to reach for a beer that I can't shut off." When asked about other problems he is dealing with, he notes that he is, and always has been, an anxious individual. In fact, he has often wondered whether drinking is a way to help him relax. "When I am bored, I feel like I am going to crawl out of my skin. I need to be doing something!" After gathering this intake information, the clinician promptly proceeds to further assess and evaluate Sam to determine the best treatment setting.

OVERVIEW OF ALCOHOL ADDICTION

As the case of Sam illustrates, alcohol abuse and addiction can wreak havoc on the lives of not only clients but also those close to them. Sam's drinking was out of control. As is the case with many clients addicted to alcohol, the fallout from excessive drinking might not be immediately realized, but over time consequences start to become severe. Sam had lost connections with his family, was struggling at work, and was becoming increasingly agitated and anxious. As in Sam's life, alcohol use and its associated consequences are a pervasive problem in U.S. society. The financial, personal, interpersonal, and occupational toll of excessive drinking is staggering. Clearly, effective and supported prevention and treatment protocols are needed to better address alcoholism.

In this chapter, I examine the effects of alcohol and provide a set of related definitions. The costs of excessive alcohol use are discussed, followed by a review of fundamental assessment and diagnostic procedures. Treatment approaches are a major focus, with an emphasis on evidence-based medications, behavioral interventions, and treatment models. The importance of support services for those struggling with alcohol addiction is stressed. This chapter concludes with resources that clinicians and clients can easily access in order to gain additional information on alcohol, its effects, its dangers, and treatment approaches.

Effects

Alcohol is classified as a central nervous system depressant and produces effects consistent with other drugs in this class, such as slurred speech, disorientation, relaxed inhibitions, and drunken (or tipsy) behavior. Overdose of central nervous system depressants can become quite serious, as these drugs impact the deeper recesses of the brain that control breathing, heart rate, and blood pressure. Symptoms of overdose include shallow respiration, cold and clammy skin, weak or rapid pulse, coma, and death. Excessive and chronic consumption of alcohol in particular can lead to alcohol poisoning; fetal alcohol syndrome; and long-term problems such as cirrhosis of the liver, cancer, and even brain damage (Hoffman & Froemke, 2007). The general withdrawal symptoms from central nervous system depressants are the opposite of the drugs' effects: anxiety, insomnia, tremors, and delirium. Suddenly stopping chronic alcohol use may even lead to seizures (Hoffman & Froemke, 2007).

Definitions

Alcohol: The type of alcohol that humans drink is referred to as *ethyl alcohol* or *ethanol*. It is generally derived from natural products such as fruit, grains, and cactus plants.

Alcohol metabolism: Alcohol metabolism begins with enzymes (alcohol dehydrogenase) that break down alcohol to acetaldehyde, which is further broken down into acetic acid, which is then broken down into carbon dioxide, water, and carbohydrates (Doweiko, 2009). The major workhorse of alcohol metabolism is the liver. Indeed, chronic alcohol use can overwhelm the liver, leading to numerous problems, including fatty liver (when fat accumulates around liver cells), alcoholic hepatitis (inflammation of the liver), and cirrhosis of the liver (hardening of the liver via scar tissue).

Alcohol use disorder: Alcohol use disorder refers to a formal clinical condition in which an individual consumes large amounts of alcohol and experiences numerous negative consequences as a result. I say more about the criteria for meeting this diagnosis in a later section.

Alcoholics Anonymous (AA): AA is a 12-step mutual support group in which individuals who struggle with controlling their drinking come together for support, communion, and encouragement. AA is *not* formal therapy, although it can provide an effective adjunct to therapy. AA is discussed more extensively in a later section.

Alcoholism: A person with alcoholism has lost control of his or her alcohol consumption and is experiencing negative consequences. Alcoholism is not an official clinical term but is common vernacular in AA circles and among the general public. The term connotes drinking at severe levels, experiencing numerous consequences, and developing signs of physical addiction such as withdrawal and tolerance.

Binge drinking: Binge drinking, also referred to as *heavy, episodic drinking*, refers to consuming five (four for women) or more drinks in a 2-hour period (National Institute on Alcohol Abuse and Alcoholism [NIAAA], 2012). Other more precise definitions may exist, but the 5+/4+ criterion is easy to understand and is commonly used across alcohol research. Binge drinking has been a concern on college campuses for a number of years, as upward of 44% of college students have reported binge drinking at least once within the previous 2 weeks (Wechsler et al., 2002). It is not surprising that this pattern of drinking is associated with a host of negative consequences.

Blood alcohol level (BAL): Also known as *blood alcohol content*, BAL is measured in milligrams of alcohol per 100 L of blood (mg/mL). Based on measured BAL, one can predict certain behavioral and/or physiological effects. Even at relatively lower levels of alcohol use (~.02 BAL), individuals experience warmth and relaxation (Doweiko, 2009) as the drug begins to take effect. At a BAL between .05 and .09, the individual becomes more talkative, feels happy, and experiences some impairment in motor skills (Doweiko, 2009). Impairment in reaction time also sets in, which is why all states in the United States demarcate a BAL of .08 as the level at which one is legally drunk and too intoxicated to drive. Above a BAL of .10, the depressant effects of alcohol become quite visible, as evidenced by slurred speech, unsteady gait, nausea, vomiting, and lowering of inhibitions. Persons reaching a BAL between .30 and .40 may experience severe stupor and even coma; a BAL above .40 most likely leads to death (Doweiko, 2009).

It is important to note that these effects are generalized to those who are infrequent drinkers. A person who has developed an addiction to alcohol may not show any behavioral effects until his or her BAL reaches well above .10. In addition, other factors can impact the speed at which alcohol is absorbed and consequently its effects, such as the presence of food in the stomach, whether the alcohol is straight or diluted in a mixed drink, the size of the person, and the person's gender.

Drink: A standard drink is .60 oz of pure alcohol (in other words, a 12-oz can of beer, a 5-oz glass of wine, or a drink made of 1.5 oz of 80-proof liquor).

Dry drunk: When a person addicted to alcohol stops drinking but continues to act in old patterns and ways that are not conducive to recovery, he or she is referred to as a *dry drunk.* Most likely coined in AA circles, *dry drunk* suggests that one might abstain from alcohol but continue to act in ways that sabotage recovery. For example, a person recovering from alcoholism might continue to avoid communication with his family, hang out with old drinking buddies, and drive by the liquor store on the way home from work. Although sober, he has not really changed his lifestyle.

Proof: The concentration of alcohol is measured in proof. *Proof* refers to twice the percentage of alcohol by volume. For example, absolute alcohol, which contains 100% alcohol, is 200 proof. A drink with 40% alcohol is 80 proof. A glass of 24-proof wine equates to 12% alcohol by volume. *Proof* is simply another way to communicate the amount of alcohol in a beverage. Today, many alcoholic beverages simply list the percentage of alcohol by volume rather than proof.

Demographics and Cost

According to the NIAAA (2012), just under 29% of women and 43.1% of men 18 years of age or older engaged in binge drinking within the past year. Current statistical trends in the United States suggest that the prevalence of alcohol use may differ by racial or ethnic group. When race and ethnicity were taken into account, it was found that a higher percentage of non-Hispanic White adults (ages 18 and older; 57%) were regular drinkers compared with Hispanic and non-Hispanic Black adults (39%). In addition, Hispanic and non-Hispanic Black adults were more likely to be lifetime abstainers compared to non-Hispanic White adults (Schiller, Lucas, Ward, & Peregoy, 2012). Across most categories of both quantity (one drink, two drinks, three drinks, etc.) and frequency (daily, nearly every day, three or four times a week, etc.) of drinking, men tend to consume alcohol in greater amounts and more frequently than women (NIAAA, 2012). Almost twice as many women as men report being lifetime abstainers.

The costs of alcohol abuse and addiction are staggering. Bouchery, Harwood, Sacks, Simon, and Brewer (2011) reported that in 2006 excessive alcohol consumption cost the United States and estimated $223.5 billion, with binge drinking accounting for more than 75% of this cost. The financial price of problematic drinking is reflected in a number of behaviors and areas, including workplace productivity (missing work), health care expenses, law enforcement expenses, and motor vehicle crashes (Bouchery et al., 2011). In terms of personal economic impact, excessive drinking in the United States is estimated to cost the average American $746 annually (Bouchery et al., 2011). Although these costs can be reasonably estimated from available statistics, the unseen costs, such as the violence and pain endured by others due to a loved one's alcohol consumption, probably underestimate the total impact and toll excessive alcohol use has on society.

Beyond direct economic costs, excessive drinking levies a heavy burden on personal health and psychological, interpersonal, and familial well-being. In the United States, 18 million people have an *alcohol use disorder* (NIAAA, 2012), defined as heavy drinking despite negative consequences and, in more severe cases, evidence of tolerance, withdrawal, and persistent and heavy daily use. One quarter of all emergency room visits and one third of all suicides are alcohol related (although emergency room estimates may be higher given that many doctors have not had training in alcohol assessment and diagnosis; Hoffman & Froemke, 2007). It has been estimated that more than half of all homicides and domestic violence incidents involve alcohol (Hoffman & Froemke, 2007). Behind smoking and obesity, problematic drinking is the third leading cause of preventable death: 75,000 Americans die each year because of excessive alcohol use (Hoffman & Froemke, 2007).

Clearly, heavy alcohol consumption continues to be a problem for policymakers, educators, and treatment providers. Continual development and support of effective alcohol prevention and treatment strategies are needed to curb this serious societal issue.

ASSESSMENT AND DIAGNOSIS

The evaluative and diagnostic processes are important steps in helping those struggling with alcohol addiction. A clinical evaluation and assessment provide a starting point from which to begin planning treatment. However, one should not assume that evaluation and diagnosis stop after the first few counseling sessions. W. R. Miller, Forcehimes, and Zweben (2011) noted that substance abuse evaluation is an ongoing process: New information constantly emerges, and it is the clinician's task to determine which information best informs practice.

Assessment of alcohol use and problems can help clinicians clarify the diagnostic picture, determine the severity of use, and propose treatment interventions. The clinician has a bevy of assessment options at his or her disposal. First and foremost is the general diagnostic (or intake) interview. Within this interview, the clinician can ask questions about quantity of alcohol use (How much do you drink on a typical occasion?), frequency of alcohol use (How often do you drink?), previous treatment history, current life functioning, and family history of use. Use of these general questions provided important information about Sam, who admitted to drinking 16 beers per day!

The clinician also can turn to screening tools and questions to get a better sense of the extent of the problem. One popular screening method for alcohol use is the CAGE assessment (Ewing, 1984). The CAGE consists of four questions: "Have you ever felt a need to cut down on your drinking?" "Have you ever felt angry or annoyed at someone because they commented that you drank too much?" "Have you ever felt bad or guilty because you drank too much? "Have you ever had a drink first thing in the morning to steady your nerves and get rid of a hangover (eye-opener)?" These questions can be asked as separate questions or infused into a diagnostic (or intake) interview. The Substance Abuse Subtle Screening Inventory–3 (SASSI-3; Lazowski, Miller, Boyce, & Miller, 1998) is another popular screening tool for both alcohol and drug addiction. The SASSI-3 takes 10 minutes to complete and can be scored by hand relatively quickly. The results help clinicians determine whether a client has a high or low probability of having a substance dependence disorder. In the case of Sam, it appears that both the CAGE and SASSI-3 would be good screening tools to use to strengthen the argument that Sam struggles with severe alcohol problems. Example items on the SASSI-3 are shown in Exhibit 2.1.

If it is determined through screening methods that a client's drinking and its associated consequences are severe, more formal assessment procedures are warranted. An excellent assessment instrument unique to alcoholism is the Alcohol Use Inventory (AUI; Horn, Wanberg, & Foster, 1986). The AUI is a 228-item multiple-

---

EXHIBIT 2.1

If a statement tends to be TRUE for you, fill in the square in the column headed T. If a statement tends to be FALSE for you, fill in the square headed F. Please try to answer all questions.

❏ T ❏ F 1. Most people would like to get what they want.
❏ T ❏ F 7. I have not lived the way I should.
❏ T ❏ F 29. Sometimes I wish I could control myself better.
❏ T ❏ F 53. I take all my responsibilities seriously.

For each item below, circle the number which reflects how often you have experienced the situation described during: (a) your entire life, (b) the past six months, (c) the six months before _____, or (d) the six months since _____. The numbers below represent 0 = *Never*, 1 = *Once or Twice*, 2 = *Several Times*, 3 = *Repeatedly*.

Alcohol

❏ 0 ❏ 1 ❏ 2 ❏ 3 1. Had drinks with lunch?
❏ 0 ❏ 1 ❏ 2 ❏ 3 5. Experienced physical problems after drinking (e.g., nausea, seeing/hearing problems, dizziness, etc.)?
❏ 0 ❏ 1 ❏ 2 ❏ 3 7. Become depressed after sobering up?
❏ 0 ❏ 1 ❏ 2 ❏ 3 11. Become nervous or had the shakes after sobering up?

Other Drugs

❏ 0 ❏ 1 ❏ 2 ❏ 3 1. Taken drugs to improve your thinking and feeling?
❏ 0 ❏ 1 ❏ 2 ❏ 3 4. Taken drugs to improve your enjoyment of sex?
❏ 0 ❏ 1 ❏ 2 ❏ 3 7. Gotten into trouble with the law because of drugs?
❏ 0 ❏ 1 ❏ 2 ❏ 3 12. Been accepted into a treatment program because of drug use?

Note. From "Efficacy of the Substance Abuse Subtle Screening Inventory-3 (SASSI-3) in Identifying Substance Dependence Disorders in Clinical Settings," by L. Lazowski, F. Miller, M. Boyce, and G. Miller, *Journal of Personality Assessment, 71*, 1998, pp. 114–128.

choice instrument that assesses direct alcohol use as well as multiple manifestations of problematic drinking, such as marital problems, drinking to cope with stress, and work problems. The AUI is easy to administer and score (computer scoring is available) and aids in clarifying the diagnostic picture. An interesting fact about the AUI is that it was normed on a population who was hospitalized for severe alcohol dependency. If a client scores high on the various scales of this test, he or she is essentially being compared to a clinical sample. Thus, the results may help clients see the need for change if they are scoring higher than the most severe cases of alcoholism. Because Sam indicated drinking extensively most days of the week, the AUI would be an appropriate assessment tool to use in his case. The feedback from this assessment could provide Sam with powerful information on the extent of his use and associated problems. Such information might spark motivation to change.

After a thorough assessment, the clinician is in a position to make a formal diagnosis. The *Diagnostic and Statistical Manual of Mental Disorders, Fifth Edition* (*DSM–5*; American Psychiatric Association, 2013) includes a chapter titled "Substance-Related and Addictive Disorders" that includes substance use disorders and substance-induced disorders (intoxication and withdrawal). The chapter includes criteria for substance use disorders, intoxication, and withdrawal relevant to each specific type of drug (e.g., alcohol, amphetamines, cocaine, opiates). Note that the *DSM–5* no longer includes separate diagnoses for abuse and dependence (e.g., alcohol abuse, alcohol dependence), replacing these instead with substance use disorder (e.g., alcohol use disorder). The *DSM–5* lists 12 classes of drugs (with the 12th class being "other"). For the purposes of this section, only alcohol use disorder is discussed.

To meet criteria for alcohol use disorder, a client must have at least two out of 11 symptoms, such as spending a great deal of time securing alcohol, taking alcohol in larger amounts than intended, or engaging in continued use despite negative consequences. Alcohol use disorder can be qualified on a continuum of severity depending on how many criteria the client meets: two or three criteria for mild severity, four or five criteria for moderate, and six or more criteria for severe. The clinician also has the option of including remission specifiers related to early remission (meets no criteria for 3–12 months) and sustained remission (has not met criteria for more than 12 months).

In general, the difference between mild and severe alcohol use is a matter of degree. A person with alcohol use disorder, mild, might engage in binge drinking on a weekend and subsequently get arrested for driving under the influence. He vows to never drink like that again and tries to cut down. Two months later, he is out partying and gets in a fight. This person has demonstrated a recurrent pattern of disruption due to alcohol. However, he is not displaying the consistent, persistent pattern of alcohol use that characterizes more severe forms of drinking. Continuing with this example, if this individual drank heavily every day, experienced both tolerance and withdrawal, had cravings for alcohol use, experienced numerous consequences, and ignored his responsibilities at work and home, alcohol use disorder, severe, would be the appropriate diagnosis. Sam appears to meet criteria for alcohol use disorder given his multiple problems, attempts to stop, daily heavy use, and tolerance. Further assessment could clarify whether his alcohol use is moderate or severe. Diagnosis is an important part of the evaluation process. It provides the clinician with information on the severity and pattern of the drinking and associated problems. A well-thought-out diagnosis is a valuable aid to treatment planning.

TREATMENT SETTINGS

Following assessment and diagnosis, the clinician determines the most appropriate treatment setting. Treatment settings are recommended by the degree of restriction or structure that clients have in their day-to-day lives (Perez, 2001; Stevens & Smith, 2013). For example, clients who exhibit severe alcohol use, who place themselves in constant danger, and who are at risk for serious injury need a restrictive environment, such as medical detoxification and stabilization. Clients who have a history of heavy drinking but are currently abstinent, are working, and have the support of family might thrive in an outpatient setting. Hence, the more severe the alcohol use, the more structure the client needs.

Inpatient

Inpatient settings include medical detox and stabilization, dual-diagnosis hospital inpatient, and some therapeutic communities and residential programs (Perez, 2001; Stevens & Smith, 2013). These settings are often quite effective in helping clients with severe alcohol problems achieve abstinence, even out, and begin the process of therapy. They include medical services, individual counseling, group counseling, 12-step mutual support groups, religious services, meals, and shelter. Unfortunately, inpatient treatment stays are temporary, and thus many hospital centers experience the revolving door phenomenon, in which clients are treated for acute alcoholism but then return a few weeks later. These experiences necessitate the need for proper referral to less restrictive environments once clients are stabilized.

Outpatient

Outpatient-type settings include partial hospitalization and day treatment, temporary recovery or halfway homes, and outpatient or intensive outpatient treatment (Perez, 2001; Stevens & Smith, 2013). These settings allow the client to carry on with some or all aspects of his or her normal, day-to-day life. For example, in a day treatment center, the client needs to attend treatment during the day but is free to spend time with his or her family at home in the evenings. Outpatient settings are an essential follow-up for clients who matriculated through an inpatient or residential alcohol program. Among other interventions, relapse prevention strategies become important at this stage and setting of treatment. Traditional outpatient counseling is once a week, although intensive outpatient, partial hospitalization, and day treatment programs might include several group and individual sessions a week.

EVIDENCE-BASED RESEARCH: TREATMENT OF ALCOHOLISM

To establish the effectiveness of an intervention, researchers typically conduct clinical trials designed to compare one treatment modality against another. In general, research has supported a number of clinical treatment approaches for alcoholism. A perusal of the ClinicalTrials.gov website (www.clinicaltrials.gov), a government database of clinical trial research supported by public funds, demonstrates hundreds of active and completed research projects examining a range of issues related to alcohol. Needless to say, a review of this entire research database is beyond the scope of this chapter; however, general conclusions and findings can be gleaned from the empirical literature. In this section, I focus on the most common approaches to the treatment of alcohol addiction, dividing the research into medications and behavioral interventions. Keep in mind that in many cases both medications and behavioral interventions are used simultaneously as part of the client's treatment plan.

Medications

Disulfiram

Disulfiram, also known as Antabuse, is primarily used to prevent alcohol relapse (Perkinson, 2012). It is the oldest medication used for this purpose on the market (more than 50 years; Perkinson, 2012). Individuals who take disulfiram and consume alcohol experience severe nausea and vomiting as toxic levels of acetaldehyde build up in the body (Perkinson, 2012). Research evidence suggests that disulfiram works better than no treatment, but only in persons who want to get better and remember to take it. Indeed, despite its effectiveness, a major weakness of disulfiram is that clients can easily avoid taking it when they feel the urge to drink impulsively.

Naltrexone

Naltrexone was originally designed as a medication to help those addicted to opioids, and its effects on alcohol addiction were discovered somewhat by accident (Perkinson, 2012). Clinical trials have shown that clients generally experience less alcohol craving and, subsequently, less potential for relapse when taking naltrexone compared to placebo (Perkinson, 2012). However, as with disulfiram, medication compliance may be an issue when clients are not monitored. To address this concern, researchers have developed a longer lasting form of naltrexone that is injected once a month by a medical specialist. This longer lasting form is thought to enhance medication compliance. In summarizing the outcome research, Perkinson (2012) reported that, in general, researchers have found that individuals who received the longer lasting form of naltrexone treatment reported reductions in quantity and frequency of drinking.

Some questions have been raised regarding naltrexone's effectiveness with severe forms of alcohol addiction, suggesting that it is effective for harm reduction but not complete abstinence. Limited research has examined the relationship between naltrexone effectiveness and level of severity of alcoholism; many studies have suggested that naltrexone is only effective in less severe clients (Pettinati et al., 2011). However, examining the effectiveness of injectable extended-release naltrexone on clients with severe alcohol problems, Pettinati et al. (2011) found that in conjunction with psychosocial interventions, naltrexone was more effective in reducing drinking behavior and maintaining abstinence than the placebo in a sample of severe alcohol users. The authors believed that their findings suggest that using naltrexone as an intervention with more severe cases of alcohol use disorders is a promising clinical strategy but warrants further investigation.

Acamprosate

Like naltrexone, acamprosate (Campral) works by decreasing alcohol craving and preventing relapse. However, acamprosate's mechanism of action in the brain is different from that of naltrexone, as it most likely exerts its effect on the GABA neurotransmitter system (Perkinson, 2012). Acamprosate is most effective for those who are highly motivated to stop drinking, as it requires several administrations a day (Perkinson, 2012). Clients who are less motivated to stop drinking may struggle with such a stringent daily regimen.

Gabapentin and Levetiracetam

Of the medications that are approved for treatment of alcohol use disorders, not all are effective with all individuals, which has led to a desire to find other options. The time immediately following cessation of drinking is the most risky for developing symptoms of withdrawal, insomnia, anxiety, depression, and concentration difficulties. These symptoms may seriously interrupt the recovery process. As a result, several authors have suggested the importance of identifying other medications that may be effective in the treatment of alcohol problems (Anton et al., 2011; Fertig et al., 2012). Two such medications are gabapentin and levetiracetam.

Anton et al. (2011) suggested that the anticonvulsant gabapentin may be useful in conjunction with already-approved naltrexone because it affects the part of the brain that is associated with alcohol withdrawal. In order to examine this hypothesis, the authors conducted a randomized controlled clinical trial in which gabapentin was added to the first 6 weeks of a 16-week regimen of naltrexone. The researchers found that when combined with naltrexone, gabapentin had positive outcomes relative to drinking behavior and withdrawal symptoms. Naltrexone alone was found to have no significant difference from the placebo. The researchers also found that the positive results of the added gabapentin were no longer present when patients stopped taking the medication, suggesting no long-term treatment effects.

In recent years, anticonvulsants have been thought to be an effective pharmacological treatment for alcohol use disorders. For this reason, Fertig et al. (2012) set out to examine the effectiveness of levetiracetam for the treatment of alcohol use because of its known effect on the areas of the brain that are associated with drinking behavior. The authors conducted a randomized, double-blind, placebo-controlled clinical trial in order to test their hypothesis that levetiracetam would be beneficial in the treatment of alcohol use. The researchers found no significant difference in drinking outcomes in an inpatient sample of heavy alcohol users who were administered the placebo versus those who received levetiracetam. However, more research is needed to establish whether levetiracetam can have a meaningful impact on treating alcohol problems.

Behavioral Interventions

The use of medication in the treatment of alcohol addiction holds promise to help clients better manage their recovery. Unfortunately, medications are not totally effective, and their use depends on client motivation. In my clinical experience, medications for alcohol abuse are initially effective but become irrelevant as client motivation to change waxes and wanes. As with medications for other mental health conditions, addiction medication can help stabilize a client and take away the craving for alcohol. Much of the work of recovery, however, depends on client characteristics, the client–counselor relationship, and treatment approaches and techniques. The importance of behavioral interventions in the treatment of substance abuse has been underscored by the National Institute on Drug Abuse (NIDA), based on decades of research. In its *Principles of Drug Addiction Treatment* (see Appendix 2.1), NIDA (2012) noted that counseling and other behavior therapies are critical components of effective treatment for substance addiction. Clinical interventions such as building motivation, enhancing relapse prevention, improving problem solving, strengthening relationships, and engaging in rewarding nondrug activities were mentioned as key benefits of addictions counseling.

W. R. Miller et al. (2011) suggested that mental health practitioners' formal training curricula, which include psychological theories, techniques, and various counseling approaches (e.g., group counseling), provide up to 80% of the knowledge and skills needed to work effectively with clients struggling with addiction. There is a mistaken notion that alcohol and drug counselors must possess secret knowledge and have extensive specialized training to be effective with addicted clients (W. R. Miller et al., 2011). In fact, many clinicians are prepared to work with addicted clients when they graduate from a graduate program. However, if they wish to focus their clinical work in the addictions, some specialized training, the remaining 20%, is critical. This includes knowledge about the classification, effects, and dangers of alcohol; the physiological mechanisms of the brain; AA philosophy; key terminology; and intervention skills such as relapse prevention. Evidence-based behavioral interventions for alcohol addiction are based on both traditional counseling theories (e.g., cognitive behavior therapy [CBT]) and unique approaches in the addictions (relapse prevention).

Several evidence-based treatments for alcoholism have been identified, including motivational interviewing (MI), CBT and its derivatives (dialectical behavior therapy and rational emotive behavior therapy), and relapse prevention. Family therapy and group therapy are considered standards as adjuncts of care for alcoholism treatment, having not amassed the same amount of research support as the other approaches. Martin and Rehm (2012) found that motivational enhancement therapy (a variation of MI), behavior therapies, CBT, and brief therapies were the most effective for alcohol use problems. In a survey of the frequency with which substance abuse treatment facilities in the United States used certain clinical approaches almost or often, 55% reported using MI, 66% used CBT, 87% used relapse prevention (heavily based on CBT), and 56% used 12-step group facilitation. In the same survey, 96% of facilities engaged in general substance abuse counseling always or often.

MI has amassed an impressive array of research (more than 200 clinical trials) that supports its effectiveness across a range of clinical problems (W. R. Miller & Rollnick, 2013). For example, Magill, Stout, and Apodaca (2012) found that MI produced better treatment outcomes (i.e., decreased drinking behavior) compared to CBT. What is interesting, however, is that the researchers found that a focus on ambivalence was not predictive of decreased drinking behavior, but emphasizing commitment to change was predictive. The authors suggested that addressing ambivalence may be beneficial at different stages of change but not others; it was recommended that a focus on ambivalence be done in phases and in the beginning stages, with decreasing emphasis throughout treatment.

Researchers have attempted to study the effectiveness of MI combined with other approaches, such as CBT (Arkowitz, Westra, Miller, & Rollnick (2007) and family therapy (Steinglass, 2008). This is primarily because MI lends itself well as a beginning approach when motivation to change is low. As motivation increases, the clinician is free to continue using MI as a standalone approach or move to other treatment strategies. Steinglass (2008) proposed a model that incorporates family therapy and MI in the treatment of alcohol addiction. Steinglass reported that not only do family factors have an impact on the development of alcohol use disorders, but the disorder also affects the family system. Although family involvement in treatment has been found in several instances to increase positive outcome, it often is difficult to work with or locate family members of individuals who are addicted, leading to this modality being underutilized.

Steinglass (2008) outlined an approach to family treatment of alcohol use that combines ideas from MI with an empirically based family systems model. The family systems model, called the *family life history model,* focuses on the family as the target of treatment rather than focusing on the individual. The goal of this model is to identify and address family rituals, family routines, and family problem-solving strategies. The idea behind this model is to better understand how these three aspects of family are altered and disrupted by alcohol use. Four treatment components are addressed within the family: assessment, detoxification, relapse prevention, and rehabilitation. MI is a critical technique in this approach because it addresses the family's ambivalence as a whole toward change. This ambivalence toward change is driven by the need for homeostasis; that is, the family members have come to need the behaviors of the alcohol-dependent member in order to maintain rituals, routines, and problem solving and have changed their behaviors to fit the addiction. According to Steinglass, in order to combine family systems models with MI, it is important to understand that alcohol use cycles exist on a family level. The systemic motivational model includes three phases: assessment, family treatment, and aftercare. Steinglass outlined strategies for implementing MI techniques and philosophy into each of these phases in order to counsel the family as a unit.

As noted previously, Martin and Rehm (2012) found that motivational enhancement therapy, behavior therapies, CBT, and brief interventions were most effective with alcohol use disorders. Consistent with psychotherapy outcome research in general, the authors reported no empirical differences in effectiveness among these treatments; however, in comparison to other forms of treatments, the aforementioned approaches have amassed more empirical evidence in support of treatment of alcohol use disorders. In addition to the type of treatment used, the clinician's effectiveness in delivering the treatment has also been found to be important. When comorbid mental health disorders are present, integrative treatment that is stage based, motivational, and long term seems to address both the mental health and alcohol/substance-related concerns (Thombs, 2006).

CBT has emerged as an evidence-based treatment for alcohol addiction. What is less well known, however, is that CBT also has been shown to help improve attitudes toward treatment among alcohol-addicted individuals. Stecker, McGovern, and Herr (2012) posited that although lifetime prevalence rates for alcohol use disorders are high (approximately 20%–22%), the rates of those who seek treatment are low (approximately 38%). The authors suggested that barriers to seeking treatment include the client's *beliefs* about treatment. They posited that negative thinking patterns related to treatment are an indicator of willingness to seek treatment. Stecker et al. attempted to study this idea by initiating a brief CBT intervention to target and challenge negative beliefs about treatment in efforts to raise rates of treatment seeking. The authors found that participants who received the CBT intervention were 3 times more likely to enter treatment. They also found that those who received the intervention were more likely to remain in treatment longer than those who did not. Thus, the authors suggested that in addition to its effectiveness as a treatment for alcohol and other substance addictions (Beck, Wright, Newman, & Liese, 1993), CBT may be a positive treatment intervention for challenging negative thinking patterns related to the treatment of alcohol use disorders.

Witkiewitz and Marlatt (2011) analyzed and discussed several evidence-based CBT-based interventions for the treatment of alcohol use disorders. Coping skills and relapse prevention training aim to identify specific triggers and teach helpful coping skills to decrease the likelihood of returning to problem drinking. Contingency management approaches draw from operant conditioning and provide positive and negative reinforcers to discourage alcohol use. Family behavior therapy explores the role of relationships in problem drinking and works with the family to improve problem solving, communication, and relationship skills. *Facilitated self-change* refers to new techniques that utilize the Internet to assist clients in monitoring their own progress in decreasing their alcohol consumption. Finally, aversion therapy aims to pair negative responses with alcohol consumption. Witkiewitz and Marlatt reported that each of these behavioral techniques is equally effective because of similar underlying cognitive and behavioral components. Similar treatment components (social support, structure and goals, reinforcement, coping skills, self-efficacy, and normative models for abstinence) have received additional empirical support and provide a framework for tailoring treatment to specific client needs rather than using a one-size-fits-all treatment (Witkiewitz & Marlatt, 2011).

In addition, there are several adjunct and supportive services for those struggling with alcohol abuse and alcoholism. NIDA (www.drugabuse.gov) and NIAAA (www.niaaa.nih.gov) are two excellent resources for both clinicians and clients. Their websites include a bevy of information on the latest in treatment, research, and resources. Because these organizations are sponsored, funded, and supported by the U.S. government, their publications are in the public domain and can be either downloaded or requested free of charge. Clients can visit these websites to learn more about alcohol addiction, specific treatment approaches, and common effects or dangers. One of the most common adjunct services for those struggling with alcoholism is AA, a not-for-profit organization designed to help those with a desire to stop drinking. Numerous alternative mutual help groups exist, including Rational Recovery, Moderation Management, and Women for Sobriety. The differences between these groups include the relative emphasis on spirituality in recovery, the use of CBT and other behavioral methods, and variations on the original 12 steps of AA. Support groups also exist for family members of those addicted to alcohol (e.g., Al-Anon). A plethora of mutual help group information is available on the Internet, including contact information, resources, and educational material. Most communities across the United States have mutual help groups. Because of the popularity of AA, and its influence on many other mutual help groups, it is given focus in the following paragraphs.

W. R. Miller et al. (2011) preferred the use of the term *mutual* help groups to *self*-help groups to describe AA and other groups based on the 12 steps. The term *mutual* is quite fitting given that the thrust of AA is about providing mutual support between and among members. The support AA provides is often critical to helping clients recover from alcohol addiction. For some, it is the most significant influence on their recovery. Many alcohol addiction theorists and researchers place AA attendance at the core of their treatment model and support a triadic counseling relationship: the client, the clinician, and AA.

Since its inception in 1935, AA has grown to more than 2 million members and 116,000 groups across 170 countries worldwide (Alcoholics Anonymous General Service Office, 2012). The foundation of AA membership is attending meetings, reading from the Big Book (the basic text for AA), and working the 12 steps. Most clients who attend AA come to treatment working on a particular step. Clinicians are encouraged to become familiar with the 12 steps of AA; a brief description of each follows:

- *Steps 1–3.* Steps 1–3 are about becoming aware of and accepting one's limitations (Stevens, 2001). In essence, these steps remind clients that (a) addictive use of alcohol is destroying their lives; (b) they do not have the knowledge or skills to handle the addiction themselves; and (c) there is a Higher Power that is a source of strength, support, and trust that can help them find a way out (Gorski, 1989). Naturally, these steps can be quite difficult for some to accept. After all, no one wants to admit to having limitations. However, the wisdom of these steps is the subtle message that what clients have tried before *is not working.* In essence, before these individuals can move on with life, they must be willing to admit they have a problem. That is the first step.

- *Steps 4–7.* These steps require honest self-assessment and behavioral actions designed to promote change (Dobmeier & Stevens, 2013), such as taking a "fearless moral inventory," admitting the exact nature of one's wrong-doings, and asking a Higher Power to remove these moral defects. Essentially, these steps are designed to help the addicted individual examine both strengths and weakness and look at all aspects of the self (Gorski, 1989), followed by corrective actions. Some clients can remain working on these steps for a significant amount of time, sometimes for years. This reflects the depth of searching that is implied within these steps in AA circles and how taking an honest look at oneself can be a scary endeavor.

- *Steps 8 and 9.* Steps 8 and 9 are about atoning for past behavior and misdeeds. Those struggling with alcoholism harbor guilt and shame for the loved ones and friends they have hurt, the lost opportunities, and the abdication of personal responsibility. Indeed, these steps are about taking personal responsibility for the hurt they have caused others (Stevens, 2001). Gorski (1989), referring to Step 9, stated that there is no "free lunch in life" (p. 137). That is, one pays either now or later for causing harm; if later, the payment can be much worse in the form of guilt and shame. Until clients make amends to others, these emotions will continue to eat away at them.

- *Steps 10–12.* The final three steps build on the previous nine steps and promote continuous self-analysis, strengthening spirituality and a connection to a higher power, and carrying what has been learned to other addicts and to other aspects of clients' lives (Dobmeier & Stevens, 2013).

AA is a critical part of recovery for many clients struggling with alcohol addiction. It is likely that most clients who present for counseling due to alcoholism also take part in AA. Thus, clinicians should familiarize themselves with AA, especially the 12 steps. Some clinicians may fear that AA will interfere with therapy, especially if the therapeutic approach and AA are at odds about the causes and assumptions of alcoholism. AA is considered an appropriate adjunct to therapy but does not replace therapy. It is important to note that discussions around AA and the 12 steps can fill in the gaps where therapy may not be as effective. AA does not need to be the entire focus of therapy; something as simple as checking in with the client regarding AA attendance shows interest and opens up the possibility for further exploration. Client worries and fears about AA attendance can be explored and addressed. A more intentional method of integration would be for the clinician and client to engage in an in-depth exploration of a particular step.

Of course, not all clients are open to attending AA and not all consider AA to be necessarily helpful. Attitudes about AA can be based on misinformation, stereotypes, negative experiences with AA, or negative stories heard about AA from others. Common stereotypes are that AA only applies to the skid-row drunk or that AA forces a person to believe what it believes. Clients who show initial reluctance, however, often soften their views after a few sessions. It is not recommended that clients leave AA because of one bad experience. For example, some clients might find members at a meeting to be relatively cold, distant, scary, or too friendly and personal. Clients need to experiment with different meetings to find a good fit.

ARMED SERVICES SUBSTANCE ABUSE TREATMENT PROGRAMS

Each branch of the U.S. military has an organized substance abuse rehabilitation program. Data are being collected regarding the efficacy of these programs. The programs are quite similar and adhere to the disease model of addictions, with alcohol being the major drug abused. The Substance Abuse Rehabilitation Program (SARP), a Navy program described here, includes a mission statement and various services. The SARP is a good example of a substance abuse program that deals with all drugs, including alcohol.

SARP's mission statement includes the delivery of quality health care to support the armed forces; maintenance of medical readiness; and the advancement of medicine through education, research, and training. In addition, the SARP includes components of alcohol and drug abuse assessment, as well as education, consultation, assessment, inpatient treatment, outpatient treatment, and continuing care services for active duty members of the military. Treatment options are available at multiple levels:

- *Impact:* A two and a half day program conducted on Monday and Tuesday, full days. This program is designed for patients who have not been diagnosed with a significant substance related disorder, but whose use of substances has created concern for the patient or the patient's command. Impact involves participation in an interactive educational curriculum and exposure to 12 step recovery programs.

- *Outpatient:* An eight day program conducted Monday through Friday on the first week and Monday through Wednesday on the second week. This program is designed primarily for patients diagnosed with Alcohol Abuse. Treatment is designed to assist the patient with the development of a responsible drinking plan, as well as providing information on healthy alternatives to substance use and abuse. Treatment involves participation in small and large group counseling, workshops and task groups, and self-help/12-Step meetings.

- *Intensive Outpatient:* A three-week program conducted Monday through Friday. This program is designed for patients diagnosed with Alcohol Dependence and/or are determined to be in need of an abstinence based treatment program. Patients will be in treatment for full days throughout the three week program. Patients coming from out of the area will be required to arrange berthing at a local BEQ [bachelor enlisted quarters]. Treatment consists of participation in small and large group counseling, workshops and task groups, physical fitness and self-help/12-Step meetings.

- *Residential:* A 34-day, 24-hour program conducted Monday through Sunday. This program is designed for patients diagnosed with Alcohol and/or Drug Dependence. All patients assigned to this treatment program, will reside in Building 500, Naval Submarine Base San Diego. Treatment consists of participation in small and large group counseling, workshops and task groups, recreational activities/fitness, medical assessments, psychological/psychiatric assessments and self-help/12-Step meetings.

- *Family Programs:* An educational, support and assistance program offered to family members of individuals enrolled in the various SARP treatment programs. This program offers family members and enrolled patients the opportunity to learn more about how substance abuse/dependence impacts their family.

- *Continuing Care:* This program is available for all patients leaving any of the formal treatment programs. Patients will attend an orientation on the first Monday after treatment is completed and will then be assigned to a weekly Continuing Care group. Patients may participate in these groups for up to one year after inpatient or outpatient treatment concludes. Weekly groups provide the patient an opportunity to work with trained professionals as they apply things learned in treatment in their daily lives. Continuing Care is also open to past patients who wish to get more support for their sobriety. (Naval Medical Center San Diego, 2013, "Services Provided")

Although many of the concepts utilized within programs like SARP are evidence based, the substance abuse programs themselves offered by the military do not meet criteria for being evidence based because of their recent adoption and difficulties related to following up with patients in recovery.

HOSPITAL TREATMENT PROGRAMS

Schick Shadel Hospital has locations in Seattle, Washington; Cooper City, Florida; and Denton, Texas, among other cities. Its counterconditioning treatment program is an example of a hospital treatment intervention that years of medical research claim is scientifically proven to work. Alcohol addiction manifests in repeated episodes of heavy drinking. As a progressive disease, alcoholism is believed to require an average of 12+ years of drinking to manifest full symptoms. Alcoholism's effects on the body include physical damage to the gastrointestinal, cardiovascular, and nervous systems. Untreated, this damage can be fatal.

The counterconditioning at Schick Shadel has its origins in an organic brain process of accidental aversion. Schick Shadel applies this natural process in an organized, scientific way, providing a medically supervised counterconditioned aversion to addictive substances as alcohol. The Schick Shadel Hospital approach is a medical alternative treatment to addiction, as it is not a 12-step program. The typical length of stay is 10 days for treatment, plus additional days for detox as needed. The Schick Shadel Hospital incorporates aspects of the following, which are considered top approaches in substance abuse treatment programs and continued care (Hester & Miller, 1995): behavioral contracting, brief interventions, chemical counterconditioning, community reinforcement, motivational enhancement, and social skills trainings. Schick Shadel's physicians and researchers have published dozens of articles on addiction and counterconditioning (e.g., Smith & Frawley, 1990, 1993; Smith, Frawley, & Polissar, 1991). Their research includes hundreds of patients who have recovered from alcohol dependence following treatment. Success is measured by total abstinence for 1 year, as determined by former patients' self-evaluation.

THE MATRIX MODEL

The Matrix Model is an evidence-based intensive outpatient treatment program for alcohol and drug addiction. It is advocated as an intensive outpatient program that any treatment center can implement.

The Matrix Model is a comprehensive, multi-format program that covers six key clinical areas
- Individual/conjoint therapy
- Early recovery
- Relapse prevention
- Family education
- Social support
- Urine testing

It's an integrated therapeutic model incorporating
- Cognitive behavioral
- Motivational enhancement
- Couples and family therapy
- Individual supportive/expressive psychotherapy and psychoeducation
- Twelve Step facilitation
- Group therapy and social support

It's a federally recognized model
- Center for Substance Abuse Treatment (CSAT)
- National Institute on Drug Abuse (NIDA)

- Office of National Drug Control Policy and Department of Justice (National Synthetic Drugs Action Plan)
- Drug Strategies
- Under review by the National Registry of Effective Programs and Practices (SAMHSA) (Hazelden, n.d.-a)

The Matrix Model treatment protocol can be extended up to 12 months through continuing care/aftercare.

It's structured differently than inpatient treatment, using methods proven-effective with stimulant addicts
- It's less confrontational
- Progress is gradual
- The focus is on the present
- "Core issues" are not immediately addressed
- The client's allegiance is to the therapist rather than the group
- A non-judgmental attitude is basis of client-therapist bond
- Change recommendations are based on scientific data
- Changes are incorporated immediately into lifestyle

It's more directive and behavior-focused than general therapy
- Visit frequency results in strong transference, which is encouraged and utilized
- Goal is stability versus comfort
- Focus is abstinence; bottom-line is always continued abstinence
- Therapeutic team approach is utilized
- Therapist frequently pursues less motivated clients
- Focus is on behavior rather than feelings; the behavior is more important than the reason behind it
- Family system support is encouraged
- Therapist functions as a coach/advocate

It's proven-effective. The organizing principles of the Matrix have been developed and modified over a 20 year period, using data from the treatment experience of 6,000 cocaine and 2,500 methamphetamine addicts. The Matrix Model works because it
- Creates explicit structure and expectations
- Establishes a positive, collaborative relationship with each patient
- Teaches information and cognitive-behavioral concepts
- Positively reinforces positive behavior change
- Provides corrective feedback when necessary/roll with resistance
- Educates family regarding stimulant abuse recovery
- Introduces and encourages self-help participation
- Uses urinalysis to monitor drug use and take the issue of use "off the table" (Hazelden, n.d.-b)

The Matrix Model is a comprehensive approach to alcohol addiction. It is an effective program for treating alcohol addiction and an evidence-based treatment for use with methamphetamine addicts.

CONCLUSIONS

Alcohol addiction plays a major role within societies across the globe. The number of individuals and families experiencing the effects of misusing alcohol continues to increase, as do costs related to this phenomenon. Alcohol addiction is considered a chronic brain disease (American Psychiatric Association, 2013; American Society of Addiction Medicine, 2011; NIDA, 2012). Therefore, the treatment of alcohol addiction and other drug addictions continues to change as the result of new neuroscience research. Further research on alcohol addiction is welcome at a time when many feel that treatment programs have failed and that individuals who have been successful in overcoming their addiction have done so on their own, or despite inadequate treatment.

However, a number of models, interventions, and programs are effective for treating alcohol addiction. Several programs are evidence based and have a history of research supporting a high degree of efficacy. NIDA (2012) identified 13 principles of effective drug addiction treatment, and most alcohol addiction programs follow these principles. Yet additional research is needed concerning the effects of alcohol on the body and brain, as well as the effectiveness of alcohol addiction treatment programs.

RESOURCES

Websites

Alcoholics Anonymous
    www.aa.org
Moderation Management
    www.moderation.org
National Institute on Alcohol Abuse and Alcoholism
    www.niaaa.nih.gov
National Institute on Drug Abuse
    www.drugabuse.gov
Rational Recovery
    www.rational.org
Resources for Therapists
    www.psychotherapy.net
Substance Abuse and Mental Health Services Administration
    www.samhsa.gov
Women for Sobriety
    www.womenforsobriety.org

Videos

Brown, S. (1997). *Treating alcoholism with Stephanie Brown, Ph.D.: Vol. 2. The developmental model in theory: A live workshop*. San Francisco, CA: Jaylen Productions.

Miller, W. R., Rollnick, S., & Moyers, T. B. (2013). *Motivational interviewing: Helping people change*. Albuquerque, NM: The Change Companies.

REFERENCES

Alcoholics Anonymous General Service Office. (2012). *A.A. at a glance*. Retrieved from http://www.aa.org/assets/en_US/f-1_AAataGlance.pdf

American Psychiatric Association. (2013). *Diagnostic and statistical manual of mental disorders* (5th ed.). Arlington, VA: Author.

American Society of Addiction Medicine. (2011). *Definition of addiction.* Retrieved from http://www.asam.org/research-treatment/definition-of-addiction

Anton, R. F., Myrick, H., Wright, T. M., Latham, P. K., Baros, A. M., Waid, L., & Randall, P. K. (2011). Gabapentin combined with naltrexone for the treatment of alcohol dependence. *American Journal of Psychiatry, 168,* 709–717.

Arkowitz, H., Westra, H., Miller, W. R., & Rollnick, S. (Eds.). (2007). *Motivational interviewing in the treatment of psychological problems.* New York, NY: Guilford Press.

Beck, A. T., Wright, F. D., Newman, C. F., & Liese, B. S. (1993). *Cognitive therapy of substance abuse.* New York, NY: Guilford Press.

Bouchery, E. E., Harwood, H. J., Sacks, J. J., Simon, C. J., & Brewer, R. D. (2011). Economic costs of excessive alcohol consumption in the U.S., 2006. *American Journal of Preventive Medicine, 41,* 516–524.

Dobmeier, R. A. & Stevens, P. (2013). Retaining sobriety: Relapse prevention strategies. In P. Stevens & R. L. Smith, *Substance abuse counseling: Theory and practice* (5th ed.). Columbus, OH: Pearson.

Doweiko, H. E. (2009). *Concepts of chemical dependency* (7th ed.). Belmont, CA: Brooks/Cole.

Ewing, J. A. (1984). Detecting alcoholism: The CAGE questionnaire. *Journal of the American Medical Association, 252,* 1905–1907.

Fertig, J. B., Ryan, M. L., Falk, D. E., Litten, R. Z., Mattson, M. E., Ransom, J., . . . Stout, R. (2012). A double-blind, placebo-controlled trial assessing the efficacy of levetiracetam extended-release in very heavy drinking alcohol-dependent patients. *Alcoholism: Clinical and Experimental Research, 36,* 1421–1430.

Gorski, T. T. (1989). *Understanding the twelve steps: An interpretation and guide for recovering people.* New York, NY: Simon & Schuster.

Hazelden. (n.d.-a). *The Matrix Model: What it is.* Retrieved from http://www.hazelden.org/web/public/matrixwhat.page

Hazelden. (n.d.-b). *The Matrix Model: Why it works.* Retrieved from http://www.hazelden.org/web/public/matrixwhy.page

Hester, R. K., & Miller, W. R. (1995). *Handbook of alcoholism treatment approaches: Effective alternatives* (2nd ed.). Needham Heights, MA: Allyn & Bacon.

Hoffman, J., & Froemke, S. (2007). Addiction is a brain disease. In J. Hoffman & S. Froemke (Eds.), *Addiction: New knowledge, new treatments, new hope* (pp. 66–69). New York, NY: Rodale.

Horn, J. L., Wanberg, K. W., & Foster, F. M. (1986). *The Alcohol Use Inventory (AUI).* Minneapolis, MN: National Computer Systems.

Lazowski, L., Miller, F., Boyce, M. & Miller, G. (1998). Efficacy of the Substance Abuse Subtle Screening Inventory-3 (SASSI-3) in identifying substance dependance disorders in clinical settings. *Journal of Personality Assessment, 71,* 114–128.

Magill, M., Stout, R. L., & Apodaca, T. R. (2012). Therapist focus on ambivalence and commitment: A longitudinal analysis of motivational interviewing treatment ingredients. *Psychology of Addictive Behaviors, 27,* 754–762. doi:10.1037/a0029639

Martin, G. W., & Rehm, J. (2012). The effectiveness of psychosocial modalities in the treatment of alcohol problems in adults: A review of the evidence. *Canadian Journal of Psychiatry/La Revue Canadienne De Psychiatrie, 57*(6), 350–358.

Miller, W. R., Forcehimes, A. A., & Zweben, A. (2011). *Treating addiction: A guide for professionals.* New York, NY: Guilford Press.

Miller, W. R., & Rollnick, S. (2013). *Motivational interviewing: Preparing people for change* (3rd ed.). New York, NY: Guilford Press.

National Institute on Alcohol Abuse and Alcoholism. (2012). *Overview of alcohol consumption.* Retrieved from http://www.niaaa.nih.gov/alcohol-health/overview-alcohol-consumption

National Institute on Drug Abuse. (2012). *Principles of drug addiction treatment: A research-based guide* (3rd ed.). Retrieved from http://www.drugabuse.gov/publications/principles-drug-addiction-treatment-research-based-guide-third-edition/principles-effective-treatment

Naval Medical Center San Diego. (2013). *Substance Abuse Rehabilitation Program (SARP)*. Retrieved from http://www.med.navy.mil/sites/nmcsd/Patients/Pages/SubstanceAbuseRehabProgram.aspx

Perez, P. J. (2001). Treatment setting and treatment planning. In P. Stevens & R. L. Smith (Eds.), *Substance abuse counseling: Theory and practice* (2nd ed., pp. 151–176). Upper Saddle River, NJ: Prentice Hall.

Perkinson, R. R. (2012). *Chemical dependency counseling: A practical guide* (4th ed.). Los Angeles, CA: Sage.

Pettinati, H. M., Silverman, B. L., Battisti, J. J., Forman, R., Schweizer, E., & Gastfriend, D. R. (2011). Efficacy of extended-release naltrexone in patients with relatively higher severity of alcohol dependence. *Alcoholism: Clinical and Experimental Research, 35*, 1804–1811.

Schiller, J. S., Lucas, J. W., Ward, B. W., & Peregoy, J. A. (2012). *Summary health statistics for U.S. adults: National Health Interview Survey, 2010* (Vital and Health Statistics Series 10, No. 252). Retrieved from http://www.cdc.gov/nchs/data/series/sr_10/sr10_252.pdf

Smith, J. W., & Frawley, P. J. (1990). Long-term abstinence from alcohol in patients receiving counter conditioning as part of a multimodal inpatient program. *Journal of Substance Abuse Treatment, 7*, 77–82.

Smith, J. W., & Frawley, P. J. (1993). Treatment outcome of 600 chemically dependent patients treated in a multimodal inpatient program including counter conditioning and pentothal interviews. *Journal of Substance Abuse Treatment, 10*, 359–369.

Smith, J. W., Frawley, P. J., & Polissar, L. (1991). Six- and twelve-month abstinence rates in inpatient alcoholics treated with counter conditioning compared with matched inpatients from a treatment registry. *Alcoholism: Clinical and Experimental Research, 15*, 862–870.

Stecker, T., McGovern, M. P., & Herr, B. (2012). An intervention to increase alcohol treatment engagement: A pilot trial. *Journal of Substance Abuse Treatment, 43*(2), 161–167.

Steinglass, P. (2008). Family systems and motivational interviewing: A systemic-motivational model for treatment of alcohol and other drug problems. *Alcoholism Treatment Quarterly, 26*(1–2), 9–29.

Stevens, P., & Smith, R. L. (2013). *Substance abuse counseling: Theory and practice* (5th ed.). Columbus, OH: Pearson.

Thombs, D. L. (2006). *Introduction to addictive behaviors* (3rd ed.). New York, NY: Guilford Press.

Wechsler, H., Lee, J. E., Kuo, M., Seibring, M., Nelson, T. F., & Lee, H. (2002). Trends in college binge drinking during a period of increased prevention efforts. *Journal of American College Health, 50*, 203–217.

Witkiewitz, K., & Marlatt, G. A. (2011). Behavioral therapy across the spectrum. *Alcohol Research & Health, 33*(4), 313–319.

APPENDIX 2.1   PRINCIPLES OF DRUG ADDICTION TREATMENT

1. *Addiction is a complex but treatable disease that affects brain function and behavior.* Drugs of abuse alter the brain's structure and function, resulting in changes that persist long after drug use has ceased. This may explain why drug abusers are at risk for relapse even after long periods of abstinence and despite the potentially devastating consequences.

2. *No single treatment is appropriate for everyone.* Treatment varies depending on the type of drug and the characteristics of the patients. Matching treatment settings, interventions, and services to an individual's particular problems and needs is critical to his or her ultimate success in returning to productive functioning in the family, workplace, and society.

3. *Treatment needs to be readily available.* Because drug-addicted individuals may be uncertain about entering treatment, taking advantage of available services the moment people are ready for treatment is critical. Potential patients can be lost if treatment is not immediately available or readily accessible. As with other chronic diseases, the earlier treatment is offered in the disease process, the greater the likelihood of positive outcomes.

4. *Effective treatment attends to multiple needs of the individual, not just his or her drug abuse.* To be effective, treatment must address the individual's drug abuse and any associated medical, psychological, social, vocational, and legal problems. It is also important that treatment be appropriate to the individual's age, gender, ethnicity, and culture.

5. *Remaining in treatment for an adequate period of time is critical.* The appropriate duration for an individual depends on the type and degree of the patient's problems and needs. Research indicates that most addicted individuals need at least 3 months in treatment to significantly reduce or stop their drug use and that the best outcomes occur with longer durations of treatment. Recovery from drug addiction is a long-term process and frequently requires multiple episodes of treatment. As with other chronic illnesses, relapses to drug abuse can occur and should signal a need for treatment to be reinstated or adjusted. Because individuals often leave treatment prematurely, programs should include strategies to engage and keep patients in treatment.

6. *Behavioral therapies—including individual, family, or group counseling—are the most commonly used forms of drug abuse treatment.* Behavioral therapies vary in their focus and may involve addressing a patient's motivation to change, providing incentives for abstinence, building skills to resist drug use, replacing drug-using activities with constructive and rewarding activities, improving problem-solving skills, and facilitating better interpersonal relationships. Also, participation in group therapy and other peer support programs during and following treatment can help maintain abstinence.

7. *Medications are an important element of treatment for many patients, especially when combined with counseling and other behavioral therapies.* For example, methadone, buprenorphine, and naltrexone (including a new long-acting formulation) are effective in helping individuals addicted to heroin or other opioids stabilize their lives and reduce their illicit drug use. Acamprosate, disulfiram, and naltrexone are medications approved for treating alcohol dependence. For persons addicted to nicotine, a nicotine replacement product (available as patches, gum, lozenges, or nasal spray) or an oral medication (such as bupropion or varenicline) can be an effective component of treatment when part of a comprehensive behavioral treatment program.

(Continued)

APPENDIX 2.1   PRINCIPLES OF DRUG ADDICTION
TREATMENT (*Continued*)

8. *An individual's treatment and services plan must be assessed continually and modified as necessary to ensure that it meets his or her changing needs.* A patient may require varying combinations of services and treatment components during the course of treatment and recovery. In addition to counseling or psychotherapy, a patient may require medication, medical services, family therapy, parenting instruction, vocational rehabilitation, and/or social and legal services. For many patients, a continuing care approach provides the best results, with the treatment intensity varying according to a person's changing needs.

9. *Many drug-addicted individuals also have other mental disorders.* Because drug abuse and addiction—both of which are mental disorders—often co-occur with other mental illnesses, patients presenting with one condition should be assessed for the other(s). And when these problems co-occur, treatment should address both (or all), including the use of medications as appropriate.

10. *Medically assisted detoxification is only the first stage of addiction treatment and by itself does little to change long-term drug abuse.* Although medically assisted detoxification can safely manage the acute physical symptoms of withdrawal and can, for some, pave the way for effective long-term addiction treatment, detoxification alone is rarely sufficient to help addicted individuals achieve long-term abstinence. Thus, patients should be encouraged to continue drug treatment following detoxification. Motivational enhancement and incentive strategies, begun at initial patient intake, can improve treatment engagement.

11. *Treatment does not need to be voluntary to be effective.* Sanctions or enticements from family, employment settings, and/or the criminal justice system can significantly increase treatment entry, retention rates, and the ultimate success of drug treatment interventions.

12. *Drug use during treatment must be monitored continuously, as lapses during treatment do occur.* Knowing their drug use is being monitored can be a powerful incentive for patients and can help them withstand urges to use drugs. Monitoring also provides an early indication of a return to drug use, signaling a possible need to adjust an individual's treatment plan to better meet his or her needs.

13. *Treatment programs should test patients for the presence of HIV/AIDS, hepatitis B and C, tuberculosis, and other infectious diseases as well as provide targeted risk-reduction counseling, linking patients to treatment if necessary.* Typically, drug abuse treatment addresses some of the drug-related behaviors that put people at risk of infectious diseases. Targeted counseling focused on reducing infectious disease risk can help patients further reduce or avoid substance-related and other high-risk behaviors. Counseling can also help those who are already infected to manage their illness. Moreover, engaging in substance abuse treatment can facilitate adherence to other medical treatments. Substance abuse treatment facilities should provide onsite, rapid HIV testing rather than referrals to offsite testing—research shows that doing so increases the likelihood that patients will be tested and receive their test results. Treatment providers should also inform patients that highly active antiretroviral therapy (HAART) has proven effective in combating HIV, including among drug-abusing populations, and help link them to HIV treatment if they test positive.

Note. From *Principles of Drug Addiction Treatment: A Research-Based Guide, Third Edition* (pp. 2–5), by National Institute on Drug Abuse, 2012, Washington, DC: National Institute on Drug Abuse. In the public domain.

CHAPTER 3

NICOTINE ADDICTION
Robert L. Smith

STUDENT LEARNING OUTCOMES

At the conclusion of this chapter students will

1. Identify why nicotine is addictive
2. Identify criteria used in determining nicotine addiction
3. Identify consequences of nicotine addiction
4. Identify treatment methods for nicotine addiction
5. Identify treatment guidelines for interventions used with nicotine addiction

CASE AND CASE DISCUSSION

Matt started smoking when he was 16. It seemed cool to smoke, and he also smoked to fit in and impress his peers. It wasn't long before he was up to a pack a day. The smoking increased as he started drinking. However, before he even graduated from high school he had lost two relatives to smoking. First his aunt died of complications associated with emphysema. Matt could still remember her visits. Each time she visited, her breathing seemed to be worse, and she would often gasp for a breath of air. Yet she continued to smoke, despite her health issues and prods from others to quit. Eventually she stopped visiting, not just because everyone would tell her to stop smoking, but because she had problems walking. Toward the end of her days she became severely depressed. Her response to quitting was "This is my only pleasure, and it's too late for me to quit." She would follow this up with "We all have to die sometime, don't we?" Matt's aunt died before his 18th birthday.

About the same time his aunt died, his grandfather, Paw Paw, passed away. His grandfather's death was also the result of a life of smoking and using chew tobacco. That was Paw Paw! Matt remembered that Paw Paw would always fix things around the home. He was a handyman who had the ability to do just about anything. Matt was not sure Paw Paw ever really accepted it when his doctor diagnosed him with emphysema as the result of continuous tobacco use. During his last years he had to carry oxygen with him wherever he went, even just around the house. The death of Paw Paw and his aunt had an indelible effect on both Matt and his dad. They both vowed to quit smoking, going cold turkey. Matt's dad lasted several years without smoking. Matt quit for 6 months.

Matt had always wanted to enlist in the service, so he did, selecting the Navy. It was soon clear to him that the "work hard, play hard" motto was a reality. He took up smoking again soon after he enlisted. That was what everyone did on breaks. His smoking habit soon increased to more than a pack of cigarettes a day. Smoking and coffee were commonplace. In later years it was smoking and alcohol. Matt smoked in the service in large part because of peer pressure, just wanting to be part of the gang. After being discharged he continued smoking, as it served as a stress reliever and was part of a habit or lifestyle he had already established.

Matt continued for the next 15 years as a heavy smoker, making weak attempts to quit on several occasions, whereas his dad became a light smoker, able to have a cigarette now and then. His dad passed away of a heart attack at the age of 57. Matt thought he was far too young to die and wondered whether the tobacco use shortened his life. He realized later that the second-hand smoke probably affected his health more. His friends had been heavy smokers, whether it was his poker buddies or the group he had hung around with at the bar or coffee shop.

After both prodding and encouragement from his wife and two daughters, Matt decided to quit this awful habit that had taken several family members. His attempts at going cold turkey this time lasted at best a couple of weeks and at worst a day or two. He met with his doctor after he began to have difficulty climbing stairs and walking. He both wanted and didn't want to know the reason for his shortness of breath. The diagnosis of light to moderate emphysema was a wakeup call. On his doctor's recommendation Matt sought behavioral counseling to cope with stress and addiction triggers. His doctor also put him on the nicotine patch. He attended some Nicotine Anonymous group sessions but received most of the support he needed from his family. After several weeks of using the nicotine patch Matt began using nicotine gum, and he has now been smoke free for several years. He sees his counselor when he experiences stress and still uses 2 mg or less of the nicotine gum per day. The support from his family and friends has been invaluable. Matt is glad he sought help and did not follow the same path as others in his family.

OVERVIEW OF NICOTINE ADDICTION

Nicotine addiction is the second leading cause of death worldwide. Fortunately for Matt, he was able to quit smoking before it was too late. The causes of smoking-related mortality are atherosclerotic vascular disease, cancer, and chronic obstructive pulmonary disease (COPD). Smoking can also contribute to other diseases, such as histiocytosis X, respiratory bronchiolitis, obstructive sleep apnea, idiopathic pneumothorax, low birth weight, and prenatal mortality (Lande, 2012).

It has been estimated that there are about 1.3 billion smokers in the world, most (84%) living in developing countries. If current smoking trends continue, tobacco will kill an estimated 10 million people each year by 2020. It is further believed that direct health care costs and loss of productivity from death and illness due to tobacco use will cost governments an estimated $200 billion per year, with a third of these costs borne by developing countries (Esson & Leeder, 2004; World Health Organization, 2005).

Similar to other addictions, an addiction to nicotine is complex. Reasons why individuals start, continue, or stop smoking are multifaceted. Factors affecting the risk of becoming addicted to nicotine are explored later in this chapter. What is known is that the nicotine in cigarette smoke is potent, affecting one's body and brain as well as one's state of being. Cigarette smoking can calm anxiety or excite (perk up) an individual, especially during the morning hours, often along with a cup of coffee. Nicotine therefore is used as both a stimulant and a depressant.

The National Institute on Drug Abuse (NIDA) and the Centers for Disease Control and Prevention cite tobacco use as the leading preventable cause of disease, disability, and death in the United States. Cigarette smoking results in more than 443,000 premature deaths in the United States each year, accounting for one in every five U.S. deaths (NIDA, 2012a). It is estimated that an additional 8.6 million people suffer with a serious illness caused by smoking and that for every one person who dies from smoking, 20 more suffer from at least one serious tobacco-related illness (Centers for Disease Control and Prevention, 2009, 2013; U.S. Department of Health and Human Services, 2006).

A disturbing fact is that the harmful effects of smoking extend far beyond the smoker. Secondhand smoke causes serious disease and death. It is estimated that 126 million Americans are regularly exposed to secondhand smoke, and almost 50,000 nonsmokers die from diseases caused by exposure to secondhand smoke (NIDA, 2012a).

NIDA (2012a), referring to a report by the Surgeon General (Novello, 1990), assessed tobacco as one of the leading health care costs in the United States. Alcohol is reported to be the leading overall cost at $185 billion. Abuse of tobacco, alcohol, and illicit drugs together is estimated to cost the United States more than $524 billion annually in terms of crime, lost work productivity, and health care (NIDA, 2008).

The 2012 Monitoring the Future study provided prevalence rates for tobacco use among eighth graders, 10th graders, and 12th graders. The study indicated a statistically significant change in cigarette use between eighth and 10th grades. Increases in the use of both cigarettes and smokeless tobacco daily, during the past month, and over the lifetime were recorded for eighth through 12th graders (Johnston, O'Malley, Bachman, & Schulenberg, 2013). The 2011 National Survey on Drug Use and Health indicated a significant increase in cigarette use between the ages of 12 and 26 (Substance Abuse and Mental Health Services Administration, 2012). Monitoring the Future has begun to survey for other methods of smoking tobacco, such as using hookah water pipes and small cigars. Findings from 2012 showed that 18.3% of 12th graders had smoked a hookah in the past year, and 19.9% had smoked a small cigar (NIDA, 2012b).

An interesting finding of the Monitoring the Future study is that after cigarette smoking by high school students peaked in 1996–1997, it has continued to decline. However, marijuana use has increased in recent years. There has been an upward trend in the use of cigarettes and marijuana among 12th graders from 1975 to 2012. In 2012, 17.1% of 12th graders were (past-month) cigarette smokers, whereas 22.9% were current marijuana smokers (NIDA, 2012b).

It is the nicotine in tobacco that leads to addiction among long-term users. This addictive drug is included in all forms of tobacco: cigarettes, cigars, pipe tobacco, snuff, and chewing tobacco. Imaging studies indicate that smoking tobacco affects the entire body, including the vital organs. Cigarette smoking has been linked to cataracts; pneumonia; acute myeloid leukemia; and cancers of the mouth, pharynx, larynx, esophagus, stomach, pancreas, cervix, kidney, and bladder (NIDA, 2012a). Cigarette smoking is linked to 90% of all cases of lung cancer, the number one cancer killer of both men and women. Nicotine, which is readily absorbed into the bloodstream, stimulates the adrenal glands to release the hormone epinephrine (adrenaline). Epinephrine in turn stimulates the central nervous system and increases blood pressure, respiration, and heart rate.

Nicotine also increases levels of the neurotransmitter dopamine, affecting the brain pathways that control reward and pleasure (NIDA, 2010). Changes in the brain occur with long-term use of tobacco, resulting in addiction. Addiction is considered a brain disease (NIDA, 2009) affecting brain circuits, such as those involved in reward, motivation, learning, memory, and behavioral control. Like with other drugs, withdrawal symptoms of irritability, attention difficulties, sleep disturbances, increased appetite, and cravings occur when a person tries to quit using tobacco. However, once someone does quit, the health benefits can be immediate, including reduced risk for cancers, heart disease, and stroke.

Tobacco addiction is a chronic disease that often requires multiple attempts to quit. Although some smokers are able to quit without help, most need assistance. Both behavioral interventions (counseling) and medication can help smokers quit, but the combination of medication with counseling is considered more effective than either alone. Tobacco (nicotine) addiction has properties similar to addictions to alcohol, heroin, gambling, sex, and food. The process of addiction involves craving, loss of control, inability to quit, continued use of the drug or behavior despite consequences, and withdrawal. The consequences of tobacco addiction are severe.

Definitions

The following definitions are provided to help the reader further understand nicotine addiction.

Acetaldehyde: Also known as *ethanol.* Acetaldehyde enters a person's system through smoking cigarettes or inhaling secondhand smoke. Acetaldehyde can negatively affect the lungs, heart, and blood vessels.

Asthma: Asthma can occur in nonsmokers as well as smokers, with symptoms similar to COPD. Smoking can make asthma worse, and smokers are particularly likely to suffer from a combination of both asthma and COPD. However, asthma patients are more likely to have allergies such as allergic rhinitis (hay fever) or atopic dermatitis (eczema). Asthma may cause shortness of breath and coughing, along with episodes of wheezing and tightness in the chest (American Academy of Allergy, Asthma and Immunology, 2013).

Chronic obstructive pulmonary disease (COPD): A progressive disease that makes it hard to breathe. *Progressive* means that the disease gets worse over time. COPD can cause coughing that produces large amounts of mucus, wheezing, shortness of breath, tightness in the chest, and other symptoms. Cigarette smoking is the leading cause of COPD. Most people who have COPD either smoke or used to smoke. Long-term exposure to other lung irritants—such as air pollution, chemical fumes, or dust—also may contribute to COPD (National Heart, Lung, and Blood Institute, 2013).

Dopamine: A neurotransmitter whose levels are increased by nicotine, cocaine, heroin, and marijuana. The increase in dopamine may improve mood and activate feelings of pleasure. When an individual experiences these effects over a long period of time, he or she becomes addicted. Changes in the brain involving the production of dopamine are often the result of this addiction.

Emphysema: A lung disease that makes it hard to breathe. Emphysema and chronic bronchitis together are referred to as *chronic obstructive lung disease,* or COPD (American Lung Association, n.d.).

Nicotine: An addictive drug found in cigarettes, cigars, pipe tobacco, snuff, and chewing tobacco. Nicotine enters the bloodstream and stimulates the adrenal glands to release epinephrine (adrenaline), which increases blood pressure, respiration, and heart rate ("What Is Nicotine Dependence?" 2013). *Nicotine* is

> a poisonous volatile alkaloid derived from tobacco (Nicotiana spp.) and responsible for many of the effects of tobacco; it first stimulates (small doses), then depresses (large doses) at autonomic ganglia and myoneural junctions. Its principal urinary metabolite is cotinine. Nicotine is an important tool in physiologic and pharmacologic investigation, is used as an insecticide and fumigant, and forms salts with most acids. ("Nicotine," n.d.)

Nicotine addiction: An addiction to nicotine, and the second leading cause of death worldwide.

Nicotine dependence: An addiction to tobacco products caused by one of its ingredients, the drug nicotine. Nicotine is an addictive drug that causes mood-altering changes in the brain that are temporarily pleasing, making people want to use it more and more ("What Is Nicotine Dependence?" 2013).

Nicotine replacement treatments (NRTs): The first pharmacological treatments (i.e., nicotine chewing gum, the nicotine transdermal patch, nasal sprays, inhalers, and lozenges) approved by the U.S. Food and Drug Administration for smoking cessation therapy. They are often used with behavior therapy.

Nicotine vaccine: A smoking cessation intervention that induces an immune response to nicotine in the bloodstream, blocking access to the brain and preventing the effects of nicotine.

Non-nicotine medications: Medications as bupropion (Zyban) and varenicline tartrate (Chantix) that do not include nicotine but target nicotine receptors in the brain to ease withdrawal symptoms and block the effects of nicotine.

Secondhand smoke: Includes exhaled smoke and smoke from the burning end of tobacco products. Because it is found in one's surroundings, it is known as *environmental tobacco smoke.* Individuals exposed to secondhand smoke increase their risk of developing heart disease, lung cancer, respiratory problems, pneumonia, and bronchitis (Centers for Disease Control and Prevention, 2013).

Smokeless tobacco: Examples include chewing tobacco and snuff, which can also increase the risk of cancer, specifically oral cancer.

Tobacco smoke: A complex grouping of chemicals, including ammonia, carbon monoxide, cyanide, formaldehyde, and tar. These carcinogens can play a role in the development of lung cancer, emphysema, bronchial disorders, and cardiovascular diseases.

Risk Factors for Nicotine Addiction

All consumers of tobacco are at risk for nicotine addiction. *Risk factors* are things that increase the likelihood of something specific occurring. For example, obesity is a risk factor for heart problems and diabetes. Two well-studied risk factors for nicotine addiction are the age at which one starts smoking and whether one's parents are smokers ("What Is Nicotine Dependence?" 2013). Some pick up the habit of smoking during childhood or adolescence. And children are more likely to smoke if their parents are smokers. The wrong circle of friends is also likely to be a risk factor for addiction.

Frequently identified risk factors for nicotine addiction include the following:

- *Parents who smoke.* Children whose parents both smoke are twice as likely than children whose parents do not smoke to become smokers themselves.
- *Friends who smoke.* Children who have friends who smoke are more likely to start using tobacco products, such as cigarettes.
- *Heredity.* Genetics plays a major role in both nicotine and alcohol addiction. Some people are able to smoke or drink occasionally throughout their lives and never seem to become addicted, whereas others are unable to stop smoking or drinking without experiencing unpleasant withdrawal symptoms. It is believed that the responses of receptors on the surface of nerve cells in the brain are influenced by genes.
- *Mental illness.* People with depression, bipolar disorder, schizophrenia, and other mental illnesses are at greater risk than others for becoming addicted to nicotine.
- *Alcohol and substance abuse.* Individuals who abuse alcohol, as well as those who take illegal drugs, are more likely than others to become addicted to nicotine.

Research findings by Hu, Griesler, Schaffran, and Kandel (2011) support the salience of these risk factors for addiction. Hu et al. found significant relationships between the age at which one initially began smoking, whether one's parents were smokers, and the smoking habits of adolescents. Numerous factors influence adolescents' decision to start smoking or use other tobacco products. These factors include individual characteristics, such as stress and low self-esteem, but also the social characteristics previously discussed, such as smoking by parents, siblings, and friends. Exposure and susceptibility to tobacco advertising, although difficult to assess, also affect smoking initiation among adolescents. The Office of Adolescent Health (2013) cited the following factors as affecting adolescents' decision to start smoking:

- *Being older.* Rates of regular cigarette smoking and other tobacco use are higher among older adolescents than younger adolescents (although the rate of smoking initiation is higher among younger adolescents).

- *Being male.* Females tend to smoke fewer cigarettes a day, use cigarettes with lower nicotine content, and inhale cigarette smoke less deeply than males.
- *Being White.* White adolescents are more likely than Black or Hispanic adolescents to use tobacco. However, multiethnic adolescents, as well as Native Americans and Alaska Natives, are more likely than adolescents of any other race or ethnicity to use tobacco.
- *Lacking college plans.* Adolescents who plan to attend 4 years of college are much more likely to be nonsmokers than their peers who lack such plans.
- *Having parents who are not college educated.* Adolescents whose parents have little or no college education are more likely to smoke than those whose parents have a college education or more.
- *Experiencing highly stressful events.* Having experienced numerous highly stressful events in childhood is linked with a greater risk of starting smoking by age 14. Examples of these stressors include being a witness or victim of abuse, experiencing a parental separation, or growing up in a household in which a family member is mentally ill or incarcerated.

Regardless of age, several signs point to whether a person has an addiction to nicotine:

- *The individual smokes and cannot stop.* The person has made at least one serious attempt to stop, but the attempt was unsuccessful.
- *The individual experiences withdrawal symptoms.* When trying to stop, the individual has physical and mood-related symptoms. There are cravings, bouts of moodiness and irritability, poor concentration, a feeling of being depressed and hollow/empty, anger, frustration, increased appetite, and insomnia. In some cases there may also be diarrhea or constipation.
- *The person continues smoking despite the emergence of health problems.* The individual continues to smoke even though he or she has developed smoking-related illnesses, such as a lung or heart condition.
- *The person makes social and/or recreational sacrifices.* Some activities are given up because of smoking (e.g., certain restaurants or pubs that are smoke free). Perhaps the individual stops visiting friends whose environments or homes are smoke free. The regular Friday night bowling get-together with friends stops because smoking is not allowed there anymore ("What Is Nicotine Dependence?" 2013).

At-risk nicotine dependence involves behavioral as well as physical factors. Behaviors and cues associated with smoking include (a) certain times of the day, such as first thing in the morning with coffee or during breaks at work; (b) after a meal, while drinking alcohol; (c) in a certain setting with friends; (d) while talking on the phone; (e) in stressful situations or when depressed; and (f) near a burning cigarette (smell and sight).

There are serious consequences for long-term smokers. Tobacco smoke contains nearly 4,800 chemicals and carcinogens that reach the body's organs during inhalation. Smoke is harmful to every organ of the body and leads to some of the most debilitating conditions:

- *Lung cancer and respiratory problems.* Nine out of 10 smokers are likely to develop lung cancer and other respiratory problems such as emphysema and bronchitis. Smoking also worsens the condition of asthmatic patients.
- *Heart disease and circulation problems.* Smoking makes a person more vulnerable to heart disease and stroke. Smoking just a couple of cigarettes daily is sufficient to double the chances of having a heart attack. Smoking worsens existing heart ailments.
- *Cancers.* Tobacco addiction leads to various cancers, including cancers of the esophagus, larynx, throat, mouth, bladder, pancreas, kidney, and cervix.
- *Changes in physical appearance.* The harmful chemicals in tobacco smoke can change the structure of the skin, leading to signs of premature aging and wrinkles. Smoking also leads to discoloration of the teeth and fingernails.
- *Infertility and impotence.* Smoking can cause infertility in women and impotence in men.
- *Complications related to pregnancy.* Pregnant women who smoke are at a greater risk of having a miscarriage, premature delivery, and stillbirth. Also, their babies are likely to be affected by sudden infant death syndrome or low birth weight.
- *Common colds and flu.* Smokers are more vulnerable to respiratory problems such as the common cold, flu, and bronchitis.
- *Diabetes.* Smoking increases insulin resistance. This can pave the way for Type II diabetes. Diabetes in turn can lead to kidney problems.
- *Impaired senses.* Smoking nullifies the senses of taste and smell. Therefore, food does not seem to be appetizing any more.
- *Risks to loved ones.* Spouses and partners of smokers are more likely to develop lung cancer and heart attacks from secondhand smoke and passive smoking. The children of smokers too are likely to experience sudden infant death syndrome, asthma, and ear infections.

DIAGNOSIS OF NICOTINE ADDICTION

The first step in treating nicotine dependence is to identify tobacco users (Ashton & Streem, 2009). Guidelines for diagnosing nicotine dependence have been put forth by the American Psychiatric Association and the U.S. Department of Health and Human Services. Emphasis is placed on asking patients systematically during each visit whether they use tobacco. It is suggested that these questions remain part of an assessment that identifies signs and symptoms and then records findings in the patient's electronic medical record. This process is believed to sharpen the clinician's recognition of nicotine dependence and assist in providing the most appropriate intervention. The criteria for diagnosing nicotine dependence or tobacco use disorder, defined under tobacco-related disorders in the *Diagnostic and Statistical Manual of Mental Disorders, Fifth Edition* (DSM–5; American Psychiatric Association), appear below. These criteria mirror those for diagnosing other substance disorders, including a consistent increase in use; unsuccessful attempts to stop; time spent securing the substance; craving; failure in meeting work, school, or other significant roles; risk taking; tolerance; and withdrawal.

A. A problematic pattern of tobacco use leading to clinically significant impairment or distress, as manifested by at least two of the following, occurring within a 12-month period:

1. Tobacco is often taken in larger amounts or over a longer period than was intended.
2. There is a persistent desire or unsuccessful efforts to cut down or control tobacco use.
3. A great deal of time is spent in activities necessary to obtain or use tobacco.
4. Craving, or a strong urge to use tobacco.
5. Recurrent tobacco use resulting in a failure to fulfill major role obligations at work, school, or home (e.g., interference with work).
6. Continued tobacco use despite having persistent or recurrent social or interpersonal problems caused or exacerbated by the effects of tobacco (e.g., arguments with others about tobacco use).
7. Important social, occupational, or recreational activities are given up or reduced because of tobacco use.
8. Recurrent tobacco use in situations in which it is physically hazardous (e.g., smoking in bed).
9. Tobacco use is continued despite knowledge of having a persistent or recurrent physical or psychological problem that is likely to have been caused or exacerbated by tobacco.
10. Tolerance, as defined by either of the following:
    a. A need for markedly increased amounts of tobacco to achieve the desired effect.
    b. A markedly diminished effect with continued use of the same amount of tobacco.
11. Withdrawal, as manifested by either of the following:
    a. The characteristic withdrawal syndrome for tobacco (refer to Criteria A and B of the criteria set for tobacco withdrawal).
    b. Tobacco (or a closely related substance, such as nicotine) is taken to relieve or avoid withdrawal symptoms.

Source. From *Diagnostic and Statistical Manual of Mental Disorders, Fifth Edition* (p. 571), by American Psychiatric Association, 2013, Arlington, VA: American Psychiatric Association. Copyright 2013 by the American Psychiatric Association. Reprinted with permission. All rights reserved.

The *DSM–5* assesses the pattern of tobacco use over a 12-month period by level of severity: mild = presence of two or three symptoms, moderate = presence of four or five symptoms, severe = presence of six or more symptoms. In addition, the *DSM–5* identifies features supporting a tobacco use disorder, including smoking within 30 minutes of waking, smoking daily, increasing the number of cigarettes smoked per day, and waking at night to smoke (American Psychiatric Association, 2013, p. 573). Three types of risk factors related to this disorder are also identified: temperamental (externalizing personality traits; attention-deficit/hyperactivity disorder or conduct disorders; depressive, bipolar, anxiety, personality, or psychotic disorders; other substance use disorders), environmental (low income and little education), and genetic and physiological (a heritability risk factor accounting for 50% of those assessed with a tobacco use disorder; American Psychiatric Association, 2013, p. 573). The *DSM–5* criteria and withdrawal indicators for a tobacco use disorder are as follows:

A. Daily use of tobacco for at least several weeks.
B. Abrupt cessation of tobacco use, or reduction in the amount of tobacco used, followed within 24 hours by four (or more) of the following signs or symptoms:
    1. Irritability, frustration, or anger.
    2. Anxiety.

 3. Difficulty concentrating.
 4. Increased appetite.
 5. Restlessness.
 6. Depressed mood.
 7. Insomnia.
C. The signs or symptoms in Criterion B cause clinically significant distress or impairment in social, occupational, or other important areas of functioning.
D. The signs or symptoms are not attributed to another medical condition and are not better explained by another mental disorder, including intoxication or withdrawal from another substance.

Source. From *Diagnostic and Statistical Manual of Mental Disorders, Fifth Edition* (p. 575), by American Psychiatric Association, 2013, Arlington, VA: American Psychiatric Association. Copyright 2013 by the American Psychiatric Association. All rights reserved. Reprinted with permission.

Several diagnostic tools can be used to assess nicotine addiction, including the Fagerström Test for Nicotine Dependence (see Table 3.1), the Hooked on Nicotine Checklist (Wheeler, Fletcher, Wellman, & Difranza, 2004), the Fagerström Test for Nicotine Dependence Smokeless Tobacco (Heatherton, Kozlowski, Frecker, & Fagerström, 1991), and breath carbon monoxide monitors. A number of tobacco cessation programs utilize and recommend these diagnostic measures (Medical Society of the State of New York, 2011; Tobacco Recovery Resource Exchange, 2009).

TABLE 3.1 FAGERSTRÖM TEST FOR CIGARETTE DEPENDENCE

Question	Points			
	3	2	1	0
How soon after you wake up do you smoke your first cigarette?	> 5 min	6–30 min	31–60 min	< 60 min
Do you find it difficult to refrain from smoking in places where it is forbidden (e.g., church, library, theater)?			Yes	No
Which cigarette would you hate most to give up?			First	Any other
How many cigarettes per day do you smoke?	≥ 31	21–30	11–20	< 10
Do you smoke more frequently during the first hours of waking than during the rest of the day?			Yes	No
Do you still smoke if you are so ill that you are in bed most of the day?			Yes	No

Total Points	Classification of Dependence
0–2	Very low
3–4	Low
5	Moderate
6–7	High
8–10	Very high

Note. From "Determinants of Tobacco Use and Renaming the FTND to the Fagerström Test for Cigarette Dependence," by K. O. Fagerström, 2011, *Nicotine & Tobacco Research,* 14, pp. 75–78. DOI: 10.1093/ntr/ntr137. Copyright 2011 by Karl O. Fagerström. Reprinted with permission. First = first cigarette in the morning.

The 5-A model is another tool used to assess tobacco use. This model, which includes five brief components, is often used in primary care settings. The 5-A model is considered an evidence-based strategy for treating tobacco dependence by the Medical Society of the State of New York (2011).

1. *Ask.* Systematically ask about tobacco use during every session, and document this information for each patient.
2. *Advise.* Advise the tobacco user to quit in a clear, strong, personalized manner.
3. *Assess.* Assess the willingness of the patient to attempt quitting.
4. *Assist.* Assist the patient in his or her attempt to quit, including through counseling, medication, and other appropriate interventions and support systems.
5. *Arrange.* Arrange follow-up contacts for individuals who are attempting to quit as well as for those who are not ready to quit.

Everyone knows one of the hundreds of millions of people who have attempted to quit smoking. Many have succeeded, yet too many have failed and have eventually lost their lives to this addiction. For a significant number of smokers, overcoming a dependence on tobacco is extremely difficult despite the benefits of quitting. It is estimated that anybody who gives up smoking before they are 50 years of age can reduce their risk of dying during the next 15 years by 50% compared with people who continue smoking. Experts say that smokers have a higher chance of permanent success if they pursue treatment that has been proven to be effective in scientific studies. Psychological therapy or medications may help; however, a combination of the two has been shown to be the most successful. Some of the benefits of quitting smoking include the following:

- *Heart rate slows down.* The benefits of giving up smoking are felt by the body just 20 minutes after stopping, when the heart rate (pulse rate) starts to drop.
- *Carbon monoxide normalizes.* Just 12 hours after one's last cigarette, blood carbon monoxide levels go back to normal.
- *Lung function improves.* Within 3 months of quitting, the individual's lung functioning starts to improve significantly.
- *Circulation improves.* Within 3 months of quitting, there are improvements in circulation.
- *Risk of heart attack decreases.* Within 12 months of quitting, the person's risk of having a heart attack falls by 50%.
- *Risk of stroke decreases.* Within 5 to 15 years, an ex-smoker's risk of having a stroke is the same as that of a lifetime nonsmoker ("What Is Nicotine Dependence?" 2013).

TREATMENT OF NICOTINE ADDICTION

Behavioral treatment and medication are the two modalities used to help clients wanting to disrupt a nicotine addiction. Counseling is often used with other interventions, including the use of medication.

Counseling

Counseling that emphasizes behavioral concepts has produced high rates of abstinence from smoking. Behavioral counseling uses a variety of methods to assist smokers in quitting, ranging from self-help materials to goal setting and contracting during individual counseling sessions. Interventions emphasize teaching individuals how to recognize and cope with high-risk situations. It is recommended that counseling interventions provide smokers with practical tools along with support and encouragement. For example, motivational interviewing (Miller & Rose, 2009) helps in the joining process and in establishing a relationship throughout counseling with clients diagnosed with an addiction, including a nicotine addiction.

The U.S. Department of Health and Human Services has established a national toll-free quitline, 800-QUIT-NOW, to serve as an access point for any smoker seeking counseling and information about quitting smoking. NIDA also supports research to expand the availability of behavioral counseling by developing interventions using alternative delivery formats, such as Web, computer, and text-based modalities, all of which may benefit hard-to-reach populations, thereby increasing access to treatment for millions of smokers.

Many smokers are daunted by the prospect of coping without cigarettes. Experts say that the first step is to think carefully about how one feels about smoking. Then compile a list of reasons for quitting, followed by a list of supportive resources, including family and friends. Finally, set a quit date and identify reinforcement systems that will help one remain smoke free. This mixture of cognitive, behavioral, and contingency management counseling is considered evidence based.

The seasoned counselor understands that thinking about giving up smoking is sometimes frightening. After all, the smoker is being asked to quit something he or she really likes to do. Smoking is the client's way of coping and often a crutch. In addition to discussing the benefits of smoking cessation, the counselor should emphasize the following suggestions:

1. *Identify factors that influence one's desire to smoke.* This includes triggers that involve other people, one's environment, and stressors.
2. *Identify activities that help in remaining smoke free.* This might include reading, exercise, spending time with family, and so on.
3. *Identify support systems.* This might include family, neighbors, friends, and colleagues.
4. *Check one's self-talk.* This includes changing one's thinking about smoking, redirecting one's thought process, and becoming aware of urges.
5. *Identify methods to mediate stress.* This could include using interventions such as meditation, deep breathing, thought stopping, and exercise.
6. *Remove oneself from activities associated with smoking.* This often involves discontinuing the use of alcohol.

For the addicted individual this process is not easy. Counseling may take time, and relapse is almost certain to occur. For both the client and the counselor, patience and persistence are necessary. It is important that counselors let clients addicted to tobacco understand that they are not alone, as hundreds of millions of people have gone through, are going through, and will go through what they are experiencing. This normalizing does not remove the addiction, but the awareness can perhaps help clients understand that they are not alone during the process of smoking cessation.

NRT

Several medications are available to help smokers quit. Some are proven to help, whereas others lack evidence of their effectiveness. It is not easy to decipher the litany of advertisements promising results for individuals who are thinking about quitting. Studies have shown that a combination of treatment modalities works best, often including the use of more than one NRT medication. The purpose of NRT is to send nicotine into the brain of a nicotine addict. NRT releases nicotine into the bloodstream at lower doses than what is obtained from tobacco smoke. NRT products help alleviate nicotine cravings that occur while one is attempting to quit smoking. Examples of NRT include the following:

- *Nicotine patch.* The nicotine patch is placed on the skin, allowing nicotine to enter the bloodstream through the skin. The patch is replaced daily. Individuals might use the nicotine patch for 8 to 12 weeks or longer. If the patch does not work, alternative medications are often recommended.
- *Nicotine gum.* Nicotine gum is a chewing gum that allows nicotine to enter the bloodstream through the mucosal lining of the mouth. Typical dosage range from 2 to 4 mg and are based on the smoker's individual habits. The gum is chewed until a mild peppery taste is detected, at which point the person places the gum between the cheek and gum line for approximately 20 minutes to release the nicotine.
- *Nicotine lozenges.* Nicotine lozenges, 2 to 4 mg in dosage, are hard candy-like tablets that dissolve in the mouth, sending nicotine into the bloodstream through the mucosal lining. Lozenges are placed under the tongue or between the gum line and cheek.
- *Nicotine inhalers.* Nicotine inhalers are cartridges that contain nicotine. Users inhale a nicotine vapor that is absorbed into the bloodstream through the mucosal lining of the mouth and throat.
- *Nicotine nasal sprays.* Nicotine nasal sprays send nicotine to the brain faster than other NRTs. Nicotine is sprayed directly into the nostril and absorbed into the bloodstream through the nasal membranes.

NRTs were the first pharmacological treatments approved by the U.S. Food and Drug Administration for use in smoking cessation therapy. NRTs deliver a controlled dose of nicotine to a smoker in order to relieve withdrawal symptoms or ease one off of nicotine during the smoking cessation process. They are most successful when used in combination with behavioral treatment.

Non-Nicotine Medications

Non-nicotine medications have been used as a treatment for smoking cessation. The following medications are most often part of a therapeutic package that includes counseling.

- *Varenicline (Chantix/Champix).* This drug interferes with receptors in the brain that attach to nicotine. The use of varenicline results in obtaining less pleasure from smoking and mitigating withdrawal symptoms. The recommended dosage includes one 0.5-mg tablet once a day for the first 3 days, then one 0.5-mg tablet twice daily for Days 4 to 7, and then one 1-mg tablet twice daily from Day 8. Varenicline is not recommended for the following individuals: persons younger than 18, pregnant women, or individuals with epilepsy or advanced kidney disease. Some of the side effects may include nausea, fatigue, headaches, constipation, and insomnia. It is recommended that clients quit completely before taking their first tablet.

- *Clonidine (Catapres).* This medication is usually recommended if other therapies have not worked. It is primarily used for treating hypertension (high blood pressure). However, the side effects, such as sedation and drowsiness, discourage the use of clonidine as a treatment.
- *Antidepressants.* Bupropion (Wellbutrin, Zyban) raises levels of dopamine and norepinephrine, as does nicotine. Some doctors recommend a combination of bupropion and the nicotine patch. This medication also reduces the risks of weight gain, a common consequence of giving up smoking. Patients with a history of seizures or serious head trauma, those younger than 18 years of age, pregnant or breastfeeding women, patients with anorexia or bulimia, individuals with a central nervous system tumor, and people with severe cirrhosis of the liver should not take bupropion. Bupropion may have side effects such as dry mouth, dizziness, headaches, and insomnia.
- *Nicotine vaccine.* The nicotine vaccine triggers the immune system to develop antibodies to nicotine, which bind to it as it enters the bloodstream, preventing the nicotine from reaching the brain. The vaccine can potentially eliminate the brain rush that smokers experience, thereby doing away with the pleasure people derive from smoking. The vaccine defeats the purpose of smoking by preventing nicotine from entering the brain.

Most studies indicate that patients who receive a combination of medication and behavioral counseling tend to have better success rates than those who receive medication or counseling by itself. Although medications may help with the immediate physical problems, behavior therapy helps people remain smoke free over the long term.

TREATMENT GUIDELINES FOR EVIDENCE-BASED PRACTICES

The clinical practice guideline *Treating Tobacco Use and Dependence: 2008 Update* (Fiore et al., 2008) is often cited when identifying evidence-based treatment strategies related to tobacco dependence. The guidelines contain strategies and recommendations meant to help professionals who work with clients with tobacco addictions, such as clinicians, tobacco treatment specialists, health care providers, administrators, and insurers. Emphasis is placed on encouraging clinicians to use the most effective counseling and medication treatments. The following guidelines provide basic information concerning tobacco dependence and evidence-based treatment strategies:

1. Tobacco dependence is a chronic disease that often requires repeated intervention and multiple attempts to quit. Effective treatments exist, however, that can significantly increase rates of long-term abstinence.
2. It is essential that clinicians and health care delivery systems consistently identify and document tobacco use status and treat every tobacco user seen in a health care setting.

3. Tobacco dependence treatments are effective across a broad range of populations. Clinicians should encourage every patient willing to make a quit attempt to use the counseling treatments and medications recommended in this Guideline.

4. Brief tobacco dependence treatment is effective. Clinicians should offer every patient who uses tobacco at least the brief treatments shown to be effective in this Guideline.

5. Individual, group, and telephone counseling are effective, and their effectiveness increases with treatment intensity. Two components of counseling are especially effective, and clinicians should use these when counseling patients making a quit attempt:

   - Practical counseling (problemsolving/skills training)
   - Social support delivered as part of treatment

6. Numerous effective medications are available for tobacco dependence, and clinicians should encourage their use by all patients attempting to quit smoking—except when medically contraindicated or with specific populations for which there is insufficient evidence of effectiveness (i.e., pregnant women, smokeless tobacco users, light smokers, and adolescents).

   - Seven first-line medications (5 nicotine and 2 non-nicotine) reliably increase long-term smoking abstinence rates: bupropion SR, nicotine gum, nicotine inhaler, nicotine lozenge, nicotine nasal spray, nicotine patch, varenicline.
   - Clinicians also should consider the use of certain combinations of medications identified as effective in this Guideline.

7. Counseling and medication are effective when used by themselves for treating tobacco dependence. The combination of counseling and medication, however, is more effective than either alone. Thus, clinicians should encourage all individuals making a quit attempt to use both counseling and medication.

8. Telephone quitline counseling is effective with diverse populations and has broad reach. Therefore, both clinicians and health care delivery systems should ensure patient access to quitlines and promote quitline use.

9. If a tobacco user currently is unwilling to make a quit attempt, clinicians should use the motivational treatments shown in this Guideline to be effective in increasing future quit attempts.

10. Tobacco dependence treatments are both clinically effective and highly cost-effective relative to interventions for other clinical disorders. Providing coverage for these treatments increases quit rates. Insurers and purchasers should ensure that all insurance plans include the counseling and medication identified as effective in this Guideline as covered benefits (Fiore et al., 2008).

The guideline update recommends that clinicians be provided with the most up-to-date intervention strategies and consider multiple methods of treatment. In addition, it is recommended that clinicians have ample institutional support to use a variety of proven options.

These guidelines include counseling (behavioral counseling), NRTs, and several non-nicotine medications as evidence-based approaches to treating nicotine addiction. Specific interventions, such as motivational interviewing, are also viewed as evidence based (Miller & Rose, 2009). Additional evidence-based interventions used to treat nicotine addiction, covered in Chapter 1 of this book, include cognitive behavior therapy, dialectical behavior therapy, aversive therapy, and support groups (e.g., Nicotine Anonymous).

CONCLUSIONS

Very few tobacco users like Matt in the case study that opened this chapter achieve permanent abstinence when attempting to quit smoking. Matt has the support of a family system, medical doctors, medication, and a professional counselor. This support is not always available to individuals who have used tobacco for many years, cycled through multiple periods of cessation and relapse, and eventually met the criteria for an addiction. According to the *DSM–5* (American Psychiatric Association, 2013), an individual with a diagnosed tobacco disorder is considered to have a chronic disease. Both the body and the brain are disrupted as the result of long-term continued use of tobacco.

Individuals addicted to tobacco go through a cycle similar to that experienced by those addicted to alcohol and other drugs. It is therefore not surprising that many of the treatment modalities used with nicotine addiction are also used with addictions to alcohol and other drugs. It is therefore incumbent on clinicians to be aware of the complexity of nicotine addiction, its destructive nature, and the availability of treatment approaches for addressing this problem.

RESOURCES

Agency for Healthcare Research and Quality
    www.ispor.org/meetings/washingtondc0512/releasedpresentations/w31-all-slides.pdf
American Heart Association, Resources for Quitting Smoking
    www.heart.org/HEARTORG/GettingHealthy/QuitSmoking/QuittingResources/
    Resources-for-Quitting-Smoking_UCM_307934_Article.jsp
American Lung Association, Getting Help to Quit Smoking
    www.lung.org/stop-smoking/how-to-quit/getting-help/
BeTobaccoFree.gov
    http://betobaccofree.hhs.gov/quit-now/
Centers for Disease Control and Prevention, Health Care Providers: How You Can Help
    Patients Quit
    www.cdc.gov/tobacco/campaign/tips/partners/health/
Centers for Disease Control and Prevention, I'm Ready to Quit!
    www.cdc.gov/tobacco/campaign/tips/quit-smoking/
Centers for Disease Control and Prevention, A Practical Guide on Tobacco-Use Treatment
    www.cdc.gov/tobacco/quit_smoking/cessation/practical_guide/index.htm
Centers for Disease Control and Prevention, Quit Smoking Resources
    www.cdc.gov/tobacco/quit_smoking/how_to_quit/resources/
National Cancer Institute
    www.cancer.gov/cancertopics/pdq/prevention/control-of-tobacco-use/
    HealthProfessional/page3
National Institutes of Health, Cigarette Smoking: Health Risks and How to Quit (PDQ®)
    www.ncbi.nlm.nih.gov/books/NBK63952/
Nicotine Anonymous
    www.nicotine-anonymous.org/

Quit Net
   www.quitnet.com/
Smokefree.gov
   http://smokefree.gov/

REFERENCES

American Academy of Allergy, Asthma and Immunology. (2013). *Asthma and COPD: Differences and similarities.* Retrieved from http://www.aaaai.org/conditions-and-treatments/library/asthma-library/asthma-and-copd--differences-and-similarities.aspx

American Lung Association. (n.d.). *Emphysema.* Retrieved from http://www.lung.org/lung-disease/emphysema/

American Psychiatric Association. (2013). *Diagnostic and statistical manual of mental disorders* (5th ed.). Arlington, VA: Author.

Ashton, K., & Streem, D. (2009). *Nicotine dependence.* Retrieved from the Cleveland Clinic Center for Continuing Education website: http://www.clevelandclinicmeded.com/medicalpubs/diseasemanagement/psychiatry-psychology/nicotine-dependence/

Centers for Disease Control and Prevention. (2009). *Tobacco use: Targeting the nation's leading killer.* Retrieved from http://www.cdc.gov/chronicdisease/resources/publications/aag/osh.htm

Centers for Disease Control and Prevention. (2013). *Health effects of cigarette smoking.* Retrieved from http://www.cdc.gov/tobacco/data_statistics/fact_sheets/health_effects/effects_cig_smoking/index.htm

Esson, L., & Leeder, S. R. (2004). *The millennium development goals and tobacco control: An opportunity for global partnership.* Geneva, Switzerland: World Health Organization.

Fagerström, K. O. (2011). Determinants of tobacco use and renaming the FTND to the Fagerström Test for Cigarette Dependence. *Nicotine & Tobacco Research, 14,* 75–78. DOI: 10.1093/ntr/ntr137.

Fiore, M. C., Jaen, C. R., Baker, T. B., Bailey, W. C., Bennett, G., Benowitz, N. L., … Williams, C. (2008). A clinical practice guideline for treating tobacco use and dependence: 2008 update. A US Public Health Service report. *American Journal of Preventive Medicine, 35*(2), 158–176.

Heatherton, T. F., Kozlowski, L. T., Frecker, R. C., & Fagerström, K-O. (1991). The Fagerström Test for Nicotine Dependence: A revision of the Fagerström Tolerance Questionnaire. *British Journal of Addiction, 86,* 1119–1127.

Hu, M. C., Griesler, P., Schaffran, C., & Kandel, D. (2011). Risk and protective factors for nicotine dependence in adolescence. *Journal of Child Psychology & Psychiatry, 52,* 1063–1072. doi:10.1111/j.1469-7610.2010.02362.x

Johnston, L. D., O'Malley, P. M., Bachman, J. G., & Schulenberg, J. E. (2013). *Monitoring the Future national results on drug use: 2012 overview, key findings on adolescent drug use.* Ann Arbor: University of Michigan, Institute for Social Research.

Lande, R. G. (2012). *Nicotine addiction.* Retrieved from the Medscape website: http://emedicine.medscape.com/article/287555-overview

Medical Society of the State of New York. (2011). *Evidence-based strategies for treating tobacco dependence.* Retrieved from https://www.medicaleducationny.com/webdocuments/courses/Evidence_Based_Strategies_for_Treating%20Tobacco_Dependence.pdf

Miller, W. R., & Rose, G. S. (2009). Toward a theory of motivational interviewing. *American Psychologist, 64,* 527–537. doi:10.1037/a0016830

National Heart, Lung, and Blood Institute. (2013). *What is COPD?* Retrieved from http://www.nhlbi.nih.gov/health/health-topics/topics/copd/

National Institute on Drug Addiction. (2008). *Addiction science: From molecules to managed care.* Retrieved from http://www.drugabuse.gov/publications/addiction-science-molecules-to-managed-care/introduction/drug-abuse-costs-united-states-economy-hundreds-billions-dollars-in-increased-health

National Institute on Drug Abuse. (2009). *DrugFacts: Treatment approaches for drug addiction*. Retrieved from http://www.drugabuse.gov/publications/drugfacts/treatment-approaches-drug-addiction

National Institute on Drug Abuse. (2010). *Monitoring the Future: National survey results on drug use, 1975–2009: Vol. 1. Secondary school students*. Retrieved from http://files.eric.ed.gov/fulltext/ED514370.pdf

National Institute on Drug Abuse. (2012a). *DrugFacts: Cigarettes and other tobacco products*. Retrieved from http://www.drugabuse.gov/publications/drugfacts/cigarettes-other-tobacco-products

National Institute on Drug Abuse. (2012b). *DrugFacts: High school and youth trends*. Retrieved from http://www.drugabuse.gov/publications/drugfacts/high-school-youth-trends

Nicotine. (n.d.). Retrieved from http://medical-dictionary.thefreedictionary.com/nicotine

Novello, A. C. (1990). *Surgeon General's report on the health benefits of smoking cessation*. Retrieved from http://www.ncbi.nlm.nih.gov/pmc/articles/PMC1580165/pdf/pubhealthrep00193-0003.pdf

Office of Adolescent Health. (2013). *Substance abuse: Risk and protective factors*. Retrieved from http://www.hhs.gov/ash/oah/adolescent-health-topics/substance-abuse/tobacco/risk-and-protective-factors.html

Substance Abuse and Mental Health Services Administration. (2012). *Results from the 2011 National Survey on Drug Use and Health: Summary of national findings* (NSDUH Series H-44, HHS Publication No. [SMA] 12-4713). Rockville, MD: Author.

Tobacco Recovery Resource Exchange. (2009). *Implementing tobacco assessment, diagnosis, and pharmacotherapy into your chemical dependency program*. Retrieved from http://www.tobaccorecovery.org/media/files/resources/implementing_121009.pdf

U.S. Department of Health and Human Services. (2006). *The health consequences of involuntary exposure to tobacco smoke: A report of the Surgeon General*. Retrieved from http://www.ncbi.nlm.nih.gov/books/NBK44324/

What is nicotine dependence? What are the dangers of smoking? (2013). Retrieved from http://www.medicalnewstoday.com/articles/181299.php

Wheeler, K. C., Fletcher, K. E., Wellman, R. J., & Difranza, J. R. (2004). Screening adolescents for nicotine dependence: The Hooked on Nicotine checklist. *Journal of Adolescent Health, 35*(3), 225–230. doi:10.1016/j.jadohealth.2003.10.004

World Health Organization. (2005). *Why tobacco is a public health priority*. Retrieved from http://www.who.int/tobacco/health_priority/en/

CHAPTER 4

MARIJUANA ADDICTION
Richard S. Balkin

STUDENT LEARNING OUTCOMES

At the conclusion of this chapter students will

1. Identify factors related to the prevalence and effects of marijuana addiction
2. Understand the biological components related to marijuana addiction
3. Recognize cannabis use, intoxication, and withdrawal disorders consistent with criteria set forth in the *Diagnostic and Statistical Manual of Mental Disorders, Fifth Edition*
4. Evaluate effective treatment modalities and apply them to the case study

CASE AND CASE DISCUSSION

Andy is a 22-year-old Caucasian man referred for partial hospitalization due to a history of cannabis use disorder, severe. Andy is employed as a certified nursing assistant for a rehabilitation hospital, working primarily with geriatric clients. Andy is seeking services because he tested positive for delta-9-tetrahydrocannabinol (THC) on a recent random drug screen and he is mandated to seek services for his substance abuse in order to continue employment. Andy admits to being angry toward his supervisor for mandating treatment. He identifies being a model employee with excellent evaluations for his job. Indeed, Andy has had positive evaluations and is valued by his colleagues for his positive interactions with the patients, particularly the elderly patients. He arrives on time for his job and works diligently throughout his shift. Andy identifies his work performance as evidence that his cannabis use is not interfering with his job functions.

Andy's parents were never married and he had minimal contact with his father, who was employed as a truck driver. Andy reports that he has not spoken with his father in 6 years and does not know his father's whereabouts.

Andy's mother worked as a registered nurse. From middle school through high school, Andy's mother worked an evening shift, so he was often home alone after school or stayed with friends. Andy reports that his marijuana use began in seventh grade, and by the time he was in eighth grade he was smoking marijuana daily. Andy's mother also smokes marijuana, and he reports having gotten high with his mother often while he was in high school.

Andy reports that he was never good at school but he also did not put much effort into school. At age 17 he was still listed as a junior because he had failed classes throughout high school. He dropped out of high school and immediately took the general equivalency diploma exam, which he passed on his first attempt. Andy began taking classes at a local community college and working in fast food restaurants. He would often get fired for neglecting his shift and not showing up. At age 19 Andy completed his course work and exam to be a certified nursing assistant, and he has been employed with the hospital since that time. He identifies quitting marijuana a few times throughout school when he would have to take drug screens in order to earn hours as a certified nursing assistant for his course work. Once employed in his current position, he started smoking marijuana again. Andy indicates that quitting was not difficult, but he enjoys smoking marijuana and his work performance was not affected.

Andy presents as ambivalent about treatment. He admits to wanting to continue to smoke marijuana, but he also does not want to lose his job. Andy indicates that he believes it is simply a matter of time before marijuana is legal, and he does not feel his employers are fair in mandating that he seek treatment. Andy admits that he has been smoking marijuana for 9 years, for 8 of those years on a daily basis. He most often uses a water pipe (i.e., bong) but may also smoke joints or blunts. He identifies that quitting marijuana completely may be difficult. Andy admits to having used cannabis last night, but did not smoke marijuana prior to his intake assessment that morning.

Cannabis users often do not exhibit acute withdrawal symptoms; however, postacute withdrawal symptoms are evident with Andy. Andy admits that he has difficulty sleeping if he does not smoke marijuana before going to bed. He identifies smoking marijuana before leaving for work each morning because it "relaxes" him. Andy believes that smoking marijuana helped him in his schoolwork while he was working on his certified nursing assistant degree because he was "able to pay attention." When asked why his marijuana use did not help him in middle school or high school, he indicates that his school failure was due to immaturity rather than his marijuana use. Given the presence of sleep disturbance, anxiety, and cravings but an absence of acute withdrawal symptoms, Andy is placed in a partial hospitalization program to address his cannabis use disorder.

OVERVIEW OF MARIJUANA ADDICTION

Perhaps no other drug is under a level of scrutiny and debate as marijuana. At the time of this writing, marijuana is legal in two states as a recreational drug and in 23 states and the District of Columbia as a medicinal drug. Unlike users of other drugs, such as cocaine or crystal methamphetamine, users of marijuana may be quick to point to the utility of the hemp plant; the medicinal benefits of marijuana for treating HIV, cancer, and glaucoma; and the less severe features of cannabis use, such as the common absence of acute withdrawal symptoms or the perceived lessened severity of marijuana intoxication. Individuals who use marijuana may point out a perception that marijuana use is less severe than alcohol use and attempt to engage in intellectual or legalistic arguments in order to rationalize their use.

Unfortunately, users of marijuana are often misinformed regarding the deleterious effects of cannabis. Cannabis affects the brain by targeting brain cells known as *cannabinoid receptors*. These receptors are normally activated by naturally occurring processes in the brain; however, when cannabis enters the system, these receptors are activated and affect parts of the brain related to brain development and functioning. Examples of processes that may be affected or impeded include pleasure, memory, thinking, concentration, learning, perception, problem solving, judgment, and physical coordination (National Institute on Drug Abuse [NIDA], 2012a). In addition, chronic marijuana use may affect learning and memory over the long term. In particular, adolescents who become chronic users of marijuana may experience permanent loss of learning and memory due to alterations in the structure and function of the brain. Unlike individuals who started smoking marijuana in adulthood, individuals who began their marijuana use as adolescents demonstrated cognitive decline, as evidenced by decreases in scores on intelligence tests between ages 13 and 38 (NIDA, 2102a).

In terms of physical effects, marijuana use raises the heart rate 20% to 100% approximately 20 minutes after use. Similar to cigarettes, marijuana is a lung irritant and can lead to similar pulmonary problems, including chronic coughing, decreased lung capacity, and increased mucus in the lungs. Marijuana smoke contains 50% to 70% more carcinogens than tobacco smoke (Office of National Drug Control Policy, 2010). In addition, marijuana is more potent now than it was 30 years ago, with increases in THC from 4% in the 1980s to 10% in 2009 (NIDA, 2012a). Increases in THC may lead to higher rates of addiction for marijuana users. Addiction rates vary depending on age at onset and frequency of use, ranging from 9% of all marijuana users to 17% if the user started at a younger age. The prevalence of marijuana addiction increases to between 25% and 50% for individuals who use marijuana on a daily basis (NIDA, 2012a).

Marijuana remains the most commonly used illicit drug in the United States. Adolescents are more likely to have smoked marijuana in the past month than cigarettes. NIDA (2012d) reported that 7% of people age 12 or older (approximately 18.1 million people) used marijuana at least one time in the past month in 2011. Use of other illicit drugs was only 2.4%, or 6.1 million individuals 12 years or older. As illicit drug use decreased from 2007 to 2011, use of marijuana increased from 5.8% to the current 7%. Miron (2010) estimated that the United States spends approximately $13.7 billion on marijuana criminalization procedures. This does not include the cost of treatment or other costs related to health care and injuries stemming from cannabis use.

Definitions

When working with clients or other mental health professionals, a rudimentary understanding of terms associated with cannabis use may be helpful.

Cannabinoid receptors: Brain cells that are targeted by THC. These brain cells are important to processes related to "pleasure, memory, thinking, concentration, sensory and time perception, and coordinated movement" (NIDA, 2012a, p. 2).

Delta-9-tetrahydrocannabinol (THC): The main psychoactive ingredient in marijuana (NIDA, 2012c).

Dronabinol: A synthetic form of THC that may decrease the severity of withdrawal symptoms from marijuana (Levin et al., 2011).

Endocannabinoids: Part of a naturally occurring communication network of the brain that is activated by cannabinoid receptors. THC has a deleterious effect on the endocannabinoid system, resulting in overactivity and functional impairment (NIDA, 2012d).

Marijuana: A substance manufactured from the hemp plant from a mix of "dry, shredded green and brown mix of leaves, flowers, stems, and seeds" (NIDA, 2012c, p. 1).

Demographics

According to the Substance Abuse and Mental Health Services Administration (2012), approximately 9.4% of adults without a mental illness and 18.4% of those with a mental health illness used marijuana over the past year (data were collected in 2011). The United Nations Office on Drugs and Crime (2009) reported that 12.3% of Americans between the ages of 15 and 64 use marijuana. NIDA (2012b) reported that 30.8% of adults ages 18–25 and 7.9% of those 26 or older used marijuana in the past year; 19% of adults ages 18–25 and 4.8% of those 26 or older used marijuana in the past month. Among adults seeking treatment for cannabis use and admitting to using marijuana daily ($N = 170,100$), 72.7% were male. With respect to ethnicity, 55.1% were White, 27.3% were African American, and 12.8% were Latino (Substance Abuse and Mental Health Services Administration, 2012). However, this study was relegated to individuals being admitted for treatment. Inconsistencies among demographic factors may be identified through consideration of individuals not in treatment. Stinson, Ruan, Pickering, and Grant (2006) conducted a nationwide study on cannabis use among adults ($N = 43,093$) and found that Native Americans had the highest prevalence rates and Asians, African Americans, and Latinos had decreased prevalence rates.

For youth, numbers are much higher. According to the Centers for Disease Control and Prevention (Kann et al., 2014), 39.9% of youth in Grades 9–12 tried marijuana at least one time in 2011. Adolescent males (42.5%, $n = 7,365$) were significantly more likely than adolescent females (37.5%, $n = 7,508$) to use marijuana at least one time. As with other substance use disorders, Native Americans are disproportionately affected. Nearly 72% of Native American youth ($n = 279$) indicated using marijuana at least once in the past year, followed by African American (43%, $n = 2,624$), Latino (42.1%, $n = 4,471$), and White (37.9%, $n = 6,043$) youth.

ASSESSMENT AND DIAGNOSIS

The American Psychiatric Association (APA; 2013) outlined criteria for cannabis-related disorders consistent with guidelines for other disorders related to illicit drug use. Hence, cannabis-related disorders consist of five classifications: cannabis use disorder, cannabis intoxication, cannabis withdrawal, other cannabis-induced disorders, and unspecified cannabis-related disorder. For the purposes of this chapter, I focus on cannabis use disorder, cannabis intoxication, and cannabis withdrawal, as unspecified cannabis-related disorders relates to other diagnostic categories of the *Diagnostic and Statistical Manual of Mental Disorders, Fifth Edition* (*DSM–5;* APA, 2013), such as schizophrenia and delirium. A client with unspecified cannabis-related disorder exhibits symptoms of the aforementioned categories and suffers from impairment but does not meet criteria.

Assessment of cannabis use disorder may be evaluated on the basis of a clinical interview as well as specialty assessments that address drug use, such as the Substance Abuse Subtle Screening Inventory–3 (SASSI-3; F. G. Miller & Lazowski, 1999). Assessments like the SASSI-3 are not specific to marijuana abuse but rather help the clinician evaluate problematic use across substances and distinguish between *use* and *dependency,* which were terms used in previous *DSM* criteria.

APA (2013) has indicated that a minimum of two criteria must be met for individuals to be diagnosed with cannabis use disorder. Of particular importance is that each symptom identified should result in "clinically significant impairment or distress . . . within a 12-month period" (p. 509). The following are the diagnostic criteria from the *DSM–5:*

1. Cannabis is often taken in larger amounts or over a longer period than was intended.
2. There is a persistent desire or unsuccessful efforts to cut down or control cannabis use.
3. A great deal of time is spent in activities necessary to obtain cannabis, use cannabis, or recover from its effects.
4. Craving, or a strong desire or urge to use cannabis.
5. Recurrent cannabis use resulting in a failure to fulfill major role obligations at work, school, or home.
6. Continued cannabis use despite having persistent or recurrent social or interpersonal problems caused or exacerbated by the effects of cannabis.
7. Important social, occupational, or recreational activities are given up or reduced because of cannabis use.
8. Recurrent cannabis use in situations in which it is physically hazardous.
9. Cannabis use is continued despite knowledge of having a persistent or recurrent physical or psychological problem that is likely to have been caused or exacerbated by cannabis.
10. Tolerance, as defined by either of the following:
    a. A need for markedly increased amounts of cannabis to achieve intoxication or desired effect.
    b. Markedly diminished effect with continued use of the same amount of cannabis.
11. Withdrawal, as manifested by either of the following:
    a. The characteristic withdrawal syndrome for cannabis.
    b. Cannabis (or a closely related substance) is taken to relieve or avoid withdrawal symptoms.

Source. From *Diagnostic and Statistical Manual of Mental Disorders, Fifth Edition* (pp. 509–510), by American Psychiatric Association, 2013, Arlington, VA: American Psychiatric Association. Copyright 2013 by the American Psychiatric Association. Reprinted with permission. All rights reserved.

Cannabis use disorder is categorized into three classifications of severity: mild, moderate, and severe. Mild refers to two or three symptoms, moderate refers to four or five symptoms, and severe is indicative of six or more symptoms.

When a client presents as *high,* or under the influence of cannabis, usually demonstrated through euphoria, sedation, grandiosity or inappropriate affect, and impaired judgment, a diagnosis of cannabis intoxication may be considered. Cannabis intoxication follows recent use of marijuana and includes at least two of the following symptoms: increased appetite, dry mouth, increased heart rate, and conjunctival injection (i.e., swollen, red eyes in the outer membrane and/or inner eyelid). Cannabis intoxication is not necessarily accompanied by cannabis withdrawal, which has a rather ambiguous description. The *DSM–5* (APA, 2013) has identified that cannabis withdrawal generally occurs after daily or near daily use over a few months. Similar to with cannabis use disorder, "clinically significant distress or impairment" in functioning occurs across three or more of the following symptoms within 1 week of heavy, prolonged use:

1. Irritability, anger, or aggression.
2. Nervousness or anxiety.
3. Sleep difficulty (e.g., insomnia, disturbing dreams).
4. Decreased appetite or weight loss.
5. Restlessness.
6. Depressed mood.
7. At least one of the following physical symptoms causing significant discomfort: abdominal pain, shakiness/tremors, sweating, fever, chills, or headache. (p. 518)

The aforementioned symptoms generally last 1 to 2 weeks, with the exception of sleep disturbance, which may last up to 30 days. The symptoms of cannabis withdrawal may not be considered as severe as those with other illicit drugs, which may require medical detox. Dronabinol is a synthetic form of THC that has been used to treat cannabis dependence (i.e., its use is consistent with *Diagnostic and Statistical Manual of Mental Disorders, Fourth Edition, Text Revision* [*DSM–IV–TR;* APA, 2000] criteria). Levin et al. (2011) identified decreases in the severity of withdrawal symptoms and increases in treatment retention in a preliminary study of 156 adults diagnosed with cannabis dependence. In most cases, individuals who use marijuana do not require an inpatient hospitalization in order to ensure medical stability during withdrawal. As a result, treatment is consistent with other treatment strategies for illicit drug use after any acute withdrawal symptoms are resolved.

TREATMENT

The probable absence of acute withdrawal symptoms results in a higher frequency of partial hospitalization, intensive outpatient, and outpatient services being utilized for cannabis use disorders. When clients continue to relapse and regress to previous high-risk behaviors, residential treatment options should be considered.

Inpatient

Typically, inpatient hospitalization for cannabis use disorders is rare. As mentioned earlier, such hospitalizations, particularly for adults, tend to be brief (e.g., 4 days or less) and focused on medical detox. Once patients are medically stable, they may be discharged to a less restrictive level of care, such as partial hospitalization. An exception may be made for children and adolescents, as the use of marijuana often accompanies other behavioral issues, such as noncompliance with parents or other authority figures, school failure and/or truancy, legal problems, and so forth. Therefore, inpatient hospitalization for minors is more common, as the comorbid issues of disruptive behavior with the marijuana use are addressed in treatment. For children and adolescents in inpatient treatment, the length of stay is usually less than 2 weeks, and 1 week is common practice. Similar to acute care with adults, the goal is still medical stability, but in the latter case, stability is often viewed as no longer being a danger to self or others (Balkin, Leicht, Sartor, & Powell, 2011; Balkin & Roland, 2007). Hence, for child and adolescent clients, stability refers to behavioral issues as well as medical issues. The client should be able to commit to safety, which in this case refers to abstaining from the use of illicit drugs; identify problems that led to hospitalization; process coping skills; and commit to follow-up (Balkin et al., 2011; Balkin & Roland, 2007).

Clients who undergo partial hospitalization attend the hospital during the day (commonly referred to as *day treatment*) and leave during the evening. This type of care provides an opportunity for the client to benefit from the structure and services of inpatient treatment throughout the day while also implementing coping skills and relapse prevention strategies in the evening. However, clients who move to this level of care without sufficient coping strategies may relapse.

Outpatient

Outpatient services are for children, adolescents, and adults who meet criteria for stability and are capable of demonstrating behavior consistent with avoiding relapse and regressing to previous high-risk behaviors. Outpatient counseling is for an undetermined amount of time, pending clients' needs and progress in counseling. In addition, the frequency of services may vary. Some individuals attend outpatient counseling once per week, whereas others attend less frequently (e.g., biweekly, monthly). More frequent service (i.e., more than once per week) is referred to as *intensive outpatient counseling.*

Residential

Longer term treatment is also available, particularly when documented failure in outpatient treatment and inpatient treatment occurs. In such cases, residential treatment may be necessary. Residential treatment may last for 28 days or longer, especially for adolescents who exhibit cannabis use disorder along with emotional or behavioral issues. In such instances, 90-day programs are not uncommon, with the potential for longer lengths of stay (e.g., 6–9 months) for severe cases. Whereas some residential treatment occurs in a medical setting, therapeutic communities offer another type of residential treatment. In therapeutic communities, the facilities are staffed and the residents are committed to a drug-free lifestyle. However, the setting may be less restrictive than a traditional residential facility. Adults may typically be in such settings 6–12 months (NIDA, 2009).

MODELS AND APPROACHES

Numerous strategies exist for treating substance use disorders, including 12-step models, Rational Recovery, cognitive behavior therapies, psychoeducational groups, approaches using medications, and so forth. However, two primary strategies appear to offer promising results for treating cannabis use disorders. Motivational enhancement therapy (MET) is a manualized method of motivational interviewing (MI; W. R. Miller, 1985; W. R. Miller & Rollnick, 1991). MET is a brief treatment modality, generally lasting two to five sessions, and is often accompanied by cognitive–behavioral components (Babor, 2004; Dennis et al., 2002, 2004; Stephens, Babor, Kadden, & Miller, 2002). Cognitive behavior therapy (CBT) also appears to be a promising modality, as evidenced by the extant research (e.g., Copeland, 2004; Liddle, Dakof, Turner, Henderson, & Greenbaum, 2008; Weinstein et al., 2010). Counselors should be cautioned, however, that approximately 50% of individuals who initiate treatment for cannabis use will relapse within 2 weeks. Of the other 50% who do not relapse, approximately half will resume cannabis use within 1 year (NIDA, 2012d).

MET

In order to understand MET, an orientation to MI is necessary. MET was outlined by W. R. Miller (1995), who was also involved in the development of MI. Both MI and MET adopt the therapeutic style of Carl Rogers's person-centered therapy. Accurate empathy is a key indicator of therapeutic success with respect to treatment, and the use of direct confrontation is discouraged (W. R. Miller, 1995). The emphasis on accurate empathy and avoidance of direct confrontation is a distinguishing element between MET and other therapeutic modalities such as CBT.

In addition to a therapeutic style consistent with person-centered therapy, MET, having emanated out of MI, is thoroughly grounded in the transtheoretical model (TTM), also commonly referred to as *stage of change* (W. R. Miller, 1995). Prochaska and DiClemente (1982, 1984, 1986) described a five-stage model of change and conducted research related to addictive behaviors using the TTM (Prochaska & DiClemente, 1984, 1986). Although the basis of this research may be dated, the TTM was foundational in the development of MI, and subsequently MET. W. R. Miller (1995) described the five-stage model of the TTM, on which MET is based:

- *Precontemplation,* which describes individuals who are not considering a change in their problematic behaviors
- *Contemplation,* which describes individuals who either have identified a problem or consider that a problem exists, as well as have identified the cost and benefits of addressing the problem
- *Determination,* which describes individuals who have made the decision to take action toward a change
- *Action,* which describes individuals engaging in new behaviors to establish change
- *Maintenance,* which describes individuals who were successful in the action stage and are now working to preserve and continue the change(s) in behavior

The counselor's approach in MET is to empathically engage the client in a manner consistent with where the client is in the TTM. W. R. Miller (1995) indicated that the contemplation and determination stages are the most critical stages. W. R. Miller (1995) identified two primary objectives of the contemplation stage:

(a) The client identifies the extent to which the substance abuse is problematic, considering both positive and negative effects of the substance use; and (b) the client considers his or her ability to make changes and the impact such changes may have in his or her life. During the determination stage, the client makes a commitment to acting to change the behavior.

The counselor's role in MET is to be supportive, even when unsuccessful attempts are made. Consistent with W. R. Miller and Rollnick (1991) for MI, W. R. Miller (1995, p. 4) identified five essential principles in MET:

1. Express empathy
2. Develop discrepancy
3. Avoid argumentation
4. Roll with resistance
5. Support self-efficacy

The expression of empathy is consistent with the Rogerian principle in person-centered therapy. Despite the problematic issues related to cannabis abuse, the counselor's role is to respect the client and the direction he or she chooses. W. R. Miller (1995) asserted that clients are more likely to become grounded in resistance and denial of the negative consequences of substance abuse when direct confrontational styles are used. Through empathic engagement, the counselor using MET should communicate acceptance of the client (i.e., unconditional positive regard; Rogers, 1957). Rather than directly confronting a client when statements of minimization and denial are made, the counselor should identify a discrepancy in the client's behavior as it relates to the client's statements, cognitions, feelings, and actions. W. R. Miller (1995) cautioned counselors that discrepancies are identified with the purpose of "raising the client's awareness" (p. 4) in such a way that the client is encouraged to engage in a discussion and further explain his or her meaning, as opposed to engaging in arguments and further grounding feelings of defensiveness, rationalization, and/or denial. In MI and MET, counselors interpret resistance similar to in other postmodern theoretical perspectives, such as solution-focused brief therapy (de Shazer & Dolan, 2007). Resistance is viewed as a normalized process and not a characteristic of pathology (W. R. Miller, 1995).

W. R. Miller and Rollnick (1991) encouraged the case for change to be a determination from the client, not the counselor. Counselors using MET should recognize that clients who move from a stance of ambivalence to a determination to change (essentially moving from precontemplation and contemplation to determination and action) require support. Encouraging the client to face a problem and initiate change is an essential role for the counselor in MET.

Each of these principles is consistent with discerning characteristics of other methods of substance abuse treatment. Counselors using MET do not argue with the client. The traditional intervention, in which family, friends, or significant others confront the client and explain how the substance abuse is affecting the individual or the relationships, is not a technique in MET. Counselors avoid confronting denial or trying to "break down" (W. R. Miller, 1995, p. 6) the client. Efforts to label the client should be avoided. The often-used mechanism of identifying the client as an addict is avoided, and the counselor does not insinuate that the client is powerless over his or her drug use. Rather, the notion of change is left entirely up to the client.

W. R. Miller's (1995) five essential principles are necessary to building motivation for change. In order to consolidate these gains and move the client through the determination and action stages of the TTM, the counselor should be aware of evidence indicating that the motivation to initiate and sustain change is sufficient. An increase in positive self-statements, an increase in statements reflecting a desire to change, and an absence of statements related to ambivalence or resistance to change are indications that the client is in the determination stage of the TTM (W. R. Miller, 1995; W. R. Miller & Rollnick, 1991). W. R. Miller (1995) included the statements in Exhibit 4.1 to address the process of "strengthening commitment to change" (pp. 26–28).

CBT

CBT was initially developed by Aaron Beck in the 1960s as an approach to working with depression and anxiety disorder (Wright, 2006). It was later modified for use with other disorders, including substance use disorders. A counselor who utilizes CBT views change as a two-way relationship. First is an examination of how cognitions influence behavior; once behavior changes, that change in behavior may influence cognitions (Wright, 2006).

Clark, Beck, and Alford (1999) posited three levels of cognitions essential to the practice of CBT. *Consciousness* refers to the extent to which an individual is fully aware when making decisions. *Automatic thoughts* refers to impulsive, subconscious, or unconscious thoughts. Because these thoughts are below the level of consciousness, the extent to which thoughts are accurate or relevant is not assessed. *Schemas* reflect the deepest level of cognition and consist of rules that provide the foundation for or govern problem solving or decision making; schemas are influenced through development and interaction with the environment (Wright, 2006). Wright (2006) suggested that one's ability to change schemas has a major influence on relapse prevention.

Treatment methods in CBT often include Socratic questioning, identification and examination of evidence related to cognitive distortions or irrational beliefs, development of alternatives, visual imagery, role play, and rehearsal (Wright, 2006). Although evidence of the efficacy of CBT interventions is present in the literature, some researchers (e.g., W. R. Miller, 1995; W. R. Miller & Rollnick, 1991) have noted that the confrontational nature of CBT practices may discourage the client

---

EXHIBIT 4.1

The changes I want to make are _____.

The most important reasons why I want to make these changes are _____.

The steps I plan to take in changing are _____.

The ways other people can help me are (persons) _____ (ways) _____.

I know that my plan is working if _____.

Some things that could interfere with my plan are _____.

and inadvertently ground the client in embracing numerous defense mechanisms (e.g., denial, rationalization).

CBT for treating cannabis use, as described by Sampl and Kadden (2001), is a skill-based treatment strategy designed to address the development of alternatives to situations and coping that impede abstinence or sobriety. In other words, CBT allows the counselor to address coping skills and strategies to decrease the likelihood of relapse. Such skills relate to the acquisition and repetition of overt behaviors related to refusing marijuana, changing social support, increasing pro-social activities, and coping with situations that trigger relapse. Some examples used in evidence-based practices follow.

Marijuana refusal skills include both nonverbal and verbal communication. Clients benefit from processing feelings of guilt when they refuse to succumb to peer pressure or advocate for themselves. In addition, Sampl and Kadden (2001) encouraged role-playing scenarios in which clients decline both firmly and directly without relying on excuses (e.g., "I have a cold," "Maybe next time"). In addition, clients should be encouraged to avoid prolonged discussions or debates related to abstaining from marijuana use.

Because smoking marijuana is commonly a social activity, enhancing social support is another pertinent coping skill. Emphasis should be placed on individuals who will be supportive, as well as individuals who have not been supportive but could be when they notice the client's efforts. Sampl and Kadden (2001) emphasized identifying and building support as opposed to focusing on individuals who may trigger relapse. In other words, this form of CBT emphasizes a positive model of building support as opposed to a negative model emphasizing likely problems and triggers for relapse.

A final common component of CBT is avoiding and managing relapse. When adapting to a lifestyle without cannabis use, difficult transitions are common. For example, clients may not obtain support from individuals who they anticipated would be supportive. This can result in boredom and loneliness, which may trigger relapse. Unintended stressors may also contribute to relapse, such as changes in a family situation, job, or school environment. Counselors who use CBT may encourage clients to identify potential scenarios that may occur or are already occurring and process approaches for managing stressors without resorting to cannabis use. In the event that a client does relapse, counselors should focus on what was learned from the relapse and process how to get back on track (Sampl & Kadden, 2001).

CBT often occurs in a group therapy milieu. Group therapy allows for the practice of skills; allows for communication of effective and ineffective processes among clients experiencing similar situations; discourages isolation; promotes risk taking; and provides feedback to clients from peers, which may likely have more of an impact than feedback from a counselor (Sampl & Kadden, 2001).

EVIDENCE-BASED RESEARCH

As mentioned before, MET is a manualized approach to MI. This manualization approach was initiated in 1992 for Project MATCH (Matching Alcoholism Treatments to Client Heterogeneity), "a multisite trial of alcoholism treatments funded as a cooperative agreement by the National Institute on Alcohol Abuse and Alcoholism" (W. R. Miller, 1995, p. ii). Since that time, numerous studies have been conducted on the efficacy of MET in relation to cannabis use.

MET as a Sole Intervention

MET as a sole intervention tends to be less efficacious than MET combined with another treatment approach. For example, Walker, Roffman, Stephens, Wakana, and Berghuis (2006) investigated the use of a two-session MET program in a school-based setting for 97 adolescents (13–17 years old) who had used marijuana at least nine times in the past month. Adolescents were randomly assigned to the two-session MET condition or a control group. At the 3-month follow-up, members of both the treatment and control groups significantly reduced their marijuana use, but no differences were evident between the groups. A similar study was undertaken by Martin and Copeland (2008), who used the two-session MET format with adolescents ages 14–19 years old. Forty individuals were randomly assigned to the two-session MET treatment or a control group. In addition, an optional component related to abstaining or reducing cannabis use was offered during the second half of Session 2. Adolescents in the treatment condition exhibited significantly less cannabis use and fewer symptoms of dependency (as identified by *DSM–IV–TR* criteria) compared to those in the control group. The group differences were both significant and meaningful (i.e., there was a moderate effect size between groups). Walker et al. (2011) also evaluated the efficacy of MET in a school-based environment. In Walker et al.'s (2011) study, participants in high school were randomly assigned to MET, educational feedback, or a control group. At the end of a 3-month period, individuals who received either educational feedback or MET had significant reductions in cannabis use and negative consequences of substance use, and these gains were sustained after a 12-month reevaluation.

The results of the aforementioned studies are indicative of some benefits of MET as a sole counseling modality, but not necessarily better than other treatment modalities. However, several studies have been conducted evaluating the efficacy of MET when combined with other therapeutic modalities.

MET Combined With CBT

Babor (2004) compared three treatment conditions in a randomized design study of 450 adult marijuana smokers. Treatment conditions included two sessions of MET; nine sessions of multicomponent therapy that included MET/CBT and case management; and a control group. Participants in the brief MET condition and the MET/CBT condition demonstrated significantly less marijuana use and associated consequences compared to those in the control group; in addition, participants in the nine-session MET/CBT format demonstrated significantly less marijuana use and associated consequences compared to those in the brief MET group.

Youth who received a combination of MET and CBT over five sessions experienced better outcomes than youth who obtained treatment in community-based programs for an indeterminate amount of time (Ramchand, Griffin, Suttorp, Harris, & Morral, 2011). Dennis et al. (2004) evaluated 12- and five-session formats of MET/CBT approaches and compared outcomes with those of other community, family, and education approaches. Although the outcomes for the 12- and five-session formats were not significantly different from those of the other formats, the MET/CBT approaches were more cost-effective because of their brevity.

CBT as a sole approach seems to be effective in reducing cannabis use but is not necessarily a better approach than other treatment strategies; however, given the length of treatment, often 12 weeks, clients may drop out of treatment with greater frequency (Weinstein et al., 2010). Hence, CBT is not as cost-effective as combined MET/CBT approaches.

CONCLUSIONS

Based on a review of evidence-based practices, the prognosis for Andy, the man in the case study that opened this chapter, is guarded. Anywhere from 10% to 30% of individuals who seek treatment for cannabis use disorders are able to abstain from further substance use after 1 year (NIDA, 2012d). Partial hospitalization, along with less restrictive levels of care on discharge from the program, is likely an appropriate intervention. "As with other addictions, a chronic care model should be considered for marijuana addiction, with treatment intensity stepped up or down based upon need" (NIDA, 2012d, p. 9).

Combining MET and CBT approaches and providing the option of additional support services and education (e.g., 12-step support) may be the most effective and cost-efficient method of treatment. With this in mind, treatment should begin by assisting Andy in identifying problems related to his cannabis use and eliciting a desire to change (W. R. Miller, 1995). For example, the counselor may work with Andy in identifying positive and negative effects of his substance use and gently identifying discrepancies. Open-ended questions should encourage him to consider how others view him or talk more about his desire to keep his job with the caveat that he must pass a drug screen. The counselor should also use reflection to encourage Andy to identify problematic areas. For example, if Andy identifies difficulty in maintaining his friendships should he quit using marijuana, the counselor may reflect the feeling (W. R. Miller, 1995): "It is hard to imagine having a social life and close friendships without marijuana."

The counselor will need to avoid confronting Andy's resistance if he expresses an unwillingness to change or abstain from marijuana. Statements from the counselor should reinforce that Andy can make the decision to change or not to change. For example, the counselor could say, "You do not have to change. You can go back to the same environment that brought you to this situation. You may believe you can handle it differently, or you can choose not to handle it differently. It is your choice."

Assuming that Andy is able to move to a determination or action phase of change, the counselor may wish to assign the Change Plan Worksheet (see Exhibit 4.1). This assignment would provide a nice segue into adopting CBT principles in Andy's treatment. Assuming that Andy is able to identify healthy support systems, discuss new behaviors, rehearse the behaviors when returning home each night, and return each day to treatment and process gains, he should be able to eventually move to a less restrictive level of care. However, should Andy relapse, he and his counselor will need to evaluate what was learned from the relapse, address continued motivation to change, and evaluate whether Andy can be successful with his current structure or requires a different level of care, such as transition to a therapeutic community.

RESOURCES

National Institute on Drug Abuse. (2009). *DrugFacts: Treatment approaches for drug addiction*. Retrieved from http://www.drugabuse.gov/publications/drugfacts/treatment-approaches-drug-addiction

National Institute on Drug Abuse. (2012). *DrugFacts: Marijuana*. Retrieved from http://www.drugabuse.gov/publications/drugfacts/marijuana

National Institute on Drug Abuse. (2012). *DrugFacts: Nationwide trends*. Retrieved from http://www.drugabuse.gov/publications/drugfacts/nationwide-trends

National Institute on Drug Abuse. (2012). *Marijuana*. Retrieved from http://www.drugabuse.gov/drugs-abuse/marijuana

National Institute on Drug Abuse. (2012). *Principles of drug addiction treatment: A research-based guide* (3rd ed.). Retrieved from http://www.drugabuse.gov/publications/principles-drug-addiction-treatment

Office of National Drug Control Policy. (n.d.). *Marijuana*. Retrieved from http://www.whitehouse.gov/ondcp/marijuana

Sampl, S., & Kadden, R. (2001). *Cannabis Youth Treatment Series: Volume 1*. Retrieved from http://store.samhsa.gov/shin/content//SMA05-4010/SMA05-4010.pdf

Substance Abuse and Mental Health Services Administration. (2012). *Results from the 2011 National Survey on Drug Use and Health: Mental health findings* (NSDUH Series H-45, HHS Publication No. [SMA] 12-4725). Retrieved from http://www.samhsa.gov/data/sites/default/files/2011MHFDT/2k11MHFR/Web/NSDUHmhfr2011.htm

Substance Abuse and Mental Health Services Administration, Center for Behavioral Health Statistics and Quality. (2012, February 2). *The TEDS report: Marijuana admissions reporting daily use at treatment entry*. Rockville, MD: Author.

United Nations Office on Drugs and Crime. (2012). *World drug report 2012*. Retrieved from http://www.unodc.org/documents/data-and-analysis/WDR2012/WDR_2012_web_small.pdf

REFERENCES

American Psychiatric Association. (2000). *Diagnostic and statistical manual of mental disorders* (4th ed., text revision). Washington, DC: Author.

American Psychiatric Association. (2013). *Diagnostic and statistical manual of mental disorders* (5th ed.). Arlington, VA: Author.

Babor, T. F. (2004). Brief treatments for cannabis dependence: Findings from a randomized multisite trial. *Journal of Consulting and Clinical Psychology, 72,* 455–466. doi:10.1037/0022-006X.72.3.455

Balkin, R. S., Leicht, D. J., Sartor, T., & Powell, J. (2011). Assessing the relationship between therapeutic goal attainment and psychosocial characteristics for adolescents in crisis residence. *Journal of Mental Health, 20,* 32–42.

Balkin, R. S., & Roland, C. B. (2007). Re-conceptualizing stabilization for counseling adolescents in brief psychiatric hospitalization: A new model. *Journal of Counseling & Development, 85,* 64–72.

Clark, D. A., Beck, A. T., & Alford, B. A. (1999). *Scientific foundations of cognitive theory and therapy for depression*. New York, NY: Wiley.

Copeland, J. (2004). Developments in the treatment of cannabis use disorder. *Current Opinion in Psychiatry, 17*(3), 161–167. doi:10.1097/00001504-200405000-00003

de Shazer, S., & Dolan, Y. (2007). *More than miracles: The state of the art of solution-focused brief therapy*. Binghamton, NY: Haworth Press.

Dennis, M., Godley, S. H., Diamond, G., Tims, F. M., Babor, T., Donaldson, J., . . . Funk, R. (2004). The Cannabis Youth Treatment (CYT) study: Main findings from two randomized trials. *Journal of Substance Abuse Treatment, 27*(3), 197–213. doi:10.1016/j.jsat.2003.09.005

Dennis, M., Titus, J. C., Diamond, G., Donaldson, J., Godley, S. H., Tims, F. M., . . . Scott, C. K. (2002). The Cannabis Youth Treatment (CYT) experiment: Rationale, study design and analysis plans. *Addiction, 97*(Suppl. 1), 16–34. doi:10.1046/j.1360-0443.97.s01.2.x

Kann, L., Kinchen, S., Shanklin, S. L., Flint, K. H., Hawkins, J., Harris, W. A., . . . Zaza, S. (2014, June). *Youth Risk Behavior Surveillance—United States, 2013.* Retrieved from the Centers for Disease Control and Prevention website: http://www.cdc.gov/mmwr/pdf/ss/ss6304.pdf

Levin, F. R., Mariani, J. J., Brooks, D. J., Pavlicova, M., Cheng, W., & Nunes, E. V. (2011). Dronabinol for the treatment of cannabis dependence: A randomized, double-blind, placebo-controlled trial. *Drug and Alcohol Dependence, 116*(1–3), 142–150. doi:10.1016/j.drugalcdep.2010.12.010

Liddle, H. A., Dakof, G. A., Turner, R. M., Henderson, C. E., & Greenbaum, P. E. (2008). Treating adolescent drug abuse: A randomized trial comparing multidimensional family therapy and cognitive behavior therapy. *Addiction, 103,* 1660–1670. doi:10.1111/j.1360-0443.2008.02274.x

Martin, G., & Copeland, J. (2008). The adolescent cannabis check-up: Randomized trial of a brief intervention for young cannabis users. *Journal of Substance Abuse Treatment, 34,* 407–414. doi:10.1016/j.jsat.2007.07.004

Miller, F. G., & Lazowski, L. E. (1999). *The Substance Abuse Subtle Screening Inventory–3 (SASSI-3) manual.* Springville, IN: SASSI Institute.

Miller, W. R. (1985). Motivation for treatment: A review with special emphasis on alcoholism. *Psychological Bulletin, 98,* 84–107.

Miller, W. R. (1995). *Motivational enhancement therapy with drug abusers.* Retrieved from http://www.motivationalinterview.net/clinical/METDrugAbuse.PDF

Miller, W. R., & Rollnick, S. (1991). *Motivational interviewing: Preparing people to change addictive behavior.* New York, NY: Guilford Press.

Miron, J. A. (2010). *The budgetary implications of drug prohibition.* Retrieved from the Harvard University website: http://scholar.harvard.edu/miron/publications/budgetary-implications-drug-prohibition-0

National Institute on Drug Abuse. (2009). *DrugFacts: Treatment approaches for drug addiction.* Retrieved from http://www.drugabuse.gov/publications/drugfacts/treatment-approaches-drug-addiction

National Institute on Drug Abuse. (2012a). *DrugFacts: Marijuana.* Retrieved from http://www.drugabuse.gov/publications/drugfacts/marijuana

National Institute on Drug Abuse. (2012b). *DrugFacts: Nationwide trends.* Retrieved from http://www.drugabuse.gov/publications/drugfacts/nationwide-trends

National Institute on Drug Abuse. (2012c). *Marijuana.* Retrieved from http://www.drugabuse.gov/drugs-abuse/marijuana

National Institute on Drug Abuse. (2012d). *Marijuana* (Research report series). Retrieved from http://www.drugabuse.gov/sites/default/files/mjrrs_2.pdf

Office of National Drug Control Policy. (2010). *Marijuana legalization.* Retrieved from http://www.whitehouse.gov/ondcp/ondcp-fact-sheets/marijuana-legalization

Prochaska, J. O., & DiClemente, C. C. (1982). Transtheoretical therapy: Toward a more integrative model of change. *Psychotherapy: Theory, Research and Practice, 19,* 276–288.

Prochaska, J. O., & DiClemente, C. C. (1984). *The transtheoretical approach: Crossing traditional boundaries of therapy.* Homewood, IL: Dow Jones/Irwin.

Prochaska, J. O., & DiClemente, C. C. (1986). Toward a comprehensive model of change. In W. R. Miller & N. Heather (Eds.), *Treating addictive behaviors: Processes of change* (pp. 3–27). New York, NY: Plenum Press.

Ramchand, R., Griffin, B., Suttorp, M., Harris, K. M., & Morral, A. (2011). Using a cross-study design to assess the efficacy of motivational enhancement therapy–cognitive behavioral therapy 5 (MET/CBT5) in treating adolescents with cannabis-related disorders. *Journal of Studies on Alcohol and Drugs, 72*(3), 380–389.

Rogers, C. R. (1957). The necessary and sufficient conditions for therapeutic personality change. *Journal of Consulting Psychology, 21,* 95–103.

Sampl, S., & Kadden, R. (2001). *Cannabis Youth Treatment Series: Volume 1.* Retrieved from http://store.samhsa.gov/shin/content//SMA05-4010/SMA05-4010.pdf

Stephens, R. S., Babor, T. F., Kadden, R., & Miller, M. (2002). The Marijuana Treatment Project: Rationale, design and participant characteristics. *Addiction, 9*(Suppl. 1), 109–124. doi:10.1046/j.1360-0443.97.s01.6.x

Stinson, F. S., Ruan, W. J., Pickering, R., & Grant, B. F. (2006). Cannabis use disorders in the USA: Prevalence, correlates and co-morbidity. *Psychology Medicine, 36,* 1447–1460.

Substance Abuse and Mental Health Services Administration. (2012). *Results from the 2011 National Survey on Drug Use and Health: Mental health findings* (NSDUH Series H-45, HHS Publication No. [SMA] 12-4725). Retrieved from http://www.samhsa.gov/data/sites/default/files/2011MHFDT/2k11MHFR/Web/NSDUHmhfr2011.htm

United Nations Office on Drugs and Crime. (2009). *World drug report 2009.* Retrieved from http://www.unodc.org/documents/wdr/WDR_2009/WDR2009_eng_web.pdf

Walker, D. D., Roffman, R. A., Stephens, R. S., Wakana, K., & Berghuis, J. (2006). Motivational enhancement therapy for adolescent marijuana users: A preliminary randomized controlled trial. *Journal of Consulting and Clinical Psychology, 74,* 628–632. doi:10.1037/0022-006X.74.3.628

Walker, D. D., Stephens, R., Roffman, R., DeMarce, J., Lozano, B., Towe, S., & Berg, B. (2011). Randomized controlled trial of motivational enhancement therapy with nontreatment-seeking adolescent cannabis users: A further test of the teen marijuana check-up. *Psychology of Addictive Behaviors, 25,* 474–484.

Weinstein, A., Miller, H., Tal, E., Avi, I., Herman, I., Bar-Hamburger, R., & Bloch, M. (2010). Treatment of cannabis withdrawal syndrome using cognitive–behavioral therapy and relapse prevention for cannabis dependence. *Journal of Groups in Addiction & Recovery, 5*(3–4), 240–263. doi:10.1080/1556035X.2010.523358

Wright, J. H. (2006). Cognitive behavior therapy: Basic principles and recent advances. *Focus, 4*(2), 173–178.

CHAPTER 5 METHAMPHETAMINE ADDICTION

Helena G. Rindone

STUDENT LEARNING OUTCOMES

At the conclusion of this chapter students will

1. Define and identify the chemical properties of methamphetamines
2. Discuss the history of drugs identified as methamphetamines and current laws
3. Identify symptoms and patterns of methamphetamine addiction
4. Identify the effects on the body of long-term use of methamphetamines
5. Identify treatment approaches used with methamphetamine addictions

CASE AND CASE DISCUSSION

Joseph is a 60-year-old man with a lengthy history of methamphetamine abuse and an abusive upbringing. Joseph's mother, the mother of four girls and one boy, bounced from marriage to marriage when he was a child. Joseph suffered many physical beatings from his alcoholic stepfathers. He was beat with belts and beat by the hands of his stepfathers. His own father, a World War II veteran, suffered from alcoholism and was absent for most of Joseph's life. At the age of 8, Joseph was abandoned by his mother, and it was because his sisters returned to find him that he was brought back into his mother's home. When Joseph was 12, he was molested and sexually abused by one of his stepfathers. His mother was unable to provide all that her children needed, and Joseph often relied on his sisters to cook and make clothing for him. Joseph spent some time from ages 13 to 16 living with his father. His father, however, was absent emotionally and did not help Joseph much with school or his personal life. This was because of his father's issues with alcoholism. At 16 Joseph returned to live with his mother until he completed high school.

Joseph was always very gifted in school and was an active athlete, musician, and drama club member. He excelled academically and was offered a scholarship to the local university when he graduated. Joseph desired greatly to attend college, but his mother kicked him out of the house at 17. He was drafted into the war when he turned 18 and was sent to fight in Vietnam. In Vietnam he was exposed to many new experiences: combat, death, strict authority, alcohol, and methamphetamine. As a soldier he was given amphetamines to assist with staying awake and alert during long stretches of combat. Joseph also discovered that while on meth his overall well-being improved and he felt less down. On exiting the war Joseph visited with a doctor to discuss his blue feelings, feelings of anxiety, and overall well-being. The doctor assessed Joseph as suffering from depression and anxiety and prescribed him a narcotics-based pill. Although this assisted him it did not compare to the effect that meth had on him.

After the war Joseph continued to work for the military and proceeded through several unsuccessful relationships and a failed marriage. Each passing year his addiction to meth and dependency on narcotics pills grew stronger to help him cope with the depression caused by his failures and the demons of his childhood.

When Joseph was 27, he met a 17-year-old girl and fell in love. Less than a year later they were married and beginning a life together. Within 5 years of marriage they had two children, a little boy and a little girl. The duties of parenthood were very anxiety inducing for Joseph given that he had never experienced a happy childhood. Also, because this was his second marriage, there were many hardships, mostly due to the large difference in age. Each fight and difficulty pushed him to use more meth. While on meth Joseph was in a zombie-like state, completely subdued. He would run away until his high came down, and on returning home he would sleep for a few days. After the effects would wear off Joseph would become very violent and angry toward his family and would often miss work because of it. Joseph struggled to maintain employment because his addiction caused him to miss work and subsequently get fired. His wife was uneducated and worked as a waitress, and therefore the responsibility to provide for the family fell to Joseph. With only a high school diploma and experience in the military, Joseph found it difficult to give his family what they needed. He was absent from his children's lives and constantly fighting with his wife; neither his wife nor his children were aware of his addiction.

After almost 15 years of marriage his family finally learned of his addiction and Joseph entered rehab. His sobriety lasted strong for a year. The family moved to a nicer town. Joseph found a new job and life was going well. However, on a trip to visit old friends Joseph relapsed and started using drugs again for almost a year. He entered rehab again. His sobriety lasted another 2 years before life became difficult again. He lost his job and for more than a year was unemployed. To cope, he used drugs throughout that time. At Christmas time of that year, Joseph tried to commit suicide while on a drug trip but was found and saved by the manager of the hotel where he was staying. Joseph entered rehab yet another time and this time remained sober for several years. He obtained another job and life seemed better for him. He and his wife had a lot of marital strife, but they remained together. His children felt the strain of the drug abuse and marital conflict, and both children began to drink and do drugs at a young age. These struggles and anxieties caused Joseph to battle for years between relapsing and maintaining sobriety.

Now that Joseph is in his 60s he has resorted to abusing narcotics-based pain medications to deal with the daily anxieties and stresses of work and his family. So how does Joseph address his substance abuse? What treatment is recommended?

OVERVIEW OF METHAMPHETAMINE ADDICTION

Antifreeze, table salt, drain cleaner, acetone, brake cleaner, engine starter, cat litter, sodium hydroxide lye, and gun scrubber. What do these materials have in common? They are some of the ingredients in a highly addictive and powerful drug known as methamphetamine. One might wonder how a person can ingest these chemicals into his or her body. The nature of addiction to methamphetamine is as complex as the chemical formula of the drug. As seen in the case example of Joseph, there is no one direct path that leads a person to begin using methamphetamine. Also, recovery is not an easy path because addiction to meth affects areas of the social, biological, and psychological domains.

The 2012 National Survey on Drug Use and Health reported that 1.2 million people reported using methamphetamine within the past year and 440,000 reported using methamphetamine within the past month (0.4% and 0.2% of the population, respectively; Office of Applied Statistics, 2012). Within the same year, 133,000 new users of meth were 12 years of age or older, a trend that remained steady from the previous year but has decreased over the past decade (Substance Abuse and Mental Health Services Administration, 2013). Meth-related emergency room visits rose from 67,954 in 2007 to 102,961 in 2011 (Substance Abuse and Mental Health Services Administration, 2014). Furthermore, the U.S. Drug Enforcement Administration reported that between 2004 and 2005 meth-related arrests increased from 5,893 to 6,055 (National Drug Intelligence Center, 2006).

An *epidemic* is a rapid spread or increase in the occurrence of something. An epidemic can be thought of as a temporary situation. There is a peak time and then a period of recovery. Methamphetamine would fit this criterion. Although numbers of reported users are decreasing, meth has a history of destruction throughout the United States. The costs are not only to the personal lives of users but also to the country as a whole. In this chapter methamphetamine is broken down into the areas of history, demographics, addiction, politics and law, and treatment. For as complicated as the drug is, it is necessary to understand the full spectrum of the drug in order to begin approaches to treatment.

Brief History

Methamphetamine is an associate of a division of drugs known as amphetamines. The chemical product amphetamine is a combination of two structures: levoamphetamine and destroamphetamine. Levoamphetamine affects the nasal passages and has no neurophysiological effects. However, destroamphetamine directly affects the brain (Halkitis, 2007). Amphetamine was first developed in the 1800s by a scientist named Lazăr Edeleano, who named it *phenylisopropylamine*, but it had no specific medical use at the time (Gahlinger, 2001). In 1919 a Japanese chemist, Akira Ogata, produced the first methamphetamine (Taylor & Covey, 2008).

During the 20th century, meth was introduced as a bronchial inhaler to treat allergies, asthma, and colds. Subsequently, by 1937 a tablet was compounded to treat children with attention-deficit/hyperactivity disorder (ADHD) and persons with narcolepsy and was also used as an appetite suppressant for women trying to lose weight (Matsumoto, Miyakawa, Yabana, Iizuka, & Kishimoto, 2000). In 1932 Benzedrine was introduced as an over-the-counter bronchial dilator. It was discovered that the plant ephedrine (the substance on which the drug is based) could be purified, and methamphetamine was formulated shortly thereafter. Scientists discovered that speed could easily be made using an ephedrine base (Suwaki, Fukui, & Konuma, 1997). During World War II, methamphetamine and amphetamine were given to Allied bomber pilots to keep them awake on long flights. Amphetamines were primarily used by soldiers to fight off fatigue and enhance their performance. The Japanese prescribed it as a means of improving the productivity of workers involved in the war (Halkitis, 2007). During this time the first maladaptive reactions were seen by soldiers who were unable to focus their performance and became irritable. After the war, Japan dealt with a meth epidemic that eventually spread to the West Coast of the United States. In the 1950s a pain alleviator, Methedrine, was prescribed (Marcovitz, 2006). It was widely used by housewives, athletes, college students, and truck drivers, to name a few. In the prescribed form of Desoxyn it was used to treat a spectrum of disorders, including attention-deficit disorder, depression, alcoholism, obesity, and even Parkinson's disease (Halkitis, 2007). During the 1960s doctors prescribed injections of meth to treat heroin addiction. American soldiers used more amphetamine during the Vietnam War than the rest of the world combined during World War II (M. A. Miller, 1997).

The first crystal amphetamine laboratories appeared in the 1960s in San Francisco. Crystal meth was first illegally produced by outlaw biker clubs such as the Hell's Angels, many of whose members were veterans of World War II, Korea, and Vietnam. The epidemic spread to Southern California because it was easy to traffic into Mexico. During the 1980s a newer form, Batu, was introduced in Hawaii. Before the 1990s, White motorcycle gangs controlled production, but since then small home labs and Mexican criminal organizations have taken over production in super-labs. In testimony to the U.S. Congress, acting administrator of the Drug Enforcement Administration Donnie R. Marshall (2000) reported that about 85% of all meth used in the United States in 2000 was produced in these super-labs. The movement and production of meth was originally contained to isolated rural locations in western and midwestern regions. However, production has since moved east because household products can easily be bought to make methamphetamine and the Internet can help show how it is done (Halkitis, 2009).

In 1959 over-the-counter amphetamines were banned by the U.S. Food and Drug Administration. By 1970 the Controlled Substances Act banned the production of injectable meth that had been used for medicinal purposes (Wermuth, 2000). The United States passed laws in 1983 that prohibited the possession of equipment for meth production. In 1986 the U.S. government passed the federal Controlled Substance Analogue Enforcement Act in an effort to stop the growing use of synthesized drugs. The Combat Methamphetamine Epidemic Act of 2005 targeted the sale of pseudoephedrine, an ingredient found in cold medicine and also an ingredient used to make meth, in order to restrict buying in large quantities. Base forms can still be found in pills to treat ADHD, but high dosages are only prescribed in extreme cases. Methamphetamine is classified as a Schedule II substance by the U.S. Drug Enforcement Administration. Schedule II substances are those that have a high potential for abuse, that have a currently accepted medical use with severe restriction, and whose abuse may lead to severe psychological or physical dependence. Meth today is calculated to be as much as 6 times as potent as meth cooked in the 1960s.

What Is Methamphetamine Made Of?

Materials commonly used to make meth are antifreeze, table salt, drain cleaner (which disintegrates the skin), acetone, hydrochloric acid (which literally eats away human flesh), cold medicine, red phosphorus, benzene, gasoline, toluene brake cleaner, ether engine starter, cat litter, sodium hydroxide lye, and trichlorethane gun scrubber (Halkitis, 2009). In a nonsmoked form this drug is referred to as *speed, meth,* and *chalk.* In a smoked form it is referred to as *ice, crystal, crank,* and *glass.* For every 1 pound of meth, 6 pounds of toxic material are produced. To produce meth, substances are broken down, bound, and combined. Because lithium and other explosive materials are used, meth lab explosions are common and result in extreme burns and even death.

Demographics

The following findings regarding admission to treatment for methamphetamine/ amphetamine addiction are from the National Survey on Drug Use and Health. Admission to substance abuse treatment by state can be monitored using the Treatment Episode Data Set, an annual compilation of demographic data on those admitted to, primarily, publicly funded treatment facilities.

As a whole, rates of substance abuse treatment admissions in the United States increased for methamphetamine/amphetamine between 1995 and 2005. The rate increased from 30 per 100,000 persons ages 12 and older to 68 per 100,000. The states that reported the highest rates in 1995 (Hawaii, Washington, Montana, and Arkansas) reported double their rates of admission in 2005. Hawaii reported 107 per 100,000 in 1995 and 244 per 100,000 in 2005 (Office of Applied Statistics, 2006). Admission rates were generally higher in the Pacific and Mountain states, with reports of 220 per 100,000 persons ages 12 or older. Of the primary admissions to treatment, 45% were women approximately 30 years old (Halkitis, 2009). The Drug Abuse Warning Network estimated that 73,400 of the 106 million emergency department visits in 2006 involved methamphetamine abuse (Office of Applied Statistics, 2006).

The TEDS and NIDA also provide statistics on the race and ethnicity of meth users. The NIDA (2014) reports between 77% and 87% of all admissions are White persons in urban areas. However, in inner cities Whites account for only 56% of admissions. Admissions for ethnic groups in larger cities are as follows: Latinos, 28%; Blacks, 5%; and Asians/Pacific Islanders, 3%. According to the Youth Risk Behavior Surveillance study (Kann et al., 2014), estimates of ever having used meth range from 1.6% to 8.9% of high school students across 35 states. Moreover, 3% of adults ages 18 to 25 and 5.5% of adults 26 and older have reported using meth in their lifetime (National Institute on Drug Abuse, 2014).

Over the years, the media has portrayed gay and bisexual men as the primary population of methamphetamine users (Halkitis, 2009). However, data collected from users and informed experts show a different trend. For example, areas like Central California show a trend of heterosexual users who begin using in their teens and move toward regular use until their 30s. Those who use into their 30s, like smaller populations in San Francisco, tend to be gay men. In June 2006 the *New York Times* published an ad for the Crystal Meth Working Group titled "Crystal Meth Manifesto." The campaign led the slogan "Buy Crystal, Get HIV for Free." There are no specific population data available for gay or bisexual persons who use meth. However, estimates from self-identified drug-using samples show numbers of gay or bisexual individuals who use meth ranging from 7.4% to as high as 62% (Halkitis & Parsons, 2002). Among men having sex with men, meth use has been reported among varying races, with higher numbers coming from White men. However, there has been an increase in meth use among other ethnic groups, such as Latinos and Asians/Pacific Islanders (Choi et al., 2005). In a 2005 study conducted among gay and bisexual men, methamphetamine use in the 6 months prior to assessment was noted in 24% of the sample. Of those 24%, 30% were Latino, 28% Black, and 15% White (Halkitis et al., 2008). These results show a progression from the 2004 Centers for Disease Control and Prevention National HIV Behavioral Surveillance System, which reported that meth use among men having sex with men tended to be among Whites versus non-Whites (50.4% vs. 43.5%, respectively; Mansergh et al., 2006).

Although meth use has been predominantly studied in men, women show significant figures as well. Methamphetamine use among incarcerated women tended to be seen among White women who had low levels of education, were mothers, were divorced or separated, and had associations with drug abuse and sexual assault (Vik & Ross, 2003). Low education can be seen as a trend, with support from a study that 76 of 204 individuals arrested in northern Utah for meth use were women and possessed a minimum of a high school degree (Senjo, 2007). Moreover, in a study of 1,104 persons, 59% of women were more likely to use meth when ages 30 or older, and 47% were more likely to be lesbian or bisexual (Parsons, Kelly, & Wells, 2006). This compares with data that indicate that Black male meth users were traditionally gay and generally had lower levels of education (Halkitis & Jerome, 2008). Although there are trends in the demographics of methamphetamine users, it is still important to understand that any person, label, or demographic can be a meth user.

Costs

Methamphetamine has at times been referred to as a poor man's cocaine. The cost to produce it depends on the costs of the household products that are used to make it. In makeshift labs and with generic chemicals, the cost to the producer can be low. Street-gathered data indicate that one fourth of a gram of meth costs approximately $25, and a gram can cost from $60 to $330 (Frontline, n.d.). An 8 ball, which is 3.5 grams, costs $200 and can last for about a week or, in the case of heavy users, only a couple of days. In a month, an addicted meth user can spend anywhere from $800 to close to $5,000.

Inpatient and outpatient residential treatment costs can vary. Intensive residential treatment at Charlie's Place, in Texas, can cost $4,500 a month. In California, a popular rehab facility, Promises, can cost a person $42,000 for the month. The Betty Ford Center costs a person around $23,000 for a month of treatment. The differences can stem from nonprofit and for-profit statuses as well as the amenities that are provided. Promises offers luxury estates for their patients to stay in along the beachfront in Malibu. A nonprofit agency like Charlie's Place may provide the essential counseling and therapy services without the luxuries of tennis courts and pools. However, there are a number of rehab facilities, and costs should not be generalized from the examples given in this section. These facilities were selected because of their popularity (Charlie's Place, 2012).

The success of treatment programs will vary also. Here my intent is not to delve into the successes and failures of the institutions but rather to give an introduction to the nature of services provided at facilities. Passages, another popular treatment facility in California, can provide its clients with personal training; private detox centers; athletic facilities; and a team of private therapists, nurses, and holistic mediators. Treatments include marriage and family therapy, nutrition therapy, art therapy, hypnotherapy, a ropes course, and even yoga. Although these amenities are luxurious, they are not synonymous with adequate and effective addiction treatment. It is important to understand also that popular facilities will boast on their websites that their successes are unparalleled and that they are the top-rated facilities in the United States. However, addiction researchers say that these boasts are very difficult to substantiate (Pringle, 2007) because follow-up data can be limited and measurements for successes are not uniform among facilities. Outcome data and follow-up statistics on abstinence and length of abstinence are more difficult to find, if not unobtainable, on facility websites. Also, reports of failures are not readily accessible either. It is important to keep this information in mind because at times referrals will need to be made for clients to attend residential treatment facilities. Also, if one is seeking employment in the field of addiction counseling, one should be knowledgeable of the efficacy of the treatment facilities one is applying to.

The Combat Methamphetamine Epidemic Act of 2005 (Office of Legislative Policy and Analysis, n.d.), a Title VII entity of the USA PATRIOT Improvement and Reauthorization Act of 2005, set regulations for retail over-the-counter sales of ephedrine, pseudoephedrine, and phenylpropanolamine products. Daily sales limits and 30-day purchase per person limits were set. This act requires that products be placed out of direct customer reach, that sale logbooks be kept, that customers' identification be verified, and that employee training be provided in order that self-certification of regulated sellers be provided.

The Methamphetamine Education, Treatment, and Hope Act of 2010 sought to enhance the responsibilities of federal offices within Substance Abuse and Mental Health Services Administration services that conduct research, education, and outreach. The act authorizes funding for grants to entities that provide residential treatment to pregnant and parenting women. It also requires the establishment of a clearinghouse for information pertaining to drug-free workplaces and requires collaboration with health care providers and youth to improve the detection and prevention of methamphetamine use. This act authorized the appropriation of $67 million for fiscal years 2012–2015 and an additional $18 million for fiscal year 2016 to fund grants to entities that provide treatment to pregnant and parenting women. A total of $39 million was disbursed over 2011–2015 and an additional $49 million after 2015.

The act clarifies a broadening of the service population from postpartum women only to include parenting women. Priority is given to applicants whose programs would serve rural areas and areas that have a shortage of mental health professionals. Areas that have a shortage of family-based treatment options and that are determined to have a high rate of addiction to methamphetamine or other drugs receive higher priority for funding. The act largely requires the expansion, intensification, and coordination of services for pregnant and parenting women who are addicted to meth or other drugs.

EFFECTS OF METHAMPHETAMINES

The Brain

To understand the complexity of what meth does to the brain, it is essential to understand, at a minimal level, how the brain functions and the relationship between its working parts and the body. The brain involves the communication among individual cells and how those communication processes are organized and synchronized (Halkitis, 2009). Neurons communicate with one another by releasing chemical messengers called *neurotransmitters*. A message originates as an electrical charge in a neuron, and when it reaches a certain threshold it triggers the transmission of an electrical and mechanical signal down a neural pathway known as an *axon*.

Different neurotransmitters have different effects on signal-receiving neurons. Some have an excitatory effect, meaning that they increase the cumulative charge inside the neuron and thus increase the likelihood that the charge will pass the threshold and create the firing of the action potential. Others are inhibitory; they act to decrease the cumulative charge inside the signal-receiving neuron after they have plugged into their specific neuroreceptor. This decreases the chances that the neuron will fire (Taylor & Covey, 2008).

Neurotransmitters match with specific neuroreceptors like puzzle pieces. They activate the receptor and change the electrical charge in the receiving neuron. The message traveling down the axon is called the *action potential*. The end of the axon is the *terminal button*, and at this spot the axon junctions with other neurons, muscles, glands, and organs. In the terminal button, the electrical and chemical message of the action potential is changed into a chemical message. This occurs as the signal of the action potential triggers storage sacs for neurotransmitter chemical messengers to travel to the inner wall of the terminal button and the signal-receiving neuron, gland, muscle, or organ (Taylor & Covey, 2008).

Catecholamines, which are dopamine, norepinephrine, and epinephrine, are neurotransmitters that are primarily affected by the action of methamphetamine. Serotonin is affected as well. All of these are excitatory, meaning that they increase the activity of the neurons they affect. Dopamine receptors are the pleasure house of the brain. Dopamine is actively involved with controlling bodily movement, thought processes, emotions, and pleasure. Dopamine receptors regulate an individual's social reactions to another's behavior or the way the person feels the emotions of another. Neurotransmitters of meth reach levels 1,500% higher than their normal levels. Norepinephrine affects alertness, attention, rest, and memory processes. Meth prevents the reuptake of it (Halkitis, 2009). Meth users describe a sense of euphoria while using the drug, a feeling that stems from overfilling levels of dopamine in the brain. Serotonin is a mood elevator as well. Although levels of dopamine and pleasure increase, meth also interferes with voluntary motor responses, making the user jittery and restless. The same is said for serotonin. When the mood elevates, psychotic processes, like hallucinations and delusions, also appear. Increases in epinephrine and norepinephrine account for increased energy and sleeplessness.

It is important to understand that the intensity of these effects will depend on the level of cognitive functioning of the person. Similar active ingredients are found in prescriptions given to persons suffering from ADHD. The excitatory effects balance out the deficiencies of ADHD, and therefore the sense of energy rush and overactivity may seem less than in a person who has a typically regulated brain. People under the influence of meth can experience elevated blood pressure, high body temperature, increased heart rate, and muscle tension. They also exhibit poor muscle control, tactile sensations, personality changes, and short-term memory deficits. These are all related to effects on the brain. Extended use and abuse of meth has detrimental effects due to neurotoxicity. These can be memory impairment, paranoia, a diminished ability to feel pleasure, and attention-related difficulties.

An easier way to think of the effects of meth is to picture the prefrontal cortex as an elastic band. Inside the band are the functioning processes—the feelings of pleasure and excitatory responses. While on meth, those functioning processes increase, and therefore the bandwidth in the brain increases to a bigger size than it would be normally in order to accommodate for the increased activity. As the effects diminish, the elastic band does not return to its normal size. It stays stretched out and now contains extra gaps and holes that the drug was filling up and expanding. The brain's normal functioning levels are not enough to fill those gaps and holes in the bandwidth. Over time, the band needs more and more meth to fill up those gaps because the increased usage means an increase in the overall width. The band becomes stretched beyond what it should be and eventually it starts to deteriorate and become tethered. After time and after much abuse, the band can break. It is then nearly impossible to fill up the space anymore because the holes cannot be fixed. The end result is that those feelings and reactions that the brain produces are lost.

The Body

Smoking has become the most common method of ingesting and abusing methamphetamine. Immediately after smoking, the drug user will experience an intense surge that lasts only a few minutes. This surge is described as extremely pleasurable, like the euphoric feeling that comes from having sex or eating chocolate, only much more intense. Snorting produces effects within 3 to 5 minutes, and oral ingestion produces effects within 15 to 20 minutes. Meth use is most often described as a binge and crash, because the effects disappear even before concentrations of the drug in the blood fall significantly. Users try to maintain the high by taking more of the drug. Most partake in a form of bingeing called a *run,* which involves forgoing sleeping and eating while continuing to abuse for several days.

The extremely toxic components of the drug affect many areas of the body, not just the brain. The drug increases wakefulness and decreases appetite. Short-term effects include increased attention, decreased fatigue, increased activity, euphoria and rush, increased respiration, rapid and irregular heartbeat, and hyperthermia.

Long-term effects can include psychosis, paranoia, hallucinations, repetitive motor activity, memory loss, loss of coordination, aggressive violent behavior, mood disturbances, dental problems, and weight loss. A person who has abused the drug extensively will have sores all over his or her face, acne, discolored skin, tooth decay, extreme weight loss, and hair loss. The sores come from formication, which is the feeling that something is crawling under one's skin, an effect of the hallucinations.

The Psychosocial Life

Think of life in terms of a mathematical equation. Substance A + Experience B = Happiness C. The brain is like a calculator. This equation is preprogrammed in a person, and A and B have specific values and components. To generate C, happiness, the brain inputs the values into the equation and sends messages throughout the body, and the person performs accordingly. Happiness, euphoria, arousal, excitement, joy, and other synonyms of the construct are subjective values. For each individual, the feelings and emotions that make up the construct are different. The feelings of euphoria that meth users experience are different for each user. One may feel the intensity experienced during sexual activity, whereas another will feel the joy that comes from receiving a gift. The extent of the happiness that a person feels is not as important as the notion that the person is training his or her brain to send the message that meth is needed in order to experience that happiness: Meth + Chemical Reaction in the Brain = "Happiness." With sustained use, the natural sense of euphoria found in the chemical dopamine depletes itself because of the toxicity of the meth. As in the example of the elastic band, more and more meth is needed to feel the euphoria and happiness. An addiction to that feeling forms. However, with sustained abuse, the user reaches a point at which that sense of happiness is unattainable.

Depression, anxiety, and aggression are but a few of the sentiments a user feels when not using meth. Methamphetamine acts as a theoretical Band-Aid for those feelings. A person may have been depressed prior to using or may not have been and as a consequence of using is in a depressed-like state when not on the drug. Meth users experience not only psychological problems but problems in their social lives as well. Addicts reach a point where without meth they have an inability to function. Their money is spent on meth; they are unable to maintain a job or a healthy group of friends. Their clothes are unwashed, their bodies are unkempt, and they have decaying teeth and sores on their bodies and face. The smell of a meth addict has been related to the smell of urine in some cases.

A study in 2004 of 350 individuals receiving treatment for methamphetamine abuse found that 84% reported weight loss, 78% sleeplessness, 73% financial problems, and 63% legal problems. Moreover, 67% reported paranoia, 61% hallucinations, 60% work problems, 57% violent behavior, 55% dental problems, and 36% skin problems (Brecht, O'Brien, von Mayrhauser, & Anglin, 2004). Although the short-term effects of usage can be highly desirable, the long-term consequences are anything but enticing. Although effects on social cognitions of meth users have been little studied, one study found that when rats were given doses of meth they exhibited lower levels of social interaction within weeks of using the drug (Clemens et al., 2006). A user's tendency to be withdrawn and aggressive is related to evidence that meth deteriorates the density of the transporter in the cortexes of the brain where emotion regulation occurs. Researchers found that acute and chronic meth use in monkeys led to extreme social withdrawal in the animals (Schiorring, 1977). For comparison, consider that a study of meth-dependent gay men reported a significantly low level of social skills as measured by social-cognitive function tests (Halkitis, Homer, Moeller, & Solomon, 2007). When people become addicted to meth, their entire lives are consumed, and often the only relationship that exists is between them and the drug.

Damages Due to Usage

A study performed by Simon et al. (2000) compared two groups of comparable nonusers to regular meth users. After 11 years of regular use, the users were found to be impaired in tasks of recalling, manipulating information, abstract thinking, and ignoring irrelevant information. The overstimulation of the nervous system creates a number of undesirable effects (Halkitis, 2009). These can include tachycardia, hypertensions, papillary dilation, diaphoresis, and hyperthermia (Meredith, Jaffe, Ang-Lee, & Saxon, 2005). Psychiatric dysfunction is linked to many of the crashing symptoms that users feel when they are withdrawing: aggression, anger, depression, and fatigue. Paranoia and hallucination have been linked to meth use as well. They are related to formication, or crank bugs, in which a person has the sensation that bugs are crawling under his or her skin, which leads to excessive picking and tearing of the skin.

Methamphetamine directly affects the functioning of the autonomic nervous system and the central nervous system, even in small doses (National Institute on Drug Abuse, 2006). As discussed already, its use can lead to increased heart rate, elevated blood pressure, and narrowing of the blood vessels. It has also been linked to strokes and heart attacks (National Institute on Drug Abuse, 2006). Traces of the drug are also linked to chest pain, shortness of breath, and myocardial infarction. Usage can also lead to hypertension, which can cause abnormalities, hemorrhages, and death (Halkitis, 2009). Chronic use of methamphetamine is associated with alterations to the dopamine system, including depletion of the chemical enzyme and a decrease in the number of transport pumps. This reduction leads to poor motor activity, decreased memory performance, and reduced verbal learning (Halkitis, 2009). It is also linked with low levels of motivation and decreases in experiences of pleasure (Halkitis, 2009).

The long-lasting and damaging effects of meth are due in part to the slow rate of metabolism in the body. Meth has a half-life of 8 to 24 hours, with 50% still remaining in the body after 24 hours (Halkitis, 2009). As discussed, the effects wear off sooner than the drug exits the body, even though users continue to put the drug in their bodies. With this basic information on the damages and effects of meth use in mind, one may begin to ask, why use and why become addicted?

ADDICTION TO METHAMPHETAMINE

There is not a generic, one-size-fits-all prototype for a methamphetamine addict. Not every user is an addict, and each person's journey with the drug is as unique as that individual. Each person has a different experience from the first time he or she chooses to use. Each time a person continues to use, that experience is altered, and therefore the complexity of the drug increases. One thing that is certain is that the drug itself is powerfully addictive. Addiction may occur after a single use or after just a few uses. Addiction can be rapid as well. Users have reported that the drug is seductive and rapid use begins quickly (Sommers, Baskin, & Baskin-Sommers, 2006). The extreme sense of pleasure pulls people to continue to use in order to experience the euphoria that they are unable to experience on their own. Because it is easy to obtain, is cheap to buy, and has seemingly good effects, it lures one in to continue to use.

Treatments for addiction are not unilateral pathways. There is not one uniform direction a user takes, nor one that is recreational. Each person experiences a different motivation for using the first time. Some may note depression, loneliness, difficult times, or a desire to belong with a certain crowd. Teenagers may experience a need to fit in or a motivation to belong with others who are using. Romantic partners may feel pressure from their significant other to partake. The promise that a person will feel good while using is enough motivation for a person to use. Whatever the intent behind using for the first time, the experience will either push the user forward to continue to use or hold him or her back.

There are commonalities in persons who receive treatment for addiction. Given that the drug provides a surge of pleasure and good feelings for a person, it is often the case that the person is unable to obtain an equal or similar sense of happiness from his or her natural, nondrug environment. Happiness is a large abstract construct that can consist of anything, and one can say that unhappiness is equally as complex. Struggles in life may involve a difficult childhood, childhood abuse, low self-esteem, loneliness, depression, anxiety, loss of jobs, loss of loved ones, pressure to fit in, and so on. The lack of positive feelings may be clear to users, and they will see a connection to their usage. For others, the relationship is subconscious, and because of extended abuse it may be difficult to discover exactly where and when they fell off the track. Important also to keep in mind is the biological perspective. People with ADHD are at times, but not always, prescribed a syndicate of the drug. The method and means do not necessarily compare with the use of a street addict. Certainly an argument can also be made that a biological predisposition from users is present, given a familial history of drug abuse.

In addition, stress—which is different from unhappiness—is important to consider in understanding meth addiction (Halkitis, 2009). The drug has been based largely in rural communities with families and individuals of low socioeconomic status. Meth has been labeled a *poor man's drug* because of the common environment users come from. Single-parent households, persons with histories of sexual and physical abuse, persons struggling to maintain a job and a house, and families with a history of generational poverty are a few of the populations affected. Urban and racial minorities may experience higher levels of stress as well due to immigration status, limited resources, poor living conditions, and discrimination (Halkitis, 2009).

The paradigm is not limited to psychological and biological components but is also significantly impacted by social influences (Halkitis, 2009). Family dynamics are important to consider when addressing a person's addiction. Hawkins, Catalano, and Miller (1992) discussed family-centered factors that were risk motivators for drug abuse in adolescents and young adults. These factors included inconsistent family regulation methods, family alcohol and drug behavior attitudes, family conflict, and poor attachment to the family. For a child living in a drug-abusing family, his or her development and growth will be directly affected by that abuse. Depending on the child's developmental stage, his or her level of understanding and rationale will be different. Adults who were admitted to treatment for drug abuse were more likely to have a family history of drug abuse (Meller, Rinehart, Cadoret, & Troughton, 1988).

Social groups can similarly act as family-type influences. In a discussion of the primary influences for adolescents who drank and used recreational drugs, it was noted that peer influences held great significance (Bahr, Hoffmann, & Yang, 2005). A similar study indicated that methamphetamine-using adolescents tend to report having peers who also use drugs (Rawson, Gonzales, Obert, McCann, & Brethen, 2005). Social networks are very significant in understanding sustained use. The phrase "Birds of a feather flock together" holds very true for meth addicts. Prolonged use can be attributed to the influence and connection that users have with other users. Users' addict families provide a secure base for their usage and provide a sense of acceptance when the rest of the world shuns them. Users' social networks are formed of individuals of different socioeconomic statuses and ethnicities. They can provide them with an escape or an outlet (Halkitis, 2009).

In light of these patterns and themes, one may wonder what constitutes addiction. In the *Diagnostic and Statistical Manual of Mental Disorders, Fifth Edition* (American Psychiatric Association [APA], 2013), the term *addiction* is not clearly defined. Substance use disorders have both psychological and physiological symptoms, such as behavioral changes and changes in the circuitry of the brain (APA, 2013). Humans have a propensity to drive themselves toward the things that make them feel good. As discussed earlier, the more people do something, the more they are training their brains to think that this is what they need to feel good. It is significant that although the nature of an addiction indicates that a person is not in control of his or her use, many addicts will state that they are in full control of their usage. When everything else around a person has turned to chaos or is even minimally outside of his or her realm of comfort, a shred of psychological control will keep the person from breaking down mentally. However, as discussed previously, users lose control of more than one area of their lives and bodies.

Dependency can be seen in many different ways—as an inability to function off the drug, an ability to maintain a job or close relationships, financial malfunctions, and so on. The path to dependency is not uniform and raises many questions about the cause of addiction and dependency. So how does treatment begin, from a universally applicable basis, when there is no one applicable formula for how a person becomes an addict?

TREATMENT

Not every methamphetamine user may need treatment. Persons may find themselves using meth recreationally for a short period of time or situationally during a brief period. When a user reaches the point at which he or she decides to receive treatment, professional help is strongly advised. Professional help comes in many different approaches and methods. A person can seek out a treatment facility for inpatient or outpatient care. A personal therapist and even clergy can be sought out as well. Here I describe some specific professional techniques and approaches to treating meth addiction. Yet it is important to keep in mind that the range of available approaches is not limited to the ones discussed in this chapter. There are numerous successful methods. Also, treatment is not limited to combining approaches with comparable methods in a multimodal approach. The following discussion provides an introduction to commonly used approaches in treating addiction.

Treatment not only addresses the amount of usage or the frequency but also focuses on other areas that reflect the nature and extent of the person's involvement with and addiction to the drug. These can include obsessive thoughts about using that give rise to cravings and the urge to use, an inability to assuredly control when and how much the person uses, the extent to which the drug impedes the person's functioning, and persistent use in the light of increasingly severe and life-damaging consequences (Washton & Zweben, 2009). Certainly to be addressed is that certain individuals have recovered from addiction without seeking professional help. Studies on this phenomenon have indicated that social support contributes to self-guided attempts to change (Sobell, Ellingstad, & Sobell, 2000). Individuals who recover without treatment utilize similar habit-breaking methods and lifestyle changes that addiction treatment programs typically promote, such as avoiding influences that previously had influenced the person to use drugs, becoming involved in positive activities to prevent boredom and unstructured time, and establishing a social network of nonusers (Latkin, Knowlton, Hoover, & Mandell, 1999).

In this section I discuss the following treatment models: 12-step facilitation therapy, cognitive behavior therapy (CBT), motivational interviewing (MI), harm reduction, and the Matrix Model for methamphetamine addiction treatment. Although there are certainly many more models that can be utilized, these five are widely used in the field of addiction therapy. Project MATCH (Matching Alcoholism Treatments to Client Heterogeneity) compared the effectiveness of 12-step facilitation therapy, CBT, and MI and found no significant differences in treatment outcomes for these approaches (Luchansky, Krupski, & Stark, 2007). This finding relates to one of the universal principles of counseling, that all models are successful in their own right. A person may choose any single one or combine a few.

12-Step and Disease Model Approaches

A substantial number of addiction programs in the United States are based on the 12-step philosophy of Alcoholics Anonymous (AA; Washton & Zweben, 2009). Affiliation with 12-step groups has consistently been linked to attainment of abstinence for persons dealing with alcohol and drug addiction (Laudet & White, 2005).

AA was founded in 1935 by Dr. Robert Holbrook and Bill Wilson when the two men met during a business trip in Ohio and Wilson was seeking support to stay sober (W. R. Miller, Zweben, & Johnson, 2005). The intent was to find a method that would assist people in their struggles to attain and maintain sobriety. In its fourth year the group had 100 members (Emmelkamp & Vedel, 2006). In 1953, Narcotics Anonymous (NA) was founded on the belief that the specific chemical was not the problem—rather, it was the common disease of addiction (Emmelkamp & Vedel, 2006). In 1988, 95% of U.S. inpatient alcohol treatment programs incorporated AA and NA into their recovery philosophy (Brown, Peterson, & Cunningham, 1988).

Enthusiasm for the 12-step approach was high among clinicians in the United States in 2001 (Forman, Bovasso, & Woody, 2001). Founder Bill Wilson noticed that a substantial number of meth addicts were attending various AA and NA meetings and thus in 1995 formed Crystal Meth Anonymous (CMA). Presently, the 12-step approach for meth addiction primarily focuses on CMA and is the standard of care for individuals seeking care within community settings (Halkitis, 2009).

Twelve-step addictions groups have established sets of goals members work toward in order to achieve the ultimate goal of attaining recovery from addiction. The following goals were identified in an outpatient survey of drug abuse programs and treatment facilities (Capuzzi & Stauffer, 2012):

- Abstinence from alcohol and other drugs
- Steady employment
- Stable social relationships
- Positive physical and emotional health
- Improved spiritual strength
- Adherence to legal mandates/requirements as applicable

The model for AA and NA emphasizes the necessity of total, immediate, and hopefully life-long abstinence from all psychoactive substances. The person must accept addiction as a life-long disease for which there is only recovery and no permanent cure. The model also ascertains that the central role of maintaining regular and meaningful involvement in a 12-step program will help a person achieve lasting recovery (Washton & Zweben, 2009). This belief rests in the idea that substance abuse is the result of a biological or psychological vulnerability, and therefore treatment is centered on the notion that substance abuse is a progressive illness that affects the body, mind, and spirit (Halkitis, 2009).

CMA comprises three main components: attendance at the 12-step meetings and the development of fellowship with peers in these groups, utilization of sponsorship from a selected individual who participates in the group to assist in the attainment of sobriety, and the provision of service and commitment to the 12-step group through active participation in group activities and services. Spirituality is an essential component in the treatment model, as the person admits that he or she is powerless to the drug and turns power over to a higher being for change. The 12 steps and 12 traditions utilized by CMA can be found on their website (CMA, 2007).

CMA is not associated with any specific religious denomination but has a faith component. The group does not discriminate against any prospective members, and nonaddicts are welcome to attend open meetings. However, only those with a chemical dependency are allowed to attend closed meetings (Capuzzi & Stauffer, 2012). There are generally six types of meetings that the counselor should be aware of (G. Miller, 2005):

1. Open meetings involve one recovering person speaking to the group about his or her addiction and recovery story. Nonaddicts are welcome and encouraged to attend.
2. Closed meetings involve addicts only.

3. Discussion or participation meetings focus on a topic discussed by the addict in attendance.
4. In speaker meetings, one addicted person speaks to the audience about his or her recovery.
5. In step meetings, the topic of discussion is one of the 12 steps.
6. In Big Book meetings, a chapter from AA is read and discussed.

Twelve-step meetings generally take place in a group setting, but at the same time individual attention is given. Open sessions are free to anyone, including nonaddicts, but closed sessions have specific groups and settings. Groups can be selected according to a variety of demographics—age, gender, or nature of the dependency. Diversity, theoretical orientations, and foundations play a significant role also.

When counselors have an in-depth knowledge of the approach of a 12-step program, they can enhance the counseling process and potential success (G. Miller, 2005). Whereas sponsors are usually recovering addicts themselves, counselors do not necessarily need to be. Effective counselors should have a thorough knowledge of the different self-help programs in the community and be able to make appropriate referrals. Counselors play an important role in educating clients about the self-help group. This includes having an extensive knowledge of not just one addiction but many types of addictions. Counselors should assess clients based on these five criteria: loss of willpower, harmful consequences, an unmanageable lifestyle, tolerance or escalation of use, and withdrawal symptoms on quitting (Capuzzi & Stauffer, 2012). Counselors should be proficient in understanding areas of diversity as well in order to make appropriate referrals for clients.

The therapist of a person attending 12-step meetings should keep some essentials in mind when working with the client. The therapist needs to have active facilitation and pay attention to the underlying beliefs of the client. The therapist should be aware of each meeting that the client has attended and his or her reactions to it. The therapist should ask the client if there were any other participants at the meeting that he or she identified with. The client should be encouraged to accept the 12-step principle that he or she is powerless over the drug and previous attempts at sobriety have failed because of this powerlessness. Given that this is an essential principle of a 12-step program, the client should remain congruent with the treatment he or she has elected to receive. The therapist should encourage the client to choose a sponsor in the 12-step program and should reinforce attendance. The therapist should of course also promote sober days and encourage continued sober days. The therapist should support change in friends and invite the client to surround himself or herself with family significant others who are supportive (Emmelkamp & Vedel, 2006).

Twelve-step programs provide a powerful outlet for their clients. They provide a safe, predictable, and chemical-free environment in which clients can learn and grow in a sober lifestyle (Capuzzi & Stauffer, 2012). Participants are able to explore freely a different lifestyle and learn more effective social skills from others. Groups encourage new behavioral changes and experimentation. Studies have noted that a 12-step model is more favorable for treating alcoholism than a CBT approach, yet a CBT approach is more favorable for treating crack cocaine addiction (Maude-Griffin et al., 1998; Ouimette, Finney, & Moos, 1997). A 2-year study that examined chemical usage in 157 chemically dependent male and female adolescents 6, 12, and 24 months after leaving AA/NA treatment programs revealed that both treatment completers and noncompleters demonstrated less chemical use after their hospitalizations than before. However, although higher rates of abstinence were seen at 6 months postdischarge for completers, those rates declined sharply 1 and 2 years after discharge (Alford, Koehler, & Leonard, 1991). Some findings have also indicated that relapse rates are as high as 70% just a couple of years after completing a 12-step program (Emmelkamp & Vedel, 2006).

It is important to note that 12-step groups do not provide formal treatment. CMA does not provide assessment, treatment plans, case management, or therapy. It is more like a social movement. Laudet and White (2005) noted that counselors in 12-step programs are not necessarily trained formally in the profession. They are trained in the nature of counseling and lack an understanding of codependency, boundaries, and necessary counseling techniques. One could also argue that recidivism is very high among group members because one of the core beliefs is that the client is powerless to the drug addiction and thus places the matter in the hands of a higher power. As discussed earlier, psychological control is vital for the regulated functioning of a person. To release that control to a higher power in a way takes away a component that provides psychological balance to a person's brain functioning. Individuals may reach a point where they believe that there is no hope because they are not in control. However, spirituality does provide a positive and advantageous component for many participants.

CBT

The cognitive–behavioral approach to substance abuse treatment is derived from the social learning theory that substance abuse is a learned maladaptive behavior. Substance abuse is theorized to be initiated and maintained by distorted beliefs about the power of the abused substance and the reinforced use of the substance to cope with stressful situations (Ouimette et al., 1997). Addiction is viewed not as a life-long irreversible disease but as a behavior that can be modified by interventions based on principles of learning, conditioning, and self-control. The most widely used CBT approach is known as the *relapse prevention* (RP) approach (Washton & Zweben, 2009).

RP was originally designed by Marlatt and colleagues at the Addictive Behaviors Research Center at the University of Washington in Seattle (Marlatt & Gordon, 1985). Strategies involve a set of interventions aimed at helping clients identify potential relapse triggers and ways to anticipate, avoid, and safely manage these relapse risk factors without returning to substance use (Washton & Zweben, 2009). It is based on social-cognitive psychology and incorporates both a conceptual model of relapse and a set of cognitive and behavioral strategies to prevent relapsing (Larimer, Palmer, & Marlatt, 1999). This method involves instructing clients in adaptive coping and problem-solving skills for managing cravings and other relapse-inducing situations.

Quitting using meth is not the only difficult task in recovery. Maintaining abstinence and avoiding relapse is a life-long struggle. Talking about using and possible outlets for using again is controversial in nature given speculation that a person may be tempted to use again from conversing about it. However, if a person does not understand when and where triggers for relapse may occur, he or she will not be well equipped to prevent them. A *relapse* is a breakdown or setback in a person's attempt to overcome or change a problem behavior (Marlatt & Gordon, 1985). Most individuals relapse in the first 6 months after treatment (Washton & Zweben, 2009), yet relapses can occur throughout the lifetime. RP strategies are designed to help individuals who are attempting to change an addictive behavior learn how to anticipate, avoid, and cope with the problem of relapse (Washton & Zweben, 2009).

Goals of the CBT model include the following:

- Clients learn how to anticipate and prevent the occurrence of a relapse after initial abstinence has been established.
- Clients learn how to respond safely to a slip or lapse before it escalates into a full-blown relapse.
- Clients learn about the relapse process and acquire problem-solving and affect management skills.

RP strategies are based on the premise that the factors that help to initiate abstinence from addictive behaviors are different from those needed to maintain abstinence (Washton & Zweben, 2009). A central approach of the method is the detailed classification of events or stimuli that can contribute to a relapse episode (Larimer et al., 1999). RP strategies are classified as maintenance, rather than action, interventions.

Treatment attempts are directed, beginning with an assessment of the environmental and emotional characteristics of situations that are proponents to relapses. Factors fall into two categories: immediate determinants (high-risk situations, coping skills, outcome expectancies, and the abstinence violation effect) and covert antecedents (lifestyle imbalances and cravings/urges). After identifying those areas, a therapist will work with the individual and assess his or her responses to these situations as well as examine the person's lifestyle to discover areas that have contributed to exposure to high-risk situations. The therapist then devises strategies to target weakness in the client's cognitive and behavioral repertoire and thereby reduce the risk of relapse (Larimer et al., 1999).

RP therapy begins by assisting the client to identify his or her own high-risk situations. Keeping a log or journal of emotional states, social interactions, cravings, and relapse is very useful in this process. Using inventories that assess client reactions in difficult situations can be helpful as well. Assessing high-risk situations is important so that clients can begin to create habitual coping strategies for difficult situations. After discussing different strategies, specific coping strategies must be considered, planned, and implemented. The strategies should be rehearsed as role-playing activities in order to prepare clients to the fullest extent for certain situations they may encounter (Capuzzi & Stauffer, 2012).

Helpful steps to follow can include the following (Capuzzi & Stauffer, 2012):

1. Be aware of intrapersonal triggers that lead one to use.
2. Use mnemonic devices to recall counterapproaches in a plan of action.

3. Obtain a system of measures that will activate the person's memory to prompt the recall of an action plan (i.e., a way in which the client can actively become aware that a situation is occurring and be able to recall the plans of action to counter a relapse trigger).
4. Develop backup plans.
5. Use multiple methods of stress relief that are nonaddictive and healthy.

A comprehensive approach includes a model that is designed to initiate and maintain changes in addictive behavior and focuses on building confidence in one's ability and promoting self-efficacy. These steps were offered by Annis and Davis (1991):

1. Develop a hierarchy of meth-risk situations.
2. Identify strengths and resources in the environment and cope with affective, behavioral, and cognitive issues.
3. Design homework in which the client is able to monitor his or her thoughts and feelings in specific situations, anticipate problematic situations, rehearse alternative responses to using, practice new behaviors within difficult situations, and reflect on personal growth and elevated levels of competence.

Possible difficulties will be found in thinking errors and psychological traps. Even seemingly irrelevant decisions can lead to a relapse (Capuzzi & Stauffer, 2012). A person may not think a situation could be a potential trigger but could inadvertently allow him or herself to be placed in an environment that is not conducive to preventing relapses. For example, choosing which direction to walk home could mean walking by an alley where meth is sold or walking where a path is clear. Simply walking by a dealer may trigger a person to buy when he or she had no preconceived notion of doing so and was merely walking home. It is important to make the client aware of all possible scenarios, even if they appear to be remote.

Another trap is the relapse violation effect. The idea is that once a rule is set, humans have a natural temptation to break it. The most common form of this is that minor infringements of a rule will justify major infringements. For example, a person has a relapse episode in which he partakes in some usage of meth. Feeling guilty, he decides that he has already broken the rule and there is no going back; therefore, he begins to use heavily again (Capuzzi & Stauffer, 2012). What is important to keep it mind in redirecting the client back to the path of abstinence and prevention is that not all lapses are preventable and some things inevitably may happen. Some therapists may note that essential to portions of addiction treatment is the idea that a client accept that he or she is powerless to the drug and therefore relapse may occur. However, making a client aware that he or she is able to manage and direct the RP may provide a psychological balance and reinforce that although a relapse has occurred, the client is able to control the path back to abstinence.

McKay (2009) contended that the effectiveness of CBT/RP-based approaches supports reducing the frequency of relapse episodes as well as the intensity of lapse. This effectiveness was particularly great in studies that compared relapse rates in patients before and after treatment or that compared relapse rates in patients receiving RP-based treatment and controls receiving no treatment. Yet

Carroll (1996) noted that despite its benefits, RP-based treatment is not associated with higher abstinence rates compared with other valid treatments. It is associated with lower usage rates among users who have experienced a relapse. RP is associated with significantly delayed emergence effects compared to other treatment approaches but only at later follow-up points (Carroll, 1996). This may be because it takes time to learn new skills associated with RP. Important to keep in mind is that RP is a method for persons who have already navigated through a rehabilitation program and is designed as a maintenance program. If a client has not fully navigated through rehab, then certainly maintenance will be much more difficult to process through. Yet CBT is congruous because it processes the individual's behavior in an attempt to change the thinking patterns that are harmful (Stevens & Smith, 2013).

MI

Motivation plays an important role in the decision to change one's behavior (Tucker, Donovan, & Marlatt, 1999), and addictive behaviors can be described as motivational problems. Change has been classified as a process that involves steps in which people recognize a problem and build the motivation to try and cure themselves (Klingemann, 1991). Poor motivation has been equated to the use of a defense mechanism, such as resistance and denial, which are universal traits among substance abusers (Tucker et al., 1999).

MI was developed by William Miller in Norway. His model focused on providing change through motivation. It honed in on responding differently to client speech with a generally empathic person-centered style. Specific attention centered round inciting and reinforcing a client's own pronounced motivation for change. In the MI framework a person who is considered to be an addict is viewed as having a diminished capacity for self-control. However, this capacity is believed to be revitalized. Volitional abstinence can interrupt a disease model basis for the destructive behavior (van Wormer & Davis, 2008).

The change-promoting value of hearing one's voice for change is linked to Festinger's (1957) development of cognitive dissonance and Bem's (1967) ideal of self-perception theory. Also similar is Rogers's (1959) theory of necessary and substantial interpersonal conditions for fostering change. The supportive atmosphere, as detailed by Rogers, is perceived as an ideal, nonthreatening facet in which clients explore their ambivalence and elicit their own desires for change. In the early 1980s Miller began trials and developed in depth the approach of MI and throughout the following decades ran trials and strengthened his treatment.

Goals of MI include the following:

- Engage in collaborative conversation to strengthen a person's own motivation for commitment to change.
- Do not attempt to persuade clients to admit that they have a problem; rather, provide a mirror for clients to look back on themselves, see the costs, and find within themselves the means to change.
- Address the common problem of ambivalence about change.
- Strengthen an individual's motivation for and movement toward a specific goal by eliciting and exploring the person's arguments for change.

Motivation is the reason individuals choose to change their addictive behavior and the strength of their desire to do so (Curry, Wagner, & Grothaus, 1990). MI is a "client-centered directive method for enhancing intrinsic motivation to change by exploring and resolving ambivalence" (W. R. Miller & Rollnick, 2002, p. 25). Clients entering counseling will have conflicting motivations to change their current behaviors and also to stay the same as they are. They may be aware of the benefits and costs but are at a crossroads in terms of the decisions they want to make for their future. Attempting to persuade clients will not be effective because it involves the clients taking a position that they are already feeling. The result of clients simply doing what they are told can be that they actually adopt the opposite behavior and decrease their likelihood for change. Motivation to change the addictive behavior comes from a combination of biological, emotional, social, and conditioning influences. It goes beyond just saying no. Pushing against resistance is seen as counterproductive; rather, the guiding principle is that clients have the voice for the argument of change.

The locus of motivation has been suggested as the variable that addresses the attributed source of motivation and the reason why an individual is seeking to change behavior patterns. MI assumes that the state of motivation may change from one time or situation to another (W. R. Miller & Rollnick, 2002). The locus can be anything for a person: a spouse, family, job, religion, or so on. States can be influenced, and therefore counselors can provide safe environments for clients and promote readiness to make positive change (Curry et al., 1990). The following model shows an example of self-determination influences (Simoneau & Bergeron, 2003).

MI uses specific strategies to enhance motivation. A key component is that the counselor does not directly persuade the client to change. The aim is to guide the client toward a resolution of ambivalence and incongruities in his or her behaviors to build motivation for change (Markland, Ryan, Tobin, & Rollnick, 2005). Great attention is paid to eliciting the person's current level of motivation instead of assuming that the person is ready to jump into action. There are five specific techniques to follow when using MI:

1. *Express empathy.* The client is seen as stuck, not pathological, and the style is respectful and accepting.
2. *Develop discrepancy.* Create and amplify the discrepancy between present behavior and important goals.
3. *Avoid argumentation.* Do not try to persuade, confront, or argue with a client who is in deep trouble and would be better off giving up his or her addictions. Breaking through denial is not the goal; rather, the goal is to explore what the terms, definitions, and conditions mean to the person.
4. *Roll with resistance.* Compliance is not the goal. It is a matter of the client's awareness of where he or she is at in the process of change and what he or she chooses to do.
5. *Support self-efficacy.* Support confidence that a person can change by removing the false idea that the counselor will change the client, showing the successes of others, and inviting the client to choose alternative approaches from what he or she has already tried.

For a more in-depth explanation, visit http://www.motivationalinterviewing.org.

Group therapy with MI has been adapted by Ingersoll and Wagner (1997) for single-session, four-session, and eight-session formats, although it has not been empirically validated. The eight-session format begins with discussing the purpose of the group. The counselor explores the members' ambivalence about substance use; assists in developing hope, changes, and discrepancies; explores change success stories; and develops a concrete plan for change. An evaluation of a single-session drinking intervention given to 167 college students found that after 3 months of monitored drinking, a significant reduction in drinking had occurred, and there were fewer alcohol-related consequences and a lower level of judicial recidivism and referrals to the university disciplinary program (LaBrie, Lamb, Pedersen, & Quinlan, 2006). The heaviest drinkers achieved the biggest reductions.

MI counselors pay close attention to three key elements: collaborating with the client, evoking the client's ideas about change, and emphasizing the autonomy of the client. Collaboration is a partnership between the client and therapist that is based on the point of view and experiences of the client. This builds rapport and facilitates trust in the helping relationship. Evocation involves the counselor drawing out the client's own thoughts and ideas rather than imposing his or her opinions on the client. The counselor recognizes that the true power to change rests in the client and his or her autonomy to make change happen. This gives the client responsibility for his or her actions (W. R. Miller & Rollnick, 2002).

Counselors should follow the principle of OARS: open-ended questions, affirmations, reflections, and summaries. Open-ended questions are those not answered with a short yes or no. Scaling questions can also be used to ascertain the client's level with regard to motivation for change. Affirmations are statements that recognize client strengths and build rapport to help the client see himself or herself in a positive light. Reflections are careful listening and reflective responses that truly show the empathy and sense of being engaged that the counselor feels with the client. They let the client know that the counselor is really there being actively engaged with him or her. Summaries are a type of reflection in which the counselor communicates interest and understanding of the important elements (W. R. Miller & Rollnick, 2002).

In MI the counselor seeks to guide the client toward expressions of change talk as a pathway to change. Change talk involves statements by the client that reveal consideration of or motivation for change. The more people talk about change, the more likely they are to change. The mnemonic DARN-CAT is an example of different types of change talk (W. R. Miller & Rollnick, 2002):

Preparatory Change Talk:
  Desire (I want to change)
  Ability (I can change)
  Reason (It's important to change)
  Need (I should change)

Implementing Change Talk:
  Commitment (I will make changes)
  Activation (I am ready to change)
  Taking steps (I am taking specific actions to change)

Counselors should ask open-ended questions and explore the pros and cons of decisions to change and decisions to stay the same. Looking backward and looking forward are both essential for discussing outcomes of changes.

Evaluations of MI have predominantly shown that implementation of the method is effective in reducing substance use (Project MATCH Research Group, 1997; Saunders, Wilkinson, & Phillips, 1995). A meta-analysis conducted of controlled clinical trials investigating adaptations of MI concluded that treatments yielded moderate effects and a 56% reduction in client usage (Burke, Arkowitz, & Menchola, 2003). Another meta-analysis of 32 controlled studies found that persons who received a brief intervention reduced their usage and were abstinent at a rate comparable to that among people who received extensive treatment (Bien, Miller, & Tonigan, 1993).

Project MATCH compared the efficacy of MI with CBT and 12-step facilitation. Results indicated that overall improvements in outcomes were achieved. In aftercare, 35% of the subjects reported continued abstinence throughout 12 months; 65% relapsed during the period. Among outpatient subjects, 19% maintained complete abstinence throughout the follow-up period, 46% had a heavy using problem, and the rest slipped out (W. R. Miller, Zweben, DiClemente, & Rychtarik, 1995). MI has an impact because its main goal is to motivate the person toward change.

Harm Reduction

Harm reduction was used as early as the 1920s, predominantly with opiate users and methadone maintenance, and in the early 1980s was used as an initial response to HIV and hepatitis epidemics (Des Jarlais, McKnight, Goldblatt, & Purchase, 2009). Harm reduction comprises education about the drug of choice along with therapy to encourage a decision in favor of abstaining or reducing harm. Harm reduction offers a different aspect of individual therapy for the person who abuses substances but is not ready to separate from the drug of choice in that the goal is to reduce risky behaviors (Stevens & Smith, 2013).

Treatment involves a nonjudgmental approach to helping substance users reduce the negative impact of drugs and alcohol in their lives (Denning, 2010). The central belief is that each person's relationship with drugs is different and develops from a unique interaction of biological, psychological, and social factors (Denning, 2010). The extent of a person's use is not the main focus; rather, it is looking at the harms consequent to use. Harm reduction is not an excuse for users to continue to use; rather, it hones in on any given reason drugs might be causing harm to the user. Most programs attend first to the most important need of an individual as a step in the direction of less risky use or, if appropriate, abstinence (van Wormer & Davis, 2012).

The goal of harm reduction strategies is to reduce the negative consequences of drug abuse, not to eliminate the use of drugs (Hilton, Thompson, Moore-Dempsey, & Janzen, 2000). Goals for harm reduction therapy include the following:

- Become familiar with the potential harms associated with drug use.
- Assess harms and risks associated with the client's drug use by becoming aware of their patterns.
- Identify what is contributing to the harms a client is experiencing in order to create motivational techniques.
- Create goals that reduce harm.

Harm reduction therapy is based on the philosophy of the five Cs, explained in the following model (harmreductiontherapy.org):

Collaboration: The client and counselor work as partners in treatment.
Continuum: Drug and alcohol use occurs on a continuum. It ranges from safe and recreational to chaotic and can vary throughout life.
Complexity: Each person's relationship with drugs and alcohol is influenced by his or her own unique biological, psychological, social, and cultural factors.
Change: Behavior change is gradual, especially for people who are using substances to cope with difficult feelings or life situations.
Compassion: Confrontation, although it dominates treatment, rarely helps people make lasting changes and often reduces trust and creates resistance.

One of the most controversial aspects of harm reduction therapy is that the low threshold for access to services does not require abstinence as a precondition for treatment. Harm reduction seeks to reduce barriers that make it less likely that people who are using or are addicted will get help. Reducing barriers is critical because estimates show that only one in six adults who inject drugs is in treatment and less than 10% of abusers receive professional treatment (Narrow, Regier, Rae, Manderscheid, & Locke, 1993). Harm reduction services are offered with the fewest possible restrictions, requirements, or goal expectations in order to appeal to the widest groups.

The harm reduction model favors the individual making positive changes in his or her life. That individual can make positive changes with the assistance of the counselor and a variety of techniques.

Harm reduction strategies meet drug users where they are by addressing conditions of use along with the use itself (Stevens & Smith, 2013). Strategies may include changing the way people consume drugs or ensuring that the environment in which they use minimizes the risks of negative consequences (Addy & Ritter, 2000).

Community-based street outreach is a popular approach for recruiting members of the targeted and desired group. Some programs use active drug users as outreach workers because they have knowledge of the governing social systems on the streets and are able to develop trusting relationships with active users (Booth, Kwiatkowski, Iguchi, Pinto, & John, 1998). Outreach usually involves providing drug education materials that tell the user how to reduce risks associated with using drugs (van Wormer & Davis, 2012). Increasing accessibility to reduction aids can be accomplished in many ways, from providing free information to passing out clean syringes to injecting users.

The first step in harm reduction is to provide accurate education about the consequences and risks of drug use. The counselor should promote behaviors that reduce risk. Education can be delivered in a variety of ways that include the physical and psychosocial risks of drug abuse. Brief interventions can be delivered in community settings and can include single-session therapy that combines other methods such as CBT and MI.

It is also essential that the counselor identify the different harms as related to the client. Drug acquisition harms are related to the risks of being exposed to high-risk situations, such as deviant behavior. Drug use harms are related to the drug used, the amount consumed, and the method of administration (injection, smoking, snorting). Drug withdrawal harms are related to effects of reducing or eliminating drug use that may impair the individual's work or social functioning. Specific focus has been given to drug users who inject given the high rate of users affected by dirty needles and HIV. In a New Jersey study in which free methadone treatment was offered for the intravenous drug user community, 59% redeemed the free treatment, and of that population 58% reported being HIV positive (Booth, Corsi, & Mikulich, 2003). Individual harm minimization strategies need to be based on the client's individual situation. The counselor should monitor the client's behavior throughout treatment and reinforce positive changes while addressing difficulties.

The following model lists effective principles for working with intravenous drug users to prevent HIV (Costigan, Crofts, & Reid, 2003):

1. Have a nonjudgmental attitude.
2. Emphasize the drug user's ability to care for himself or herself.
3. Use short-term pragmatic goals and a scale of behaviors to achieve the goals.
4. Provide information about the transmission of HIV, its prevention, and its connection with risk behaviors.
5. Focus on concrete risk behaviors and connect those with the individual's reality (his or her own risk behaviors).
6. Provide different options to reduce the risk of infection.
7. Provide a supportive environment (professionals, family, peers, etc.).
8. Have a team of experienced professionals involved in designing and implementing harm reduction programs and strategies.

In a methadone maintenance program with 12 sessions and 220 patients, patients were more likely to be abstinent from using during treatment and reported fewer unsafe sex practices during treatment. After treatment, patients reported having higher levels of self-efficacy (Avants, Margolin, Usubiaga, & Doebrick, 2004). Ritter and Cameron (2006) reviewed more than 650 articles related to harm reduction therapy and concluded that there is sufficient evidence to support the widespread adoption of harm reduction interventions in relation to illicit drugs. Logan and Marlatt (2010) reviewed dozens of studies and concluded that there is substantial support for the effectiveness of harm reduction. Important to keep in mind is that resistance skills training in drug prevention, similar to harm reduction therapy, has been seen in programs like DARE (Drug Abuse Resistance Education). Studies show that DARE produced no effects, and in some cases students who received the education were more likely to become illicit drug users than those who did not receive the education (Lilienfeld, 2007). Other similar programs, such as the School Health and Alcohol Harm Reduction Project, have also reported no significant changes in long-term prevalence of drug use or abstinence, but short-term reductions in use can be seen (McBride, Farringdon, Midford, Meuleners, & Phillips, 2004; Poulin & Nicholson, 2005).

The Matrix Model

The outpatient Matrix Model derived from collaboration between the Matrix Institute on Addictions group and the National Institute on Drug Abuse during the 1980s. The term *matrix* developed from the use of components of different evidence-based models such as CBT, MI, the 12-step model, and so on. The model is intended to integrate the different interventions into one comprehensive approach.

The Matrix Model is a 16-week nonresidential psychosocial approach (Rawson et al., 1995). It is delivered in individual and group settings. Patients learn about the problems that are pertinent to addiction and relapse. Treatment manuals typically contain worksheets for individual sessions. Subsequent parts involve family education groups, social support groups, combined sessions, early recovery skills groups, RP and analysis, and urine tests (Rawson et al., 1995).

The foundation of the Matrix Model is based on the following cognitive–behavioral principles and goals (Rawson et al., 2002):

- Stop drug use.
- Learn issues critical to addiction and relapse.
- Receive education for family members affected by addiction and recovery.
- Become familiar with self-help programs.
- Receive weekly monitoring in the form of urine toxicology and breathalyzer alcohol testing.

The content is tailored to individual needs but incorporates structured elements. The Matrix Model counselor serves as a teacher and a coach. Counselors foster a positive behavior change that boosts self-esteem and is not confrontational. Sessions are about 45 minutes long and are used to set goals and verify that goals are being attained (Yudko & Gagnet, 2003). Early recovery groups take place in the beginning, with RP groups at the start and end of each week. The goal of the open sessions is to teach participants about maintaining sobriety.

A 1994 study by Shoptaw, Rawson, McCann, and Obert of 146 patients 6 months after they had received treatment showed that those who stayed in a long-term treatment program had positive abstinence outcomes. The Center for Substance Abuse Treatment, coordinated by the University of California, Los Angeles, funded a large-scale evaluation of the Matrix Model in 1999 in which around 1,000 meth-dependent individuals were admitted to treatment, with about half of them receiving the Matrix Model treatment. The researchers found that the individuals receiving the Matrix Model treatment obtained more treatment services, were retained in treatment much longer, and completed treatment at a higher rate than those not in the treatment (Rawson et al., 2002). However, Rawson et al. (1995) found that participants in Matrix Model treatment fared no better than those who received random treatment programs. They concluded that this was because of the highly variable treatment experiences that patients had.

Quitting Strategies

Washton and Zweben (2009) examined a large portion of clinical and educational materials as well as pulled from theoretical frameworks to devise specific strategies for quitting. This challenging excursion requires adequate amounts of support, motivation, and oversight in the beginning. To fully achieve abstinence, one must replace the rituals of drug using with healthy ones. For more in-depth explanations, refer to Washton and Zweben's text.

Time management is a necessary part of treatment for people in recovery. When individuals abuse meth, their days and nights become muddled from staying awake and sleeping for days at a time. Structured time starts with keeping track of days simply at the times of sleeping and waking up each day. Stabilizing and structuring sleep is very important because the stability of activities will transcend into other daily activities. These activities must be carefully planned so as to avoid potential triggers for relapse (Taylor & Covey, 2008).

Community-Based Treatment

Although the bulk of this has chapter focused on individual treatment for meth addiction, families and the community play a significant role in the individual treatment of an addict. The need for support seems obvious, and many family members may say, of the individual they are close to, "I have supported them. I have paid their bills, bought them food, bailed them out, etc., etc." To the family and/or community member this may seem like support, but in actuality it is more of a perpetuation of the user's continued drug use. Deception, manipulation, isolation, and taking advantage of ones close to the addict are common themes among persons who would claim to have supported the addict. Although intentions are certainly genuine, support needs to come in a different form. Addicts begin to rely on using people as they do drugs. When those supporters take an all-or-nothing stance—"Get clean or we are gone!"—change can finally begin.

As discussed at the beginning of the chapter, many meth users come from difficult backgrounds. Relationships with family, friends, and close ones were probably not the best all the time. Positive feelings were most likely absent, and a feeling of closeness with someone caring may have been nonexistent as well. The drugs fill that void by causing the user to feel good. Misery loves company in the same sense that users who are down and out will easily find similar users. A strong, stable, healthy, and sober support system is not always available to a user, especially given that many addicts have experienced broken ties, isolation, and an inability to form relationships. This inability becomes even more severe as cognitive functioning becomes damaged, as discussed earlier in the chapter. An addict can certainly reach the point where he or she says that there is no hope. Family members and community members reach that point as well. This feeling is not helped by the sense that addicts are viewed as criminals. This comes from a lack of understanding of the depth and complexity of what makes up an addict. It is important to keep in mind that many addicts are aware that treatment exists, but many of them may not know where to find it. One can postulate, though, that if the beginnings of addiction stem from a lack of quality relationships and self-esteem, the beginnings of treatment can be found in those same constructs. A therapist alone can do many wonderful things for an addict that can bring about change, and with the support of the community and any family-type relationship, that wonderful change can explode tenfold.

This chapter does not specify specific family-based treatments, but it is nonetheless important to consider the dynamics of the addict's family and to ask how the family would feel with the addict back in the home. Are the family members willing to work with the addict and community/therapist partnerships? The first step is for the addict to be placed among a sober community, which can be composed of family, friends, professionals, neighbors, and any network of caring individuals. One must always be cognizant, though, that just as sober communities are hesitant, addicts are hesitant as well. Many are accustomed to being around untrusting, manipulative, lying, stealing, insincere users. An addict may not be completely open and receptive to genuine people, let alone able to accept that he or she needs to find happiness and positive interaction while sober with these people. It is essential that addicts are around a stable sober community, otherwise relapse is almost inevitable. Addicts most certainly are aware that what they do is illegal and are creative in trying not to get caught. They develop a lack of responsibility for their emotions and mental functioning and replace it with a deviant mentality that what they are doing is wrong in the same sense that theft is. Community partners are not exempt from thinking in the same light and believing that change will not come. However, with a positive, consistent connection from the community and the individual, success can be found.

Effective treatment serves, creates, and helps addicts produce real and long-lasting changes in their behaviors and lives. Addicts affect the community and society they live in. If addicts continue to go along untreated, the community as a whole will suffer. One can also hypothesize that more addicts will be produced as well. Perpetuated cycles produce further generations of hopelessness and desolation. For these reasons, it is imperative that the community be involved with treatment (Taylor & Covey, 2008). The community is in charge of providing a theoretically based and evidence-based program that will help the addict maintain a lifestyle and behavior that support continued abstinence (Taylor & Covey, 2008).

There are several notable problems with community action–based programs. The first has to do with the availability of funding for nonprofits, for struggling families, and for the individual. Earlier in the chapter I noted that the government provides millions of dollars for treatment, but for pregnant and parenting women. However, numbers show that most addicts are men. Treatment facilities charge tens of thousands of dollars a month—the average addict cannot realistically afford these facilities. Although some entities do offer low-cost and even free treatment, the efficacy of these programs is seriously questioned. Which is better: no care or inadequate and even dangerous care? The efficacy of community programs is also a problem. Although evidence-based models do exist, there is a lack of research on these models. Taylor and Covey (2008) noted that programs tend to use a partial implementation of a program, and there is no evidence-based support for using a partial program. If partial programs are to be used, then specific research needs to be done on their efficacy, and from there programs can be developed based on that partial structure.

Community-based models should follow treatment strategies that address and provide treatment based on biological, psychological, and social goals. Biological goals include establishing regular eating and sleeping patterns. Psychological goals include changing expectations about meth and sobriety, learning to feel natural pleasure, and learning to cope without meth. Social goals include stopping hanging out with addicts and developing a sober social support group (Taylor & Covey, 2008). Specific exercises target changes in these domains in order to provide treatment for them. However, simply enhancing skills is not enough. Specific in-depth digging into a person's hierarchy of needs will help discover where the need for meth developed and became vital to the addict.

Three principles are essential to a community model: case management, outpatient success, and substance abuse treatment. Case management is about helping individuals who are trying to stop using meth be able to meet their needs and understand their hierarchy of needs. Case management is the base of quality meth care because people in treatment have to be motivated and provided with the training, resources, and opportunities to be able to take care of themselves (Taylor & Covey, 2008). Communities have to reach a level of comfortableness in which they can team up to provide resources, ideas, and strategies for adequate treatment.

As discussed previously, numerous inpatient treatments are available to addicts, and many can bring much success. However, level of treatment, quality of care, and efficacy between inpatient and outpatient treatment facilities can become confusing to communities and families affected by addictions. People can be told about all of the tools available and how to use them, but if they are thrown into a construction zone without leadership or guidance, they are lost. This means that communities and families have a responsibility to help the addict recover in the same way that the treating therapist does.

Controlled environments are available, such as sober living homes, residential treatment facilities, and sober companionship. The use of these entities should be short term in nature in order that addicts reach a point at which they can function on their own and be responsible for their own needs. Individuals also need to see that inpatient treatment is really the support for continued outpatient treatment, which does not end (whereas residential treatment does).

Outpatient treatment is difficult. As discussed previously, one may contemplate all the possible triggers for relapse, but essentially anything may be a trigger. Daily life throws curveballs at people, and it requires constant awareness and learning by the addict to be able to deal with day-to-day life. This is why it is crucial to have reinforcement from communities, therapists, and sober persons. It is a take-it-as-you-go kind of structure, but the greatest success is that the person not only learns to maintain sobriety but little by little be able to integrate back into society as a functioning person (Taylor & Covey, 2008). For a complete breakdown of how to begin community involvement and family treatments, refer to Taylor and Covey (2008).

CONCLUSIONS

This chapter was designed to serve as an introduction to the drug methamphetamine, how individuals become addicted, and how they can be treated. I highly encourage readers to look into supplemental texts and resources for an even more in-depth look at these topics. The literature is never stagnant, and as years go by more resources are added on drug treatment and addiction.

Addiction is overwhelming. Meth addiction is no less devastating. As seen with the different treatment models discussed, the likelihood of relapse can be very high and long-term abstinence can be very low. Resources and funding, although they have come a long way, still do not reach all demographics of users. It would also be naïve not to consider the implications of drug production and a cycle of users that come with each generation. You can take the addict off the streets and clean him up, but what about the individuals who are at risk for becoming addicts? When does early prevention need to begin? If most production happens outside of U.S. borders, how can the population of addicts be decreased if production is still up and running? The "what if" game can be played continuously. As counselors and educators, we must decide where we want to stand in the formula for success and treatment. We can be a community partner, a counselor, an educator, a network, and more. Tools and tips are in great abundance, but without proper implementation, they can be useless.

RESOURCES

The Meth Project
    http://foundation.methproject.org/
Montana Meth Project
    www.montanameth.org/
National Center on Substance Abuse and Child Welfare
    www.ncsacw.samhsa.gov/
National Institute on Drug Abuse, DrugFacts: Methamphetamine
    www.drugabuse.gov/publications/drugfacts/methamphetamine
Rural Assistance Center, Meth Information Resources
    www.raconline.org/rural-monitor/meth-information-resources/

REFERENCES

Addy, D., & Ritter, A. (2000). *Clinical treatment guidelines for alcohol and drug clinicians: No 2. Motivational interviewing*. Fitzroy, Victoria, Australia: Turning Point Alcohol and Drug Centre.

Alford, G. S., Koehler, R. A., & Leonard, J. (1991). Alcoholics Anonymous–Narcotics Anonymous model inpatient treatment of chemically dependent adolescents: A 2-year outcome study. *Journal of Studies on Alcohol and Drugs, 52*(2), 118–126.

American Psychiatric Association. (2013). *Diagnostic and statistical manual of mental disorders* (5th ed.). Arlington, VA: Author.

Annis, H. M., & Davis, C. S. (1991). Relapse prevention. *Alcohol Health & Research World, 15*, 204–212.

Avants, S. K., Margolin, A., Usubiaga, M. H., & Doebrick, C. (2004). Targeting HIV-related outcomes with intravenous drug users maintained on methadone: A randomized clinical trial of a harm reduction group therapy. *Journal of Substance Abuse Treatment, 26*(2), 67–78.

Bahr, S. J., Hoffmann, J. P., & Yang, X. (2005). Parental and peer influences on the risk of adolescent drug use. *Journal of Primary Prevention, 26*, 529–551.

Bem, D. J. (1967). Self-perception: An alternative interpretation of cognitive dissonance phenomena. *Psychological Review, 74*(3), 183–200.

Bien, T. H., Miller, W. R., & Tonigan, J. S. (1993). Brief interventions for alcohol problems: A review. *Addiction, 88*(3), 315–336.

Booth, R. E., Corsi, K. F., & Mikulich, S. K. (2003). Improving entry to methadone maintenance among out-of-treatment injection drug users. *Journal of Substance Abuse Treatment, 24*, 305–311.

Booth, R. E., Kwiatkowski, C., Iguchi, M. Y., Pinto, F., & John, D. (1998). Facilitating treatment entry among out-of-treatment injection drug users. *Public Health Reports, 113*, 116–128.

Brecht, M. L., O'Brien, A., von Mayrhauser, C., & Anglin, M. D. (2004). Methamphetamine use behaviors and gender differences. *Addictive Behaviors, 29*, 89–106.

Brown, H. P., Peterson, J. H., & Cunningham, O. (1988). Rationale and theoretical basis of a behavioral/cognitive approach to spirituality. *Alcoholism Treatment Quarterly, 5*, 47–59.

Burke, B. L., Arkowitz, H., & Menchola, M. (2003). The efficacy of motivational interviewing: A meta-analysis of controlled clinical trials. *Journal of Consulting and Clinical Psychology, 71*, 843–861.

Capuzzi, D., & Stauffer, M. D. (2012). *Foundations of addiction counseling* (2nd ed.). Boston, MA: Pearson Education.

Carroll, K. M. (1996). Relapse prevention as a psychosocial treatment: A review of controlled clinical trials. *Experimental and Clinical Psychopharmacology, 4*(1), 46–54.

Charlie's Place. (2012). *Treatment programs.* Retrieved from http://charliesplaceonline.com/services/treatment/

Choi, K., Operario, D., Gregorich, S. E., McFarland, W., MacKeller, D., & Valleroy, L. (2005). Substance use, substance choice, and unprotected anal intercourse among young Asian American and Pacific Islander men who have sex with men. *AIDS Education and Prevention, 17,* 418–429.

Clemens, K., Van Nieuwenhuyzen, P., Li, K., Cornish, J., Hunt, G., & McGregor, I. (2006). MDMA ("ecstasy"), methamphetamine and their combination: Long-term changes in social interaction and neurochemistry in the rat. *Psychopharmacology, 173,* 318–325.

Combat Methamphetamine Epidemic Act of 2005, Title VII of Pub. L. No. 109-177.

Controlled Substance Analogue Enforcement Act of 1986, Pub. L. No. 99-570

Controlled Substances Act of 1970, 21 U.S.C. § 801 et seq.

Costigan, G., Crofts, N., & Reid, G. (2003). *The manual for reducing drug related harm in Asia.* Melbourne, Australia: Centre for Harm Reduction.

Crystal Meth Anonymous. (2007). *Twelve steps.* Retrieved from http://www.crystalmeth.org/home/twelve-steps.html

Curry, S., Wagner, E. H., & Grothaus, L. C. (1990). Intrinsic and extrinsic motivation for smoking cessation. *Journal of Consulting and Clinical Psychology, 58*(3), 310–316.

Denning, P. (2010). Harm reduction therapy with families and friends of people with drug problems. *Journal of Clinical Psychology: In Session, 66,* 164–174. doi:10.1002/jclp.20671

Des Jarlais, D. C., McKnight, C., Goldblatt, C., & Purchase, D. (2009). Doing harm reduction better: Syringe exchange in the United States. *Addiction, 104,* 1441–1446.

Emmelkamp, P. M., & Vedel, E. (2006). *Evidence-based treatment for alcohol and drug abuse: A practitioner's guide to theory, methods, and practice.* New York, NY: Routledge.

Festinger, L. (1957). *A theory of cognitive dissonance.* Evanston, IL: Row & Peterson.

Forman, R. F., Bovasso, G., & Woody, G. (2001). Staff beliefs about addiction treatment. *Journal of Substance Abuse Treatment, 21,* 1–9.

Frontline. (n.d.). *Frequently asked questions.* Retrieved from http://www.pbs.org/wgbh/pages/frontline/meth/faqs/

Gahlinger, P. M. (2001). *Illegal drugs: A complete guide to their history, chemistry, use and abuse.* Las Vegas, NV: Sagebrush Press.

Halkitis, P. N. (2007). Behavioral patterns, identity, and health characteristics of self-identified barebackers: Implications for HIV prevention and intervention. *Journal of LGBT Health Research, 3,* 37–48.

Halkitis, P. N. (2009). *Methamphetamine addiction: Biological foundations, psychological factors, and social consequences.* Washington, DC: American Psychological Association.

Halkitis, P. N., Homer, B. D., Moeller, R. W., & Solomon, T. M. (2007, March). *Methamphetamine and social cognition: Findings from project MASC.* Paper presented at the New York University Development Psychology Colloquium, New York, NY.

Halkitis, P. N., & Jerome, R. (2008). A comparative analysis of methamphetamine use: Black gay and bisexual men in relation to men of other races. *Addictive Behaviors, 33,* 83–93.

Halkitis, P. N., Moeller, R. W., Siconolfi, D. E., Jerome, R. C., Rogers, M., & Schillinger, J. (2008). Methamphetamine and poly-substance use among gym-attending men who have sex with men in New York City. *Annals of Behavioral Medicine, 35*(1), 41–48.

Halkitis, P. N., & Parsons, J. T. (2002). Recreational drug use and HIV-risk sexual behavior among men frequenting gay social venues. *Journal of Gay & Lesbian Social Services, 14,* 19–38.

Hawkins, J. D., Catalano, R. F., & Miller, J. Y. (1992). Risk and protective factors for alcohol and early adulthood: Implications for substance abuse prevention. *Psychological Bulletin, 112*, 64–105.

Hilton, B. A., Thompson, R., Moore-Dempsey, L., & Janzen, R. G. (2000). Harm reduction theories and strategies for control of human immunodeficiency virus: A review of the literature. *Journal of Advance Nursing, 33*(3), 357–370.

Ingersoll, K., & Wagner, C. (1997). *Motivational enhancement groups for the Virginia Substance Abuse Treatment Outcome Evaluation (SATOE) model: Theoretical background and clinical guidelines.* Richmond: Virginia Addiction Technology Transfer Center.

Kann, L., Kinchen, S., Shanklin, S. L., Flint, K. H., Hawkins, J., Harris, W. A., . . . Zaza, S. (2014, June). *Youth Risk Behavior Surveillance—United States, 2013.* Retrieved from the Centers for Disease Control and Prevention website: http://www.cdc.gov/mmwr/pdf/ss/ss6304.pdf

Klingemann, H. K. H. (1991). The motivation for change from problem alcohol and heroin use. *British Journal of Addiction, 86*, 727–744.

LaBrie, J. W., Lamb, T. F., Pedersen, E. R., & Quinlan, T. (2006). A group motivational interviewing intervention reduces drinking and alcohol-related consequences in adjudicated college students. *Journal of College Student Development, 47*(3), 267–280.

Larimer, M. E., Palmer, R. S., & Marlatt, G. A. (1999). Relapse prevention: An overview of Marlatt's cognitive–behavioral model. *Alcohol Research and Health, 23*(2), 151–160.

Latkin, C. A., Knowlton, A. R., Hoover, D., & Mandell, W. (1999). Drug network characteristics as a predictor of cessation of drug use among adult injection drug users: A prospective study. *American Journal of Drug and Alcohol Abuse, 25*, 463–473.

Laudet, A., & White, W. (2005). An exploratory investigation of the association between clinicians' attitudes towards twelve-step groups and referral rates. *Alcoholism Treatment Quarterly, 23*, 31–45.

Lilienfeld, S. O. (2007). Psychological treatments that cause harm. *Perspectives on Psychological Science, 2*(1), 53–70.

Logan, D. E., & Marlatt, G. A. (2010). Harm reduction therapy: A practice-friendly review of research. *Journal of Clinical Psychology, 66*(2), 201–214.

Luchansky, B., Krupski, A., & Stark, K. (2007). Treatment response by primary drug of abuse: Does methamphetamine make a difference? *Journal of Substance Abuse Treatment, 32*(1), 89–96.

Mansergh, G., Purcell, D. W., Stall, R., McFarlane, M., Semaan, S., Valentine, J., & Valdiserri, R. (2006). CDC consultation on methamphetamine use and sexual risk behavior for HIV/STD infection: Summary and suggestions. *Public Health Reports, 121*, 127–132.

Marcovitz, H. (2006). *Methamphetamine.* Farmington Hills, MI: Thomson Gale.

Markland, D., Ryan, R. M., Tobin, V. J., & Rollnick, S. (2005). Motivational interviewing and self-determination theory. *Journal of Social and Clinical Psychology, 24*, 811–831.

Marlatt, G. A., & Gordon, J. R. (1985). *Relapse prevention: Maintenance strategies in the treatment of addictive behaviors.* New York, NY: Guilford Press.

Marshall, D. R. (2000, July 6). *Congressional testimony to the Senate Judiciary Committee.*

Matsumoto, T., Miyakawa, T., Yabana, T., Iizuka, H., & Kishimoto, H. (2000). A clinical study of comorbid eating disorders in female methamphetamine abusers: The final report. *Clinical Psychiatry, 42*, 1153–1160.

Maude-Griffin, P. M., Hohenstein, J. M., Humfleet, G. L., Reilly, P. M., Tusel, D. J., & Hall, S. M. (1998). Superior efficacy of cognitive behavioral therapy for crack cocaine abusers: Main and matching effects. *Journal of Consulting and Clinical Psychology, 66*, 832–837.

McBride, N., Farringdon, F., Midford, R., Meuleners, L., & Phillips, M. (2004). Harm minimization in school drug education: Final results of the School Health and Alcohol Harm Reduction Project (SHAHRP). *Addiction, 99*(3), 278–291.

McKay, J. R. (2009). Continuing care research: What we've learned and where we're going. *Journal of Substance Abuse Treatment, 36,* 131–145.

Meller, W. H., Rinehart, R., Cadoret, R. J., & Troughton, E. (1988). Specific familial transmission in substance abuse. *International Journal of Addiction, 10,* 1029–1039.

Meredith, C. W., Jaffe, C., Ang-Lee, K., & Saxon, A. J. (2005). Implications of chronic methamphetamine use: A literature review. *Harvard Review of Psychiatry, 13,* 141–154.

Methamphetamine Education, Treatment, and Hope Act of 2010, H. R. 2818, 111th Cong.

Miller, G. (2005). *Learning the language of addiction counseling.* Englewood Cliffs, NJ: Wiley.

Miller, M. A. (1997). History and epidemiology of methamphetamine abuse in the US. In H. Klee (Ed.), *Amphetamine misuse* (pp. 113–133). Amsterdam, The Netherlands: Harwood Academic.

Miller, W. R., & Rollnick, S. (2002). *Motivational interviewing: Preparing people for change.* New York, NY: Guilford Press.

Miller, W. R., Zweben, A., DiClemente, C. C., & Rychtarik, R. G. (1995). *Motivational enhancement therapy manual* (Project MATCH Monograph, No. 2). Rockville, MD: U.S. Department of Health and Human Services.

Miller, W. R., Zweben, J. E., & Johnson, W. (2005). Evidence-based treatment: Why, what, where, when, and how? *Journal of Substance Abuse Treatment, 29,* 267–276.

Narrow, W. E., Regier, D. A., Rae, D. S., Manderscheid, R. W., & Locke, B. Z. (1993). Use of services by persons with mental and addictive disorders. *Archives of General Psychiatry, 50,* 95–107.

National Drug Intelligence Center. (2006, October). *National drug threat assessment 2007.* Retrieved from http://www.justice.gov/archive/ndic/pubs21/21137/index.htm

National Institute on Drug Abuse. (2006). *Methamphetamine abuse and addiction* (National Institutes of Health Publication No. 06-4210). Retrieved from http://www.nida.nih.gov/PDF/RRMetham.pdf

National Institute on Drug Abuse. (2014). *Methamphetamine.* Retrieved from http://www.drugabuse.gov/drugs-abuse/methamphetamine

Office of Applied Statistics. (2006). *The DASIS report: Methamphetamine/amphetamine treatment admissions in urban and rural areas: 2004.* Rockville, MD: Substance Abuse and Mental Health Services Administration.

Office of Applied Statistics. (2012). *The National Survey on Drug Use and Health report.* Rockville, MD: Substance Abuse and Mental Health Services Administration.

Office of Legislative Policy and Analysis. (n.d.). *Combat Meth Act of 2005.* Retrieved from http://olpa.od.nih.gov/legislation/109/pendinglegislation/combatmeth.asp

Ouimette, P. C., Finney, J. W., & Moos, R. H. (1997). Twelve-step and cognitive–behavioral treatment for substance abuse: A comparison of treatment effectiveness. *Journal of Consulting and Clinical Psychology, 65,* 230–240.

Parsons, J. T., Kelly, B. C., & Wells, B. E. (2006). Differences in club drug use between heterosexual and lesbian/bisexual females. *Addictive Behaviors, 31,* 2344–2349.

Poulin, C., & Nicholson, J. (2005). Should harm minimization as an approach to adolescent substance use be embraced by junior and senior high schools? Empirical evidence from an integrated school- and community-based demonstration intervention addressing drug use among adolescents. *International Journal of Drug Policy, 16,* 403–414.

Pringle, P. (2007, October 9). The trouble with rehab, Malibu-style: Lawsuits and violations reveal problems in a luxury cottage industry for the addicted. *Los Angeles Times.* Retrieved from http://articles.latimes.com/2007/oct/09/local/me-rehab9

Project MATCH Research Group. (1997). Matching alcoholism treatment to client heterogeneity: Project MATCH post-treatment drinking outcomes. *Journal of Studies on Alcohol, 58,* 7–29.

Rawson, R. A., Gonzales, R., Obert, J. L., McCann, M. J., & Brethen, P. (2005). Methamphetamine use among treatment-seeking adolescents in Southern California: Participant characteristics and treatment response. *Journal of Substance Abuse Treatment, 29,* 67–74.

Rawson, R. A., Huber, A., McCann, M., Shoptaw, S., Farabee, D., Reiber, C., & Ling, W. (2002). A comparison of contingency management and cognitive–behavioral approaches during methadone maintenance treatment for cocaine dependence. *Archives of General Psychiatry, 59,* 817–824.

Rawson, R. A., Shoptaw, S. J., Obert, J. L., McCann, M. J., Hasson, A. L., Marinelli-Casey, P. J., . . . Ling, W. (1995). An intensive outpatient approach for cocaine abuse treatment: The Matrix Model. *Journal of Substance Abuse Treatment, 122,* 117–127.

Ritter, A., & Cameron, J. (2006). A review of the efficacy and effectiveness of harm reduction strategies for alcohol, tobacco and illicit drugs. *Drug and Alcohol Review, 25,* 611–624.

Rogers, C. (1959). A theory of therapy, personality and interpersonal relationships as developed in the client-centered framework. In S. Koch (Ed.), *Psychology: A study of a science: Vol. 3. Formulations of the person and the social context* (pp. 184–256). New York, NY: McGraw-Hill.

Saunders, B., Wilkinson, C., & Phillips, M. (1995). The impact of a brief motivational intervention with opiate users attending a methadone programme. *Addiction, 90,* 415–424.

Schiorring, E. (1977). Changes in individual and social behavior induced by amphetamine and related compounds in monkeys and man. In E. H. Ellinwood Jr. & M. M. Kilbey (Eds.), *Cocaine and other stimulants* (pp. 481–522). New York, NY: Raven.

Senjo, S. R. (2007). The insidious allure of methamphetamine: Female patterns of purchasing, use, consequences of use and treatment. In G. H. Toolaney (Ed.), *New research on methamphetamine abuse* (pp. 53–68). New York, NY: Nova Science.

Shoptaw, S., Rawson, R. A., McCann, M. J., & Obert, J. L. (1994). The Matrix Model of outpatient stimulant abuse treatment: Evidence of efficacy. *Journal of Addiction Disorders, 13*(4), 129–141.

Simon, S., Domier, C., Carnell, J. C., Brethen, P., Rawson, R., & Ling, W. (2000). Cognitive impairment in individuals currently using methamphetamine. *American Journal on Addictions, 9,* 222–231.

Simoneau, H., & Bergeron, J. (2003). Factors affecting motivation during the first six weeks of treatment. *Addictive Behaviors, 28,* 1219–1241.

Sobell, L. C., Ellingstad, T. P., & Sobell, M. B. (2000). Natural recovery from alcohol and drug problems: Methodological review of the research with suggestions for future directions. *Addiction, 95,* 749–764.

Sommers, I., Baskin, D., & Baskin-Sommers, A. (2006). Methamphetamine use among young adults: Health and social consequences. *Addictive Behavior, 31,* 1469–1476.

Stevens, P., & Smith, R. (Eds.). (2013). *Substance abuse counseling: Theory and practice* (5th ed.). New York, NY: Pearson.

Substance Abuse and Mental Health Services Administration. (2013). *Results from the 2013 National Survey on Drug Use and Health: Summary of national findings* (NSDUH Series H-48, HHS Publication No. [SMA] 14-4863). Retrieved from http://www.samhsa.gov/data/sites/default/files/NSDUHresultsPDFWHTML2013/Web/NSDUHresults2013.pdf

Substance Abuse and Mental Health Services Administration, Center for Behavioral Health Statistics and Quality. (2014). *Emergency department visits involving methamphetamine: 2007 to 2011.* Retrieved from http://www.samhsa.gov/data/sites/default/files/DAWN_SR167_EDVisitsMeth_06-12-14/DAWN-SR167-EDVisitsMeth-2014.pdf

Suwaki, H., Fukui, S., & Konuma, K. (1997). The history of methamphetamine abuse in Japan. In H. Klee (Ed.), *Amphetamine misuse: International perspectives on current trends* (pp. 200–214). Amsterdam, The Netherlands: Harwood Academic.

Taylor, T. T., & Covey, H. C. (2008). *Helping people addicted to methamphetamine: A creative approach for families and communities.* Westport, CT: Praeger.

Tucker, J. A., Donovan, D. M., & Marlatt, G. A. (1999). *Changing addictive behavior.* New York, NY: Guilford Press.

USA PATRIOT Improvement and Reauthorization Act of 2005, H. R. 3199, 109th Cong.

van Wormer, K., & Davis, D. R. (2008). *Addiction treatment: A strengths perspective* (2nd ed.). Belmont, CA: Thomson.

van Wormer, K., & Davis, D. (2012). *Addiction treatment*. New York, NY: Cengage Learning.

Vik, P. W., & Ross, T. (2003). Methamphetamine use among incarcerated women. *Journal of Substance Use, 8*(2), 69–77.

Washton, A. M., & Zweben, J. E. (2009). *Cocaine and methamphetamine addiction: Treatment, recovery, and relapse prevention*. New York, NY: Norton.

Wermuth, L. (2000). Methamphetamine use: Hazards and social influences. *Journal of Drug Education, 3*, 423–433.

Yudko, E., & Gagnet, T. (2003). *Treatment of methamphetamine abuse: Lack of evidence for the efficacy of any of the models currently in use*. Retrieved from http://catbull.com/alamut/Bibliothek/Yudko/1477_17.pdf

CHAPTER 6 # PRESCRIPTION DRUG ADDICTION

Todd F. Lewis

STUDENT LEARNING OUTCOMES

At the conclusion of this chapter students will

1. Identify key terms and definitions related to prescription drug addiction and treatment
2. Comprehend the costs of prescription drug abuse and addiction in the United States
3. Understand key sociodemographic characteristics often associated with prescription drug abuse
4. Describe and apply treatment approaches for prescription drug abuse
5. Summarize the literature on prescription drug addiction treatment

CASE AND CASE DISCUSSION

Ashley, a 32-year-old Caucasian woman, enters counseling under her own volition. During the intake interview, it is clear that Ashley has struggled with drug abuse and addiction since she was in her early 20s. She reports periods of severe alcohol abuse, cocaine abuse, and dabbling with heroin use, although she reports currently being clean from these substances.

Earlier in the year, Ashley fell at home and threw out her back. She was in intense pain and notes that she "couldn't function" at home, let alone on the job. She went to her doctor, who prescribed Vicodin to help relieve the pain. Of course, Ashley was well aware of her substance-abusing past but neglected to tell her doctor, as she believed those times were over. When Ashley took her first dose of Vicodin, it provided quick and effective relief of her pain. However, she also noticed another unexpected effect: She felt that her stress seemed to melt away, she didn't get as upset as usual, and she felt at ease with herself. "When I took my pain pills, I thought, 'This is how I should feel—I feel normal,'" she says.

If one Vicodin could be that effective for her pain and help her feel "normal," then she reasoned that more would be even better. Soon Ashley found herself taking more than what was prescribed and returning to the doctor asking for more medication. She knew that over time her doctor would get suspicious, so she started making appointments with other physicians claiming that she was in pain and needed medication. Tolerance quickly set in, and before she knew it she was taking several Vicodin a day so as not to experience any withdrawal symptoms. Ashley soon ran out of doctors she could meet with and found herself searching the underground market for pain pills. She hit up friends, family, and the streets in order to get her pills.

Ashley's husband Roger was no stranger to substance use and abuse. However, he was solidly in recovery and, at some level, knew what Ashley was doing. He finally confronted her after he discovered several unusual withdrawals from their savings account (which was not checked very often). In fact, Ashley had pretty much wiped out what limited savings they had. Roger and Ashley had a decent marriage, and they both wanted to save some money before they had children. When Roger confronted Ashley, she was in tears. She agreed to seek help and came to the agency to inquire about the buprenorphine (Suboxone) program.

OVERVIEW OF PRESCRIPTION DRUG ADDICTION

The case of Ashley illustrates many of the realities clients face when they abuse prescription drugs. Often these drugs are secured via legitimate prescriptions from doctors, which can confuse patients even more when they develop an addiction. As this case demonstrates, prescription medications can be quite effective for what they are intended to relieve; Ashley's pain dissipated greatly when she took Vicodin. However, other effects are overlooked, such as feeling "normal" and having the sense that all her stresses "melted away." Clients may reason that more is better, and soon they are in the throes of an addiction.

Prescription drug abuse and addiction is often unnoticed by friends, family, and coworkers (Colvin, 2008). What is interesting is that the abusing of pills is an "intensely private affair" that is in contrast to other forms of drug addiction (Colvin, 2008, p. 18), such as binge drinking or meth parties. The privacy of the act makes it difficult for others to know exactly what is going on until the consequences begin to mount, as in the case of Ashley. Because prescription medications are provided legally by a doctor and can be easily accessed, many assume that it must be safe to take them (Byrne, Lander, & Ferris, 2009)—even a little more than prescribed. Over time, however, access to medications may take a darker turn (e.g., securing pills via illegal means) as the person becomes desperate to maintain his or her habit.

In this chapter, the effects of prescription drug addiction are covered along with a definition of terms. The costs of prescription drug addiction are presented, followed by a review of common assessment and diagnostic procedures. Treatment approaches are given major attention, with an emphasis on evidence-based medications and behavioral interventions used for prescription drug addictions. The importance of support services for those struggling with prescription drug addiction is stressed. The chapter concludes with several resources that clinicians and clients can easily access for more information on prescription medications, their effects, their dangers, and treatment approaches.

Effects

According to the Drug Abuse Warning Network (as cited in Colvin, 2008), prescription drug abuse is quite common, with rates exceeding rates of heroin and cocaine abuse combined. Prescription drug abuse most commonly occurs with pain relievers, sedatives, and stimulants (Perkinson, 2012). These drugs can and do produce tolerance and withdrawal. Thus, each has a unique effect on the central nervous system, behavior, and emotions.

Pain Relievers

An estimated 1.7 million individuals in the United States are addicted to prescription pain pills (Burson, 2010). Thus, pain pills are one of the most commonly abused prescription medications in the United States. Researchers have noted an increased prevalence in prescription pain pill abuse in the past several years, with rates tripling over a 10-year span (Back et al., 2009). Pain medication abuse is becoming increasingly more prevalent among college-age populations (McCabe, Cranford, Boyd, & Teter, 2007; McCabe, Teter, & Boyd, 2005). Pain relievers (or *painkillers*) are from the opioid family of drugs (also called *opiates*) and are prescribed to help clients block pain from any number of sources. For example, doctors prescribe pain relievers after surgery or for chronic back pain. Opiates are usually prescribed for a brief period of time, up to 4 weeks, to address acute pain (Colvin, 2008). The danger with pain relievers is twofold: (a) They have a high abuse and addiction potential (Colvin, 2008), and (b) subsequent withdrawal is exceedingly uncomfortable. In addition to having a high abuse potential, pain relievers also numb emotional pain so that individuals feel greater pleasure in their lives. Indeed, this feeling of euphoria is a large reason these pills become so addicting and is a significant reason why Ashley struggles to control her use.

Examples of prescription pain relievers include oxycodone, Oxycontin, Percocet, Percodan, and Vicodin. They work in the brain by binding to opiate receptors; however, these opiate receptors do not all have the same intensity level (Kuhn, Swartzwelder, & Wilson, 2008). Thus, doctors must assess the intensity of pain to determine whether the patient should receive a stronger opiate (e.g., fentanyl) or a moderately effective agent (e.g., oxycodone). As one might imagine, astute clients might feign the extent of their pain in order to procure stronger drugs. Prescription pain medications can be taken orally, snorted, or injected (Hoffman & Froemke, 2007).

People assume that because a doctor prescribes pain relievers, these drugs are safe to use as they wish. This is a serious mistake, as opiates are powerful drugs, and their misuse can cause significant damage. Prescription pain medications do not produce the initial rush that one might experience with heroin or morphine, although other effects are similar if varied. Common effects aside from pain relief include euphoria, drowsiness, constricted pupils, lack of motivation, constipation, violent yawning, and depressed breathing (Colvin, 2008; Hoffman & Froemke, 2007; Kuhn et al., 2008; Smith, 2013). Overdose from opiate medications can be lethal (Kuhn et al., 2008). Byrne et al. (2009) noted that prescription pain pills have contributed to more deaths related to overdose than substances such as heroin. Chronic abuse of pain medications can lead to physical and psychological addiction. Withdrawal symptoms produce significant discomfort: vomiting, runny nose, nausea, and flu-like symptoms. They are a large reason why many cannot quit cold turkey. Indeed, several of my clients have testified that opiate withdrawal is one of the worst experiences they have gone through.

Sedatives

Sedatives are central nervous system depressants used to treat problems such as anxiety, sleep problems, and epilepsy. Before the 1960s, barbiturates were the most commonly used sedatives to treat many sleep and anxiety disorders (and they are still used today for these purposes; Doweiko, 2009); however, their high abuse potential and small therapeutic index (the ratio of a drug's effectiveness to its lethality) make them dangerous if misused. Common types of barbiturates include Phenobarbital, Secobarbital, and Amobarbital (Kuhn et al., 2008). The small ratio between their effective dose and lethal dose suggests that taking slightly more drugs than prescribed can be lethal; barbiturates slow down the central nervous system, including the areas of the brain that control breathing. Breathing might become shallow or thin and in severe cases stop completely. Besides slowing down the nervous system, they have initial effects similar to those of alcohol: impaired judgment, lowered inhibitions, and enhanced confidence (Smith, 2013). However, because of the depressant nature of the drugs, psychoactive effects also include periods of sorrow and depression (Erickson, 2001). Abuse and addiction to barbiturates are not as common as they once were with the advent of benzodiazepines (Erickson, 2001).

In the early 1960s benzodiazepines (or *benzos*) were marketed as a safer alternative to barbiturates. Benzodiazepines have a milder sedation effect compared to barbiturates, and many people concluded that one could not abuse them or develop an addiction. Unfortunately, benzodiazepines are among the most commonly prescribed and abused prescription medications in the United States (Colvin, 2008). Despite their effectiveness in treating conditions like anxiety, their potential to produce a physiological dependence is well documented (Doweiko, 2009). Thus, doctors must balance the effectiveness of benzodiazepines with their potential for abuse.

Common benzodiazepines include Ativan, Valium, Xanax, Halcion, and Restoril (Colvin, 2008). They are usually prescribed for short-term use (a few weeks), although debate continues regarding safe, long-term use (Colvin, 2008). Benzodiazepines are rarely lethal when abused (Newton & Gomez, 2011). However, the combination of benzodiazepines with alcohol can be quite dangerous (Colvin, 2008). Effects of benzodiazepines include overall relaxation, lowered anxiety, and less worry.

Stimulants

Stimulants, also referred to as *uppers*, are a class of drugs that raise activity levels within the central nervous system. Common effects include increased alertness; feelings of euphoria; and activation of the fight-or-flight response—increased heart rate, increased blood pressure, and enhanced energy. Stimulants are dangerous at high doses, leading to extreme hostility, hallucinations, convulsions, and possibly death. Perhaps the greatest risk among those who abuse stimulant drugs is the excess demand on the heart and cardiovascular system.

Many stimulants exert their influence by affecting two key neurotransmitters in the brain: norepinephrine and dopamine (Colvin, 2008). Norepinephrine is responsible for increasing heart rate and blood pressure, and dopamine is responsible for inducing feelings of euphoria, well-being, motivation, and pleasure. Susceptible people can easily become addicted to stimulants because of the heightened sense of energy and pleasure these drugs produce. Managing cravings can be especially difficult with clients addicted to stimulants.

Stimulants are prescribed for conditions such as attention-deficit/hyperactivity disorder, suppression of appetite, and narcolepsy (Colvin, 2008). Common stimulant medications include Ritalin, Cylert, Concerta, and Adderall. In adults, stimulants such as Pro-Fast and Didrex are prescribed as appetite suppressants.

A troubling trend with prescription stimulant abuse is their abuse by young people, especially college students (Narconon International, 2012). For example, college students abuse Ritalin and Adderall to help study for exams or simply to get high. They can crush tablets and insufflate the powder, or dissolve and inject them to reach a desired effect (Narconon International, 2012). The underground market for selling stimulant drugs on college campuses poses a serious risk to students; these drugs can be abused and can produce tolerance, withdrawal, and dependency.

Definitions

Medical use: Using medications to treat a diagnostic condition. The medication usually makes life better for the patient. The pattern of appropriate medical use is steady, reasonable, and based on doctor recommendation. The use of medication via a doctor's prescription is legal, and control of use is determined jointly between the doctor and patient (Dupont, as cited in Colvin, 2008).

Nonmedical use: Using medications to change mood or feel better. Nonmedical use usually does not make life better for the patient. The pattern of nonmedical use is often inconsistent, including dangerously high doses. The activity is illegal, and control of use is determined by the patient rather than the physician (Dupont, as cited in Colvin, 2008).

Prescription: A note written by a medical specialist that allows a patient to legally purchase (or be given) a medicine or medical treatment.

Prescription drug abuse: The intentional use of a medication in a manner different from the reason it was prescribed. It also entails using medication without a prescription or to experience its positive effects (National Institute on Drug Abuse [NIDA], 2014).

Unwitting addict: Many individuals who become addicted to prescription pain medication are as surprised as anyone. They often have no history of drug abuse and never plan on becoming addicted, hence the term *unwitting addict* (Colvin, 2008). They take the medicine for legitimate pain or anxiety but over time take it in increasing amounts because it makes them feel good. Such is the situation with Ashley in the beginning case study.

Demographics and Cost

Using medication beyond its intended reason appears quite common. According to NIDA (2014), in 2010 approximately 4.5% of Americans (16 million) reported using prescription medications for nonmedical purposes within the past year.

Americans are abusing prescription medications in greater numbers than they are using cocaine, hallucinogens, inhalants, and heroin combined (Colvin, 2008). A survey of 12th graders indicated that among illegal drugs, prescription and over-the-counter medications (e.g., Vicodin, Oxycontin) were the most commonly used (NIDA, 2014).

Colvin (2008) noted that women, older adults, and young people are at particular risk for prescription drug addiction. Women are more likely than men to experience chronic pain and seek medical help for emotional conditions, leading to increased risk of prescription pain medication abuse (Back et al., 2009; Colvin, 2008). Older adults, on average, take more medication than younger people. In addition, they may not be able to fully metabolize the medication in their systems (Colvin, 2008), resulting in a diminished effect. This may lead to taking increased doses of medication, placing them at greater risk for addiction.

Young people abuse prescription medications for a variety of reasons. However, one factor seems particularly relevant: availability. From 1991 to 2010, prescriptions for stimulants increased sevenfold (from 4 million to 45 million), and those for opioids increased almost threefold (from 75.5 million to 209.5 million; NIDA, 2014). The significant increase in abuse of prescription pain medications has primarily been seen among young people (ages 12–25; Byrne et al., 2009). Prescription medications can be easily accessed not only from doctors. Most teenagers acquire prescription medications from a relative or friend for free (NIDA, 2014). Clearly, the easy availability of prescription medication for a host of issues that teenagers experience—inability to sleep, attention-deficit/hyperactivity disorder, lack of concentration, anxiety—sets up a slippery slope, resulting in increased abuse or addiction potential.

Back, Lawson, Singleton, and Brady (2011) found differences in the characteristics and correlates of prescription opioid abuse among men and women. Specifically, females ages 12–17 were more likely than males of the same age to abuse prescription opioid drugs. However, males ages 18–25 were more likely to abuse these drugs than females of the same age. Women were more likely than men to use prescription pain medications in conjunction with other drugs. Whereas women commonly consumed prescription opioids orally, men were more likely to explore alternative routes of administration (Back et al., 2011). The authors also found that women were more likely to report using prescription opioids as a means of coping with stress or difficult emotions and were more likely to use first thing in the morning than men, who were more likely to use in the early evening. Men were significantly more likely than women to abuse alcohol in addition to prescription pain medication (Back et al., 2009). In another study by McCabe et al. (2005), White men were found to be more likely than Asian men to engage in illicit use of prescription pain medications. Inconsistent with national trends, McCabe et al. (2005) found that African American college men were not at a lower risk for prescription pain medication abuse. Among college students, members of fraternities were more likely to engage in illicit prescription opioid abuse. A majority of college students reported that they obtained prescription pain pills from their peers (McCabe et al., 2007).

The economic costs of prescription drug abuse are staggering. The Coalition Against Insurance Fraud (as cited in Burson, 2010) noted that the movement of prescription medications to those who abuse them costs insurance companies *billions* of dollars per year. Prescription pain relievers cost $8.6 billion in 2001 (Baldasare, 2011). Much of this cost is through the diversion of prescription drugs, which is the "the transfer of a prescription drug from a lawful to an unlawful channel of distribution or use" (Inciardi, Surratt, Cicero, & Beard, 2009, p. 538). Increases in new nonmedical users and emergency department visits related to prescription drug abuse have skyrocketed since the 1990s. According to Inciardi et al. (2009), the U.S. Drug Enforcement Administration has estimated that the diversion of prescription drugs yields approximately $25 billion each year and is occurring throughout the drug delivery process. Studying this phenomenon, the researchers found that the most common source of diversion was by older adults (by feigning pain to get prescriptions from their physicians), pain patients, and "doctor shoppers" working in conjunction with dealers and brokers to sell their prescriptions. The authors posited that the popularity of prescription medications may be due to the fact that they are seen as less stigmatizing, they seem less dangerous (because they are controlled), and the legal consequences are not as severe as they are with other substances. Because the researchers found that prescriptions from physicians play an important role in the pill-brokering process, they considered education for medical personnel to be an important step in decreasing the abuse of prescription drugs.

One also cannot ignore the costs and negative effects that long-term abuse of prescription drugs, especially painkillers, has on the brain. New research has suggested that the brains of regular, chronic opiate users function abnormally (Kuhn et al., 2008), and similar findings have been found for those who abuse stimulant drugs. For example, basic cognitive functioning, such as complex decision making, tends to be more difficult among chronic narcotic and stimulant users, leading to poor decisions and choices. The constant suppression of breathing caused by opiates may lead to hypoxia (low blood oxygen), most likely rooted in drug-induced changes in the brain (Kuhn et al., 2008). The fact that changes in the brain occur as a result of exposure to chemicals is one of the main reasons drug addiction is considered a brain disease by many in the medical community.

These cost estimates are based on what can be measured—lost workdays, medical expenses and tests, and so on. In reality, the costs of prescription drug abuse and addiction are probably much higher, as fraudulent prescriptions, pharmacy thefts, and state prescription drug monitoring programs, among other factors, are difficult to monitor and calculate (Baldasare, 2011). It is the uncalculated costs, however, that lead to untold misery. The nonmonetary costs are the damaged marriages, lost jobs, damaged health, and ruined reputations that create despair for the addicted person as well as close friends and family members (Burson, 2010).

ASSESSMENT, DIAGNOSIS, AND TREATMENT SETTINGS

The assessment and diagnosis of prescription drug abuse follow similar procedures as for other drugs of abuse. However, it is important to remember that the assessment process also depends on the clinician's unique training and preference, agency protocol, and client needs. For example, some clinicians may favor certain assessment tools, whereas others may rely solely on the diagnostic interview. Regardless of which method or tools a clinician uses, the goals of assessment are to conceptualize the problem with prescription drug abuse, clarify the diagnostic picture, and provide direction for treatment planning.

Assessment

Assessing prescription drug addiction may be more difficult than assessing other forms of drug addiction. This is because many clients rationalize that overconsumption of prescription medications is acceptable and safe because these drugs have been legally prescribed (and because the clients need them for medical purposes; NIDA, 2014). Thus, clients may not be forthcoming about their prescription drug use. In the assessment process, clinicians may need to speak with collaterals or other individuals in the client's life to secure a more complete picture of his or her use.

Given the unique nature of prescription drug abuse, the diagnostic interview should be tailored to ensure that the clinician is getting relevant information. Aside from asking questions regarding quantity and frequency of use, previous treatment history, current life functioning, and family history of use, the clinician should hone in on specific aspects of prescription drug abuse and addiction. Examples of questions might include the following:

- Have you ever lied to a doctor to obtain prescription medication?
- Do you use prescription drugs in a way that is not intended?
- Has your school, job, or family life suffered because of your prescription drug use?
- Have you ever stolen prescription drugs?
- Have you ever thought that you might have a problem with prescription drug use?
- Have you ever gotten angry when others have suggested that you have a prescription drug use problem?
- Have you ever used more prescription drugs than you needed for your condition?
- Do you panic at the thought of not having your prescription drugs?

This list is certainly not exhaustive; the clinician's task is to narrow in on aspects of prescription drug use that could indicate a problem (e.g., lying to one's doctor). Although it may seem obvious, clinicians also should be clear on exactly which medications the client is taking. This can get complicated given that many clients are on multiple medications and some cannot remember their names and dosage levels. Clinicians need to avoid rushing through the assessment process and ensure that they are clear on the information provided. Because mental health clinicians are usually not medical doctors, it is tempting to skip over these details. However, doing so could lead to improper assessment and inaccurate diagnoses.

Unlike problems with alcohol and other drugs, there are not many assessment tools or instruments that specifically and uniquely assess for prescription drug abuse and addiction. However, there are assessments that query about problems and consequences of drug use and that include prescription drugs among a cadre of other drugs. An example is the Drug Abuse Screening Test (DAST; Skinner, 1982), which currently comes in 10-item and 20-item versions (the original DAST had 28 items). The DAST is a brief screening tool designed to detect possible substance abuse and dependence (Alcohol and Drug Abuse Institute, 2012). The DAST is readily available online. Example items from the DAST are presented in Exhibit 6.1.

Another tool is the NIDA-Modified Alcohol, Smoking, and Substance Involvement Screening Test (NIDA-Modified ASSIST), designed to assess the frequency of substance use across alcohol, tobacco, prescription drugs, illegal drugs, and

---

EXHIBIT 6.1   EXAMPLE ITEMS FROM THE DRUG ABUSE SCREENING TEST

❏ Yes ❏ No   1.   Have you used drugs other than those required for medical reasons?

❏ Yes ❏ No   2.   Have you abused prescription drugs?

❏ Yes ❏ No   5.   Are you always able to stop using drugs when you want to?

❏ Yes ❏ No   12. Has drug abuse ever created problems between you and your spouse?

Note. Clinicians can easily access the Drug Abuse Screening Test online (www. drtepp.com/pdf/substance_abuse.pdf). Although it is copyrighted, it may be reproduced for noncommercial use (clinical, research, or training purposes) if credit is given to the author, Dr. Harvey A. Skinner, Dean, Faculty of Health, York University, Toronto, Canada. It was created in 1982.

---

controlled medications (NIDA, 2002). Higher scores on the NIDA-Modified AS-SIST indicate a need for intervention. An excellent free online tool is the NIDA Quick Screen (NIDA, 2013), which can help determine whether more thorough assessment is warranted. The NIDA Quick Screen is set up so that the client is taken directly to the full NIDA-Modified ASSIST if he or she indicates problematic use. Example items on the NIDA Quick Screen are presented in Exhibit 6.2.

EXHIBIT 6.2   EXAMPLE ITEMS FROM THE NIDA QUICK SCREEN

In the past year, how often have you used the following?

Alcohol (for men, 5 or more drinks a day; for women 4 or more drinks a day)

❏ Never   ❏ Once or twice   ❏ Monthly   ❏ Weekly   ❏ Daily or almost daily

Tobacco products

❏ Never   ❏ Once or twice   ❏ Monthly   ❏ Weekly   ❏ Daily or almost daily

Prescription drugs (for nonmedical reasons)

❏ Never   ❏ Once or twice   ❏ Monthly   ❏ Weekly   ❏ Daily or almost daily

Illegal drugs

❏ Never   ❏ Once or twice   ❏ Monthly   ❏ Weekly   ❏ Daily or almost daily

---

Note. The NIDA Quick Screen can help determine whether a client is at risk for substance use. If so, then the clinician should move immediately to the more involved NIDA-Modified Alcohol, Smoking, and Substance Involvement Screening Test (NIDA-Modified ASSIST). A free online assessment using the NIDA Quick Screen that transitions seamlessly into the NIDA-Modified ASSIST can be found at www.drugabuse.gov/nmassist/. NIDA = National Institute on Drug Abuse.

The Addiction Severity Index (ASI; McLellan, Luborsky, O'Brien, & Woody, 1980) is a semistructured, comprehensive tool used to assess client functioning across seven domains, including alcohol and drug use, legal issues, medical/ health issues, work problems, family issues, and psychiatric problems. Because of its comprehensiveness, the ASI is an excellent screening tool for dual diagnoses and assists in treatment planning. Although not specifically designed for prescription medication abuse, the drug questions on the ASI inquire about a range of chemicals, including legal and illegal sedatives, opioids, and stimulants. The ASI can be accessed free on the Internet (www.tresearch.org/tools/download-asi-instruments-manuals/) and includes user-friendly short- and long-version manuals.

The substance abuse clinician is encouraged to screen clients for prescription drug problems and, if warranted, follow up with more formal procedures. For example, the clinician may want to start with questions from the diagnostic interview and the DAST. If the results indicate a possible problem, the use of more thorough methods, such as the ASI, should be considered. Whatever the protocol, assessment for prescription drug abuse should aid in diagnosis and treatment planning efforts.

Diagnosis

Based on assessment information, the clinician is in a position to make a diagnosis based on the *Diagnostic and Statistical Manual of Mental Disorders, Fifth Edition* (*DSM–5*; American Psychiatric Association, 2013). As noted in Chapter 4, the *DSM–5* no longer uses the terms *abuse* and *dependence* in relation to substance use disorders. In addition, there is no overall diagnosis for prescription medication addiction. The appropriate diagnosis for any prescription medication addiction depends on the class of drug to which the medication belongs. For example, if a client abuses Adderall, then the diagnosis would be amphetamine use disorder rather than Adderall abuse because Adderall is a stimulant medication that contains amphetamine. Prescription pain medication abuse, such as overconsumption of Oxycontin, would be diagnosed as opioid use disorder. If a client abuses Valium, a benzodiazepine, then the appropriate diagnosis would be sedative, hypnotic, or anxiolytic use disorder. If a client abuses a prescription medication that does not fit into one of the classifications outlined in the *DSM*, the diagnosis would be other (or unknown) substance use disorder. Several specifiers are available for the clinician to consider when making a diagnosis of substance use disorder. For example, severity specifiers can be used based on the number of symptoms (criteria) a client meets (mild = two or three symptoms, moderate = four or five symptoms, severe = six or more symptoms). Remission specifiers can be used to document whether the client has been in remission for at least 3 months but less than 12 (in early remission) or whether the client has been in remission for 12 months or longer (in sustained remission; American Psychiatric Association, 2013).

As with alcohol and other drugs, the difference between mild and severe prescription drug use is a matter of degree. A person with mild prescription drug use might take too many sleeping pills one night and not be able to get up in the morning for work. After vowing to never take so many pills again, he repeats this behavior 2 weeks later and is again late for work. A client with severe prescription drug use experiences increased tolerance, craving, daily consumption of pills, continued use despite negative consequences, and failed attempts at quitting and actively seeks pills to secure a high. In my clinical experience, clients addicted to pain medications will go to great lengths to secure more pills, including stealing from family and friends, forging prescriptions, and shopping for doctors.

The diagnostic process is an important component of the overall evaluation of the client. In general, the clinician needs to determine whether the client's prescription drug use is consistent with a physician's approval or places the client and others at risk. This can be a tricky process: Clients may not be forthcoming about their prescription drug use because they assume it is safer than abusing illegal drugs like heroin or cocaine. After all, because the doctor prescribed the medication, they reason, it must be safe. However, a thorough exploration of clients' medication use, information from collaterals (e.g., family members), consequences of use, and other criteria often helps clients see that their use is out of control.

Inpatient Versus Outpatient Treatment Settings

After a thorough assessment and diagnosis, the clinician is in a position to recommend the most appropriate treatment setting based on the severity of the client's addiction. Severe cases of prescription drug addiction (e.g., clear evidence of tolerance/withdrawal, active seeking out of the drug, intense cravings, and numerous consequences) would require that the client be placed in a restrictive environment with significant structure (e.g., medical detoxification; Smith & Garcia, 2013). For less severe cases, the client would most likely benefit from less restriction and structure, such as outpatient counseling.

In my clinical experience, however, most clients addicted to prescription drugs will first be seen in outpatient settings. This is because prescription drug abuse is not as obvious as abuse of harder, illegal drugs. Those addicted to prescription drugs may be described as silent abusers because others generally do not notice their abuse. They may function relatively well by holding a job and maintaining a home. After all, their medication was legally prescribed by a physician, so family members believe that they are just following the doctor's orders. It is not until the consequences begin to mount (e.g., relationship problems, employment problems, lack of motivation) that others begin to speculate that there could be a problem. The case of Ashley demonstrates the insidious nature of addiction to prescription medications: Her husband only became concerned when their bank savings account showed an unusually low balance.

Despite the silent nature of prescription drug abuse, there are situations in which a more restrictive setting is warranted. If a client is abusing other substances in addition to prescription medications, or has concomitant mental health problems, more structure may be necessary. In addition, if the prescription drug abuse is severe, limiting the client's ability to function, a more restrictive environment should be considered. Smith and Garcia (2013) noted that inpatient settings include medical detox and stabilization, dual-diagnosis hospital inpatient programs, and some therapeutic communities and residential programs. These settings include a bevy of services for the client, including medication management, individual therapy, group therapy, 12-step mutual support groups, close contact with treatment staff, and medical supervision.

TREATMENT OF PRESCRIPTION DRUG ADDICTION

Unlike other substances such as alcohol, there is a dearth of empirical outcome research on effective interventions for prescription drug abuse and addiction. Available options for successful treatment of prescription drugs are based on the drug being abused (NIDA, 2014). For example, clinical approaches for the treatment of prescription pain medication addiction are extrapolated from empirical studies on heroin addiction (NIDA, 2014). Interventions used for prescription depressant abuse are taken from research on other central nervous system depressants, such as alcohol.

Medication and behavioral interventions seem to be the most common methods for treating prescription drug problems (NIDA, 2014). Medications are readily available to treat addictions to prescription pain medications; however, there are no medications as of yet to treat addictions to prescribed central nervous system depressants or stimulants (although NIDA is currently examining studies to determine safe medications for stimulant prescription drugs; NIDA, 2014). Psychological and behavioral therapies found to be effective with other drug use problems also can be effective with prescription drug addiction. In this section, I focus on the most common approaches to the treatment of prescription drug abuse and addiction, dividing them into medications and behavioral interventions. Where appropriate, evidence for their effectiveness is noted.

Medications

Pain is one of the leading causes of physician visits, and the use of prescription opioids to manage pain is on the rise (Ling, Mooney, & Hillhouse, 2011). Medications to treat prescription opioid abuse and addiction (e.g., methadone, buprenorphine) have become increasingly popular components of care in the treatment process (Perkinson, 2012). In essence, these prescription drugs help clients stabilize their dependency, minimize their experience of craving, and ease the withdrawal process. Two of the most common medications are methadone and buprenorphine.

Methadone
Methadone is a synthetic, long-lasting opioid that is primarily implicated in heroin detoxification and treatment programs (Perkinson, 2012) but can be used to treat addiction to any analgesic medication/drug. Methadone works by activating the same receptors as narcotic drugs, minimizing the painful withdrawal syndrome (WebMD, 2013). Methadone also lessens cravings and does not provide the intense high that one might reach with heroin use (WebMD, 2013).

Unfortunately, methadone is not without its dangers. A casual perusal of the Internet suggests that there is increasing concern over the use of methadone for treating pain. Using existing survey data, Maxwell and McCance-Katz (2010) found that the amount of methadone sold, the number of methadone-related emergency room visits, and the amount of methadone-related deaths all increased between 2000 and 2008. Another disadvantage of methadone is the relatively short amount of time the effects last, from 12 to 24 hours (although this is longer lasting than the effects of many other opiate drugs; Kuhn et al., 2008). Thus, clients who choose to attend methadone maintenance clinics must return *daily* to receive their specific dose. Counseling is usually a part of many methadone treatment programs, but unfortunately not all of them. Many of the clients I see in my clinical practice have revealed their frustrations at having to return to a clinic every day to secure their medication and, depending on the clinic, receiving little to no psychosocial support.

Buprenorphine (Suboxone/Subutex)

The U.S. Food and Drug Administration approved buprenorphine for the treatment of opiate addiction in 2002. The advantage of buprenorphine is that it can be prescribed in a doctor's outpatient office. This is a significant advantage for many clients. Rather than securing medication every day at a methadone clinic, a patient can now get a 30-day prescription for buprenorphine and take it in daily doses like one would take any other medication.

The effectiveness of buprenorphine is well documented (Perkinson, 2012). It is an opiate medication but does not produce the high or euphoria that one experiences from prescription pain medications, making abuse difficult (Byrne et al., 2009). In addition, it is safer than methadone (Perkinson, 2012). It works well for detoxification because it can ease withdrawal symptoms, manage cravings, and stabilize dependency because it blocks the effects of opioids on the brain (Byrne et al., 2009). Common routes of administration include oral tablets or sublingual film strips. A recent clinical trial funded and reported by NIDA (2014) demonstrated that extended Suboxone (buprenorphine with added naloxone, a narcotic antagonist) treatment helped roughly half of participants lower their pain medication abuse.

I have been astonished at how effective buprenorphine therapy can be for those struggling with prescription pain medication. Roughly half of the clients in my clinical practice are addicted to prescription pain medications, and almost all are taking buprenorphine as part of their care. Many of my clients have extolled the virtues of buprenorphine, claiming that it has "saved my life" or "given my life back." I have found buprenorphine to be particularly effective in managing opiate craving, which allows clients to focus on other important issues of recovery during counseling.

Like any medication, however, buprenorphine is not for everyone. For starters, it is quite expensive, which may alienate clients who do not have the means to pay for a prescription. In addition, clients may depend psychologically on buprenorphine and fail to address other lifestyle issues associated with their addiction. Many clients are frightened to stop using it lest they go back to misusing pain pills. Although buprenorphine is safer than methadone (e.g., methadone is more readily abused), Maxwell and McCance-Katz (2010) found that, as with methadone, buprenorphine emergency room visits increased between 2004 and 2007. Given the increasing number of prescriptions for buprenorphine (buprenorphine is being prescribed more readily as a treatment for opioid addiction than as a treatment for pain), the authors recommended continual monitoring of adverse effects (Maxwell & McCance-Katz, 2010). However, fewer adverse consequences related to methadone and buprenorphine occur when these medications are monitored by physicians rather than self-administered (Maxwell & McCance-Katz, 2010).

Behavioral Interventions

Medications *may* be effective for treating prescription drug abuse and addiction, but they are not the entire answer. They do not treat the thoughts, feelings, and behaviors that maintain addictive problems (Byrne et al., 2009). Counseling is generally regarded as an essential component of treatment for prescription pain (and other drug) addiction (Byrne et al., 2009), although Weiss et al. (2011) found that the addition of counseling along with medication treatment did not improve outcomes among those addicted to prescription pain pills. Individual therapy, group therapy, and 12-step mutual support groups are thought to be important adjuncts to prescription medication (Moss-King, 2013). Further empirical evidence is needed, however, to support counseling as a value-added component of buprenorphine and other medication maintenance programs.

Behavioral interventions for prescription drug abuse and addiction are similar to those used for other drug addictions. Essential components of any addictions treatment are establishing a strong therapeutic alliance, helping the client address dysfunctional thoughts that maintain the addictive behavior, developing coping resources and self-efficacy, and providing support. The nature of prescription drug addiction also requires that the clinician be sensitive to what classification of drug is being abused, what others (i.e., collaterals) notice in terms of the drug abuse, and what information can be gleaned from detailed assessment questions (see "Assessment, Diagnosis, and Treatment Settings"). Next I provide a brief review of evidence-based procedures for working with chemical dependency with a focus on prescription drug abuse and addiction: motivational interviewing (MI), cognitive behavior therapy (CBT), relapse prevention, and 12-step mutual support groups.

MI

MI is a collaborative, person-centered form of guiding to elicit and strengthen motivation to change (Rollnick, Butler, Kinnersley, Gregory, & Mash, 2010). MI was born out of the substance addictions field and thus has direct relevance for clients abusing a wide range of chemicals. A key aspect of MI is the "spirit of MI," which consists of honoring client autonomy, evocation (i.e., eliciting client ideas and thoughts), collaboration, and compassion (W. R. Miller & Rollnick, 2013). The spirit of MI serves as the foundation of MI; all techniques and strategies emanate from this stance in the therapeutic setting. The overall goals of MI are to (a) lower resistance, (b) resolve ambivalence about change, and (c) enhance intrinsic motivation to change.

MI has amassed an impressive array of empirical evidence to support use of the approach across an ever-increasing application of problems. A number of studies have supported the use of MI with alcohol and other drug problems (Burke, Arkowitz, & Dunn, 2002). Related to prescription drug abuse, Zahradnik et al. (2009) found that MI plus individualized written feedback resulted in reductions in defined daily doses of prescription drugs at 3 months among general hospital patients compared to a control group. However, in a 12-month follow-up to this study, Otto et al. (2009) found no significant differences between treatment and control groups, suggesting that periodic check-ins and MI booster sessions may be needed to extend its effects past 3 months. In a randomized controlled trial, Satre, Delucchi, Lichtmacher, Sterling, and Weisner (2013) tested the effectiveness of an MI intervention among those who abused alcohol and other drugs and struggled with clinical depression. At the 3-month follow-up, participants in the MI group were less likely than those in the control group to report hazardous drinking. Although this study did not specifically focus on prescription drug abuse, alcohol is classified as a central nervous system depressant, similar to prescription benzodiazepines or barbiturates. Thus, the effectiveness of MI may carry over to prescription drugs in the same class as alcohol, although more research is needed to substantiate this claim. Readers interested in the extensive evidence base for MI and substance abuse problems are encouraged to consult W. R. Miller and Rollnick (2002, 2013), Burke et al. (2002), and W. R. Miller, Forcehimes, and Zweben (2011).

CBT

CBT is an effective intervention for those struggling with prescription medication abuse and addiction. An attractive feature of CBT is that it can be readily folded into already existing forms of treatment (Lee & Rawson, 2008). In clinical settings, it does not take long to realize that maladaptive thinking is at the heart of many substance abuse problems and is a significant reason why individuals maintain their addictive patterns. CBT is the foundation of many substance abuse treatment approaches: relapse prevention, controlled drinking programs, behavioral marital therapy, and token economies (Thombs, 2006). For a review of the techniques and procedures of CBT, see Chapter 2.

CBT has amassed empirical support for its effectiveness with clients struggling with stimulant abuse. In a study comparing CBT with acceptance and commitment therapy among methamphetamine abusers, Smout et al. (2010) found that CBT had better treatment outcomes. Siqueland et al. (2004) found that cocaine users rated cognitive therapy as more favorable compared to psychoeducation and supportive therapy. In a review of treatments for methamphetamine use, Lee and Rawson (2008) found that those who received CBT interventions showed less methamphetamine use. In addition, those who received CBT treatment showed more positive changes, even after a brief time in treatment, compared to controls. Although these studies did not specifically include prescription stimulant medications, CBT would most likely be an effective behavioral intervention for abuse of both prescribed and nonprescribed stimulant drugs. However, additional clinical trial research on the effectiveness of CBT across the spectrum of prescription drug problems is needed. For an excellent review of the practice of cognitive therapy and CBT approaches in the treatment of substance abuse, see Beck, Wright, Newman, and Liese (1993).

Relapse Prevention

Relapse prevention strategies are critical to any substance abuse treatment program. *Relapse,* or the return to pretreatment levels of use, poses a constant risk, and upward of 60% of individuals return to using substances after treatment (McLellan, Lewis, O'Brien, & Kleber, 2000). Numerous relapse prevention models exist (for an excellent review of relapse prevention models, see Dobmeier & Stevens, 2013), many of which are grounded in CBT. Thus, relapse prevention can be used as a stand-alone strategy or infused into other treatment methods. Relapse prevention approaches and techniques are appealing because they have a strong theoretical foundation (i.e., CBT), and several models have been empirically validated (Rawson, Obert, McCann, & Marinelli-Casey, 1993).

In examining effective relapse prevention strategies, Fisher and Harrison (2009) noted four critical components, based on Gorski's (1989) Center for Applied Sciences model and other cognitive–behavioral models:

1. *Assessing high-risk situations.* High-risk situations include any environmental conditions in which the client is tempted to return to drug use. For example, in the case of Ashley, a high-risk situation might be meeting with an old friend who she knows uses pain medication. In some cases, Ashley may make poor choices without even noticing. These apparently irrelevant decisions can operate beyond the client's awareness but slowly add up to a dangerous situation. For example, Ashley may decide to drive by her friend's house on the way home just to see if she wants to talk. However, if Ashley is honest with herself, she also wants to ask her friend for pain medication.

   Fisher and Harrison (2009) stated that assessing high-risk situations is critical. The clinician should explore with the client all potential environmental triggers and coconstruct a plan to cope with them. Triggers, however, are not limited to the environment. Dobmeier and Stevens (2013) discussed several other determinants of relapse, including behavioral, cognitive, and affective variables. For example, a behavioral determinant may be having few coping skills, a cognitive determinant may be low motivation to change, and an emotional determinant may be a serious depressive illness.

2. *Coping with high-risk situations.* Once the client is aware of high-risk situations, he or she may need help learning skills to better cope with these situations. For example, Ashley could learn skills to better manage anger and promote relaxation. She could learn and practice refusal skills in the event that a friend pressures her to take pain pills. Coping skills should be relevant and useful for clients and include education about relapse, enhancing awareness, and learning healthier cognitions when faced with a challenging situation.

3. *Establishing support systems.* Addiction can be an isolating disease and thrives when clients are without social support. The chance of relapse diminishes if the client feels supported in his or her life. Exploring and cultivating relationships and promoting a stable support system (sometimes this is done through mutual help groups, like Alcoholics Anonymous) help clients realize that they are not alone in their struggles. Ashley's addiction to Vicodin is eroding not only her relationship with her husband but relationships with her coworkers and friends as well. Of course, in a metaphorical sense, isolation is what the addiction wants; social support is the antidote to addictive behavior.

4. *Making lifestyle changes.* Lifestyle imbalance is a risk factor for relapse. Marlatt, Parks, and Witkiewitz (2002) defined a *lifestyle imbalance* as having more "shoulds" than "wants." Shoulds include multiple demands, negative emotions, and negative self-talk that increase stress and contribute to relapse. Wants are simple, everyday pleasures (or extended pleasurable activities, like a vacation) that decrease stress and make life fun. Clients addicted to drugs often have many more shoulds than wants. Of course, we can't get rid of all shoulds (and we wouldn't want to), and we can't engage in all wants. However, the key is balance: Cultivating a balanced lifestyle includes building up the wants and decreasing irrational self-statements and beliefs. Assume that Ashley is attending two Narcotics Anonymous meetings a day, is taking on more than necessary at work, berates herself about how bad a spouse she is, and is extremely hard on herself when she has the slightest urge to use pain medication. Furthermore, assume that she reports no pleasurable activities

in her life. Encouraging her to let go of some of her shoulds and balance her life with more wants will ease her stress and place her at less risk for relapse. She could clearly benefit from more wants—relaxing, taking time to herself, and enjoying life without prescription drugs.

12-Step Mutual Support Groups

Byrne et al. (2009) stated that the combination of buprenorphine treatment and 12-step therapy, or pharmacological management coupled with a mutually supportive group environment to address unhealthy emotions and cognitions related to use, may be a well-rounded approach to treating prescription pain pill abuse. Although 12-step mutual support groups may not be for everyone, they can provide a venue of support for those open to attending. For those suffering from prescription drug addiction, support groups such as Narcotics Anonymous or Cocaine Anonymous may be good options, as these groups, despite their names, do not focus on any particular drug—they welcome those who are struggling with addiction to any substance.

CONCLUSIONS

Working with individuals abusing prescription drugs is complicated because many struggle with significant pain and are dependent on opiate medications. Many would suffer greatly if these medications were suddenly removed. N. S. Miller and Gold (2007) reported an increase in prescription opioid dependence and addiction in the past several years. They stated that opiates are being prescribed more frequently for pain relief, and when they are used for chronic pain, the potential for tolerance and addiction increases significantly. The authors posed the question of whether the use of opiate prescriptions really improves pain symptoms in individuals who are dependent on prescription pain medications. Little research has been done related to this question, but Miller and Gold believed that prescription opioids may not decrease chronic pain but could actually increase the experience of pain. The authors suggested that *it can be difficult to differentiate between drug-seeking behavior and the actual experience of increased pain.* Tolerance can further skew these differences because increasing dosages based on increased tolerance can exacerbate addiction. It is interesting that Miller and Gold cited past studies in which perceptions of pain decreased when opioid medications were discontinued.

N. S. Miller and Gold's (2007) analysis resonates with my clinical experiences counseling those struggling with pain. I recall counseling Martin (a pseudonym), a client in his mid-30s who was in excruciating pain from an accident. His list of physical problems would fill several sheets of paper, including a reconstructed hip that would flare up daily, causing pain in his lower back and down his leg. Martin had consulted with several doctors and tried numerous procedures to address his pain issues, *but nothing was more effective than pain medication.* Of course, I was concerned that Martin was addicted to pain medication (which he most certainly was), but I was even more concerned about what he would do if the medications were taken away—complicating Martin's picture was frequent suicidal ideation. This case begs the question: Is it justified for clients who are in considerable pain to continue using prescription pain medication, even if they are clinically dependent on those medications? I never want to see anyone addicted to drugs, but in some cases is the alternative worse? How do mental health clinicians promote responsible prescription drug use when physicians continue to prescribe these drugs to clients? Does prescription pain medication actually increase the experience of pain, as Miller and Gold suggested? The management of chronic pain in a client who is addicted to opiates is "one of the most challenging tasks of addiction medicine" (Perkinson, 2012, p. 672).

There are several adjunct and supportive services for those struggling with prescription medication abuse or addiction. In today's technological age, the Internet is quickly becoming an excellent resource and supportive aid for clients. Government-sponsored agencies, such as NIDA and the Substance Abuse and Mental Health Services Administration, are excellent resources for clinicians and clients. Other organizations, such as the American Association for the Treatment of Opioid Dependence, provide clients with specific information regarding addiction and the treatment of opioids, including prescription pain medications.

There is no direct analog to Alcoholics Anonymous among prescription drug abuse support groups. However, Narcotics Anonymous would be the most relevant mutual help group for clients who struggle with prescription medication addiction. The principles of Narcotics Anonymous closely resemble those of Alcoholics Anonymous, and Narcotics Anonymous models the 12 steps of Alcoholics Anonymous. A plethora of mutual help group information is available on the Internet, including contact information, resources, and educational material. Communities across the United States, both large and small, hold daily mutual help group meetings.

RESOURCES

The following are resources available for substance abuse clinicians who work with clients struggling with prescription drug abuse. Some resources are geared specifically toward prescription pain medications, whereas others include information applicable to the wide spectrum of substances.

Websites

American Association for the Treatment of Opioid Dependence
    www.aatod.org
American Society of Addiction Medicine
    www.asam.org
Buprenorphine (Suboxone) Treatment Peer Support
    www.addictionsurvivors.org/vbulletin/forumdisplay.php?f=45
Narcotics Anonymous
    www.na.org
National Alliance for Medication Assisted Recovery
    www.methadone.org
National Center on Addiction and Substance Abuse
    www.casacolumbia.org
National Institute on Drug Abuse
    www.drugabuse.gov
Rational Recovery
    www.rational.org

Substance Abuse and Mental Health Services Administration
  www.samhsa.gov
Women for Sobriety
  www.womenforsobriety.org

Videos

Miller, W. R., Rollnick, S., & Moyers, T. B. (2013). *Motivational interviewing: Helping people change*. Albuquerque, NM: The Change Companies.

This is an excellent DVD resource for learning MI. The creators of MI take the viewer through the basic aspects of MI and include several demonstrations. More information can be found at www.changecompanies.net/motivational_interviewing.php

REFERENCES

Alcohol and Drug Abuse Institute. (2012). *Drug Abuse Screening Test (DAST)*. Retrieved from http://bit.ly/DAST_inst

American Psychiatric Association. (2013). *Diagnostic and statistical manual of mental disorders* (5th ed.). Arlington, VA: Author.

Back, S. E., Lawson, K. M., Singleton, L. M., & Brady, K. T. (2011). Characteristics and correlates of men and women with prescription opioid dependence. *Addictive Behaviors, 36*, 829–834.

Back, S. E., Payne, R. A., Waldrop, A. E., Smith, A., Reeves, S., & Brady, K. T. (2009). Prescription opioid aberrant behaviors: A pilot study of sex differences. *Clinical Journal of Pain, 25*, 477–484.

Baldasare, A. (2011, November). *United States drug policy*. Retrieved from http://sai-dc.com/wp-content/uploads/2014/07/US-Drug-Policy-Fact-Sheet-Final.pdf

Beck, A. T., Wright, F. D., Newman, C. F., & Liese, B. S. (1993). *Cognitive therapy of substance abuse*. New York, NY: Guilford Press.

Burke, B. L., Arkowitz, H., & Dunn, C. (2002). The efficacy of motivational interviewing and its adaptations: What we know so far. In W. R. Miller & S. Rollnick (Eds.), *Motivational interviewing: Preparing people for change* (2nd ed., pp. 217–250). New York, NY: Guilford Press.

Burson, J. (2010). *Pain pill addiction: A prescription for hope*. Indianapolis, IN: Dog Ear.

Byrne, M. H., Lander, L., & Ferris, M. (2009). The changing face of opioid addiction: Prescription pain pill dependence and treatment. *Health & Social Work, 34*(1), 53–56.

Colvin, R. (2008). *Overcoming prescription drug addiction: A guide to coping and understanding* (3rd ed.). Omaha, NE: Addicus Books.

Dobmeier, R. A., & Stevens, P. (2013). Retaining sobriety: Relapse prevention strategies. In P. Stevens & R. L. Smith (Eds.), *Substance abuse counseling: Theory and practice* (5th ed., pp. 51–92). New York, NY: Pearson.

Doweiko, H. E. (2009). *Concepts of chemical dependency* (7th ed.). Belmont, CA: Brooks/Cole.

Erickson, S. (2001). The major substances of abuse and the body. In P. Stevens & R. L. Smith (Eds.), *Substance abuse counseling: Theory and practice* (2nd ed., pp. 33–76). Columbus, OH: Merrill Prentice Hall.

Fisher, G. L., & Harrison, T. C. (2009). *Substance abuse: Information for school counselors, social workers, therapists, and counselors* (4th ed.). New York, NY: Pearson.

Gorski, T. T. (1989). Special issue: Relapse: Conceptual, research, and clinical perspectives. *Journal of Chemical Dependency Treatment, 2*, 153–169.

Hoffman, J., & Froemke, S. (2007). Addiction is a brain disease. In J. Hoffman & S. Froemke (Eds.), *Addiction: New knowledge, new treatments, new hope* (pp. 66–69). New York, NY: Rodale.

Inciardi, J. A., Surratt, H. L., Cicero, T. J., & Beard, R. A. (2009). Prescription opioid abuse and diversion in an urban community: The results of an ultrarapid assessment. *Pain Medicine, 10,* 537–548.

Kuhn, C., Swartzwelder, S., & Wilson, W. (2008). *Buzzed: The straight facts about the most used and abused drugs from alcohol to ecstasy* (3rd ed.). New York, NY: Norton.

Lee, N. K., & Rawson, R. A. (2008). A systematic review of cognitive and behavioural therapies for methamphetamine dependence. *Drug and Alcohol Review, 27,* 309–317.

Ling, W., Mooney, L., & Hillhouse, M. (2011). Prescription opioid abuse, pain and addiction: Clinical issues and implications. *Drug and Alcohol Review, 30,* 300–305.

Marlatt, G. A., Parks, G. A., & Witkiewitz, K. (2002). *Clinical guidelines for implementing relapse prevention therapy: A guideline developed for the Behavioral Health Recovery Management Project.* Retrieved from http://www.bhrm.org/guidelines/RPT%20guideline.pdf

Maxwell, J., & McCance-Katz, E. F. (2010). Indicators of buprenorphine and methadone use and abuse: What do we know? *American Journal on Addictions, 19*(1), 73–88.

McCabe, S., Cranford, J. A., Boyd, C. J., & Teter, C. J. (2007). Motives, diversion and routes of administration associated with nonmedical use of prescription opioids. *Addictive Behaviors, 32,* 562–575.

McCabe, S., Teter, C. J., & Boyd, C. J. (2005). Illicit use of prescription pain medication among college students. *Drug and Alcohol Dependence, 77*(1), 37–47. doi:10.1016/j.drugalcdep.2004.07.005

McLellan, A. T., Lewis, D. C., O'Brien, C. P., & Kleber, H. D. (2000). Drug dependence, a chronic medical illness: Implications for treatment, insurance, and outcome evaluation. *Journal of the American Medical Association, 284,* 1689–1695.

McLellan, A. T., Luborsky, L., O'Brien, C. P., & Woody, G. E. (1980). An improved diagnostic instrument for substance abuse patients: The Addiction Severity Index. *Journal of Nervous Mental Disorders, 168,* 26–33.

Miller, N. S., & Gold, M. S. (2007). Opiate prescription medication dependence and pain perceptions. *Journal of Addictive Diseases, 26,* 65–71.

Miller, W. R., Forcehimes, A. A., & Zweben, A. (2011). *Treating addiction: A guide for professionals.* New York, NY: Guilford Press.

Miller, W. R., & Rollnick, S. (2002). *Motivational interviewing: Helping people change* (2nd ed.). New York, NY: Guilford Press.

Miller, W. R., & Rollnick, S. (2013). *Motivational interviewing: Helping people change* (3rd ed.). New York, NY: Guilford Press.

Moss-King, D. A. (2013). Individual treatment. In P. Stevens & R. L. Smith (Eds.), *Substance abuse counseling: Theory and practice* (5th ed., pp. 188–201). New York, NY: Pearson.

Narconon International. (2012). *Prescription stimulants.* Retrieved from http://www.narconon.org/drug-information/prescription-stimulants.html

National Institute on Drug Abuse. (2002). *Screening for drug use in general medical settings: Resource guide.* Retrieved from http://www.drugabuse.gov/sites/default/files/resource_guide.pdf

National Institute on Drug Abuse. (2013). *The NIDA Quick Screen.* Retrieved from http://www.drugabuse.gov/publications/resource-guide-screening-drug-use-in-general-medical-settings/nida-quick-screen

National Institute on Drug Abuse. (2014). *DrugFacts: Prescription and over-the-counter medications.* Retrieved from http://www.drugabuse.gov/publications/drugfacts/prescription-over-counter-medications

Newton, C., & Gomez, H. (2011). *Benzodiazepine abuse.* Retrieved from http://www.emedicinehealth.com/benzodiazepine_abuse/article_em.htm

Otto, C., Crackau, B., Lohrmann, I., Zahradnik, A., Bischof, G., Ulrich, J., & Rumpf, H. (2009). Brief intervention in general hospital for problematic prescription drug use: 12-month outcome. *Journal of Drug and Alcohol Dependence, 105,* 221–226.

Perkinson, R. R. (2012). *Chemical dependency counseling: A practical guide* (4th ed.). Los Angeles, CA: Sage.

Rawson, R. A., Obert, J. L., McCann, M. J., & Marinelli-Casey, P. (1993). Relapse prevention strategies in outpatient substance abuse treatment. *Psychology of Addictive Behaviors, 7,* 85–95.

Rollnick, S., Butler, C. C., Kinnersley, P., Gregory, J., & Mash, B. (2010). Competent novice: Motivational interviewing. *British Medical Journal, 340,* 1242–1245.

Satre, D. D., Delucchi, K., Lichtmacher, J., Sterling, S. A., & Weisner, C. (2013). Motivational interviewing to reduce hazardous drinking and drug use among depression patients. *Journal of Substance Abuse Treatment, 44,* 323–329.

Siqueland, L., Crits-Christoph, P., Barber, J. P., Gibbons, M. B., Gallop, R., Griffin, M., . . . Liese, B. (2004). What aspects of treatment matter to the patient in the treatment of cocaine dependence? *Journal of Substance Abuse Treatment, 27,* 169–178.

Skinner, H. A. (1982). The Drug Abuse Screening Test. *Addictive Behavior, 7,* 363–367.

Smith, R. L. (2013). The major substances of abuse and the body. In P. Stevens & R. L. Smith (Eds.), *Substance abuse counseling: Theory and practice* (5th ed., pp. 51–92). New York, NY: Pearson.

Smith, R., & Garcia, E. (2013). Treatment setting and treatment planning. In P. Stevens & R. L. Smith (Eds.), *Substance abuse counseling: Theory and practice* (pp. 155–187). New York, NY: Pearson.

Smout, M. F., Longo, M., Harrison, S., Minniti, R., Wickes, W., & White, J. M. (2010). Psychosocial treatment for methamphetamine use disorders: A preliminary randomized controlled trial of cognitive behavior therapy and acceptance and commitment therapy. *Substance Abuse, 31,* 98–107.

Thombs, D. L. (2006). *Introduction to addictive behaviors* (3rd ed.). New York, NY: Guilford Press.

WebMD. (2013). *Treating an addiction to painkillers.* Retrieved from http://www.webmd.com/mental-health/breaking-an-addiction-to-painkillers-treatment-overvew

Weiss, R. D., Potter, J. S., Fiellin, D. A., Byrne, M., Connery, H. S., Dickinson, W., . . . Ling, W. (2011). Adjunctive counseling during brief and extended buprenorphine-naloxone treatment for prescription opioid dependence: A 2-phase randomized controlled trial. *Archives of General Psychiatry, 68,* 1238–1246.

Zahradnik, A., Otto, C., Crackau, B., Löhrmann, I., Bischof, G., John, U., & Rumpf, H-J. (2009). Randomized controlled trial of a brief intervention for problematic prescription drug use in non-treatment-seeking patients. *Addiction, 104,* 109–117.

CHAPTER 7

PATHOLOGICAL GAMBLING

Stephen Southern and Katherine Hilton

STUDENT LEARNING OUTCOMES

At the conclusion of this chapter students will

1. Identify key terms and diagnostic criteria for a gambling disorder
2. Describe clinical interviewing, self-monitoring, and assessment approaches
3. Discuss two major types of pathological gambling and potentially effective treatment
4. Apply concepts of concurrent and integrative treatment approaches to a complex clinical case involving pathological gambling and comorbid depression and posttraumatic stress disorder

CASE AND CASE DISCUSSION

Sarah is a 35-year-old Caucasian woman, married 10 years and employed full time as an administrator in a social service agency. Her husband is an allied health professional who works shifts in a local hospital and drills periodically with his National Guard unit. They sustain a distant marriage, rarely share sexual relations, and practice birth control in order not to have children. Sarah complains of symptoms of depression and anxiety. She has no close friends and maintains a secretive lifestyle in which she loses relatively large sums of money playing slot machines in a nearby casino.

She conceals losses from her husband by securing new credit cards and borrowing money, forging his name to applications. She depleted their savings account and has overdrawn the checking account during weekend binges at the casino. She stays at the casino hotel when her husband is with his guard unit. He is aware of some of her gambling losses and saves the family from financial crises by working extra shifts at the hospital.

Recently Sarah engaged in a costly binge in which she bet increasingly large sums of money in an irrational attempt to recoup her losses. She used most of the funds available to her and dreaded being discovered by her husband. She met a man in the hotel and engaged in compulsive sexual activities for the rest of the weekend. When she returned home, she began to meet anonymous partners on the Internet and engage in risky sexual behaviors. She borrowed money from her aging parents to conceal her recent losses. Experiencing sleep disturbance, loss of appetite, crying spells, and passing thoughts of suicide, she sought help from her family doctor, who prescribed Prozac for depression. Her doctor referred her to a local therapist.

Sarah reluctantly revealed to her female therapist the extent of her pathological gambling. During the clinical interview and history taking, she disclosed that she had been date raped at 15 years of age when she was intoxicated at a party. She withdrew from family and friends, becoming involved in compulsive Internet use of more than 20 hours a week. She continued this pattern of withdrawal throughout her high school and college years. As an adult, she discovered Internet gambling and eventually felt compelled to play slot machines at the casino.

Sarah met her husband in a graduate course at the state college. They had a rapid courtship characterized by intense sexual relations. However, shortly after their marriage, Sarah's husband began to withdraw into his work while she dedicated herself to her new position in the agency. Sarah returned to Internet role-playing games and gambling until she began to focus her attention on casino gambling. Tension would build up in her otherwise devitalized life as she fantasized about a big score at the casino. Inevitably she would continue gambling even after sustaining significant losses. She increased her gambling binges to twice weekly, leaving during the night or calling in sick at work and gambling for hours in spite of headaches, weight loss, and other physical symptoms. Her most recent binge resulted in a weekend sexual relationship with a stranger, which intensified her shame until she started hooking up with anonymous partners. This switching of addictive disorders prompted enough distress that she sought help from her family doctor and then an experienced therapist.

OVERVIEW OF PATHOLOGICAL GAMBLING

Pathological gambling is a multifaceted clinical disorder generally treated as an impulse control disorder not elsewhere classified in the *Diagnostic and Statistical Manual of Mental Disorders, Fourth Edition, Text Revision* (*DSM–IV–TR;* American Psychiatric Association [APA], 2000), which nevertheless presents characteristics of addictive disorders. It is the only process addiction included under the "Non-Substance-Related Disorders" heading of the "Substance-Related and Addictive Disorders" section of the *Diagnostic and Statistical Manual of Mental Disorders, Fifth Edition* (*DSM–5*) because the diagnostic criteria for gambling disorder fit clearly the model for addiction (APA, 2013). This chapter covers (a) important definitions related to pathological gambling/gambling addiction, (b) considerations for special populations, (c) diagnosis and assessment, and (d) evidence-based treatments for use with clients.

Pathological gambling is called *problem gambling* and *compulsive gambling* by some treatment providers. The concept of problem gambling incorporates public health concerns such as harm to the individual and community (Svetieva & Walker, 2008). Generally speaking, the 12-step or recovery community considers gambling disorder to be gambling addiction. The 12-step fellowship addressing this disorder, Gamblers Anonymous (GA), was modeled after Alcoholics Anonymous and Narcotics Anonymous. Because most research and clinical publications included in this review use the term *pathological gambling*, this label is retained even though current diagnostic criteria are applied. Several definitions will be helpful in reviewing the literature and examining the clinical case study.

Definitions

Abstinence: Goals for outcomes in treating pathological gambling range from total abstinence, in which the recovering client refrains from all gambling, to controlled gambling, a harm reduction strategy in which the client may engage in recreational or responsible gambling behavior.

Chasing losses: Characteristic of the progression of gambling disorder, the gambler engages in increasingly risky gambling behaviors, wagering larger sums of money, in order to recover lost funds and possibly conceal losses.

Comorbidity: Pathological gambling is usually encountered in clinical settings with one or more comorbid or co-occurring disorders in descending likelihood of occurrence: substance use disorder, mood disorders, personality disorders (including antisocial personality disorder), posttraumatic stress disorder (PTSD), anxiety disorder, and other process addictions or addictive disorders.

Concurrent treatment: Given comorbidity and complex presentations in clinical practice, many care providers combine treatment of pathological gambling and co-occurring disorder(s) in concurrent, sequential, and integrative treatment formats. Concurrent treatment involves addressing clearly defined treatment components in the same treatment package. Sequential treatment involves stabilizing one problem (usually gambling disorder) before moving to another component. Integrative treatment reflects a seamless combination of treatment models and techniques in one process.

Empirically supported treatment: Receiving a designation of *empirically supported treatment* requires outcome research studies in which minimum criteria for random assignment, meaningful control group(s), measurement of change, and analysis of results are achieved. Effect sizes from empirically supported treatments are reviewed and combined in meta-analyses to establish particular interventions in evidence-based practice.

Gambler's fallacy: The gambler's fallacy is a typical cognitive distortion that maintains compulsive gambling. In the gambler's fallacy, the gambler predicts based on one event that the next event will be in one's favor or advantage. For example, after a run of heads on coin flips, the compulsive gambler will believe the next flip will produce a tail even though it is a chance or random event.

Gambling disorder: Gambling disorder is the only addictive disorder that meets criteria for inclusion in the *DSM–5* (APA, 2013), including criteria for tolerance, unmanageability of consequences, progression, and severity of symptoms.

Illusion of control: The pathological gambler maintains the distortion that he or she can control gambling behavior, including wagering, and can influence the results of games based entirely on chance or randomness.

Internet gambling: Most land-based forms of gambling, but especially casino games, are available on the Internet for potential use, abuse, and progression of compulsive gambling behaviors. The accessibility of Internet gambling increases the likelihood that more persons could develop problems with gambling.

Pathological gambling: In the *DSM–IV–TR*, pathological gambling was considered an impulse control disorder (APA, 2000). Because *pathological gambling* is the term most frequently used in the research literature, it is used throughout this chapter to discuss compulsive gambling, problem gambling, and *gambling addiction*, the term most often used in the self-help recovery community. *Gambling disorder* is the term presented in the *DSM–5* (APA, 2013).

Prevalence and Demographics

According to data considered in the preparation of the *DSM–5* (APA, 2013, p. 587), the past-year prevalence of gambling disorder was 0.2%–0.3% of the general population, with a lifetime prevalence of 0.4%–1.0%. Males (0.6%) were more likely to be diagnosed with the disorder than females (0.2%). Gambling disorder is estimated to be more prevalent among African Americans (0.9%) than Whites (0.4%) or Hispanics (0.3%). Age and gender contribute to two basic manifestations of pathological gambling in those who develop the disorder.

Younger and male gamblers are more likely to be impulsive, energetic, restless, and easily bored. There appear to be temperamental, genetic, and physiological risk factors with co-occurrence of alcohol use disorder, antisocial personality disorder, and early onset (APA, 2013, p. 588). When pathological gambling emerges in adolescence, some of these individuals will resolve problems with increasing age over time. Another manifestation or type of pathological gambling is more often encountered in older, female, and later-stage-of-progression gamblers. These individuals are depressed and lonely. They may feel helpless and guilty about their behavior. This type of gambler is less motivated by the high associated with risk taking and the excitement associated with the behavior. Instead, he or she continues to gamble with increasing distress and hardship in maladaptive attempts to escape from consequences and negative emotions (APA, 2013; Korman, Toneatto, & Skinner, 2010).

The pathogenesis or etiology of pathological gambling has a known course of development. The onset of some of the most serious cases begins in adolescence or young adulthood, with 10%–15% of children estimated to be at risk for pathological gambling (Hardoon & Derevensky, 2002). There is a gradual progression of consequences characterized by extent of losses, functional impairment, and concealment. The most rapid progression occurs in women at midlife. Pathological gamblers typically report problems with one or two types of gambling, but access to certain types of gambling (e.g., those associated with Internet gambling) may increase the number, frequency, and duration of gambling behaviors. Younger and male gamblers are most often involved in sports betting, cards, and horse racing, whereas older gamblers engage in games of chance, such as slot machines and bingo. Time spent in gambling and amounts of money wagered are not necessarily indicative of gambling disorder, as there are recreational and professional gamblers. Rather, extent of losses, distress, and impairment are the primary determinants of pathological gambling. Younger and male gamblers are the least likely to seek treatment. Older and female gamblers seek help more often and sooner, but treatment seeking is less than 10% among those with gambling disorder (APA, 2013; Korman et al., 2010).

Beginning in the mid-1990s Internet gambling led to dramatic increases in worldwide gambling. Internet gambling presents virtually all forms of traditional land-based gambling. In a study of Internet gambling (Wood & Williams, 2011), as many as 10.5% of individuals in the United Kingdom participated in at least one type of online gambling, with poker having the highest rate of participation (54.1%). Internet gamblers engaged in 4.1 types of gambling, whereas non-Internet gamblers engaged in 2.6 types. Online gamblers tended to be younger, male, single, and employed full time with a higher than average income (p. 1127). The study group presented higher rates of substance use disorders (13.0%) and addictive disorders (10.4%). Using the Canadian Problem Gambling Index, 16.4% of Internet gamblers could be classified as moderate to severe problem gamblers (p. 1129). Only 39.9% of Internet gamblers were classified as non–problem gamblers compared to 82.1% of non-Internet gamblers (p. 1129). Therefore, engaging in gambling on the Internet appears to hasten the progression of problems for some individuals (Wood & Williams, 2011).

Pathological gambling, which is known as *gambling disorder* in the *DSM–5* (APA, 2013), is a complex addictive disorder. Although it affects 1% or less of the population, pathological gambling produces significant problems for the individual, his or her family, and the community. Internet gambling has increased access to a range of opportunities for the problem to develop with increasing consequences. Errors in thinking lead to increased involvement in gambling behaviors in spite of negative consequences. Pathological gamblers lie or conceal their activities and chase losses by making larger bets in highly risky circumstances in a desperate attempt to regain money needed to keep playing. Pathological gambling co-occurs with other clinical disorders, including anxiety and depression; therefore, differential diagnosis is indicated. Nevertheless, pathological gambling produces emotional and behavioral symptoms and may lead to suicidal ideation. There are two major types of pathological gamblers: (a) younger male gamblers whose gambling behaviors involving games of skill may have started in adolescence or college and (b) older female gamblers whose gambling in games of chance progresses rapidly after manifesting at midlife. There are also other populations for whom pathological gambling has produced severe consequences in an unhealthy lifestyle.

SPECIAL POPULATIONS OF PATHOLOGICAL GAMBLERS

Several populations of pathological gamblers deserve special attention. The characteristics of these groups tend to support the differentiation of pathological gamblers into two major types: younger, male, and impulsive gamblers versus older, female, and later-stage-of-progression gamblers.

Trauma Survivors

A review of pathological gamblers in institutional, outpatient, and community treatment settings established a history of trauma in many individuals (Kausch, Rugle, & Rowland, 2006). For example, 64% of pathological gamblers in a gambling treatment program in a Veterans Affairs medical center reported a history of emotional trauma. In addition, 40.5% of the program participants reported physical abuse trauma and 24.3% reported sexual trauma. High-trauma patients in this treatment program were more depressed, anxious, and likely to abuse drugs and alcohol. In a related study that examined the co-occurrence of PTSD and substance use disorders in 20,611 veterans, 63% of women and 25% of men had experienced lifetime physical abuse, and 51% of women and 8% of men reported lifetime sexual abuse (Kausch et al., 2006).

In an outpatient treatment program for pathological gambling, reviewed by Kausch et al. (2006), 60% of women and 16% of men were diagnosed with PTSD and other mental disorders arising from sexual abuse. Moreover, 29% of pathological gamblers admitted to a private psychiatric treatment program reported physical and/or sexual abuse in childhood. Finally, 13% of GA members in the United States and Canada had been abused as a child.

Najavits et al. (2013) described a pilot outcome study in which her Seeking Safety therapy was implemented on an outpatient basis for PTSD and pathological gambling. PTSD is a prevalent disorder (it has a 7% lifetime rate in the general population), whereas pathological gambling is underreported and undiagnosed (Kessler et al., 2005; Najavits, 2010). Overall, PTSD is estimated to occur in 12.5%–29% of pathological gamblers in treatment for the disorder (Ledgerwood & Petry, 2006). Najavits (2010) estimated that a significant subset of pathological gamblers need treatment for underlying PTSD and can benefit from concurrent treatment when patient needs and preferences are carefully identified. Concurrent treatment of PTSD arising from a history of physical and/or sexual abuse and pathological gambling seems to be indicated, especially for women who present co-occurring mental disorders in inpatient and outpatient treatment settings.

Older Gamblers

Older (age 60 and over) veterans in a Veterans Affairs residential gambling treatment program had similar scores on the Addiction Severity Index to younger problem gamblers. They also evidenced about the same rates of co-occurring mental disorders as the younger cohort with lifetime histories of depression and suicidal ideation (Kausch, 2004). Active older adults (age 65 and older) given the South Oaks Gambling Screen (SOGS) presented lifetime rates of combined problem and pathological gambling of 10.6%–12.9% (Ladd, Molina, Kerins, & Petry, 2003). Three fourths of pathological gamblers older than age 60 in a community sample indicated an interest in gambling treatment because they feel depressed and lonely (Pietrzak & Petry, 2006).

It is likely that older pathological gamblers engage in sedentary games of chance to alleviate feelings of distress, including depression and anxiety. Their physical health and fitness may be impaired. Older gamblers progress toward troubling consequences as personal and financial losses increase. Nevertheless, this population may be amenable to treatment. They could be recruited from bingo halls, slot machine sites, and senior community centers.

Forensic Populations

Although antisocial personality disorder has been associated with gambling disorder, the prevalence of gambling in correctional facilities (40%) is lower than in the general population (94%; Shaffer, Hall, & Bilt, 1999). However, 50% of the crimes committed by pathological gamblers in this forensic population were reportedly committed to support gambling. Those in the forensic population who gamble attempt to gamble frequently and may represent problem gamblers in need of specialized treatment (Williams, Royston, & Hagen, 2005).

Gambling may not be tolerated in correctional facilities, with monitoring and disciplinary actions to reduce gambling behaviors. Yet it is likely that there is an active subset of pathological gamblers in adult correctional and juvenile justice settings. They may evade detection and gamble on games of chance and skill. Losses and debts in detention centers, jails, and prisons pose significant problems because of risks for coercion and aggression. Some pathological gamblers in forensic settings are experiencing the legal consequences of progressive losses in which they engage in illegal and criminal activity in order to continue gambling. Therefore, an intervention for pathological gambling might be especially warranted for some individuals.

DIAGNOSIS AND ASSESSMENT

A central diagnostic feature of gambling disorder is persistent, recurrent involvement in gambling behaviors in spite of financial hardships and interference with personal, family, educational, and career goals (Korman et al., 2010). The *DSM–5* diagnostic criteria for gambling disorder are as follows:

A. Persistent and recurrent problematic gambling behavior leading to clinically significant impairment or distress, as indicated by the individual exhibiting four (or more) of the following in a 12-month period:
   1. Needs to gamble with increasing amounts of money in order to achieve the desired excitement.
   2. Is restless or irritable when attempting to cut down or stop gambling.
   3. Has made repeated unsuccessful efforts to control, cut back, or stop gambling.
   4. Is often preoccupied with gambling (e.g., having persistent thoughts of reliving past gambling experiences, handicapping or planning the next venture, thinking of ways to get money with which to gamble).
   5. Often gambles when feeling distressed (e.g., helpless, guilty, anxious, depressed).
   6. After losing money gambling, often returns another day to get even ("chasing" one's losses).
   7. Lies to conceal the extent of involvement with gambling.
   8. Has jeopardized or lost a significant relationship, job, or educational or career opportunity because of gambling.
   9. Relies on others to provide money to relieve desperate financial situations caused by gambling.

Source. From *Diagnostic and Statistical Manual of Mental Disorders, Fifth Edition* (p. 585), by American Psychiatric Association, 2013, Arlington, VA: American Psychiatric Association. Copyright 2013 by the American Psychiatric Association. Reprinted with permission. All rights reserved.

The diagnosis of pathological gambling is rendered complex because of its frequent incidence with several comorbid or co-occurring disorders. There are high rates of comorbidity with mental disorders, such as substance use disorders, depressive disorders, anxiety disorders, and personality disorders (APA, 2013, p. 589). In particular, differential diagnosis must rule out poor judgment and excessive gambling associated with a manic episode, substance-related intoxication, and medical conditions such as Parkinson's disease that require dopaminergic medications. Finally, gambling disorder has been associated with poor general health, with symptoms of tachycardia and angina, even when tobacco use and other lifestyle disorders are controlled (APA, 2013, p. 589).

According to a comprehensive literature review conducted by Korman et al. (2010), comorbidity is a major concern in pathological gambling, with some issues arising prior to the onset of problem gambling, some issues concurrent with gambling disorder, and other conditions occurring as results or consequences of pathological gambling. Substance use disorders occur in approximately 50% of pathological gamblers. Anxiety disorders, including obsessive-compulsive disorder, agoraphobia, and panic, are more common in pathological gamblers than in the general population. For example, 72%–76% of pathological gamblers were found to suffer from depression, 93% met criteria for a personality disorder in descending rank order: obsessive compulsive (59%), borderline (57%), histrionic (54%), avoidant (50%), and narcissistic (47%). Moreover, 15%–40% of pathological gamblers met criteria for the diagnosis of antisocial personality disorder. Pathological gamblers with concurrent borderline personality disorder or antisocial personality disorder presented more psychosocial dysfunction, impulsivity, and severity of symptoms than other problem gamblers.

A systematic review and meta-analysis of population surveys established the prevalence of comorbid disorders in 11 rigorous studies identified between January 1998 and September 2010 (Lorains, Cowlishaw, & Thomas, 2011). The studies confirmed that the majority of pathological gamblers presented comorbid disorders. The highest mean prevalence was 60.1% for nicotine dependence, followed by substance use disorder (57.5%), any type of mood disorder (37.9%), and any type of anxiety disorder (37.4%; pp. 492–494). Because there were high prevalence rates for comorbid disorders, the reviewers recommended that treatments be tailored to subtypes of problem gamblers (p. 496).

Gambling disorder is manifested in episodic and persistent patterns. The severity of the disorder is estimated by the presence of symptoms: four or five diagnostic criteria (mild), six or seven criteria (moderate), or eight or nine criteria (severe). The most common symptoms of gambling disorder are preoccupation with gambling and chasing losses, characterized by an urgent need to keep gambling with even larger bets or heightened risks in order to undo a series of losses (APA, 2013, p. 586). Individuals who present severe gambling disorder rely on others to provide money to offset losses, lie or cover up gambling losses, and jeopardize relationships or career opportunities (APA, 2013, pp. 586–589). Some of these individuals may progress to forgery, fraud, theft, or embezzlement to conceal increasing financial consequences. There are major impacts on home and family life in cases of severe gambling, including foreclosure, repossession, bankruptcy, divorce, and homelessness.

Underlying gambling disorder is the core belief that money is the cause and solution of problems in life. There are distorted and maladaptive thoughts, including denial and minimization, superstitious and ritualistic behavior, an illusory sense of power or control over chance events, and overconfidence or grandiosity

(APA, 2013, p. 587). Accumulating consequences lead half of those in treatment to have suicidal ideation, and 17% have attempted suicide (p. 587).

Assessment of Pathological Gambling

Assessing pathological gambling begins with differentiating pathological gambling from professional and social/recreational gambling as well as brief periods of problem gambling that do not meet the diagnostic criteria for gambling disorder (APA, 2013). Next there should be careful assessment of potentially comorbid or co-occurring disorders. If the gambling behavior can be better explained by a manic episode, personality disorder, or substance intoxication, then the other mental disorder should be the primary focus of ongoing assessment. Additional psychological evaluation and/or psychosocial history may be indicated.

The clinical interview to specify the nature of pathological gambling should address the following concerns: criminal history, financial status, overall functional impairment, occupational and relational consequences, current social support, and history of suicidality (ideation, planning, and attempt). Several clinical interview formats have been used in assessment; however, they are based on *DSM–IV–TR* (APA, 2000) criteria: the Diagnostic Interview for Gambling Severity (Winters, Specker, & Stinchfield, 1997) and the Diagnostic Interview Schedule Pathological Gambling Module (Govoni, Frisch, & Stinchfield, 2001). Two additional instruments are frequently used to assess pathological gambling, especially in research studies.

The SOGS (Lesieur & Blume, 1987; Stinchfield, 2002) is one of the most frequently used self-report screening tools. The SOGS, a 20-item questionnaire, identifies "probable pathological gambling" with a score of five or more positive answers. The SOGS has been used in almost all problem gambling research in the United States (Young & Wohl, 2011). It has acceptable psychometric properties but produces a large number of false positives (Stinchfield, 2002; Thompson, Walker, Milton, & Djukic, 2005). The SOGS has been used with adolescents (Chiesi, Galli, & Primi, 2013), college students (Fortune & Goodie, 2010), veterans (Nelson & Oehlert, 2008), and gamblers from many countries (de Oliveira et al., 2009; Tang, Wu, Tang, & Yan, 2010; Vassar, 2008) Compared to the Diagnostic Interview for Gambling Severity, the SOGS seems to better fit *DSM–IV–TR* (APA, 2000) diagnostic criteria and to be more reliable, especially with college students (Fortune & Goodie, 2010).

The Canadian Problem Gambling Index is the other major self-report measure for assessing gambling behavior. This measure has 31 items in three sections: gambling involvement, problem gambling assessment, and correlates of problem gambling (Ferris & Wynne, 2001). It identifies five categories of gamblers: nongamblers, non–problem gamblers, low-risk gamblers, moderate-risk gamblers, and problem gamblers. Although the Canadian Problem Gambling Index incorporates items from the *DSM–IV–TR* (APA, 2000) and SOGS, it includes some items that address individual and community harm, which makes the assessment more problem centered in a public health model instead of addiction focused (Svetieva & Walker, 2008; Young & Wohl, 2011). The following are example items from the Canadian Problem Gambling Index:

1. Have you bet more than you could really afford to lose?
3. Have you gone back another day to try and win back the money you lost?
6. Have you felt that gambling has caused you health problems, including stress and anxiety?

7. Have people criticized your betting or told you that you have a gambling problem, whether or not you thought it was true? (Ferris & Wynne, 2001)

These items help clients self-assess their risk of problem gambling; however, an in-depth clinical interview conducted by a trained professional may be needed to accurately identify cases of pathological gambling or gambling disorder (Svetieva & Walker, 2008; Young & Wohl, 2011).

Several other instruments are useful in assessing the nature of pathological gambling. The following instruments measure attitudes and beliefs in disordered gambling: Gambling Attitudes Scale, Gambling Attitudes and Belief Survey, Gambler's Belief Questionnaire, and Gambling Self-Efficacy Questionnaire (Korman et al., 2010, p. 294). These scales are particularly relevant to targeting particular errors in thinking for treatment planning and cognitive–behavioral outcome studies.

Another cognition measurement has promise for the assessment of pathological gambling processes. The Gambling Related Cognitions Scale is a 23-item, well-validated tool for assessing particular cognitions across five factors: interpretive control/bias, illusion of control, predictive control, gambling-related expectancies, and perceived inability to stop gambling (Raylu & Oei, 2004). These five factors accounted for 70% of the total variance in scores in an exploratory factor analysis of the reliable and valid instrument (Raylu & Oei, 2004, p. 761). The Gambling Related Cognitions Scale has proven to be useful in screening for pathological gambling among community members as well as clinical populations.

A final scale, the University of Rhode Island Change Assessment (URICA), can be used to determine readiness for or amenability to treatment and to match interventions to the stage of change presented by potential clients (Petry, 2005a). The URICA-Gambling Scale was originally developed for use with incarcerated drug-using women, but it has application with a wide range of populations (El-Bassel et al., 1998). The 32 items are rated on a 5-point Likert scale from 1 (*strongly disagree*) to 5 (*strongly agree*).

The URICA-Gambling Scale is available for download and use from PsycTESTS, a database of the American Psychological Association (Petry, 2005b). The scale follows the stages of change model. Stages of change model concepts from the URICA are presented in Exhibit 7.1.

EMPIRICALLY SUPPORTED TREATMENTS

Previous literature reviews (e.g., Blaszczynski & Silove, 1995; Lopez-Viets & Miller, 1997) have established that gamblers responded well to treatments, with at least short-term abstinence from pathological gambling. Walker (1992) reviewed results from numerous studies using several treatments, including GA, psychotherapy, behavior therapy, and psychoanalysis. Across all modalities, 72% of participants were in control of their gambling behavior 6 months after treatment, 50% were in control at the 1-year follow-up, and 27% were in control at the 2-year posttreatment review (Walker, 1992). The uncontrolled nature of the studies included in the descriptive review hampered generalization and led to some improvements in subsequent studies.

EXHIBIT 7.1 URICA GAMBLING SCALE EXAMPLES

Precontemplation
The person does not think they have a problem or knows they do but does not want to change. They may feel pressure by others to seek treatment, may admit to a problem, but still have no desire to change.

Contemplation
The person is beginning to be aware that a problem exists. They are struggling to understand the problem and seeking information. However, there is no commitment to change.

Action
The person has actively begun to change their behavior or environment. They are struggling to change but have not been successful on their own and need help.

Maintenance
The person has changed and made significant gains; however, they are having difficulty maintaining changes (new behaviors and attitudes) and is seeking help.

Toneatto and Ladouceur (2003) identified from the Medline and PsycLIT databases 11 randomized controlled trials of treatments for problem or pathological gambling. Although they did not report effect sizes, the reviewed studies provided some empirical validation of effectiveness. The critical appraisal established that behavioral interventions resulted in improvements in 30%–50% of individuals receiving imaginal desensitization, aversion therapy, or imaginal relaxation (Toneatto & Ladouceur, 2003, pp. 285–286). Improvement included controlled gambling, in which there was an absence of impaired controlled and financial hardship. Three studies of exposure and response prevention, in which gamblers were exposed in vivo to slot machine play and required to exert stimulus control over gambling behavior, produced paradoxical results. Although there was some benefit from exposure and response prevention, which is a key component of relapse prevention, gamblers in a cognitive restructuring group and a control group showed considerable improvement. Apparently, the commitment to become involved in treatment and a willingness to explore the illusion of control produced benefits, including spontaneous remission (pp. 286–288).

Cognitive interventions resulted in fewer symptoms and diagnostic criteria, as well as improvement in self-efficacy expectation; however, dropout rates of up to 30% confound the determination of clinically significant change mechanisms (Toneatto & Ladouceur, 2003, p. 288). Pharmacological treatments were promising but limited because of the presence of side effects and placebo influences (pp. 288–289). Open-label trials of selective serotonin reuptake inhibitors reduced compulsive symptoms. Naltrexone, an opioid antagonist, reduced cravings and seemed to interfere with the powerful reinforcement values of gambling behavior.

Self-help approaches, involving treatment manuals with cognitive and behavioral techniques known to be potentially effective, produced some initial declines in problem gambling. However, the treatment gains were not maintained or were found not to differ significantly from the natural recovery occurring in the control groups (pp. 289–290).

Toneatto and Ladouceur (2003) offered a summary of key findings. They indicated that the generalizability of study results was affected by methodological flaws, including small sample sizes, lack of direct behavioral measures of gambling, inconsistency in treatment goals (from abstinence to controlled gambling), lack of follow-up, lack of process evaluations, and the assumption that pathological gamblers are a homogeneous group. They called for the construction of standardized treatment manuals and the careful selection of assessment tools and outcome measures. In addition, Toneatto and Ladouceur recommended that future treatments focus on subtypes of pathological gambling. Najavits (2003) offered specific recommendations for improving clinical outcome research that promise to address threats to internal and external validity.

Ledgerwood and Petry (2005) reviewed current trends and future directions in psychosocial treatments for pathological gambling. They listed a sample of studies ranging from descriptive accounts in which there was no comparison (or control) group to more rigorous research reports meeting basic standards for random assignment, sufficient sample size and power, and one or more comparison groups to establish treatment effects. Cognitive therapy and cognitive behavior therapy (CBT) conducted during the period 1991–2004 produced the best treatment outcomes compared to GA and self-help interventions (Ledgerwood & Petry, 2005).

GA, a peer-support self-help group based on the 12 steps and traditions of Alcoholics Anonymous, produced up to 48% abstinence 2 months into treatment; however, abstinence was 8% at the 1-year follow-up and 7% at the 2-year follow-up (Ledgerwood & Petry, 2005, pp. 89–91). Most participants (70%) dropped out after the 10th GA session. There was some evidence that GA attendance primed pathological gamblers to benefit from individual professional treatment through improving participation in therapy sessions and maintaining abstinence (pp. 90–91). Ledgerwood and Petry (2005) found one study in which self-guided treatment, using a self-help workbook, plus an initial telephone motivational interview decreased gambling problems. It appears that self-help approaches can be useful, particularly when they address ambivalence, resistance to change, and commitment to ongoing care (pp. 90–91).

Cognitive and behavioral approaches produced the best outcomes, with 75%–79% initial abstinence and 50%–69% abstinence at the 1-year follow-up (Ledgerwood & Petry, 2005, pp. 90–92). There were declines in diagnostic criteria, gambling symptom severity, and consequences of gambling. CBT helped gamblers identify particular gambling distortions, overall superstition, and misattributions. CBT also addressed nonaddictive coping and problem-solving skills, as well as psychoeducation about problems with gambling. Ledgerwood and Petry (2005) discussed how their integrative CBT model combined effective behavior change techniques into a treatment package. Their model emphasizes behavioral principles of functional analysis, stimulus control, and environmental contingency management (pp. 91–92). After the CBT therapist and patient complete a functional analysis of the antecedents, behaviors, and consequences, gamblers are taught to identify their gambling triggers, modify ruminative thoughts about gambling, overcome rationalizations and distortions, and examine selective recollections about past wins and losses. Finally, pathological gamblers are encouraged to restructure their environments to include more positive life events, including hobbies and social interactions (pp. 91–92).

Given the reluctance of most gambling addicts to seek treatment, it is difficult to conduct controlled outcome studies to determine effectiveness. A comprehensive review of treatment techniques (Korman et al., 2010) included a few randomized clinical trials or other studies in which treatments were empirically validated. Nevertheless, it is possible to identify treatments supported by some research data.

Cognitive and behavioral treatments have been used to effectively reduce gambling urges, frequency, and expenditures (Korman et al., 2010, pp. 294–295). There was empirical support for the following techniques: stimulus control, in vivo exposure and response prevention, cognitive restructuring, coping skills training, and problem solving. Emotion-based treatment was developed for emotionally vulnerable, out-of-control gamblers. Emotion-based treatment targeting anger reduction and emotion regulation was superior to CBT, which was treated as a therapy-as-usual control group. Korman et al. (2010) recommended concurrent treatment for comorbid conditions in order to enhance treatment efficacy. Comorbid or co-occurring diagnoses, such as depression, anxiety, substance use disorder, and personality disorder, should be assessed and targeted in treatment as moderating variables (p. 295).

Self-help approaches using treatment manuals or telephone support were found to be effective in enhancing motivation to change and reducing symptoms of pathological gambling (Korman et al., 2010, pp. 295–296). Although GA did not produce significant or long-lasting results, primarily because of high rates of attrition from the self-help group sessions, GA appeared to help with commitment to change, an important motivational factor (p. 296). GA produced the best results for members who had bottomed out or suffered the most severe consequences from gambling addiction or pathological gambling. Interventions consistent with the stages of change model may be required in the initial process of treatment (p. 297).

Several studies have supported the use of medications in treating pathological gambling (Korman et al., 2010, pp. 296–297). Antidepressants targeting serotonergic and dopaminergic neurotransmitter functioning have been used with some modest results, but the medications have not been approved for the treatment of pathological gambling. Anti-manic medications such as lithium have not yielded significant results in terms of affecting symptoms of pathological gambling. Naltrexone, which interferes with the rewarding aspects of gambling, has demonstrated some good results, with as many as 75% of one sample reporting decreases in urges and other symptoms (pp. 296–297). Additional research will be required to establish pharmacological treatments for gambling pathology.

Results of three major literature reviews have established some empirically supported and promising treatments (Korman et al., 2010; Ledgerwood & Petry, 2005; Toneatto & Ladouceur, 2003). Empirically supported treatments include the following:

- Behavioral treatments (stimulus control, exposure and response prevention)
- Cognitive–behavioral treatments (cognitive restructuring, motivational interviewing, relapse prevention, mindfulness therapy)
- Emotion-focused treatment (affect regulation)
- Self-help treatments (self-help manuals, GA)
- Pharmacotherapy (selective serotonin reuptake inhibitors, naltrexone, stimulants)
- Integrative treatment (individual, group, and family interventions; self-help and professional treatment; pharmacotherapy and psychotherapy)

Each of these empirically supported treatments can contribute something promising to an omnibus treatment package for pathological gambling and gambling disorder. A meta-analysis of various psychological treatments of pathological gambling (Pallesen, Mitsem, Kvale, Johnson, & Molde, 2005) established that self-help, eclectic, and cognitive–behavioral interventions produced significant outcome and follow-up effect sizes, especially when there were more therapy sessions and randomized clinical trials. It is possible to identify potentially effective components for treatment packages tailored to the needs of pathological gamblers encountered in clinical practice.

TREATMENT PACKAGES FOR PATHOLOGICAL GAMBLING

Based on evidence of beneficial outcomes, several components should be considered for inclusion in an omnibus or integrative treatment package. Although 10% or less of pathological gamblers seek treatment, those who reach out for help may have suffered severe emotional, financial, occupational, and familial consequences (*bottoming out* in the 12-step model). Gambling helplines, offered by nonprofit groups in some states, afford opportunities for pathological gamblers to seek assistance when they are acutely suffering.

Treatment Initiation

Treatment initiation frequently involves a telephone call to a gambling helpline, which serves as an essential frontline resource for intervention. The goal is to disrupt gambling behavior and refer the caller to a provider for assessment and initial treatment if indicated. In one study (Weinstock et al., 2011), more than 76% of callers accepted a referral, and 55% of all callers attended an in-person assessment appointment. More women than men called the helpline, but men were more likely to attend the assessment session. Women may have lacked transportation and child care resources. However, men who called usually faced severe losses, legal consequences, and coercion by family members. Utilization of assessment resources appeared to be a function of "warm transfer" rapport building and information giving by trained helpline staff, as well as offering the follow-up appointment at no charge within 72 hours (Weinstock et al., 2011, p. 377).

Another study carefully examined treatment initiation in gambling helpline callers (Ledgerwood et al., 2013). In this study, 67% of callers attended at least one treatment session (92.7% attending formal treatment and 28.1% attending peer-support group meetings). Callers were more likely to attend a follow-up interview if they had previously sought help for gambling problems (p. 35). The researchers verified the finding that men were more likely to follow up based on the severity of their financial problems and the encouragement of family members (p. 36). The 15- to 20-minute helpline contacts were effective in motivational enhancement, which appears to be an essential component of the treatment package.

Face-to-face and telephone counseling sessions emphasizing motivational interviewing (Miller & Rollnick, 2002; Prochaska & DiClemente, 1986) have demonstrated effectiveness in reducing total hours spent in gambling (effect size [d] = 0.89), percentage of total money gambling to income (d = 0.89), and scores on the Gambling Attitudes and Beliefs Survey (d = 0.78; Tse et al., 2013). There were no significant differences between the modes of delivery of the motivational enhancement (pp. 62–63). Each group (face-to-face with manualized motivational enhancement, or telephone counseling with manualized motivational enhancement) completed up to six counseling sessions based on an intervention manual: building rapport, raising insight/awareness, instilling hope, acknowledging feelings, setting goals, advising on budget management, and avoiding high-risk situations for relapse (p. 59). More than half of the study participants dropped out before completing the face-to-face or telephone sessions. Participants viewed both types of sessions as helpful and effective (p. 62). In this multisite, manualized treatment study, participants valued the opportunity to be matched with a counselor of the same ethnic background if they so wished (p. 62).

A clinical case study of a 36-year-old male gambler confirmed the value of a guided self-change approach (Lipinski, Whelan, & Meyers, 2007). The brief treatment involved five sessions focused on motivation building through cognitive–behavioral exercises. Gambling symptoms decreased, consistent with a harm reduction model for problem gambling behaviors. Brief intervention may help in initial treatment compliance and dropout prevention.

Treatment initiation is an important component of an integrative treatment package. Recent studies have established that helpline calls and telephone contacts could be effective in reducing harmful gambling behaviors or establishing abstinence from pathological gambling. Initial contacts are most effective for men facing severe consequences and family/legal coercion. Telephone contacts followed up with professional face-to-face interviews conducted by counselors matched with client types and needs may produce initial motivational benefit and postpone the tendency to drop out of treatment. Internet contacts, which may be preferred by electronic media/Internet gamblers, may be helpful in initiating treatment (Wood & Williams, 2011). Initial interventions should be based on motivational interviewing or motivational enhancement therapy, which has been implemented with many addictive disorders or process addictions.

Pharmacological Treatment

Although some may view pharmacological treatment as contraindicated in treating substance use and addictive disorders, there are a few promising medications for reducing urges and/or treating underlying emotional problems in pathological gambling (Korman et al., 2010; Toneatto & Ladouceur, 2003). Naltrexone was effective in reducing gambling urges and other symptoms (Grant, Kim, & Potenza, 2003). Although placebo-controlled trials of fluvoxamine, lithium, and valproate have not evidenced strong results (Korman et al., 2010), paroxetine (Paxil) was effective in an 8-week trial (Kim, Grant, Adson, Shin, & Zaninelli, 2002).

Bupropion (Wellbutrin) has been effective with a wide range of substance use and addictive disorders, including alcohol dependence, nicotine dependence, cocaine dependence, and excessive Internet use/game playing (Han & Renshaw, 2012, p. 690). Bupropion reduces compulsive behavior and improves mood in individuals presenting comorbid depression and addictive disorder (p. 690). The medication reduced symptoms of pathological gambling in one study (Dannon, Lowengrub, Musin, Gonopolski, & Kotler, 2005), but the promising results were not replicated in another (Black, 2004; Black et al., 2007). Antidepressants, such as paroxetine or bupropion, may be most helpful in helping depressed pathological gamblers improve their mood and modify the potential reinforcement or mood-altering excitement of gambling behavior.

Another pharmacological treatment study produced promising results for reducing gambling behaviors while demonstrating possible underlying physiological pathways for the impulsive, risk-taking subtype of pathological gambler most frequently encountered among younger, male gamblers, who may abuse alcohol or other substances (Zack & Poulos, 2009). Modafinil (Provigil), a wakefulness-promoting (sympathomimetic-like) agent used to treat narcolepsy and excessive daytime sleepiness, increases dopamine levels in the treatment of cocaine abuse and attention-deficit/hyperactivity disorder. Modafinil decreased desire to gamble, disinhibition, and risky decision making in high-impulsivity pathological gamblers engaged in slot machine gambling but actually increased the symptoms in low-impulsivity pathological gamblers (pp. 663–667). Consistency of the bidirectional effects on behavior, attention, and working memory suggests that the drug acts on a substrate that differentiates high- and low-impulsivity gamblers (p. 669).

Pharmacological treatment represents a promising adjunct to an integrative treatment package for pathological gambling. Naltrexone could be used to reduce the urge to gamble and early relapse. Failing to follow treatment recommendations and dropping out of potentially effective treatment may be functions of unmanageable urges and/or strong reinforcement values associated with gambling behavior. Among younger, more impulsive, early-onset males, modafinil or another stimulant could be helpful. Older, later onset women who present comorbid depression may benefit from the administration of paroxetine or bupropion. Pharmacological treatment could threaten a polyaddicted individual's recovery from especially the devastating substance use disorders. Therefore, the use of medications in early treatment for pathological gambling should be limited to those individuals who would be likely to maintain a strong recovery program.

GA and Self-Help

GA and self-help interventions (Ledgerwood & Petry, 2005) reflect another strong perspective in the treatment of pathological gambling. GA produces some immediate benefits in terms of abstinence from gambling addiction. GA enhances motivation to participate in treatment and primes a client to receive benefits from individual psychotherapy. However, most individuals drop out of GA, and those who remain in recovery for 1 or 2 years are likely to experience relapse. Therefore, GA is unlikely to be sufficient to produce long-term abstinence. Additional treatment is indicated.

Self-help approaches include completing step work in the Big Book of GA (GA, 2007), self-guided cognitive–behavioral exercises in a book (Hodgins, Currie, &

el-Guebaly, 2001; Lipinski et al., 2007), or homework exercises from an empirically supported treatment manual (Ladouceur & Lachance, 2007). These self-help approaches help the pathological gambler develop and maintain motivation, examine cognitive distortions and errors in thinking, and monitor gambling urges and behaviors. For many suffering addicts, completion online of the 20 questions of GA (GA, n.d.) begins the reflection and self-examination needed to enter recovery. Then behavioral and cognitive interventions can be introduced into the treatment package.

Cognitive–Behavioral Interventions

Cognitive and behavioral approaches produce good treatment outcomes at program completion and 1-year follow-up (Ledgerwood & Petry, 2005, pp. 90–92). Behavioral interventions, which tend to focus on skill development and environmental contingency management, help to bring compulsive gambling behavior under initial control (Korman et al., 2010). CBT helps the pathological gambler identify gambling distortions, especially the illusion of control (perceiving more personal control over events than is warranted by the facts). CBT also targets distortions related to the gambler's fallacy, or the belief that after a string of one event, such as a coin landing heads, an alternative event, such as the coin landing tails, becomes more likely in a genuinely chance environment (Goodie & Fortune, 2013). Another class of cognitive distortions represents gambling affinity, in which problem gamblers pursue betting strategies based on overestimation of their knowledge and skills (Goodie & Fortune, 2013). In the comprehensive CBT model, nonaddictive skills development and psychoeducation generally precede cognitive interventions.

Ledgerwood and Petry (2005) discussed how their integrative CBT model combines effective behavior change techniques into a treatment package. Their model emphasizes behavioral principles of functional analysis, stimulus control, and environmental contingency management (pp. 91–92). The client completes a functional analysis of the antecedents, behaviors, and consequences. Through a combination of therapist consultation and self-directed homework exercises, gamblers identify their gambling triggers, tolerate urges and negative emotions, prevent responses that would lead to reinforcement of gambling behavior, and practice in vivo alternative coping and decision making. In addition, gamblers are taught how to increase positive life events, including hobbies and social interactions (pp. 91–92).

Ladouceur and Lachance (2007) offered an empirically supported treatment manual with homework exercises for effective CBT treatment. At the outset of treatment, the client completes the Diagnostic Interview on Pathological Gambling (pp. 107–124) in order to specify problems and estimate their severity, raise awareness of change-worthy behaviors, and enhance motivation to continue the treatment process. The Diagnostic Interview addresses motivation for consultation, games that lead to partial or complete loss of control, information on the development of gambling habits, *DSM–IV–TR* (APA, 2000) diagnostic criteria, consequences of the gambling problem, suicidal ideation, current living conditions, other dependencies (present or past), mental health-prior experiences, strengths and available resources, and other comments. Information obtained in the interview assists in the functional analysis of gambling in the context of the overall lifestyle. The results of the interview help with differential diagnosis and clinical decision making regarding the treatment of comorbid disorders.

The next step in the integrative CBT treatment process is engaging the client in the Daily Self-Monitoring Diary (Ladouceur & Lachance, 2007, pp. 17–18) to measure the treatment process and outcomes, the Perceived Self-Efficacy Questionnaire (p. 16) to measure confidence in controlling gambling behaviors, and workbook exercises intended to enhance motivation through examination of consequences of gambling (pp. 25–27). Subsequent sessions initiate the behavior change process.

In general, pathological gamblers are taught how to effectively avoid high-risk situations, such as going to a casino and gambling through slot machines (Ladouceur & Lachance, 2007, pp. 33–36). Obviously it is desirable to avoid triggers and high-risk situations early in recovery. However, the treatment program also teaches gamblers how to refuse opportunities to gamble and how to use nonaddictive coping skills when exposed to triggers (pp. 33–38). Frequently, relationship difficulties elicit a chain of behaviors that lead to a gambling episode (pp. 38–39). However, the Overcoming Pathological Gambling program (Ladouceur & Lachance, 2007) does not directly address relationship issues in early relapse. Other triggers are targeted, such as having a lack of competing activities; consuming alcohol or drugs (i.e., disinhibition); and experiencing frustration, failure, or rejection. The integrative treatment program addresses problem solving, rational decision making, participation in self-help and help-seeking actions (e.g., attending GA), and careful specification of the chain of behaviors that lead to relapse in pathological gambling (pp. 42–46). Following this initial process of functional analysis and problem specification, the cognitive interventions are implemented.

Cognitive interventions in the Overcoming Pathological Gambling program (Ladouceur & Lachance, 2007) include seven sessions and corresponding homework assignments. Program participants continue to self-monitor using the Daily Self-Monitoring Diary, focusing on relating cognitive distortions to triggers, urges, and slips. In order to neutralize, refute, or test out distorted beliefs, the therapist asks clients to evaluate their ability to outsmart chance, estimate chances of winning, determine whether they are applying strategies or rituals to win, and use superstitions and premonitions (Ladouceur & Lachance, 2007, p. 50). One beneficial intervention involves carefully analyzing a gambling session. Additional sessions involve psychoeducation regarding the concept of chance, overconfidence and overestimation of skill, and avoiding gambling traps in which distortions lead gamblers to engage in particular actions in a futile attempt to control chance events.

Using the ABCD model, clients learn how to accurately assess high-risk situations and self-manage behaviors (Ladouceur & Lachance, 2007, pp. 58–60). Illusions of control, some particular to games such as slot machines, are explored and refuted in depth (pp. 67–71). Remaining sessions in confronting cognitive distortions help the recovering gambler improve his or her decision-making skills. The final section of the empirically supported treatment package addresses relapse prevention.

Relapse prevention involves additional skill building to self-manage ongoing behavior change. The sessions and homework exercises address each client's unique cycle of behaviors that could lead to a slip or a full-blown relapse, such as a gambling binge. The pathological gambler learns to identify risky situations and decisions that constitute warning signs. Next the recovering gambler develops tools for managing a slip, enacting emergency measures, and returning to abstinence. At the close of the treatment process, program participants complete a posttreatment assessment to document personal change and to facilitate ongoing outcome evaluation.

The Overcoming Pathological Gambling program (Ladouceur & Lachance, 2007) represents a comprehensive treatment package that has empirical support and clinical relevance. The treatment package includes ongoing monitoring and outcome evaluation with the following treatment components: motivational enhancement, behavioral interventions, cognitive interventions, and relapse prevention. Depending on the needs of the pathological gambler, the integrative treatment approach for pathological gambling will likely incorporate treatment initiation strategies and participation in self-help efforts such as GA. Pharmacological treatment may be indicated for pathological gamblers who are unable to quit gambling or who experience severe comorbid disorders, such as depression or PTSD. Although the basic CBT package will assist most gamblers in establishing abstinence or reducing harm in gambling behaviors, some clients will require specialized treatment.

CONCURRENT TREATMENT OF TRAUMA AND PATHOLOGICAL GAMBLING

A significant subset of pathological gamblers experience unresolved life trauma, which contributes to relapse in recovery for pathological gambling. Unresolved trauma also contributes to the severity of comorbid conditions, especially substance use disorders (Kausch et al., 2006). It is likely that women who develop pathological gambling later in life present histories of emotional, physical, and sexual trauma (Kausch et al., 2006; Ledgerwood & Petry, 2006; Najavits, 2010; Najavits et al., 2013). The concurrent treatment of trauma and pathological gambling produces better outcomes for many women gamblers.

Seeking Safety is an evidence-based treatment program for concurrent treatment of PTSD and addiction (Najavits, 2002). Twenty-four outcome studies, including randomized controlled trials, have established the efficacy of Seeking Safety with women and men from various ethnic and socioeconomic backgrounds in treatment for PTSD and addictive disorders (Najavits, 2009). Seeking Safety may be administered in individual and group formats in inpatient, residential, and outpatient settings. The program develops coping skills and emotion regulation through psychoeducation, therapy, and homework exercises. Seeking Safety addresses 25 topics in the treatment manual and client worksheets, including safety, asking for help, setting boundaries in relationships, getting others to support recovery, healthy relationships, compassion, creating meaning, coping with triggers, self-nurturing, and detaching from emotional pain (grounding).

All 25 topics were offered in a 6-month period to male and female patients in a pilot study (Najavits et al., 2013). This was the first trial of Seeking Safety for concurrent treatment of pathological gambling and PTSD. The trial resulted in improvements in PTSD/trauma; anxiety, dissociation, and sex problems; benevolent views; psychopathology; addiction severity; and gambling cognitions and behaviors (pp. 13–15). Results were best for clients who participated in the most sessions and who developed a strong helping (therapeutic) alliance (p. 15). Attendance was excellent in this concurrent treatment model for comorbid PTSD and pathological gambling. Seeking Safety enjoyed high acceptability, and attendance at sessions was excellent. Therapist adherence with the manualized treatment program was maintained through a review of session videotapes.

Najavits (2010) explored treatment preferences for another group of 106 people with PTSD and pathological gambling. PTSD treatments were rated higher than pathological gambling components. Among pathological gambling treatments, self-help interventions, including the use of books and homework, were highly valued. Individual therapy was preferred over group therapy. Medications were rated lower than other treatment types. Additional components available for individually tailored treatment packages include computerized treatment, coaching, family therapy, and alternative therapies.

Mindfulness-based interventions represent a very promising treatment for emotion regulation and distress tolerance in concurrent treatment approaches. If behavior therapy represents the first wave in treatment for pathological gambling, and cognitive therapy the second wave, then mindfulness approaches reflect the third wave of treatment innovations (Hayes, Follette, & Linehan, 2004). Mindfulness therapy may supplement cognitive–behavioral interventions in order to improve relapse prevention through focus on the process of thinking rather than the content of cognitive errors (Sauer & Baer, 2009). The process of being mindful involves letting go of preoccupations in order to observe the body and mind and accept changes in moment-to-moment experiencing. Five facets of mindfulness therapy include nonreactivity to inner experience, observing and attending to sensations and perceptions, acting with awareness, describing with words, and nonjudging of experience (Baer, Smith, Hopkins, Kreitemeyer, & Toney, 2006). Although there has been no randomized controlled study to establish the efficacy of mindfulness therapy for pathological gambling, Segal, Williams, and Teasdale (2002) reported good results for mindfulness-based cognitive therapy applied to problem gambling (de Lisle, Dowling, & Allen, 2011). Mindfulness meditation reduces automatic gambling behaviors and assists problem gamblers in observing cognitive errors and problem emotions rather than engaging in habitual behavior patterns. The utility of mindfulness meditation suggests that other alternative therapies, such as yoga or movement therapy, may be helpful in treatment-resistant cases of pathological gambling.

A neglected treatment component of the prevalent CBT approaches for pathological gambling is couples/family therapy. Pathological gambling has many effects on the family system, requiring an integrative treatment approach involving biological, psychological, social, spiritual, economic, and environmental contexts (Grant Kalischuck, Nowatzki, Cardwell, Klein, & Solowoniuk, 2006). There are problems in parental bonding with children, who may experience pervasive loss (Darbyshire, Oster, & Carrig, 2001; Grant & Kim, 2002). Spouses and partners of pathological gamblers experience a wide range of addictive and mental disorders as well as relationship difficulties and domestic violence (Grant Kalischuck, 2010). Couples and family therapy are needed to deal with secrecy, deception, manipulation, neglect, and abuse. In addition, spouses and partners contribute to triggers for compulsive gambling and relapse after treatment for pathological gambling (Grant Kalischuck, 2010).

A grounded theory study of themes among family members of problem gamblers identified the following impacts: trauma and trigger (the *problem gambling platform*), transition, tension and turmoil, transcendence, and termination (Grant Kalischuck, 2010). Couples therapy has been adapted to specifically address the interpersonal problems and consequences of pathological gambling (Bertrand, Dufour, Wright, & Lasnier, 2008). Many women who are pathological gamblers will require couples therapy to stabilize the home environment, reduce complementary substance use and mental disorders, educate family members about the recovery process, and prevent relapse. Female trauma survivors who develop pathological gambling to cope with the consequences of neglect, physical abuse, or sexual abuse will benefit from couples and family therapy. Relational therapy will help to protect children, promote parental bonding, and mitigate against an intergenerational pattern of trauma and addiction.

INTEGRATIVE TREATMENT IN THE CASE OF SARAH

Sarah was motivated to see her family doctor and accept a referral to a therapist after she bottomed out in her pathological gambling and experienced negative emotional consequences from compulsive sexual behavior. Sarah's therapist suggested that she had temporarily fixed her feelings by engaging in sexual addiction. The therapist indicated that Sarah would probably return to a pattern of self-injurious behavior not manifested since adolescence if her underlying sexual abuse trauma was not addressed. The therapist increased awareness of the severity of the unresolved trauma by emphasizing the function of compulsive behaviors in Sarah's particular firing order of addictions. Over the course of several weeks, the Prozac prescribed by her doctor helped Sarah deal with urges to gamble and act out sexually. Her mood improved and she committed to a course of integrative treatment.

Sarah continued taking Prozac and visited GA. She felt like a guy at the GA meeting was being seductive (i.e., "trying to Thirteenth Step me"), so she decided to attend meetings online. At times she felt tempted to visit hookup and role-playing sites on the Internet, but she used grounding and containment techniques taught by her therapist as well as mindfulness meditation she practiced in the office. Sarah completed the Diagnostic Interview on Pathological Gambling and began keeping the Daily Self-Monitoring Diary. Her therapist estimated the severity of her gambling disorder as 8, or severe. Sarah completed psychoeducational sessions, CBT, and homework exercises from the Overcoming Pathological Gambling program. She focused on cognitive distortions that maintained compulsive slot machine gambling, including the gambler's fallacy and illusion of control. Sarah reported a history of magical thinking, superstitions, and rituals that extended back to her days of immersion in compulsive fantasy (role-playing) games on the Internet as a college student. She recalled how she had met her husband during this period and he had "pulled me out of my fog" in an intense sexual courtship. After 7 weeks of abstinence from pathological gambling and compulsive sexual behavior, Sarah was encouraged to begin Seeking Safety in twice-weekly individual therapy sessions. She continued her pharmacological treatment and GA recovery. Sarah was engaged in reading the GA Big Book and working the steps toward recovery.

Seeking Safety helped Sarah to see that she was not alone in recovering from pathological gambling and sexual abuse trauma. She completed the worksheets and worked with her therapist to maintain boundaries while slowly exposing herself to the reality of the date rape. She recalled that there had been some earlier abuse incidents in elementary school when an older boy would secretly touch her body under her clothes. She always felt ashamed and awkward around peers. She blamed herself for the date rape, but her therapist assisted her in examining mistaken beliefs and misattributions arising from a history of sexual abuse. Slowly Sarah developed a more resilient sense of self. As she addressed her trauma issues, Sarah noted that urges to act out through gambling returned. However, she was able to use nonaddictive coping skills, the ABCD model, and mindfulness approaches to avoid relapse. Sarah began to yearn for a stronger relationship with her husband and asked her therapist to work with her on intimacy issues.

The therapist conducted a collateral contact interview with the husband, who remarked that he was pleased and surprised by Sarah's progress in overcoming pathological gambling. The therapist discussed with the husband the ongoing treatment for sexual abuse trauma. The husband was aware of the date rape but did not understand how the PTSD was related to the compulsive gambling. At this stage in her recovery, Sarah and her therapist decided to postpone disclosure until she worked her steps in the spiritual growth process of GA. Sarah and her husband committed to beginning once-weekly couples therapy sessions with a male colleague of her therapist.

The couples therapy addressed improvements in communication and emotional intimacy. Slowly they progressed toward physical and sexual intimacy. Sarah's husband expressed regret from withdrawing from his work and admitted that he had had some one-night stands while spending weekends with his guard unit. Sarah admitted her recent sexual binges. The therapist maintained the holding environment of the therapeutic alliance and reassured the couple that they could work through their shame and pain. The therapist helped them to see that each responded to the demands of intimacy by withdrawing to work or fantasy, becoming preoccupied with emergency conditions, or seeking soothing in intense sexual contacts. Sarah and her husband collaborated in establishing new relational boundaries, recovering a satisfying sex life, and pursuing shared spiritual activities.

Sarah's treatment can be characterized by concurrent holistic and intensive treatments aimed at addressing her compulsive gambling and sexual behavior and maintenance of abstinence. Treatment initiation enhanced motivation and laid the foundation for effective CBT. Furthermore, Sarah found her medication and mindfulness meditation to be essential to avoiding relapse in early recovery.

Although there was substantial upheaval during the period of disclosing and working through extramarital affairs, the breech in the relationship established Sarah's resilience, overall improvement, and readiness for increasing intimacy in her marriage. She was able to use internal skills and external boundaries to prevent relapse and move toward genuine intimacy in a fulfilling relationship with her husband, who similarly benefited from the process in overcoming his complementary work addiction. They exited the fog of addition and embraced together the promises of recovery.

CONCLUSIONS

Pathological gambling, treated as an impulse control disorder in the *DSM–IV–TR* (APA, 2000), fits the criteria for an addictive disorder or process addiction. The contemporary term *gambling disorder,* included in the *DSM–5* (APA, 2013), will be the future search term for research studies and clinical reports. Although the prevalence of gambling disorder is 1.0% or less, pathological gambling produces severe consequences for individuals and families.

Younger and male gamblers present temperamental risk factors that predispose them to substance use disorders and antisocial personality disorder. Some of these pathological gamblers age out of the disorder, whereas others progress to later stages in which chasing losses and avoiding negative emotions maintain the risky gambling behavior. Another type of pathological gambling is found among older, female, and later-stage-of-progression gamblers. In this type, there is a greater likelihood of trauma history, comorbid mental disorders, and involvement in sedentary games of chance. Internet gambling may increase the prevalence and severity of gambling problems in the population.

Pathological gamblers exhibit cognitive distortions that maintain compulsive gambling in spite of financial losses and interpersonal consequences. Three major categories of cognitive distortions must be addressed in treatment: gambling affinity, gambler's fallacy, and the illusion of control. Given the centrality of cognitive distortions in pathological gambling, cognitive interventions are essential to treatment. Cognitive and behavioral approaches produced the best outcomes in treatment, with 75%–79% of clients achieving initial abstinence and 50%–69% maintaining abstinence at the 1-year follow-up (Ledgerwood & Petry, 2005).

GA, a self-help group based on the 12 steps and 12 traditions of Alcoholics Anonymous, appears to assist out-of-control gamblers achieve abstinence in the early months of recovery. However, the outcome research literature (Korman et al., 2010) indicates that most participants drop out after 10 sessions. Nevertheless, participation in GA may serve a priming function in that it encourages gamblers to seek and continue professional treatment.

Early abstinence in pathological gambling requires attention to motivational enhancement. Treatment initiation approaches that work include gambling helpline calls, motivational interviewing, and initiation of self-monitoring and homework exercises. Internet gamblers may prefer online treatment initiation, whereas older gamblers can be motivated through outreach contacts at senior centers, bingo parlors, or casinos.

Pathological gamblers who cannot achieve abstinence goals may benefit from pharmacological treatment. Bupropion (Wellbutrin) has shown some potential for helping gamblers who struggle with comorbid mood disorders. Younger and male gamblers may benefit from a trial of modafinil (Provigil), a wakefulness-promoting agent. Naltrexone has been used with some good results (Korman et al., 2010).

Effective treatment of pathological gambling requires implementation of a treatment package tailored to the needs of the individual and his or her family. The Overcoming Pathological Gambling program (Ladouceur & Lachance, 2007) was explored in depth here in order to specify behavioral interventions, including exposure and response prevention and environmental contingency management, and cognitive therapy components. The treatment package requires attention to relapse prevention and transitioning from therapist direction to self-management of behavior change in the natural environment.

Although the basic CBT package assists most pathological gamblers in establishing abstinence, some clients require concurrent treatment of gambling disorder and comorbid disorders, most frequently depression and PTSD. Seeking Safety, a manualized treatment program (Najavits, 2002), has produced beneficial outcomes in treating addictive disorders and PTSD. There has been a promising pilot testing of Seeking Safety with pathological gamblers who suffer with symptoms of PTSD (Najavits et al., 2013). Seeking Safety is a concurrent treatment package that can reduce the risk of relapse in pathological gambling by attending to the emotional and relational consequences of unresolved life trauma.

Neglected components of most treatment packages for pathological gambling include couples/family therapy and mindfulness therapy, an alternative therapy approach. The case of Sarah was presented in order to indicate helpful components of a treatment package for pathological gambling. Marital therapy and mindfulness-based exercises augmented the empirically supported cognitive–behavioral interventions used in her case.

Pathological gambling or gambling disorder can be treated effectively in most clients by implementing the best practices of cognitive–behavioral interventions. The treatment package must be tailored to individual needs. Most pathological gamblers benefit from treatment initiation and self-help approaches. Participation in GA meetings enhances commitment to change and increases the likelihood of completing professional treatment, especially individual therapy. Pharmacological interventions, which are not preferred by most recovering clients, should be reserved for clients who cannot manage urges or maintain abstinence. Relational techniques and alternative treatments hold promise for integration of new approaches. Randomized controlled trials and meta-analyses will establish best practices for the treatment of gambling disorder in the future.

RESOURCES

Websites

Canadian Problem Gambling Index
   http://classes.uleth.ca/201201/hlsc3700a/The%20Canadian%20Problem%20Gambling%20Index.pdf
Evergreen Council on Problem Gambling
   www.evergreencpg.org/training/
Gam-Anon
   www.gam-anon.org
Gamblers Anonymous
   www.gamblersanonymous.org
Gamblers Anonymous, 20 Questions: Are You a Compulsive Gambler?
   www.gamblersanonymous.org/ga/content/20-questions
Gambling Addiction
   www.gamblingaddiction.org
Motivational Interviewing Training
   www.motivationalinterviewingtraining.com
National Council on Problem Gambling
   www.ncpgambling.org
Northwest Frontier Addiction Technology Treatment Center Guide to Gambling Addiction
   www.nfattc.org
Problem Gambling Helpline
   www.ncpgambling.org/programs-resources/resources/

Seeking Safety
  http://www.seekingsafety.org
University of California at Los Angeles Gambling Studies Program
  http://www.uclagamblingprogram.org

Books

Ladouceur, R., & Lachance, S. (2007). *Overcoming your pathological gambling: Workbook.* New York, NY: Oxford University Press.

Videos

Compulsive Gambling and Addiction
  http://www.nyproblemgambling.org/resources/videos
Gambling Addiction
  http://www.problemgamblingguide.com/gambling_addiction_videos.html
Gambling Addiction in America
  http://www.cbsnews.com/video/watch/?id=3438648n
Mindfulness for Life: An Interview With Jon Kabat-Zinn
  http://www.psychotherapy.net/video/Mindfulness-Kabat-Zinn
Motivational Interviewing
  http://www.motivationalinterview.org/
Problem Gambling
  http://www.apa.org/pubs/videos/4310738.aspx
Stages of Change for Addictions
  http://www.psychotherapy.net/video/norcross-stages-change-addictions

REFERENCES

American Psychiatric Association. (2000). *Diagnostic and statistical manual of mental disorders* (4th ed., text rev.). Washington, DC: Author.

American Psychiatric Association. (2013). *Diagnostic and statistical manual of mental disorders* (5th ed.). Arlington, VA: Author.

Baer, R. A., Smith, G. T., Hopkins, J., Kreitemeyer, J., & Toney, L. (2006). Using self-report measures to explore facets of mindfulness. *Assessment, 13,* 27–45.

Bertrand, K., Dufour, M., Wright, L., & Lasnier, B. (2008). Adapted couple therapy (ACT) for pathological gamblers: A promising avenue. *Journal of Gambling Studies, 24,* 390–409.

Black, D. W. (2004). An open-label trial of bupropion in the treatment of pathological gambling. *Journal of Clinical Psychopharmacology, 24,* 108–110.

Black, D. W., Arndt, S., Coryell, W. H., Argo, T., Forbush, K. T., Shaw, M. C., . . . Allen, J. (2007). Bupropion in the treatment of pathological gambling: A randomized, double-blind, placebo-controlled, flexible-dose study. *Journal of Clinical Psychopharmacology, 27,* 143–150.

Blaszczynski, A., & Silove, D. (1995). Cognitive and behavioral therapies of pathological gambling. *Journal of Gambling Studies, 11,* 195–219.

Chiesi, F. D., Galli, M. A., & Primi, C. (2013). The suitability of the South Oaks Gambling Screen–Revised for Adolescents (SOGS-RA) as a screening tool: IRT evidence. *Psychology of Addictive Behaviors, 27,* 287–293.

Dannon, P. N., Lowengrub, K., Musin, E., Gonopolski, Y., & Kotler, M. (2005). Sustained-release bupropion versus naltrexone in the treatment of pathological gambling: A preliminary blind-rater study. *Journal of Clinical Psychopharmacology, 25,* 593–596.

Darbyshire, P., Oster, C., & Carrig, H. (2001). The experience of pervasive loss: Children and young people living in a family where parental gambling is a problem. *Journal of Gambling Studies, 17,* 23–45.

de Lisle, S. M., Dowling, N. A., & Allen, J. S. (2011). Mindfulness-based cognitive therapy for problem gambling. *Clinical Case Studies, 10*(3), 210–228.

de Oliveira, M. P., de Carvalho, D. X., Collakis, S. V. B., Bizeto, S. T., Silva, J., & Araujo, M. T. (2009). Reliability, validity and classification of the South Oaks Gambling Screen in a Brazilian sample. *Journal of Gambling Studies, 25,* 557–568.

El-Bassel, N., Schilling, R. F., Ivanoff, A., Chen, D., Hanson, M., & Bidassie, B. (1998). Stages of change profiles among incarcerated drug-using women. *Addictive Behaviors, 23,* 389–394.

Ferris, J., & Wynne, H. (2001). *The Canadian Problem Gambling Index: Final report.* Ottawa, Ontario, Canada: Canadian Centre on Substance Abuse.

Fortune, E. E., & Goodie, A. S. (2010). Comparing the utility of a modified Diagnostic Interview for Gambling Severity (DIGS) with the South Oaks Gambling Screen (SOGS) as a research screen in college students. *Journal of Gambling Studies, 26,* 639–644.

Gamblers Anonymous. (n.d.). *20 questions: Are you a compulsive gambler?* Retrieved from www.gamblersanonymous.org/ga/content/20-questions

Gamblers Anonymous. (2007). *GA: Sharing recovery through Gamblers Anonymous.* Los Angeles, CA: Author.

Goodie, A. S., & Fortune, E. E. (2013). Measuring cognitive distortions in pathological gambling: Review and meta-analysis. *Psychology of Addictive Behaviors, 27,* 730–743. doi:10.1037/a0031892

Govoni, R., Frisch, G., & Stinchfield, R. (2001). *A critical review of screening and assessment instruments for problem gambling.* Windsor, Ontario, Canada: University of Windsor Problem Gambling Research Group.

Grant, J. E., & Kim, S. W. (2002). Parental bonding in pathological gambling disorder. *Psychiatric Quarterly, 73,* 239–247.

Grant, J. E., Kim, S. W., & Potenza, M. N. (2003). Advances in the pharmacological treatment of pathological gambling. *Journal of Gambling Studies, 19,* 85–109.

Grant Kalischuck, R. (2010). Cocreating life pathways: Problem gambling and its impact on families. *The Family Journal: Therapy for Couples and Families, 18,* 7–17.

Grant Kalischuck, R., Nowatzki, N., Cardwell, K., Klein, K. K., & Solowoniuk, J. (2006). Problem gambling and its impact on families: A literature review. *International Gambling Studies, 6,* 31–60.

Han, D. H., & Renshaw, P. F. (2012). Bupropion in the treatment of problematic online game play in patients with major depressive disorder. *Journal of Psychopharmacology, 26,* 689–696.

Hardoon, K. K., & Derevensky, J. L. (2002). Child and adolescent gambling behavior: Current knowledge. *Clinical Child Psychology & Psychiatry, 7,* 263–281.

Hayes, S. C., Follette, V. M., & Linehan, M. M. (Eds.). (2004). *Mindfulness and acceptance: Expanding the cognitive tradition.* New York, NY: Guilford Press.

Hodgins, D. C., Currie, S. R., & el-Guebaly, N. (2001). Motivational enhancement and self-help treatments for problem gambling. *Journal of Consulting and Clinical Psychology, 69,* 50–57.

Kausch, O. (2004). Pathological gambling among elderly veterans. *Journal of Geriatric Psychiatry and Neurology, 17,* 13–19.

Kausch, O., Rugle, L., & Rowland, D. Y. (2006). Lifetime histories of trauma among pathological gamblers. *American Journal on Addictions, 15,* 35–43.

Kessler, R. C., Berglund, P., Demler, O., Jin, R., Merikangas, K. R., & Walters, E. E. (2005). Lifetime prevalence and age-of-onset distributions of *DSM–IV* disorders in the National Comorbidity Survey Replication. *Archives of General Psychiatry, 62,* 593–602.

Kim, S. W., Grant, J. E., Adson, D. E., Shin, Y. C., & Zaninelli, R. (2002). A double-blind placebo-controlled study of the efficacy and safety of paroxetine in the treatment of pathological gambling. *Journal of Clinical Psychiatry, 63,* 501–507.

Korman, L. M., Toneatto, T., & Skinner, W. (2010). Pathological gambling. In J. E. Fisher & W. T. O'Donohue (Eds.), *Practitioner's guide to evidence-based psychotherapy* (pp. 291–300). New York, NY: Springer.

Ladd, G. T., Molina, C. A., Kerins, G. J., & Petry, N. M. (2003). Gambling participation and problems among older adults. *Journal of Geriatric Psychiatry and Neurology, 16,* 172–177.

Ladouceur, R., & Lachance, S. (2007). *Overcoming pathological gambling: Therapist guide.* New York, NY: Oxford University Press.

Ledgerwood, D. M., Arfken, C. L., Wiedermann, A., Bates, K. E., Holmes, D., & Jones, L. (2013). Who goes to treatment? Predictors of treatment initiation among gambling help-line callers. *American Journal on Addictions, 22,* 33–38.

Ledgerwood, D. M., & Petry, N. M. (2005). Current trends and future directions in the study of psychosocial treatments for pathological gambling. *Current Directions in Psychological Science, 14,* 89–94.

Ledgerwood, D. M., & Petry, N. M. (2006). Psychological experience of gambling and subtypes of pathological gamblers. *Psychiatry Research, 144*(1), 17–27.

Lesieur, H., & Blume, S. (1987). The South Oaks Gambling Screen: A new instrument for the identification of pathological gamblers. *American Journal of Psychiatry, 144,* 1184–1188.

Lipinski, D., Whelan, J. P., & Meyers, A. W. (2007). Treatment of pathological gambling using a guided self-change approach. *Clinical Case Studies, 6,* 394–411.

Lopez-Viets, V. C., & Miller, W. R. (1997). Treatment approaches for pathological gamblers. *Clinical Psychology Review, 17,* 689–702.

Lorains, F. K., Cowlishaw, S., & Thomas, S. A. (2011). Prevalence of comorbid disorders in problem and pathological gambling: Systemic review and meta-analysis of population surveys. *Addiction, 106,* 490–498.

Miller, W. R., & Rollnick, S. (2002). *Motivational interviewing: Preparing people to change addictive behavior* (2nd ed.). New York, NY: Guilford Press.

Najavits, L. M. (2002). *Seeking Safety: A treatment manual for PTSD and substance abuse.* New York, NY: Guilford Press.

Najavits, L. M. (2003). How to design an effective treatment outcome study. *Journal of Gambling Studies, 19,* 317–337.

Najavits, L. M. (2009). *Seeking Safety: An implementation guide—The clinician's guide to evidence-based practice.* Hoboken, NJ: Wiley.

Najavits, L. M. (2010). Treatments for PTSD and pathological gambling: What do patients want? *Journal of Gambling Studies, 27,* 229–241.

Najavits, L. M., Smylie, D., Johnson, K., Lung, J., Gallop, R. J., & Classen, C. C. (2013). Seeking Safety therapy for pathological gambling and PTSD: A pilot outcome study. *Journal of Psychoactive Drugs, 45*(1), 10–16.

Nelson, K. G., & Oehlert, M. E. (2008). Evaluation of a shortened South Oaks Gambling Screen in veterans with addictions. *Psychology of Addictive Behaviors, 22*(2), 309–312.

Pallesen, S., Mitsem, M., Kvale, G., Johnson, B., & Molde, H. (2005). Outcome of psychological treatments of pathological gambling: A review and meta-analysis. *Addiction, 100,* 1412–1422.

Petry, N. M. (2005a). Stages of change in treatment-seeking pathological gamblers. *Journal of Consulting and Clinical Psychology, 73*(2), 312–322.

Petry, N.M. (2005b). *URICA-Gambling Scale.* Retrieved from http://www.apa.org/pubs/databases/psyctests/

Pietrzak, R. H., & Petry, N. M. (2006). Severity of gambling problems and psychosocial functioning in older adults. *Journal of Geriatric Psychiatry and Neurology, 19,* 106–113.

Prochaska, J. O., & DiClemente, C. C. (1986). Toward a comprehensive model of change. In W. R. Miller & N. Heather (Eds.), *Treating addictive behaviors: Processes of change* (pp. 3–27). New York, NY: Plenum Press.

Raylu, N., & Oei, T. P. (2004). The Gambling Related Cognitions Scale (GRCS): Development, confirmatory factor validation and psychometric properties. *Addiction, 99,* 757–769.

Sauer, S. E., & Baer, R. (2009). Responding to negative internal experience: Relationships between acceptance and change-based approaches and psychological adjustment. *Journal of Psychopathology and Behavioral Assessment, 31,* 378–386.

Segal, Z. V., Williams, J. M. G., & Teasdale, J. D. (2002). *Mindfulness-based cognitive therapy: A new approach to preventing relapse.* New York, NY: Guilford Press.

Shaffer, H. J., Hall, M. N., & Bilt, J. V. (1999). Estimating the prevalence of disordered gambling behavior in the United States and Canada. *American Journal of Public Health, 89,* 1369–1376.

Stinchfield, R. (2002). Reliability, validity, and classification accuracy of the South Oaks Gambling Screen (SOGS). *Addictive Behaviors, 27,* 1–19.

Svetieva, E., & Walker, M. (2008). Inconsistency between concept and measurement: The Canadian Problem Gambling Index (CPGI). *Journal of Gambling Issues, 22,* 157–173.

Tang, C. S.-K., Wu, A. M. S., Tang, J. Y. C., & Yan, E. C. W. (2010). Reliability, validity, and cut scores of the South Oaks Gambling Screen (SOGS) for Chinese. *Journal of Gambling Studies, 26,* 145–158.

Thompson, A. W., Walker, M., Milton, M., & Djukic, E. S. (2005). Explaining the high false positive rate of the South Oaks Gambling Screen. *International Gambling Studies, 5*(1), 45–56.

Toneatto, T., & Ladouceur, R. (2003). Treatment of pathological gambling: A critical review of the literature. *Psychology of Addictive Behaviors, 17*(4), 284–292.

Tse, S., Campbell, L., Rossen, F., Wang, C., Jull, A., Yan, E., & Jackson, A. (2013). Face-to-face and telephone counseling for problem gambling: A pragmatic multisite randomized study. *Research on Social Work Practice, 23,* 57–65.

Vassar, M. (2008). Characterizing score reliability for the South Oaks Gambling Screen. *South African Journal of Psychology, 38,* 541–549.

Walker, M. B. (1992). *The psychology of gambling.* Oxford, England: Pergamon Press.

Weinstock, J., Burton, S., Rash, C. J., Moran, S., Biller, W., Krudelbach, N., . . . Morasco, B. J. (2011). Predictors of engaging in problem gambling treatment: Data from the West Virginia Problem Gamblers Help Network. *Psychology of Addictive Behaviors, 27,* 372–379.

Williams, R. J., Royston, J., & Hagen, B. F. (2005). Gambling and problem gambling within forensic populations: A review of the literature. *Criminal Justice and Behavior, 32,* 665–689.

Winters, K., Specker, S., & Stinchfield, R. (1997). *Brief manual for the use of the Diagnostic Interview for Gambling Severity.* Minneapolis: University of Minnesota Medical School.

Wood, R. T., & Williams, R. J. (2011). A comparative profile of the Internet gambler: Demographic characteristics, game-play patterns, and problem gambling status. *New Media & Society, 13,* 1123–1141.

Young, M. M., & Wohl, M. J. A. (2011). The Canadian Problem Gambling Index: An evaluation of the scale and its accompanying profiler software in a clinical setting. *Journal of Gambling Studies, 27,* 467–485.

Zack, M., & Poulos, C. X. (2009). Effects of the atypical stimulant modafinil on a brief gambling episode in pathological gamblers with high versus low impulsivity. *Journal of Psychopharmacology, 23,* 660–671.

CHAPTER 8

SEXUAL ADDICTION

Stephen Southern, Dawn Ellison, and Mark Hagwood

STUDENT LEARNING OUTCOMES

At the conclusion of this chapter students will

1. Identify key terms and diagnostic criteria for sexual addiction and hyper-sexual disorders
2. Describe clinical interviewing, self-monitoring, and assessment approaches in specifying problems with sexual addiction
3. Discuss three major types of sexual addiction and potentially effective treatment components
4. Apply integrative treatment approaches to a complex clinical case

CASE AND CASE DISCUSSION

Sarah is a 35-year-old Caucasian woman, married 10 years and employed full time as an administrator in a social service agency.[1] Her husband is an allied health professional who works shifts in a local hospital and drills periodically with his National Guard unit. They sustain a distant marriage, rarely share sexual relations, and practice birth control in order not to have children. Sarah complains of symptoms of depression and anxiety. She has no close friends and maintains a secretive lifestyle in which she loses relatively large sums of money playing slot machines in a nearby casino.

Recently she met a man in the casino's hotel and engaged in compulsive sexual activities for the rest of the weekend. When she returned home, she began to meet anonymous partners on the Internet and engage in risky sexual behaviors. She borrowed money from her aging parents to conceal her recent

---

[1]This case study was introduced in Chapter 7, "Pathological Gambling." It represents the co-occurrence of mental disorder and a firing order of process addictions used to escape from the pain and shame of sexual abuse trauma.

losses. Experiencing sleep disturbance, loss of appetite, crying spells, and passing thoughts of suicide, she sought help from her family doctor, who prescribed Prozac for depression. Her doctor referred her to a local therapist.

Sarah reluctantly revealed to her female therapist the extent of her pathological gambling and compulsive sexual behavior. During the clinical interview and history taking, she disclosed that she had been date raped at 15 years of age when she was intoxicated at a party. She withdrew from family and friends, becoming involved in compulsive Internet use of more than 20 hours a week. She continued this pattern of withdrawal throughout her high school and college years. During her adolescence, she became obsessed with role-playing games in which she would portray a damsel in distress awaiting rescuing by a dominant partner. She frequently masturbated while visiting Internet sites devoted to spanking videos. She would engage in cybersex with partners she met online, especially with dominant men with whom she could engage in submissive, masochistic activities. As an adult, she discovered Internet gambling and eventually felt compelled to play slot machines at the casino. Therefore, the pathological gambling emerged from a long history of compulsive Internet use and cybersex.

Sarah met her husband in a graduate course at the state college. They had a rapid courtship characterized by intense sexual relations. However, shortly after their marriage, Sarah's husband began to withdraw into his work while she dedicated herself to her new position in the agency. Sarah returned to Internet role-playing games and gambling until she began to focus her attention on casino gambling. Her most recent binge resulted in a weekend sexual relationship with a stranger, which intensified her shame until she started hooking up with anonymous partners. This switching of addictive disorders prompted enough distress that she sought help from her family doctor and then an experienced therapist.

OVERVIEW OF SEXUAL ADDICTION

Sexual addiction is a controversial clinical disorder, generally treated as a sexual disorder not elsewhere classified in the *Diagnostic and Statistical Manual of Mental Disorders, Fourth Edition, Text Revision* (DSM–IV–TR; American Psychiatric Association [APA], 2000). With the publication of a groundbreaking book, Carnes (1983) introduced the term *sexual addiction* to the recovery (12-step) community and the general public. However, the underlying assumptions in the conceptualization of the disorder and the lack of consensus-based diagnostic criteria have slowed the acceptance of this process addiction in the professional psychotherapy and mental health treatment communities.

The concept of disordered sexual behavior has been discussed and labeled for hundreds of years. Terms such as *satyriasis, nymphomania, Don Juanism, perversion, paraphilia, compulsive sexual behavior, sexual addiction, impulse control disorder,* and *sin* have all been used to categorize or describe sexual behavior considered abnormal (Garcia & Thibaut, 2010). Early in the evolution of the term, professionals criticized *sexual addiction* as a thinly veiled attempt by dominant culture to pathologize or restrict sexual minorities and those presenting alternative sexual lifestyles (Coleman, 1987, 1990, 1991; Schwartz & Southern, 1999). Although historical terms appear to be judgmental, contemporary labels attempt to classify certain sexual behaviors as harmful to oneself or others. Similarly, the designation of sexual behavior as problematic or change worthy may be based on the criterion that participation in the behavior contributes to impairment in social or occupational functioning or adversely affects significant relationships. Ultimately, sexual addiction, similar to other addictive behaviors, is best determined by self-diagnosis based on the accumulation of negative consequences. This chapter covers (a) important definitions, (b) prevalence and demographics, (c) assessment and diagnosis, and (d) treatment methods related to sexual addiction.

One of the main barriers to understanding sexual addiction is that there is no clear definition of what constitutes addictive sexual behavior. Carnes (1983) applied the 12-step model of Alcoholics Anonymous to the problem, arguing that there is evidence of loss of control, powerlessness, unmanageability, tolerance, and disease progression. In his initial model, he hypothesized that there may be three levels of progression, starting with relatively mild or common forms of hypersexuality, such as becoming involved in affairs or viewing pornography while masturbating; progressing to voyeurism, exhibitionism, and other paraphilias; and concluding in victimizing behaviors such as incest, pedophilia, or rape. The construct of disease progression is not supported. The paraphilias are discrete disorders with an etiology and diagnostic criteria particular to each classification (e.g., voyeuristic disorder, sexual masochism disorder, fetishistic disorder). The paraphilic disorders are included in the *Diagnostic and Statistical Manual of Mental Disorders, Fifth Edition* (DSM–5; APA, 2013, pp. 685–705), whereas sexual addiction and hypersexuality are not addressed.

The concept of sexual addiction has both supporters and detractors. There is much discussion in the literature concerning the difficulty of labeling sexual behavior as addictive, compulsive, or even problematic. In the mid-1980s the senior author (Stephen Southern) attended the initial conferences on sexual addiction and compulsivity held at the University of Minnesota Medical School in Minneapolis. Patrick Carnes (1983) and colleagues from Golden Valley Health Center advocated adoption of the term *sexual addiction* with a corresponding addiction model, whereas Mark Schwartz and colleagues from the Masters and Johnson Institute advised conference attendees to treat *sexual compulsivity* from a trauma-based intimacy dysfunction model (cf. Schwartz, Galperin, & Masters, 1995; Schwartz & Southern, 1999). Eli Coleman and colleagues from the University of Minnesota Medical School considered the concept of sexual addiction to be somewhat misleading, as anxiety disorders, including obsessive-compulsive disorder, impulse control disorders, and particular sexual disorders, would account for the problem sexual behaviors (cf. Coleman, 1987, 1990). Later, conference attendees formed an association (now known as the Society for the Advancement of Sexual Health) and developed a publication, *Sexual Addiction & Compulsivity*, that bears witness to the several perspectives of the disorder.

Public awareness of sexual addiction has grown from increased media attention, particularly in the cases of celebrities in treatment and fallen political figures. Several 12-step groups offer help and support, including Sex Addicts Anonymous, Sexaholics Anonymous, and Sex and Love Addicts Anonymous. These groups perceive that sexual addiction qualifies as an addictive disorder by fitting well within the addiction model. Clinicians who work within an addiction model or have been trained by Carnes and colleagues assert the reality of sexual addiction in the lives of suffering persons and their families (Carnes, 2004; Laaser, 2004). Some definitions are used in this chapter to communicate constructs in a consistent manner.

Definitions

Abstinence: In recovery from sexual addiction, *abstinence* refers to refraining from sexual behaviors that are problematic. Similar to eating disorders, the goal is not to refrain completely from sexual behavior; rather, it is to avoid unmanageable hypersexual behavior. Each sexual addict must define for himself or herself the boundaries of sexual health.

Addictive cycle: The sexually addictive cycle, presented by Carnes (2004), is composed of preoccupation, ritualization, compulsive sexual behavior, and despair. The components of the cycle produce powerlessness (loss of control) and unmanageability. Once the cycle is complete, the despair drives the addict back to the preoccupation to cope with the shame of the sexual act and the cycle begins again.

Comorbidity: Co-occurring mental and addictive disorders are common in cases of sexual addiction. The most frequently co-occurring disorders are mood disorders, anxiety disorders, substance abuse disorders, attention-deficit disorder, personality disorder, and impulse control disorder (Kafka & Hennen, 2002; Kafka & Prentky, 1994).

Compulsive sexual behavior: Compulsive sexual behavior or *sexual compulsivity* is a term advocated by some professionals. The construct offers an alternative to *sexual addiction* by emphasizing either underlying anxiety (Coleman, 1987, 1990, 1991, 1992) or a history of trauma and intimacy dysfunction (Schwartz et al., 1995; Schwartz & Southern, 1999).

Hypersexual disorder: Kafka (2010) and colleagues proposed specific diagnostic criteria for hypersexual disorder, but the condition was not included in the *DSM–5* (APA, 2013).

Paraphilic sexual addiction: Compulsive sexual behavior focusing on one or more paraphilias (i.e., variant erotic activities or objects) can be treated as a type of sexual addiction. Paraphilias limit options for sexual health because they become over time the primary or exclusive means for sexual outlet.

Sexual addiction: Behaviors vary based on the individual who presents for treatment. Some common behaviors that are part of the addictive cycle for many addicts are fantasy or sexual preoccupation; compulsive masturbation; the use of pornography; participation in the adult sex industry; sexual contact with casual or anonymous partners; involvement in a pattern of extra-relationship affairs; the trading of sex for money; cybersex; and selected paraphilias, such as voyeurism, exhibitionism, or masochism.

Sexual trauma: Sexual trauma refers to personal experience with unwanted, premature, or invasive sexual activities that overwhelm the coping resources of the individual. Sexual abuse typically involves a sense of betrayal or exploitation by someone charged by society with the responsibility of protecting or supporting the vulnerable person.

Prevalence and Demographics

Commentators in the field (Kuzma & Black, 2008) estimate that between 3% and 6% of the adult population in the United States engage in behaviors consistent with the classification of sexual addiction. Hagedorn (2009) estimated that 17–37 million people present sexual addiction or compulsive sexual behavior. It is difficult to estimate the prevalence because of the private nature of sexual behavior and the potential social stigma associated with reporting out-of-control sexual behavior. In an effort to characterize hypersexual behavior, Kafka (1997) attempted to measure the frequency of orgasms per week. He argued that seven or more orgasms per week involving 1–2 hours daily in sexual activity over a 6-month period of time constituted hypersexual disorder as proposed for the *DSM–5* (APA, 2013). This was criticized in another study (Långström & Hanson, 2006) that found that high rates of sexual contact within the context of a stable relationship was associated with good psychological functioning. A better means for measuring sexually problematic behavior would include the criterion of continued engagement in sexual outlet in spite of negative consequences (Kuzma & Black, 2008).

In terms of prevalence, most self-identified sexual addicts are male. For example, 80% of 290 persons surveyed regarding sexual addiction were male (Kuzma & Black, 2008). Kaplan and Krueger (2010) reported that an estimated 8% to 20% of hypersexual individuals are female. In a study investigating psychiatric comorbidity in pathological gambling, Grant and Potenza (2006) found that 59% of gay or bisexual men had a lifetime prevalence rate for compulsive sexual behaviors compared to the heterosexual men in the study.

Types of compulsive or hypersexual behaviors vary by gender. Men are more likely than women to engage in compulsive masturbation, use of pornography, paraphilic behaviors, paying for sex (prostitution, strip clubs, etc.), and anonymous sex or one-night stands (Kuzma & Black, 2008). In a sample of 42 men recruited from "John schools," after being arrested for solicitation, one third would have qualified for a diagnosis of sexual addiction using the Sexual Addiction Screening Test (Gordon-Lamoureux, 2007). Women are more likely to engage in fantasy sex, to engage in sadomasochism, to use sex as a business or exchange in a relationship, and to refer to themselves as love addicts (Kuzma & Black, 2008).

In a retrospective chart review, Levine (2010) attempted to answer the question "What Is Sexual Addiction?" by constructing the following six subdivisions based on the perceptions of the patient or partner: no sexual excess beyond breaking the spouse's restrictive rules, discovery of the husband's long-standing sexual secrets, new discovery of the joys of commercial or chat room sex, the bizarre or paraphilic, a different concept of masculinity, and spiraling deteriorating dependence of commercial or illicit sex.

Only about 25% of men with sexual presenting problems could be considered sexual addicts. This group experienced significant psychological deterioration in conjunction with their sexual behavior. Another 25% of the patients could be described as paraphilic. Half of the men in this clinical sample would not have been classified as sexually addictive. Instead, their sexuality produced some personal or relational concerns that could be addressed outside the addiction model (Levine, 2010). Responding to this study, Kafka (2010) proposed a more robust diagnosis, *hypersexual disorder,* which assimilates aspects of sexual addiction and avoids some of the controversies associated with *sexual addiction.*

Carnes (2004) reported that sexual addiction can be traced to adolescence in most of the sexual addicts in his clinical practice. Paraphilic behaviors have an earlier onset than nonparaphilic behaviors (Bergner, 2002). Sexual addiction tends to progress to more frequent, intense, or extreme behaviors over time but may be interrupted by circumstances or involvement in other addictive behaviors. Each sexual addict has a cycle that can be described and understood by the recovering person (Schneider & Irons, 2001).

SPECIAL POPULATIONS OF SEXUAL ADDICTS

Several populations of sexual addicts deserve special attention. The characteristics of these groups tend to support the differentiation of sexual addicts into three major types: hypersexual, impulsive partner-oriented males; paraphilic sexual addicts; and female trauma survivors with comorbid substance use and mental disorders.

Hypersexual Men

Men who engage online or in person in hypersexual behavior that is partner oriented probably constitute the largest group of sexual addicts. Typical forms of sexual outlet involve viewing pornography, compulsively masturbating, visiting strip clubs and adult sex businesses, and repeatedly engaging in affairs. A biopsychosocial model of hypersexual disorder or sexual addiction (cf. Samenow, 2010) asserts that there may be underlying neurological or physiological factors contributing to the behavior. Although there is a lack of research support, there is some speculation that sexual addiction may be a function of disturbance in the dopaminergic reward pathways of the brain (Levine, 2010).

There is an emerging perspective that nonsubstance behavioral addictions, such as sexual addiction, may be understood in terms of brain systems pathology (Karim & Chaudhri, 2012), which can be measured by brain imaging or related medical tests (Amen, Willeumier, & Johnson, 2012). Men with impulsive or out-of-control sexual behavior not explained by mania or substance intoxification may account for the largest group of sexual addicts. In this group, some hypersexual men, similar to individuals who present attention-deficit/hyperactivity disorder, engage in impulsive or dysregulated sexual behavior to self-stimulate or overcome aversive internal states (Blankenship & Laaser, 2004).

Women Survivors Presenting Sexual Addiction

In a study that examined the co-occurrence of posttraumatic stress disorder and substance use disorders in 20,611 veterans, 63% of women and 25% of men experienced lifetime physical abuse, and 51% of women and 8% of men reported lifetime sexual abuse (Kausch, Rugle, & Rowland, 2006). Another study of patients admitted to an inpatient addictions unit (Charney, Palacios-Boix, & Gill, 2007) found that 23% of patients reported a history of sexual abuse. This group presented higher rates of comorbid psychological problems and impaired family relationships. Alcohol and other drug counselors reported high rates of co-occurring substance use disorders, mental disorders, and sexual addiction in women who sought treatment for chemical addiction (Kiepek, 2008). Among 99 self-identified female sexual addicts, there were high rates of childhood abuse, depression, and substance abuse (Opitz, Tsytsarev, & Froh, 2009). In addition, these women recalled poor cohesion in the family of origin and a lack of positive relationships with their fathers.

Women who engage in out-of-control sexual behavior despite adverse consequences are likely to present adult attachment disorder (cf. Schwartz et al., 1995; Schwartz & Southern, 1999) characterized by vulnerability to stress, inability to tolerate the demands of intimacy, and emotion dysregulation (Faisandier, Taylor, & Salisbury, 2012; Katehakis, 2009; Schneider & Schneider, 2004). Women who turn to compulsive sexual behavior may be trying to self-soothe or fix feelings while engaging in a less threatening fantasy world in which various roles, especially masochism, can be enacted (Southern, 2002). With the growth of the Internet and sex-based websites, women have been afforded additional opportunities to engage in sexually addictive behaviors. The accessibility, anonymity, and affordability of the Internet have contributed to less difference in prevalence rates of sexually addictive behaviors between women and men (Cooper, Delmonico, & Griffin-Shelley, 2004; Schneider & Weiss, 2001). Therefore, cybersex addicts may represent a special subgroup within female sexual addicts.

The term *cybersex* includes an array of online sexual activity associated with Internet use: viewing explicit or pornographic images on websites, exposing private details of one's sex life by uploading images or written descriptions of oneself or one's partner, interacting with sex workers on specialized websites, interacting with anonymous partners through instant messages or chat rooms, meeting potential sexual partners for offline contacts, and violating interpersonal boundaries by engaging in unwanted sexually oriented contacts through e-mail or social networking sites (Southern, 2008, p. 697).

Cybering behavior typically occurs between consenting partners in private spaces accessed through e-mail, instant messaging, real-time exchanges via websites, or other electronic means. However, cybercontacts for the purposes of sexual outlet may cause adverse consequences to the extent that they are secretive or illicit (e.g., extramarital affairs) or illegal (e.g., engaging minors in sexual interactions). Particular cybersex behaviors range from solitary acts, such as masturbation, to involvement with anonymous or dangerous sexual partners online or in subsequent face-to-face contact. Women who engage in compulsive cybersex may engage in sexual fantasies in which they repeat or recreate salient aspects of earlier life traumas (Schwartz & Southern, 2000; Southern, 2002, 2008). Studies of cybersex addiction suggest that there may be nearly equal numbers of women and men engaged in this secretive world (Carnes, Delmonico, & Griffin, 2001; Cooper et al., 2004; Schneider & Weiss, 2001; Schwartz & Southern, 2000). Sexual sites on the Internet also afford opportunities for persons with paraphilic sexual preferences to explore their preferences.

Paraphilic Sexual Addicts

Paraphilia (from the Greek, "other love") "denotes any intense and persistent sexual interest other than sexual interest in genital stimulation or preparatory fondling with phenotypically normal, physically mature, consenting human partners" (APA, 2013, p. 685). A *paraphilic disorder* is a paraphilia involving distress, impairment, personal harm, or the harm of another person (APA, 2013, pp. 685–686). Paraphilias typically involve erotic activity preferences or choices of targets for sexual contact and gratification. Paraphilic disorders include voyeuristic disorder, exhibitionistic disorder, frotteuristic disorder, sexual masochism disorder, sexual sadism disorder, pedophilic disorder, festishistic disorder, transvestic disorder, other specified paraphilic disorders, and unspecified paraphilic disorders (APA, 2013, pp. 685–705).

Paraphilic sexual addiction includes hypersexual or compulsive behaviors involving variant or atypical sexual activities or objects/targets for erotic preferences. Some paraphilic behaviors are relatively common among couples, such as biting, spanking, or power exchange role play in sadomasochism. Other behaviors are rare or criminal, such as pedophilia or child molesting. A key determinant in identifying the severity of paraphilic sexual addiction is the extent to which involvement with the variant activity/object interferes with the expression of intimacy in a consenting adult couple. Thus, paraphilic sexual addiction emphasizes hypersexual behavior as intimacy dysfunction.

Sexual addiction involving a paraphilia embodies the essence of impairment in intimate functioning. Birchard (2011) described historical contexts and modern clinical cases of paraphilic sexual addiction. He noted that the particular paraphilia emerges in the context of a patient being unable to tolerate distress or negative effects. In addition, the sexual addict cannot handle the demands of intimacy. Each paraphilia has a function determined by the individual's history of childhood trauma.

According to Birchard (2011, p. 162), 95% of paraphilias are practiced by men and may arise out of distortions of the masculine gender role (Becerra, Robinson, & Balkin, 2011). Nevertheless, some female sexual addicts present paraphilias arising from the pain and shame of sexual abuse or exploitation. Sadomasochism is one paraphilia encountered regularly among women who present sexual addiction (Southern, 2002).

In the classic sense, a paraphilia is a perversion, an eroticized sense of hatred (Stoller, 1975) in which an abused child fails to master object relations required for secure attachment. Consequently, there are problems maintaining a coherent sense of identity, establishing a capacity for self-soothing, and integrating the skills needed to venture forth into the demanding world of intimate relationships (Schwartz & Southern, 1999, 2000; Southern, 2002). Therefore, the woman or man who survives child abuse develops a distorted "lovemap" that organizes information about erotic relational opportunities; omits, distorts, displaces, or incorporates unusual preferences into the developing template for eroticism; and motivates the person to engage in sexual behaviors consistent with the abused sense of self (cf. Money, 1986). Consequently, the sexually addicted trauma survivor cannot establish or maintain a pair bond with an intimate partner. There is impairment in capacity for intimacy with dysregulation of the sexual appetite, characterized by preoccupation with paraphilic fantasies, periodic disinhibition of sexual impulses, and recurrent hypersexual behavior (Kafka, 2007).

DIAGNOSIS OF SEXUAL ADDICTION AND HYPERSEXUAL DISORDER

The *Diagnostic and Statistical Manual of Mental Disorders, Third Edition* (APA, 1987), classified sexual addiction under the heading "Sexual Disorders Not Otherwise Specified" and stated that the individual shows distress at the pattern of repeated sexual conquests or other forms of nonparaphilic sexual addiction involving a succession of people who exist only as things to be used (p. 296). The *DSM–IV–TR* (APA, 2000) kept the concept of sexual disorders not otherwise specified but highlighted distress about a pattern of repeated sexual relationships involving a succession of lovers. Although the *DSM–5* (APA, 2013) excludes hypersexual disorder and sexual addiction, the criteria proposed here could be used by researchers and treatment providers to share a common language.

Criteria for Hypersexual Disorder

Criterion A. Over a period of at least 6 months, recurrent and intense sexual fantasies, sexual urges, and sexual behaviors in association with four or more of the following five criteria:

A.1. A great deal of time is consumed by sexual fantasies and urges, and by planning for and engaging in sexual behavior.

A.2. Repetitively engaging in sexual fantasies, urges, or behaviors in response to dysphoric mood states (e.g., anxiety, depression, boredom, irritability).

A.3. Repetitively engaging in sexual fantasies, urges, or behaviors in response to stressful life events.

A.4. Repetitive but unsuccessful efforts to control or significantly reduce these sexual fantasies, urges, or behaviors.

A.5. Repetitively engaging in sexual behaviors while disregarding the risk for physical or emotional harm to self or others.

Criterion B. There is clinically significant personal distress or impairment in social, occupational, or other important areas of functioning associated with the frequency and intensity of these sexual fantasies, urges, or behaviors.

Criterion C. These sexual fantasies, urges, or behaviors are not due to the direct physiological effect of an exogenous substance (e.g., a drug of abuse or a medication).

Specify if:
Masturbation
Pornography
Sexual behavior with consenting adults
Cybersex
Telephone sex
Strip clubs
Other (including specific paraphilias)

Source. From "Hypersexual Disorder: A Proposed Diagnosis for *DSM–5*," by M. P. Kafka, 2010, *Archives of Sexual Behavior, 39*, p. 379. Copyright 2010 by Springer. Reprinted with kind permission from Springer Science and Business Media.

Although hypersexual disorder is not included in the final version of the *DSM–5*, it represents the efforts of the Sexual and Gender Identity Disorders Work Group for the *DSM–5* to establish diagnostic criteria for disordered sexual behavior (Kafka, 2010). This diagnosis represents an improvement over the construct of sexual addiction in that it incorporates research and clinical experiences from sexuality therapy. Diagnostic criteria for hypersexual disorder also take into account the extensive literature on treating sexual offending (Samenow, 2010). Therefore, we advocate using criteria for hypersexual disorder when estimating in clinical settings the severity of sexual addiction presented by a distressed patient.

An alternative view in the diagnosis of sexual addiction and specification of problematic hypersexuality is to compare current behavior to goals or ideals for sexual health. "Sexual health is the integration of the somatic, emotional, intellectual, and social aspects of sexual well-being, in ways that are positively enriching and that enhance personality, communication, and love" (World Health Organization, as cited in Firestone, Firestone, & Catlett, 2006, p. 11). The sexual health model asserts that the pursuit of meaningful sexuality is a human right.

Manley (1999), a major contributor to understanding and treating sexual addiction, emphasized the importance of positive sexual behaviors in recovery. For Manley, sexual health consists of progress in five interrelated domains:

- Spirituality: the core of sexuality, rejecting sexual shame and affirming that sex is good
- Personhood: the development of autonomy, accepting one's sexual self and respecting boundaries
- Roles and relationships: the expression of trust, vulnerability, and mutuality
- Behaviors: the initiation of safe and pleasurable sexual activities
- Physical function: the opportunity to experience the full range of human sexual response

Edwards (2012) described the evolution of a sexual health model in the assessment and treatment of Internet sexual compulsivity. This approach was derived from a sexual health promotion model of HIV prevention (Robinson, Bockting, Rosser, Miner, & Coleman, 2002). Edwards adapted this model to the treatment of sexual compulsivity in residential and outpatient treatment.

The components of the sexual health model identify treatment goals beyond breaking the addiction cycle or establishing abstinence. The treatment of sexual addiction or hypersexual disorder from the sexual health perspective involves communication, positive body image, recognition of culture, enjoyment of sexual fulfillment, and maintenance of intimacy and spirituality in the process. Within the context of identifying sexual health goals for each client, the clinician may seek additional data for problem specification and treatment planning.

ASSESSMENT METHODS

Given the ambiguous and controversial nature of sexual addiction diagnosis, assessment becomes a critical element in understanding the type and severity of sexual problems presented in clinical practice. Assessing sexual addiction begins with differentiating the disorder from gainful employment in the adult sex industry as well as brief periods of excessive or atypical sexual behavior that do not meet the diagnostic criteria for hypersexual disorder. Next there should be careful assessment of potentially comorbid or co-occurring disorders. If the sexual behavior can be better explained by a manic episode, personality disorder, or substance intoxication, then the other mental disorder should be the primary focus of ongoing assessment. Additional psychological evaluation and/or psychosocial history may be indicated.

A clinical interview is needed to specify the nature of the sexual presenting problem. Several psychometric scales have been used to screen or specify sexual addiction and compulsive sexual behavior as well.

The Clinical Interview

The first step in the assessment of sexual addiction or hypersexual disorder involves a respectful, sensitive clinical interview conducted by a clinician trained and experienced in discussing sexuality and initiated with the client's informed consent. The effective clinical interview establishes rapport and the commonality of goals characteristic of an initial therapeutic alliance. Woody (2011) described a sexuality-focused interview through which important information regarding hypersexual behavior could be obtained. Some of the general domains of the clinical interview advocated by Woody include the client's range of sexual behaviors in daily life, sexual behaviors causing distress and in what context, the incongruence of current sexual behavior and the personal value system, overall sexual and relationship history, current substance use and history of substance use disorders, and amenability to treatment for hypersexual disorder.

Clinical interviewing for sexual addiction should include collateral contact with a partner or family member whenever possible (Woody, 2011). The shameful nature of sexual concerns makes it likely that the client will withhold information or minimize the severity of the sexual problem. The use of psychometric instruments can assist the clinician with problem specification in sexual addiction treatment.

Tests and Measures

Sexual behavior that qualifies as sexual addiction is not determined by type, frequency, or lack of social acceptability but rather by the impact of the behavior pattern on the individual's life. Hook, Hook, Davis, Worthington, and Penberthy (2010) identified "the key features that distinguish sexual addiction from other patterns of sexual behavior" (p. 228) as a lack of control over the sexual behavior and continuation in the behavior despite significant harmful consequences. Instruments designed to assess sexual addiction include these features and distinguish between addictive and other types of sexual behavior (Carnes, Green, & Carnes, 2010).

Three types of information typically included in sexual addiction assessment instruments are (a) objective sexual addiction symptoms, (b) subjective sexual addiction symptoms, and (c) consequences associated with sexual addiction. *Objective symptoms* refers to observable or tangible activities present in sexual addiction, such as time spent in the activity or number of orgasms per week. *Subjective symptoms* are those perceived by the client: thoughts, feelings, behaviors, and the ability to control them. *Consequences* refers to the negative outcomes resulting from engagement in the activity, including relationship problems and health problems (Hook et al., 2010). Several existing measures of sexual addiction are currently available. These measures include self-report measures (scales and checklists) and clinician-administered instruments.

Self-Report Instruments

Because the designation of sexual behavior as problematic is based on the subjective experience of symptoms, assessment of sexual addiction is often determined by self-report. Self-report measures are quick and easy to use in both research and practice, but there are disadvantages that must be kept in mind when evaluating a person's perception of sexuality as problematic. For example, individuals may provide socially acceptable answers to avoid the shame and embarrassment of being labeled a sex addict. Likewise, some individuals may overreport symptoms, seeking a diagnostic label to avoid responsibility for their actions. Finally, inaccurate answers may be given based on a misunderstanding of the questions themselves (Hook et al., 2010). Self-report instruments are divided into self-report rating scales of symptoms, self-report checklists of symptoms, and self-report measures of consequences associated with sexual addiction.

Self-Report Rating Scales

Self-report rating scales are designed to assess an individual's experience of problematic thoughts, behaviors, and feelings. Items are typically rated on a Likert-type scale, and scores are summed to form a total score. Subscales assessing particular aspects of sexual addiction are included in some instruments (Hook et al., 2010).

Sexual Addiction Scale of the Disorders Screening Inventory. The Sexual Addiction Scale is a five-item scale that produces a total score for measuring sexual addiction. Each item is rated on a 5-point Likert-type scale from 0 (*never*) to 4 (*all the time [1–2 times per day]*). Total scores range from 0 to 20, with higher scores indicating a higher probability of addiction. Scores from 0 to 5 indicate a low probability, 6 to 11 indicate a moderate probability, and 12 to 20 indicate a high probability of sexual addiction (Carter & Ruiz, 1996). The Sexual Addiction Scale is "a brief, face-valid measure of sexual addiction" (Hook et al., 2010, p. 236) with evidence of both discriminant validity and internal consistency. Because it has only been tested in one study of male psychotherapy clients, its psychometric properties are considered weak.

Compulsive Sexual Behavior Inventory. The Compulsive Sexual Behavior Inventory is a 28-item scale that produces a total score and three subscale scores: Control (sexual behavior), Abuse (past history), and Violence (experiences of violence). Each item is rated on a 5-point Likert-type scale ranging from 1 (*very frequently*) to 5 (*never*). Total scores range from 28 to 140. Higher total scores indicate a lower probability of sexual addiction. The Compulsive Sexual Behavior Inventory is a brief instrument that has been evaluated with heterosexual men and women and with gay men. It demonstrates evidence of convergent validity and criterion-related validity (Coleman, Miner, Ohlerking, & Raymond, 2001).

Sexual Dependency Inventory–Revised. The Sexual Dependency Inventory–Revised is a 179-item scale that produces a total score, two composite scores, and 10 subscale scores. It measures 10 distinct categories: fantasy, voyeurism, paying for sex, pain exchange, exploitive sex, seductive role play, exhibitionism, trading sex, intrusive sex, and anonymous sex. Each item has two questions. The first item allows individuals to report the frequency of experience of each thought, feeling, or fantasy. Items are rated on a 6-point Likert-type scale ranging from 0 (*never*) to 5 (*very often*). The second item measures the power of each thought, feeling, or fantasy, with respondents again rating each item on a 6-point scale ranging from 0 (*no power*) to 5 (*very high power*). Higher scores indicate a higher probability of sexual addiction (Delmonico, Bubenzer, & West, 1998).

The Sexual Dependency Inventory–Revised has been evaluated with mostly heterosexual psychotherapy clients, sex offenders, and members of the community. It demonstrates internal consistency for the total score and subscale scores. There is also evidence of convergent validity and criterion-related validity. The Sexual Dependency Inventory–Revised is a long, in-depth measure of sexual addiction, providing detailed information about the individual's experience. The length of the assessment, however, often makes it an impractical tool for use in clinical settings (Hook et al., 2010).

Perceived Sexual Control Scale. The Perceived Sexual Control Scale is a 20-item scale that provides a total score along with two subscale scores. It was designed to measure problems with sexual self-control in which the individual may not be able to stop the behavior even when that is the stated goal (Kingston & Firestone, 2008). The two subscales are (a) Control of Sex Drive and (b) Control of Risk Behavior. Each of the 20 items is rated on a 5-point Likert-type scale from 1 (*strongly agree*) to 5 (*strongly disagree*). Higher scores on the full scale and the subscales indicate greater perceived control over the addiction and therefore a lower probability of sexual addiction (Exner, Meyer-Bahlburg, & Ehrhardt, 1992).

The Perceived Sexual Control Scale has been evaluated mostly with gay men in community and college settings. It has demonstrated evidence of internal consistency, convergent validity, discriminant validity, and criterion-related validity. Hook et al. (2010) indicated that some of the items on the scale are "double barreled (e.g., 'Sex is important to me, but it doesn't rule my life' . . .) making these items difficult for respondents to interpret" (p. 240).

Garos Sexual Behavior Index. The Garos Sexual Behavior Index is a 70-item scale (35 core items and 35 masking items) that produces four subscale scores measuring constructs of sexual control and frequency: Discordance (extent of conflict about sexual desires), Sexual Obsession (degree of preoccupation with sexual stimuli), Permissiveness (general values about sexual issues), and Sexual Stimulation (comfort level with sexual stimulation/arousal). Each item is rated on a 5-point Likert-type scale ranging from 1 (*strongly agree*) to 5 (*strongly disagree*). Lower subscale scores indicate stronger endorsement of the constructs (Garos & Stock, 1998a, 1998b).

The Garos Sexual Behavior Index has been evaluated primarily with heterosexual males and females in college, psychotherapy, and community settings. It has also been administered to inmates and sex offenders. It demonstrates internal consistency and some evidence of convergent validity. Like the Perceived Sexual Control Scale, the Garos Sexual Behavior Index provides detailed information but is a lengthy measure that is time consuming to administer (Hook et al., 2010).

Sexual Compulsivity Scale. The Sexual Compulsivity Scale is a 10-item scale producing a total score that measures the "insistent, repetitive, intrusive, and unwanted urge to perform specific acts often in a ritualized or routine fashion" (Hook et al., 2010, p. 242). Items are rated on a 4-point Likert-type scale ranging from 1 (*not at all like me*) to 4 (*very much like me*). Total scores range from 10 to 40, with higher total scores indicating greater problems with sexual addiction (Hook et al., 2010). A cutoff score of 24 has been utilized to indicate problems with sexual addiction (Benotsch, Kalichman, & Pinkerton, 2001).

The Sexual Compulsivity Scale has been evaluated with both heterosexual and gay men and women in community settings, college students, and individuals with HIV. It demonstrates internal consistency, convergent validity, and discriminant validity. Because it is a brief measure with strong evidence of validity, the Sexual Compulsivity Scale is the most widely used research measure of sexual addiction (Hook et al., 2010).

Sex Addicts Anonymous Questionnaire. The Sex Addicts Anonymous Questionnaire is a 16-item scale derived from an existing questionnaire utilized to determine appropriateness for referral to 12-step Sex Addicts Anonymous groups. Each item is rated on a 3-point Likert-type scale ranging from 0 (*never*) to 2 (*often*). The range of total scores is from 0 to 32, with higher scores indicative of sexual addiction. The Sex Addicts Anonymous Questionnaire has been mostly evaluated on male clients in psychotherapy or college settings (Mercer, 1998). It has substantial psychometric weaknesses, lacking internal consistency and temporal stability. There are no norms for the measure (Hook et al., 2010).

Sexual Symptom Assessment Scale. The Sexual Symptom Assessment Scale is a 12-item scale that measures sexual addiction defined as "a clinical syndrome involving excessive sexual thoughts, sexual urges, or sexual activities that cause distress or impairment" (Hook et al., 2010, p. 244). It samples both subjective (i.e., "How strong were your urges?") and objective ("How much time did you spend engaging in problematic sexual behaviors?") symptoms. Items are rated on a 5-point Likert-type scale ranging from 0 to 4 with anchors dependent on the particular question. Total scores range from 0 to 48, with higher scores more indicative of sexual addiction (Raymond, Lloyd, Miner, & Kim, 2007).

The Sexual Symptom Assessment Scale has been evaluated in male psychotherapy clients. It demonstrates internal consistency, temporal stability, and convergent and discriminant validity. It is the first measure to address subjective and objective symptoms. Potential problems exist with the combination of subjective and objective scores into one total score (Hook et al., 2010).

Self-Report Checklists

Like self-report rating scales, self-report checklists contain items that assess subjective symptoms: the individual's experience of problematic behaviors. Respondents acknowledge the presence or absence of particular items by marking "yes" or "no." Checklists are time efficient and cover a wide array of symptoms. However, they do not provide detailed information, as the individual cannot clarify his or her degree of agreement or disagreement with the item (Hook et al., 2010).

Sexual Addiction Screening Test (SAST). The SAST is a 25-item scale that measures sexual addiction defined as "a pathological relationship with a mood-altering experience" (Hook et al., 2010, p. 245). Affirmative answers to each item are summed to yield a total score, which ranges from 0 to 25. A cutoff score of 13 is considered an indicator of sexual addiction (Carnes et al., 2010). The SAST has been evaluated in multiple populations (college students, sex offenders, veterans, physicians), but selected samples were mostly heterosexual males. It has demonstrated internal consistency, convergent validity, and discriminant validity. The instrument is widely used in clinical settings but, based on norms, is limited in scope (Hook et al., 2010).

Sexual Addiction Screening Test–Women (WSAST). The WSAST was developed from the original SAST utilizing the 25-item format. Total scores range from 0 to 25, with a cutoff score of 6 (or higher) indicating sexual addiction (Seegers, 2003). No basis is given for the arbitrary cutoff score. The WSAST was evaluated mostly in heterosexual college women. Internal consistency has not been reported for the measure, and there is no evidence of convergent, criterion-related, or discriminant validity. The low threshold produces problems for comparing the WSAST to the original SAST (Hook et al., 2010).

Sexual Addiction Screening Test–Gay Men (GSAST). Like the WSAST, the GSAST is a 25-item measure based on the original SAST. It also utilizes a cutoff score of 6 (or higher) as indicative of sexual addiction. Total scores range from 0 to 25, with higher scores suggestive of the presence of addiction (Chaney & Dew, 2003). The GSAST was evaluated on a sample of gay male community members. There is no reported internal consistency and no evidence of convergent, criterion-related, or discriminant validity for the measure (Hook et al., 2010).

Internet Sex Screening Test. The Internet Sex Screening Test is a 25-item scale designed to measure problematic online behavior. It has five factors measured on five subscales: (a) Online Sexual Compulsivity, (b) Online Sexual Behavior–Social, (c) Online Sexual Behavior–Isolated, (d) Online Sexual Spending, and (e) Interest in Online Sexual Behavior (Delmonico & Miller, 2003). Affirmative answers to items are summed to formulate a total score that ranges from 0 and 25. Higher scores are indicative of sexual addiction. The Internet Sex Screening Test has been evaluated in community samples of heterosexual men and women and in gay men. The instrument has limited evidence of validity and reliability. It is the only sexual addiction measure designed to assess online sexual behavior (Hook et al., 2010).

Self-Report Instruments Measuring Consequences
"The presence or absence of consequences cannot alone determine whether a person has a sexual addiction" (Hook et al., 2010, p. 252). Consequences associated with sexual addiction do, however, provide information about the negative outcomes related to the addiction. In therapeutic settings, assessment of consequences can help the client become aware of the destructive nature of his or her behavior. Self-report rating items that focus on consequences measure the degree to which individuals experience negative effects of addiction (Hook et al., 2010).

Cognitive and Behavioral Outcomes of Sexual Behavior Scale. The Cognitive and Behavioral Outcomes of Sexual Behavior Scale is a 36-item measure consisting of two scales: Cognitive Outcomes (20 items) and Behavioral Outcomes (16 items). Each scale produces a total score and scores for six subscales: Legal/Occupational, Social, Financial, Physical (pain/injury), Psychological/Spiritual, and Physical (disease/pregnancy). The cognitive scale measures the degree to which individuals worry about specific outcomes of sexual behaviors. Items are rated on a 4-point Likert-type scale ranging from 1 (*never*) to 4 (*always*). Total scores range from 20 to 80, with higher scores indicating greater concern over the consequences of the behavior (McBride, Reece, & Sanders, 2007).

The behavior scale measures whether individuals have experienced specific consequences as a result of their behavior. Items can be checked "yes" or "no." Affirmative answers are summed, producing a total score that ranges from 0 to 16, with higher scores indicative of more consequences (McBride et al., 2007). The Cognitive and Behavioral Outcomes of Sexual Behavior Scale has been tested on college students and has limited support for validity and reliability (Hook et al., 2010).

Compulsive Sexual Behavior Consequences Scale. The Compulsive Sexual Behavior Consequences Scale is a 21-item scale adapted from the Inventory of Drug Use Consequences. Two versions of the measure exist: One assesses lifetime consequences, and the other assesses consequences in the past 90 days. Items are rated on a 5-point Likert-type scale ranging from 0 (*never*) to 4 (*always*). Total scores range from 0 to 84. Higher scores are associated with more consequences of addiction (Tonigan & Miller, 2002). The Compulsive Sexual Behavior Consequences

Scale has been evaluated in a community sample of gay and bisexual men. The measure has limited support for validity and reliability (Hook et al., 2010).

Clinician Rating Scales

Clinician rating scales include questions that assess objective symptoms of sexual addiction. Clinician-administered instruments offer several advantages over self-report assessments. Trained clinicians can explain items that are confusing to individuals, creating the potential for more accurate results with less measurement error. Also, administration of the assessment provides an opportunity for clinicians to establish rapport with clients. Finally, potential bias in answering (e.g., effects of social desirability) is reduced. The disadvantages of utilizing clinician-administered scales are that they are time consuming and some individuals may feel uncomfortable discussing sexual issues with the clinician early in the treatment process (Hook et al., 2010).

Sexual Outlet Inventory

The Sexual Outlet Inventory is a six-item scale that documents the incidence and frequency of sexual behaviors, fantasies, and urges in a designated week. Behaviors are divided into conventional and unconventional categories. Conventional behaviors include those that occur within the context of a mutually consenting relationship. Unconventional behaviors include paraphilias and nonparaphilic sexual addictions. Clinicians rate the sum of all sexual behaviors leading to orgasm. Hypersexual desire is indicated by an output of seven or more orgasms a week sustained for at least 6 months. The Sexual Outlet Inventory has been normed on male psychotherapy patients, making generalizability questionable. The instrument has very little psychometric support (Hook et al., 2010).

Diagnostic Interview for Sexual Compulsivity

The Diagnostic Interview for Sexual Compulsivity is a semistructured interview based on the Structured Clinical Interview for the DSM–IV substance abuse and dependence model. The instrument does not measure the degree of sexual addiction symptoms but is designed to establish whether diagnostic criteria are met. It has six sections assessing "(a) period of time bothered, (b) seven problem behaviors, (c) abuse and dependence criteria, (d) presence of distress or interference, (e) age of onset, and (f) course of the problem" (Hook et al., 2010, p. 250). Items are rated on a 4-point Likert-type scale ranging from 0 (*absent or false*) to 3 (*threshold or true*). The Diagnostic Interview for Sexual Compulsivity has been administered in gay and bisexual community members. Reliability and validity evidence is limited to a single study (Hook et al., 2010).

Yale-Brown Obsessive Compulsive Scale–Compulsive Sexual Behavior

The Yale-Brown Obsessive Compulsive Scale–Compulsive Sexual Behavior is a 10-item scale adapted from the Yale-Brown Obsessive Compulsive Scale. Subjective and objective symptoms are rated. The instrument yields a total score between 0 and 40, with individual items being rated on a 5-point Likert-type scale ranging from 0 to 4 (anchors vary based on the question). Higher total scores indicate higher sexual addiction. The scale has been tested in samples of gay and bisexual men. There is limited evidence of validity and reliability, and generalizability to different populations is uncertain. "The development of the [Diagnostic Interview for Sexual Compulsivity] represents a major step in developing a set of diagnostic criteria representing sexual addiction" (Hook et al., 2010, p. 252).

Clients typically present for sexual addiction treatment because they cannot tolerate consequences of hypersexual behavior, which may be incongruent with their values and other lifestyle choices. The sexual behavior should be assessed carefully within the context of the emerging diagnostic model for hypersexual disorder. Change-worthy behaviors and problems can be specified through clinical interviewing and additional testing. The clinician and client establish a therapeutic alliance in which specific treatments are implemented.

TREATMENT OF SEXUAL ADDICTION AND HYPERSEXUAL DISORDER

Most of the literature on sexual addiction describes treatment components from the perspective of addiction recovery. The original description of sexual addiction (Carnes, 1983) advocated application of the 12 steps and traditions of Alcoholics Anonymous to disordered sexual behavior. Over the years, Carnes (1989, 1997, 2000, 2004) modified his treatment approach to incorporate shame reduction and trauma resolution as well as means for improving the quality of life in recovery. Various modalities have been applied to sexual addiction treatment, including motivational interviewing, psychotropic medication, group therapy, psychoeducation, eye-movement desensitization and reprocessing (EMDR), and family therapy. Self-help groups and bibliotherapy have been emphasized in sexual addiction recovery as well.

Sexual addiction recovery, originally developed by Carnes (1983) and based on 12-step principles, seems to be indicated in cases of hypersexual behavior, especially in men. Carnes (2000) described initial and long-term treatment of sexual addiction. His treatment model emphasized confronting cycles of shame and compartmentalizing. In a study of recovery over a 5-year period, sexual addicts reported little measurable improvement in the first year beyond achieving some periods of abstinence and decreasing negative consequences (pp. 6–7). In the second and third years, a rebuilding process occurred in which there were benefits in coping with stress, spirituality, career, and capacity for friendship. The third through fifth years in recovery produced healing in damaged relationships with partners, children, parents, siblings, and other family members affected by the hypersexual disorder. Life satisfaction and general sense of well-being increased in the later period of sexual addiction recovery.

Carnes (2000, pp. 8–9) described six stages of recovery: the developing stage (lasts up to 2 years), crisis/decision stage (1 day–3 months), shock stage (the first 6–8 months), grief stage (6 months), repair stage (18–36 months), and growth stage (2 years or more). The developing stage involves overcoming denial and minimization, coming to understand the consequences of sexual addiction. The early stages of recovery typically include a crisis or catastrophe in which the accumulating consequences and unmanageability of the addictive lifestyle produce readiness to change (e.g., an *unfreezing* of habitual thoughts and behaviors). During the shock stage, there is increasing distress, hopelessness, and despair. The focus of treatment is living one day at a time. A grief stage may follow cessation of hypersexual behavior and experiencing emotional awareness of losses in the current life and the family of origin. A repair stage follows a "paradigm shift" (p. 9) in which sexual addicts come to view their lives and choices through new, healthy perspectives. This stage is characterized by heightened responsibility and accountability. The growth stage evolves out of a genuine recovery program in which there is the promise of intimacy and integrity. Overall, the stages of sexual addiction recovery correspond to progress through the 12 steps.

Recovery from sexual addiction is facilitated by attendance at 12-step groups in the community. Twelve-step fellowships include Sexaholics Anonymous, Sex Addicts Anonymous, and Sex and Love Addicts Anonymous. There are also groups for partners and family members of sex addicts, such as COSA (www.cosa-recovery.org). These groups focus on spiritual growth, assisting family members to refrain from engaging in behaviors that trigger the addiction cycle and to address the underlying addictive behaviors of the coaddict. Frequently, the coaddicted family member has his or her own addiction, which has been covered or hidden by the preoccupation and attention placed on the sexual addict. For example, a sexual addict may be married to a woman who has a hidden eating disorder. Each partner manages the demands of the relationship by avoiding intimacy through addictive behavior.

Motivational interviewing helps the sexual addict prepare for entry into recovery or treatment. Sexual addiction is characterized by a core belief system in which shame, unworthiness, secrecy, and avoidance interfere with seeking help and support (Carnes, 1983). Therefore, interventions from motivational interviewing and enhancement increase awareness of negative consequences, lack of life satisfaction, powerlessness, and impairment sufficient for the sexual addict to take steps toward a recovery program. Movement toward action in the change process is embedded in step work within the 12-step recovery group. In addition to readiness to change, motivational interviewing encourages a strong therapeutic alliance with a therapist, sponsor, or other caregiver (Del Guidice & Kutinsky, 2007). Partners and family members have benefited from a motivational approach, invitational intervention, to help them examine life with the sexual addict and engage them in the change process at a systems level (Landau, Garrett, & Webb, 2008).

Psychotropic medication is used to help the recovering sexual addict gain initial control over acting-out behaviors, set initial boundaries, and establish abstinence or celibacy. Similar to the treatment of other addictive disorders or process addictions, a variety of medications have been used in initial and ongoing recovery. Frequently, sexual addicts, especially those who have suffered childhood sexual abuse or other life trauma, present comorbid or co-occurring mental disorders such as posttraumatic stress disorder, depression, or anxiety disorder. Medication is especially indicated in those cases in which the hypersexual behavior represents the client's effort to fix feelings or escape inner emptiness. Medications used in treating sexual addiction include naltrexone, citalopram (Celexa), and bupropion (Wellbutrin; Muench, Blain, Morgenstern, & Irwin, 2011).

Selective serotonin reuptake inhibitors have shown promise in reducing sexually addictive behaviors and comorbid conditions (Kafka & Prentky, 1992; Raymond, Grant, Kim, & Coleman, 2002; Suarez et al., 2002). Bupropion (Wellbutrin) has been used with a wide range of substance use and addictive disorders and could be especially helpful in dealing with compulsive Internet use in sexual addiction (Han & Renshaw, 2012, p. 690). Bupropion improves depressed mood and reduces compulsive behavior in clients presenting co-occurring depression and addictive disorder.

Group therapy is the key modality in sexual addiction recovery. Extending the hope, shame reduction, and ongoing fellowship afforded by participation in the 12-step recovery community, group therapy provides a microcosm of society with opportunities for disclosure, self-expression, accountability, and closeness. Therapy groups that focus on shame reduction and trauma resolution must maintain high levels of confidentiality and safety for members who may be sharing their stories for the first time. Ongoing process-oriented groups (e.g., long-term group psychotherapy) provide a life laboratory in which sexual addicts can learn from relationships how to manage urges and acting-out behaviors, explore their addiction and relapse cycles, and develop genuine intimacy with others (Hook, Hook, & Hines, 2008).

Psychoeducational interventions complement 12-step group attendance and group therapy participation. Psychoeducation is typically completed in groups with recovering sexual addicts or their family members. It is important to help sexual addicts and family members understand the compulsive sexual behavior, which is incongruent with other aspects of the client's life. Psychoeducation in sexual addiction usually includes lectures and readings from books such as Carnes's *Out of the Shadows: Understanding Sexual Addiction* (originally published in 1983). Topics of psychoeducation include examining core beliefs, breaking the addictive cycle, and completing 12-step work. Carnes (2012) developed and advocated "a gentle path through the 12 steps," which has been implemented in his proprietary sexual addiction treatment programs offered in clinics and hospital systems around the United States.

EMDR and trauma resolution methods have been used in sexual addiction recovery in order to reduce underlying compulsivity associated with childhood sexual abuse and other life traumas. Bilateral or dual attention stimulation is the central feature of EMDR. When Shapiro (1991) first developed EMDR, the emphasis was placed on using eye movements in the processing of trauma memories. Later, other mechanisms were found to produce the bilateral brain stimulation needed for therapeutic effect, including tapping of the knees, legs, or hands; shifting auditory tones; and even pulsating devices that the client holds in his or her hands. Cox and Howard (2007) described the application of EMDR in a case study of a sexually addicted trauma survivor. They emphasized how early trauma experiences not only disrupt information processing but also distort relationships with family members and others.

Carnes (1997) conducted a study of more than 1,000 recovering sexual addicts and their partners. Sexual addicts had mothers (25%), fathers (38%), and siblings (46%) who had significant substance use problems. In addition, 18% of mothers, 38% of fathers, and 50% of siblings acknowledged problems with sexual acting out. Study participants also reported eating disorders, pathological gambling, compulsive working, and other addictive disorders. Only 13% of the sexual addicts in the study came from families in which there was no addiction. Therefore, families of sexual addicts are troubled by addiction and present dynamics that contribute to the development and course of sexual addiction.

Moreover, 77% of study participants stated that they came from a family with a rigid or disengaged family structure (Carnes, 1997). These families were described as dogmatic and inflexible, evoking problems with limit setting and closeness. Disengaged families were characterized as being detached, uninvolved, and emotionally absent or distant. Most families of sexual addicts were both rigid and disengaged. Persons who grow up in such families develop sexual addiction as a survival mechanism to navigate threatening demands for intimacy in subsequent adolescent and adult relationships.

Although sexual addiction, like other substance use and addictive disorders, is considered a family disease, relatively little attention has been paid to couples and family treatment (Phillips, 2006). Schneider and Schneider (2004) discussed couples issues involved in sexual addiction. Similarly, Laaser (2002) described a 12-step recovery models for couples affected by sexual addiction. Couples affected by sexual addiction reported problems in maintaining communication, physical closeness, and sexual contact; handling finances; and engaging in recreation.

The sense of betrayal and breach of trust implicit in sexual activity outside of a committed relationship may lead the partner of a sexual addict to withdraw physically or emotionally, discontinue sexual relations, or discontinue the pair bond. Many of the wives or partners of sexual addicts come from families of origin in which there was addiction, intimacy dysfunction, or abuse (Phillips, 2006). Sexual addicts and their partners repeat the pattern of disengaged family relations many of them experienced during their childhoods. The pain and shame of addiction are delineated to children and passed on to succeeding generations.

The intergenerational nature of addictive disorders is manifested in sexual addiction through shame and secrecy. It is difficult in American society to pursue open and age-appropriate communication and education about sexual health. Therefore, children in families affected by sexual addiction are especially deprived of healthy information and interaction. Corley and Schneider (2003) indicated that age-appropriate disclosure of sexual acting-out behavior could help in overcoming shameful secrets in sexually addictive family systems.

INTEGRATIVE TREATMENT PACKAGE FOR SEXUAL ADDICTION AND LIFE TRAUMA

The life histories of most sexual addicts, especially women and paraphilic sexual addicts, are testimonies to the power of symptoms to serve as survival mechanisms, paradoxically escaping the pain and shame of childhood traumas while engendering adverse and shameful consequences. The case of Sarah speaks to her attempts to survive sexual abuse trauma while constructing a restrictive, addictive lifestyle in which she repeats salient aspects of her abuse and avoids growth potentials in intimate relationships. Over the course of nearly 30 years, clinicians trained at the Masters and Johnson Institute (e.g., Schwartz & Southern, 1999, 2000) have offered together and independently integrative treatment of sexual abuse and sexual addiction as well as other trauma-based addictive disorders. The following treatment program, which was developed by the senior author (Stephen Southern), has been offered in inpatient, residential, day treatment, intensive outpatient, and weekly outpatient settings.

Residential treatment in the continuum of care seems ideally suited to simultaneously treating life trauma and addictive disorders. The Life Trauma Treatment Workshop is implemented in the second or third month of residential treatment in order to reduce trauma-related factors, such as emotion dysregulation and dissociation, that might otherwise contribute to relapse. When sexual addiction is the primary presenting problem, there is a need for concurrent treatment of life trauma (i.e., neglect, physical abuse, sexual abuse, and other childhood adverse events) and the addictive disorder. Comprehensive screening and admissions criteria need to be used in clinical decision making for a case such as that presented by Sarah in which there are comorbid mental, addictive, and sexual disorders, including masochistic (paraphilic) sexual addiction.

Several of the screening criteria should incorporate conventional wisdom in sequential addiction treatment, including a period of sobriety, establishment of structure and a plan for aftercare, the ruling out of severe mental disorders that would interfere with treatment, basic compliance with previous medical regimens, a willingness to commit to treatment rules and contracting, and practice of safe and respectful behaviors in a sanctuary-like environment (cf. Bloom, 1997).

In the Life Trauma Treatment Workshop, 2 weeks are invested in active treatment combining psychoeducational sessions, nonaddictive coping skills training, exposure-based treatment, cognitive restructuring, narrative therapy, art therapy, 12-step work, relapse prevention, and aftercare planning. The goal of the workshop is to prepare the participant to address trauma issues before they naturally arise in ongoing recovery so that the thoughts and feelings can be processed in a safe, supportive environment. In addition, it is best to practice nonaddictive coping skills, distress tolerance, and relapse prevention when the recovering sexual addict is experiencing activation of trauma-related schemas and controlled emotional upheaval. The Life Trauma Treatment Workshop involves daily group and individual therapies, skill building and psychoeducational sessions, recreation therapy, creative arts therapy, and spiritual development exercises. These programs are highly structured during the day, and homework exercises are provided for each evening, 7 days per week.

In the preparation week, there is screening and selection of participants from applicants in the residential treatment center. Participants learn enough about the model of treatment and the process so that they can provide informed consent and complete a treatment contract. They secure childhood photos and memorabilia and initiate a life history review that contextualizes trauma experiences and the progression of addictive behaviors. In preparation for the active phase of treatment, clients practice effective coping and problem-solving skills.

During the first week of active treatment, participants organize a portfolio for maintaining homework exercises and recording important aspects of their emerging life stories. Depth of sharing in groups is emphasized. Creative arts and experiential therapies instigate recollection and processing of difficult feelings, and participants use nonaddictive skills to regulate emotions and avoid addictive cycles or relapse chains of behavior. In particular, each client develops skills in grounding, containment, and switching to counteract disorganizing anxiety and even dissociation in cases of extreme trauma. Bibliotherapy and therapeutic media, as well as disclosures by group members, instill hope and provide evidence that change is possible. Each participant begins to tell his or her story while others learn vicariously and integrate their stories in the collective narrative experience of the group. Trust and increasing group cohesiveness are major curative factors. Additional experiential techniques, such as constructing a genogram, producing a kinetic family drawing, engaging in family sculpting, and participating in psychodrama, increase the intensity of the treatment process.

The second week of active treatment builds on the experiential and regressive therapies. Participants reveal the pain and shame of their childhood experiences in a safe, structured environment that can contain and make meaning from suffering. Fantasies, urges, and ritualized behaviors, which could trigger the client's addictive cycle, are unearthed and disclosed in the mutuality of the healing process. The client participates in imagery-based trauma reconstruction and reprocessing with an experienced therapist who participates in recovery and supervision to manage countertransference issues. Each group member presents a First Step for addictive survival mechanisms in an addictive behavior treatment group and tells his or her story in the process-oriented group. One or more group members lead in the development of healing rituals and collective stories that will memorialize their shared healing. Toward the end of the week, members develop plans for self-adoption (self-care through self-parenting) and relapse prevention based on insight into their addictive cycles.

The final week in the intensive workshop involves debriefing. The overall structure of the work reflects the change process in which one prepares by building structural supports, instigates and catalyzes trauma material and addictive urges, processes content and makes meaning from life trauma and adverse consequences, and debriefs participants who are sharing experiences and reconstructing their lives.

INTEGRATIVE TREATMENT IN THE CASE OF SARAH

Sarah was motivated to see her family doctor and accept a referral to a therapist after she bottomed out in her pathological gambling and experienced negative emotional consequences from compulsive sexual behavior. Sarah's therapist suggested that she had temporarily fixed her feelings by engaging in sexual addiction. The therapist indicated that Sarah would probably return to a pattern of self-injurious behavior not manifested since adolescence if her underlying sexual abuse trauma was not addressed. The therapist increased awareness of the severity of the unresolved trauma by emphasizing the function of compulsive behaviors in Sarah's particular firing order of addictions. Over the course of several weeks, the Prozac prescribed by her doctor helped Sarah deal with urges to gamble and act out sexually. Her mood improved and she committed to a course of integrative treatment.

Sarah continued taking Prozac and visited Gamblers Anonymous (GA). She felt like a guy at the GA meeting was being seductive (i.e., "trying to Thirteenth Step me"), so she decided to attend meetings online. At times she felt tempted to visit hookup and role-playing sites on the Internet, but she used grounding and containment techniques taught by her therapist as well as mindfulness meditation she practiced in the office. Sarah maintained boundaries in pathological gambling through psychoeducational sessions, cognitive behavior therapy, and homework exercises from the Overcoming Pathological Gambling program (Ladouceur & Lachance, 2007). After 7 weeks of abstinence from pathological gambling and compulsive sexual behavior, Sarah was encouraged to begin Seeking Safety, an integrative approach involving concurrent treatment for trauma and addictive behavior (Najavits, 2002), in twice-weekly individual therapy sessions. She continued her pharmacological treatment and GA recovery. Sarah was engaged in reading the GA Big Book and working the steps toward recovery.

Seeking Safety helped Sarah to see that she was not alone in recovering from pathological gambling and sexual abuse trauma. She completed the worksheets and worked with her therapist to maintain boundaries while slowly exposing herself to the reality of her date rape. She recalled that there had been some earlier abuse incidents in elementary school when an older boy would secretly touch her body under her clothes. She always felt ashamed and awkward around peers. She blamed herself for the date rape, but her therapist assisted her in examining mistaken beliefs and misattributions arising from a history of sexual abuse. Slowly Sarah developed a more resilient sense of self. As she addressed her trauma issues, Sarah noted that urges to act out through gambling returned. She slipped or lapsed by visiting some gambling and role-playing game sites on the Internet. In the past, increased Internet use would lead to preoccupation with masochism and compulsive masturbation while viewing spanking and bondage videos. However, she was able to continue participation in the Seeking Safety program.

Sarah began to realize that compulsive Internet use, compulsive masturbation, pathological gambling, and extramarital sex represented survival mechanisms. She realized that she was programmed through childhood sexual abuse to view herself as an object for exploitation. She derived gratification from the attention of dominant partners and opportunities to be submissive. Involvement in pathological gambling intervened in her addictive process of retreating into a fantasy world, which was constructed through compulsive Internet use, role play, and finally compulsive masturbation. The recent sexual addiction binge occurred as she bottomed out in pathological gambling. She returned to the well-developed pattern of escape from pain and shame though Internet activity. After a period of 90 days of sobriety, Sarah's therapist concluded that she was ready to participate in exposure therapy, in which she would relive salient aspects of the date rape.

Exposure-based therapy and response prevention helped Sarah face the reality of the date rape experience. She had apparently been touched and penetrated by two peers while she was intoxicated. One of the adolescents had taken photographs of her during the episode. Experiencing these memories intensified her shame and triggered urges to act out sexually through masochistic fantasies and masturbation. She was able to refrain from Internet use and interaction with potentially exploitive partners.

This component of treatment embraced harm reduction. She was increasingly able to tolerate distress and regulate emotions through mindfulness meditation. Sarah set and maintained boundaries to reduce all of her addictive behaviors. As she addressed the underlying sexual abuse trauma, she was better able to abstain from pathological gambling and sexual addiction. Fantasies and urges to engage in role play while spending increasing amounts of time on the Internet were most resistant to change. Because she had established some external or exclusive boundaries, she began to work with internal boundaries regarding choices of what to include in a healthier lifestyle. She became aware of some core emptiness and lack of intimacy. Sarah began to yearn for a stronger relationship with her husband and asked her therapist to work with her on intimacy issues.

The therapist conducted a collateral contact interview with the husband, who remarked that he was pleased and surprised by Sarah's progress in overcoming pathological gambling. The therapist discussed with the husband the ongoing treatment for sexual abuse trauma. The husband was aware of the date rape but did not understand how the posttraumatic stress disorder was related to the compulsive gambling. At this stage in her recovery, Sarah and her therapist decided to postpone disclosure until she worked her steps in the spiritual growth process of GA. Sarah and her husband committed to beginning once-weekly couples therapy sessions with a male colleague of her therapist.

The couples therapy addressed improvements in communication and emotional intimacy. Slowly they progressed toward physical and sexual intimacy. Sarah's husband expressed regret about withdrawing from her in his work and admitted that he had some one-night stands while spending weekends with his guard unit. Sarah admitted her recent sexual binges. The therapist maintained the holding environment of the therapeutic alliance and reassured the couple that they could work through their shame and pain. The therapist helped them to see that each responded to the demands of intimacy by withdrawing to work or fantasy, becoming preoccupied with emergency conditions, or seeking soothing in intense sexual contacts. Sarah and her husband collaborated in establishing new relational boundaries, recovering a satisfying sex life, and pursuing shared spiritual activities.

Integrative treatment of pathological gambling, sexual addiction, compulsive Internet use, and sexual abuse trauma was effective in helping Sarah maintain abstinence and evolve effective boundaries. Sarah and her husband were able to enjoy increasing intimacy and spirituality in a meaningful lifestyle. Sarah continued to practice skills she learned in the Overcoming Pathological Gambling and Seeking Safety programs. Periodically, when under a lot of stress, she would slip by spending increasing amounts of time on the Internet, which led to some visiting of spanking sites. However, she did not experience a full relapse in sexual addiction or pathological gambling. She continued to take medication as prescribed and to participate in weekly outpatient psychotherapy. Concurrent treatment of trauma and addiction reduced her compulsive urges and restored her capacity for intimacy.

CONCLUSIONS

Sexual addiction is a complex clinical disorder that has been treated primarily from the perspective of sexual recovery based on the work of Patrick Carnes and his colleagues. Hypersexual men can be treated through the sexual recovery model consisting of group work and individual consultation using the 12 steps (Carnes, 1983, 1997, 2004). Women who present sexual addiction and paraphilic sexual addicts have underlying sexual abuse trauma that should be addressed to reduce the risk of relapse in recovery.

There is no consensus on the diagnosis of sexual addiction. Criteria for diagnosing hypersexual disorder (Kafka, 2010) should replace the controversial and ambiguous label of *sexual addiction*. In addition, self-diagnosed sexual addiction should not focus exclusively on abstinence or the reduction of problem behaviors. Rather, the emerging concepts of sexual health (e.g., Edwards, 2012) provide a context for lifestyle change and sexual fulfillment as treatment goals.

The lack of agreement regarding what constitutes sexual addiction increases the importance of sensitive clinical interviewing and assessment. Although a number of assessment instruments or tools are described in the literature (Hook et al., 2010), there is no standard battery or protocol for problem specification in planning sexual addiction treatment.

Sexual addiction treatment includes 12-step group attendance and step work, motivational interviewing, bibliotherapy and psychoeducation, group therapy, pharmacological treatment of comorbid conditions, and family therapy. Sexual addiction typically affects the partners and family members of clients; therefore, couples and family therapy should be implemented in most cases. Because sexual addiction is a trauma-based intimacy disorder, especially among women who engage in hypersexual behavior, concurrent treatment of trauma and addiction is indicated. Integrative treatment of sexual abuse trauma and hypersexual disorder was described here in the Life Trauma Treatment Workshop as well as the case of Sarah. Integrative treatment helps sexual addicts realize the promises of sexual recovery.

RESOURCES

Websites

Association for the Treatment of Sexual Abusers
    www.atsa.com/
COSA
    www.cosa-recovery.org/
Cybersex Addiction Screening Test
    www.sexualrecovery.com/resources/self-tests/csat.php
International Institute for Trauma & Addiction Professionals, Am I a Sex Addict?
    www.sexhelp.com/am-i-a-sex-addict
Internet Behavior Consulting, Cybersex Addiction and Online Sex Offender Resources
    www.internetbehavior.com/index.htm
Men's Sexual Addiction Screening Test
    www.sexualrecovery.com/resources/self-tests/gsast.php
Partners of Sex Addicts Screening Test
    www.sexualrecovery.com/resources/self-tests/psast.php
PATHOS Questionnaire
    http://sexualhealth-addiction.com/questionnaire/
Recovering Couples Anonymous
    www.recovering-couples.org/
S-Anon
    www.sanon.org/
Safer Society Foundation, Inc.
    www.safersociety.org/
Sex Addiction Support Groups
    www.porn-free.org/support_groups.htm
Sex Addicts Anonymous
    https://saa-recovery.org/
Sex and Love Addicts Anonymous
    www.slaafws.org/
Sexaholics Anonymous
    www.sa.org/
Sexual Compulsives Anonymous
    www.sca-recovery.org/

Sexual Offender Treatment Journal
www.sexual-offender-treatment.org/
Sexual Recovery Anonymous
www.sexualrecovery.org/
Society for the Advancement of Sexual Health (resource page)
http://sash.net/?q=groups-and-meetings
Women's Sexual Addiction Screening Test
www.sexualrecovery.com/resources/self-tests/wsast.php
Your Brain on Porn
www.yourbrainonporn.com/

Videos

Are You a Hurting Partner of a SA With Carol the Coach
www.blogtalkradio.com/sexhelpwithcarolthecoach/2013/04/09/sexual-addiction-can-be-managed-with-carol-the-coach
Dr. Patrick Carnes, Leading Sex Addiction Expert, Video Interview
www.youtube.com/watch?v=i1pQfGD_MQI
Ex-Porn Star Shelley Lubben, The Truth Behind the Fantasy of Porn: PornHarms.com Briefing
www.youtube.com/watch?v=B9P4a3uhcUQ
How to Treat Sex Addiction: Sexual Addiction Treatment With Dr. Clark
www.youtube.com/watch?v=QwoCWAdvkdk
Kids Access Porn Sites at 6, Begin Flirting Online at 8
www.usatoday.com/story/cybertruth/2013/05/14/childrens-online-safety-porn/2158015/
Maria's Story: How Porn Ended Her Marriage
www.youtube.com/watch?v=cQR4FF6qLBk
The Science of Pornography Addiction
www.youtube.com/watch?v=SQ_fIv019fs
Sex Addicts' Dark World
www.youtube.com/watch?v=0gavSBX926M
Sex Addicts Informational Video
www.sexualrecovery.com/resources/videos.php
Spouses of Sex Addicts Informational Video
www.sexualrecovery.com/resources/videos.php

REFERENCES

Amen, D. G., Willeumier, K., & Johnson, R. (2012). The clinical utility of brain SPECT imaging in process addictions. *Journal of Psychoactive Drugs, 44,* 18–26. doi:10.1080/02 791072.2012.660101

American Psychiatric Association. (1987). *Diagnostic and statistical manual of mental disorders* (3rd ed.). Washington, DC: Author.

American Psychiatric Association. (2000). *Diagnostic and statistical manual of mental disorders* (4th ed., text rev.). Washington, DC: Author.

American Psychiatric Association. (2013). *Diagnostic and statistical manual of mental disorders* (5th ed.). Arlington, VA: Author.

Becerra, M. D., Robinson, C., & Balkin, R. (2011). Exploring relationships of masculinity and ethnicity as at-risk markers for online sexual addiction in men. *Sexual Addiction & Compulsivity, 18,* 243–260. doi:10.1080/10720162.2011.627284

Benotsch, E. G., Kalichman, S. C., & Pinkerton, S. D. (2001). Sexual compulsivity in HIV-positive men and women: Prevalence, predictors, and consequences of high-risk behaviors. *Sexual Addiction & Compulsivity, 8,* 83–99.

Bergner, R. M. (2002). Sexual compulsion as attempted recovery from degradation: Theory and therapy. *Journal of Sex & Marital Therapy, 28*(5), 373–387.

Birchard, T. (2011). Sexual addiction and the paraphilias. *Sexual Addiction & Compulsivity, 18*, 157–187. doi:10.1080/10720162.2011.606674

Blankenship, R., & Laaser, M. (2004). Sexual addiction and ADHD: Is there a connection? *Sexual Addiction & Compulsivity, 11*, 7–20. doi:10.1080/10720160490458184

Bloom, S. L. (1997). *Creating sanctuary: Toward the evolution of sane societies.* New York, NY: Routledge.

Carnes, P. (1983). *Out of the shadows: Understanding sexual addiction.* Minneapolis, MN: CompCare.

Carnes, P. (1989). *Contrary to love: Helping the sexual addict.* Minneapolis, MN: CompCare.

Carnes, P. J. (1997). *The betrayal bond: Breaking free of exploitive relationships.* Deerfield Beach, FL: Health Communications.

Carnes, P. (2000). Sexual addiction and compulsion: Recognition, treatment and recovery. *CNS Spectrums, 5*(10), 1–16.

Carnes, P. (2004). *Out of the shadows: Understanding sexual addiction* (Rev. ed.). Center City, MN: Hazelden.

Carnes, P. (2012). *A gentle path through the twelve steps: The classic guide for all persons in the process of recovery* (3rd ed.). Center City, MN: Hazelden.

Carnes, P., Delmonico, D. L., & Griffin, E. (2001). *In the shadows of the net: Breaking free of compulsive online sexual behavior.* Center City, MN: Hazelden.

Carnes, P., Green, B., & Carnes, S. (2010). The same yet different: Refocusing the Sexual Addiction Screening Test (SAST) to reflect orientation and gender. *Sexual Addiction & Compulsivity, 17*, 17–30. doi:10.1080/10720161003604087

Carter, D. R., & Ruiz, N. J. (1996). Discriminant validity and reliability studies on the Sexual Addiction Scale of the Disorders Screening Inventory. *Sexual Addiction & Compulsivity, 3*, 332–340.

Chaney, M. P., & Dew, B. J. (2003). Online experiences of sexually compulsive men who have sex with men. *Sexual Addiction & Compulsivity, 10*, 259–274.

Charney, D. A., Palacios-Boix, J., & Gill, K. J. (2007). Sexual abuse and the outcome of addiction treatment. *American Journal on Addictions, 16*, 93–100. doi:10.1080/10550490601184225

Coleman, E. (1987). Sexual compulsivity: Definition, etiology, and treatment considerations. *Journal of Chemical Dependency Treatment, 1*, 189–204.

Coleman, E. (1990). The obsessive-compulsive model for describing compulsive sexual behavior. *American Journal of Preventive Psychiatry and Neurology, 2*, 9–14.

Coleman, E. (1991). Compulsive sexual behavior: New concepts and treatments. *Journal of Psychology & Human Sexuality, 4*, 37–52.

Coleman, E. (1992). Is your patient suffering from compulsive sexual behavior? *Psychiatric Annals, 22*, 320–325.

Coleman, E., Miner, M., Ohlerking, F., & Raymond, N. (2001). Compulsive Sexual Behavior Inventory: A preliminary study of reliability and validity. *Journal of Sex and Marital Therapy, 27*, 325–332.

Cooper, A., Delmonico, D. L., & Griffin-Shelley, E. (2004). Online sexual activity: An examination of potentially problematic behaviors. *Sexual Addiction & Compulsivity, 11*, 129–143.

Corley, M. D., & Schneider, J. P. (2003). Sex addiction disclosure to children: The parents' perspective. *Sexual Addiction & Compulsivity, 10*, 291–324.

Cox, R. P., & Howard, M. D. (2007). Utilization of EMDR in the treatment of sexual addiction: A case study. *Sexual Addiction & Compulsivity, 14*, 1–20. doi:10.1080/10720160601011299

Del Guidice, M. J., & Kutinsky, J. (2007). Applying motivational interviewing to the treatment of sexual compulsivity and addiction. *Sexual Addiction & Compulsivity, 14*, 303–319. doi:10.1080/10720160701710634

Delmonico, D. L., Bubenzer, D. L., & West, J. D. (1998). Assessing sexual addiction with the Sexual Dependency Inventory–Revised. *Sexual Addiction & Compulsivity, 5*, 179–187.

Delmonico, D. L., & Miller, J. A. (2003). The Internet Sex Screening Test: A comparison of sexual compulsives versus non-sexual compulsives. *Sexual and Relationship Therapy, 18*, 261–276.

Edwards, W. (2012). Applying a sexual health model to the assessment of treatment of Internet sexual compulsivity. *Sexual Addiction & Compulsivity, 19*, 3–15. doi:10.1080/10720162.2012.660433

Exner, T. M., Meyer-Bahlburg, H. F. L., & Ehrhardt, A. A. (1992). Sexual self-control as a mediator of high-risk sexual behavior in a New York City cohort of HIV+ and HIV- gay men. *Journal of Sex Research, 29*, 389–406.

Faisandier, K. M., Taylor, J. E., & Salisbury, R. M. (2012). What does attachment have to do with out-of-control sexual behaviour? *New Zealand Journal of Psychology, 41*, 19–29.

Firestone, R. W., Firestone, L. A., & Catlett, J. (2006). *Sex and love in intimate relationships.* Washington, DC: American Psychological Association.

Garcia, F. D., & Thibaut, F. (2010). Sexual addictions. *American Journal of Drug and Alcohol Abuse, 36*, 254–260. doi:10.3109/00952990.2010.503823

Garos, S., & Stock, W. A. (1998a). Investigating the discriminant validity and differentiating capability of the Garos Sexual Behavior Index. *Sexual Addiction & Compulsivity, 5*, 251–267.

Garos, S., & Stock, W. A. (1998b). Measuring disorders of sexual frequency and control: The Garos Sexual Behavior Index. *Sexual Addiction & Compulsivity, 5*, 159–177.

Gordon-Lamoureux, R. J. (2007). Exploring the possibility of sexual addiction in men arrested for seeking out prostitutes: A preliminary study. *Journal of Addiction Nursing, 18*, 21–29. doi:10.1080/10884600601174458

Grant, J. E., & Potenza, M. N. (2006). Sexual orientation of men with pathological gambling: Prevalence and psychiatric comorbidity in a treatment-seeking sample. *Comprehensive Psychiatry, 47*, 515–518.

Hagedorn, W. B. (2009). The call for a new *Diagnostic and Statistical Manual of Mental Disorders:* Addictive disorders. *Journal of Addictions & Offender Counseling, 29*, 110–127.

Han, D. H., & Renshaw, P. F. (2012). Bupropion in the treatment of problematic online game play in patients with major depressive disorder. *Journal of Psychopharmacology, 26*, 689–696.

Hook, J. N., Hook, J. P., Davis, D. E., Worthington, E. L., Jr., & Penberthy, J. K. (2010). Measuring sexual addiction and compulsivity: A critical review of instruments. *Journal of Sex & Marital Therapy, 36*, 227–260. doi:10.1080/00926231003719673

Hook, J. N., Hook, J. P., & Hines, S. (2008). Reach out or act out: Long-term group therapy for sexual addiction. *Sexual Addiction & Compulsivity, 15*, 217–232. doi:10.1080/10720160802288829

Kafka, M. P. (1997). Hypersexual desire in males: An operational definition and clinical implications for males with paraphilias and paraphilia-related disorders. *Archives of Sexual Behavior, 26*, 505–526.

Kafka, M. P. (2007). Paraphilia-related disorders: The evaluation and treatment of non-paraphilic hypersexuality. In S. Leiblum (Ed.), *Principles and practice of sex therapy* (4th ed., pp. 442–476). New York, NY: Guilford Press.

Kafka, M. P. (2010). Hypersexual disorder: A proposed diagnosis for *DSM–5. Archives of Sexual Behavior, 39*, 377–400.

Kafka, M. P., & Hennen, J. (2002). A *DSM–IV* Axis I comorbidity study of males (*n* = 120) with paraphilias and paraphilia-related disorders. *Sexual Abuse, 14*(4), 349–366.

Kafka, M. P., & Prentky, R. (1992). Fluoxetine treatment of nonparaphilic sexual addictions and paraphilias in men. *Journal of Clinical Psychiatry, 53*, 351–358.

Kafka, M. P., & Prentky, R. A. (1994). Preliminary observations of *DSM–III–R* Axis I co-morbidity in men with paraphilias and paraphilia-related disorders. *Journal of Clinical Psychiatry, 55,* 481–487.

Kaplan, M. S., & Krueger, R. B. (2010). Diagnosis, assessment, and treatment of hyper-sexuality. *Journal of Sex Research, 47*(2–3), 181–198.

Karim, R., & Chaudhri, P. (2012). Behavioral addictions: An overview. *Journal of Psychoactive Drugs, 44,* 5–17. doi:10.1080/02791072.2012.662859

Katehakis, A. (2009). Affective neuroscience and the treatment of sexual addiction. *Sexual Addiction & Compulsivity, 16,* 1–31. doi:10.1080/10720160802708966

Kausch, O., Rugle, L., & Rowland, D. Y. (2006). Lifetime histories of trauma among pathological gamblers. *American Journal on Addictions, 15,* 35–43.

Kiepek, N. (2008). Interactions between substance use and sexual behaviours for women receiving alcohol and other drugs services. *New Zealand Journal of Psychology, 37,* 49–55.

Kingston, D. A., & Firestone, P. (2008). Problematic hypersexuality: A review of conceptualization and diagnosis. *Sexual Addiction & Compulsivity, 15,* 284–310. doi:10.1080/107201802289249

Kuzma, J. M., & Black, D. W. (2008). Epidemiology, prevalence, and natural history of compulsive sexual behavior. *Psychiatric Clinics of North America, 31,* 603–611.

Laaser, M. R. (2002). Recovery for couples. In P. J. Carnes & K. M. Adams (Eds.), *Clinical management of sex addiction* (pp. 125–136). New York, NY: Brunner-Routledge.

Laaser, M. (2004). *Healing the wounds of sexual addiction.* Grand Rapids, MI: Zondervan.

Ladouceur, R., & Lachance, S. (2007). *Overcoming pathological gambling: Therapist guide.* New York, NY: Oxford University Press.

Landau, J., Garrett, J., & Webb, R. (2008). Assisting a concerned person to motivate someone experiencing cybersex into treatment. *Journal of Marital and Family Therapy, 34,* 498–511.

Långström, N., & Hanson, R. K. (2006). High rates of sexual intercourse in the general population: Correlates and predictors. *Archives of Sexual Behavior, 35,* 37–52.

Levine, S. B. (2010). What is sexual addiction? *Journal of Sex & Marital Therapy, 36,* 261–275.

Manley, G. (1999). Treating chronic sexual dysfunction in couples recovering from sex addiction and sex coaddiction. *Sexual Addiction & Compulsivity, 6,* 111–124.

McBride, K. R., Reece, M., & Sanders, S. A. (2007). Predicting negative outcomes of sexuality using the Compulsive Sexual Behavior Inventory. *International Journal of Sexual Health, 19,* 51–62.

Mercer, J. T. (1998). Assessment of the Sex Addicts Anonymous Questionnaire: Differentiation between the general population, sex addicts, and sex offenders. *Sexual Addiction & Compulsivity, 5,* 107–117.

Money, J. (1986). *Lovemaps—Clinical concepts of sexual/erotic health and pathology, paraphilia, and gender transposition in childhood, adolescence, and maturity.* New York, NY: Prometheus Books.

Muench, R., Blain, L., Morgenstern, J., & Irwin, T. (2011). Self-efficacy and attributions about change in persons attempting to reduce compulsive sexual behavior with medication vs. placebo. *Sexual Addiction & Compulsivity, 18,* 232–242. doi:10.1080/10720162.2011.625912

Najavits, L. M. (2002). *Seeking Safety: A treatment manual for PTSD and substance abuse.* New York, NY: Guilford Press.

Opitz, D. M., Tsytsarev, S. V., & Froh, J. (2009). Women's sexual addiction and family dynamics, depression and substance abuse. *Sexual Addiction & Compulsivity, 16,* 324–340. doi:10.1080/10720160903375749

Phillips, L. A. (2006). Literature review of research in family systems treatment of sexual addiction. *Sexual Addiction & Compulsivity, 13,* 241–246. doi:10.1080/10720160600870794

Raymond, N. C., Grant, J. E., Kim, S. W., & Coleman, E. (2002). Treatment of compulsive sexual behaviour with naltrexone and serotonin reuptake inhibitors: Two case studies. *International Clinical Psychopharmacology, 17*, 201–205.

Raymond, N. C., Lloyd, M. D., Miner, M. H., & Kim, S. W. (2007). Preliminary report on the development and validation of the Sexual Symptom Assessment Scale. *Sexual Addiction & Compulsivity, 14*, 119–129.

Robinson, B. E., Bockting, W. O., Rosser, B., Miner, M., & Coleman, E. (2002). The Sexual Health Model: Application of a sexological approach to HIV prevention. *Health Education Research, 17*(1), 43–57.

Samenow, C. P. (2010). A biopsychosocial model of hypersexual disorder/sexual addiction. *Sexual Addiction & Compulsivity, 17*, 69–81. doi:10.1080/10720162.2010.481300

Schneider, J. P., & Irons, R. R. (2001). Assessment and treatment of addictive sexual disorders: Relevance for chemical dependency relapse. *Substance Use & Misuse, 36*, 1795–1820.

Schneider, J. P., & Schneider, B. H. (2004). *Sex, lies, and forgiveness: Couples speak out on healing from sex addiction* (3rd ed.). Tucson, AZ: Recovery Resources Press.

Schneider, J., & Weiss, R. (2001). *Cybersex exposed: Simple fantasy or obsession.* Center City, MN: Hazelden.

Schwartz, M., Galperin, L., & Masters, W. (1995). Sexual trauma within the context of traumatic and inescapable stress, neglect, and poisonous pedagogy. In M. Hunter (Ed.), *Adult survivors of sexual abuse: Treatment innovations* (pp. 1–19). Thousand Oaks, CA: Sage. doi:http://dx.doi.org/10.4135/9781483345352.n1

Schwartz, M. F., & Southern, S. (1999). Manifestations of damaged development of the human affectional systems and developmentally based psychotherapies. *Sexual Addiction & Compulsivity, 6*, 163–175.

Schwartz, M. F., & Southern, S. (2000). Compulsive cybersex: The new tea room. *Sexual Addiction & Compulsivity, 7*, 127–144.

Seegers, J. A. (2003). The prevalence of sexual addiction symptoms on the college campus. *Sexual Addiction & Compulsivity, 10*, 247–258.

Shapiro, F. (1991). Eye movement desensitization and reprocessing procedure: From EMD to EMDR: A new treatment model for anxiety and related trauma. *Behavioral Therapist, 14*, 133–135.

Southern, S. (2002). The tie that binds: Sadomasochism in female addicted trauma survivors. *Sexual Addiction & Compulsivity, 9*, 209–229.

Southern, S. (2008). Treatment of compulsive cybersex behavior. *Psychiatric Clinics of North America, 31*, 697–712.

Stoller, R. (1975). *Perversion: The erotic form of hatred.* New York, NY: Pantheon Books.

Suarez, T., O'Leary, A., Morgenstern, J., Allen, A., Hollander, E., & O'Leary, A. (2002). Selective serotonin reuptake inhibitors as a treatment for sexual compulsivity. In A. O'Leary (Ed.), *Beyond condoms: Alternative approaches to HIV prevention* (pp. 199–220). New York, NY: Kluwer Academic/Plenum.

Tonigan, J. S., & Miller, W. R. (2002). The Inventory of Drug Use Consequences (InDUC): Test–retest stability and sensitivity to detect change. *Psychology of Addictive Behaviors, 16*, 165–168.

Woody, J. D. (2011). Sexual addiction/hypersexuality and the *DSM*: Update and practice guidance for social workers. *Journal of Social Work Practice in the Addictions, 11*, 301–320. doi:10.1080/1533256X.2011.619926

CHAPTER 9

DISORDERED EATING
Tamara Duarte and Fredericka DeLee

STUDENT LEARNING OUTCOMES

At the conclusion of this chapter students will

1. Outline the demographic characteristics of those with an eating disorder
2. Identify symptoms that characterize an eating disorder
3. Identify the different assessments used to diagnose eating disorders
4. Identify evidence-based approaches for working with this population

CASES AND CASE DISCUSSION

Sharon is a 38-year-old woman who is attending counseling because she feels "down." Sharon has been married for 8 years and reports no marital issues other than her husband is worried about her and urged her to attend counseling. Sharon is slim and dressed appropriately. She admits she struggled with anorexia nervosa when she was in high school. After attending counseling for 6 months she was able to overcome her eating disorder. Sharon states that she does not know why she feels down. She reports having a great relationship with her husband, enjoying her work, and having a close-knit group of friends. She states that her husband is supportive of her and often tells her that her weight means nothing to him. Sharon admits that she has difficulty believing this and thinks that "he may leave if I get really fat."

In five sessions of individual counseling Sharon shares a significant amount about her life in an effort to explore her down experiences. Sharon reports that she has lost weight recently, approximately 20 pounds. She states that she is not on a diet per se but tends to "watch what I eat." Sharon goes on to admit that since her eating disorder she has maintained a specific weight for 20 years, up until a few months ago, when she gained "too much weight." Sharon reports that she has weighed herself every morning "at 7 a.m., immediately after using the restroom, but before brushing my teeth" for the past 20 years. She states that when her weight was "up" she would eat only vegetables and water that day, and when it was "down" she would eat regularly. Sharon states that this "worked great" for many years until recently, when the number on the scale "kept going up." She reports being disappointed in herself for gaining the extra weight. Sharon states that she "had to do something drastic or else." Sharon reports that she is now about 5 pounds under her typical weight. She states that she feels comfortable at her current weight but would not mind if it went down a bit more. When questioned about how she would feel about gaining back the 5 pounds in order to be back at her prior weight, she states, "That cannot happen."

After further discussion Sharon reveals that she spends a significant amount of time talking about her body and her weight. Throughout her session she discusses the food she has eaten for the day, which includes mainly a portion of low-fat and nonfat items, and she restricts her caloric intake to less than 800 calories per day. Sharon mentions that she is not a vegetarian but avoids eating meat because it makes her "feel weighed down." She discusses the sadness she experiences when she avoids the foods she used to love and confesses that she is afraid to eat them because she does not want to gain weight again. Sharon states that some days she has difficulty eating even "safe foods."

Sharon states that she started feeling down when she initially gained weight but does not understand why she does not feel better now that she has lost it. When she discusses her life before the weight gain she admits to having been happy. Sharon states that this is the first time since her teenage years that she has worried about her weight, but she does not think she has an eating disorder. Sharon talks considerably about the immense feeling of failure she felt when she realized she had gained 20 pounds.

Charles is a 17-year-old male referred by his school counselor. Charles's mother fills out his paperwork and indicates that the school counselor is concerned with Charles's recent weight loss. She indicates that the school counselor is worried that Charles might be depressed. Charles is tall and lean, has good hygiene, and is dressed in baggy pants and a loose hooded sweatshirt. He denies any symptoms of depression. Charles states that he is sleeping well, enjoys school, and engages in activities he enjoys. Charles states that he is a straight-A student and that he hopes to attend one of the state schools on an academic scholarship.

Charles is eager to discuss his recent weight loss. He admits he was "out of shape" and wanted to "get healthier and lose weight." Charles states that his desire to change the way he looked started over the summer when he went to the beach with classmates and he "felt like a butterball compared to the other guys." Charles states that he has lost approximately 20 pounds over the past 2 months. Charles has an athletic body type and appears healthy. He states he exercises fairly regularly and enjoys food.

Charles is not in a romantic relationship and admits that he would like to be. Charles states that most girls are not interested in a guy who is not in shape. He admits that this prompted his new healthy lifestyle, and although he does not have a girlfriend yet he feels certain he will be able to "get one" soon enough.

Charles admits that he struggles with his new lifestyle. He discusses his difficulty resisting urges to eat "bad" food such as pizza, donuts, chips, and other carbohydrate-laden foods. He discusses his "intense love/hate relationship" with these types of foods, admitting he has difficulty controlling how much he eats once he starts. He states that he does pretty well avoiding these foods during the week, but he tends to become anxious once the weekend approaches. He states that he has a tendency to "let loose" over the weekend and eat whatever he wants. Charles admits to "going overboard" at times. He reports that when this occurs he will increase his amount of exercise until he feels he has "gotten rid of all the extra calories." When asked for a specific example, Charles recounts an episode from the prior Saturday when he consumed two cheeseburgers with fries and a milkshake for lunch after having just finished a "snack" of Oreo cookies with milk, two bowls of cereal, half a bag of potato chips, and three pieces of leftover pizza from the night before. Charles admits he felt "out of control" and attempted to induce vomiting, which he had never tried before, but he could not "get anything to come up." He reports that he went to the gym instead and exercised on various cardio machines for almost 5 hours. Charles states that he typically only exercises for 2.5 hours per day, so the extra couple of hours "helped get rid of all those calories."

OVERVIEW OF DISORDERED EATING

Eating disorders are serious mental illnesses affecting approximately 5% of the population, often causing long-lasting or deadly medical and psychological problems (Berg, Peterson, & Frazier, 2012). Eating disorders have the highest mortality rate of any mental illness (National Association of Anorexia Nervosa and Associated Disorders, 2013), and prevalence rates are 0.6% for anorexia, 1.0% for bulimia, and 2.8% for binge eating (National Institute of Mental Health, 2012). Of those individuals with anorexia or bulimia who seek treatment, typically only half ever recover, defined as achieving an appropriate weight and an absence of symptoms (Fursland et al., 2012; Safer, Telch, & Chen, 2009; Seligman & Reichenberg, 2012). Approximately 20% to 30% will have persistent symptoms, although they will no longer meet diagnostic criteria for an eating disorder (Fursland et al., 2012). A chronic disorder will persist in about 20% to 25%, and it is estimated that 10% will die as a result of their disorder (Fursland et al., 2012). This chapter covers (a) important definitions related to disordered eating, (b) costs associated with disordered eating, (c) demographic information, (d) etiology, (e) diagnosis and assessment of disordered eating, and (f) clinical treatments for clients with diagnoses of disordered eating.

Definitions

According to the *Diagnostic and Statistical Manual of Mental Disorders, Fourth Edition, Text Revision* (DSM–IV–TR; American Psychiatric Association [APA], 2000), the three classifications of eating disorders are anorexia nervosa, bulimia nervosa, and eating disorder not otherwise specified (EDNOS). The *DSM–IV–TR* does not classify binge eating as an eating disorder; a discussion of this behavior is found in Appendix B, "Criteria Sets and Axes Provided for Further Study." The *Diagnostic and Statistical Manual of Mental Disorders, Fifth Edition* (*DSM–5*; APA, 2013a) classifies anorexia nervosa, bulimia nervosa, and binge-eating disorder (BED) as feeding and eating disorders, with the criteria for each diagnosis significantly revised from the previous edition.

The American Society of Addiction Medicine classifies addiction as a disease engaging areas of the brain associated with reward, motivation, memory, and circuitry (Smith, 2012). A primary characteristic of an addiction is a dependence on a drug, whereby the body adapts to this additional stimulus, resulting in tolerance or dependence (Karim & Chaudhri, 2012). For some time addiction has been associated with substance use only. The American Society of Addiction Medicine's definition of addiction broadens this understanding in that it does not focus specifically on a substance but emphasizes the neurobiology associated with addiction. Recent research on compulsive and impulsive disorders supports the conjecture that addiction can be applied to constructs outside of substance use. In fact, the state of addiction engages the same neural circuits associated with compulsive and impulsive behaviors (Volkow & Fowler, 2000). The term *process addiction* refers to those behavioral constructs and mental health issues that fall under impulse control disorders, including gambling, sex, disordered eating, and the like (Smith, 2012).

People with food addiction have been shown to exhibit similar neurobiological pathologies to those with substance abuse or dependence (Karim & Chaudhri, 2012). Food addiction typically refers to BED; however, other forms of disordered eating tend to accompany substance abuse. In 2010, Root et al. performed a study examining the relationship between substance use and eating disorders. Root et al. found that 50% of those whose primary diagnosis was an eating disorder had a history of substance use. In addition, 35% of those whose primary diagnosis was a substance use disorder had an eating disorder (Root et al., 2010). People with specific eating disorders have similar behavior traits as those with substance use disorders (Ram, Stein, Sofer, & Kreitler, 2008). Ram et al. (2008) found that those with bulimic tendencies and those with a diagnosed substance use disorder shared similar attitudes regarding core beliefs, such as attitudes about the self, goals, reality, and others. These studies point to the similarities among the disorders, their underlying issues, and the idea that *addiction* is a term that can be applied to constructs other than substance use.

Cost

The actual cost incurred by eating disorders is unclear (Hay & Mond, 2005). Stuhldreher et al. (2012) investigated the number of publications addressing the cost of eating disorders. The researchers concluded that the number of such publications has increased somewhat, although there remains a dearth of research and knowledge on this topic. The lack of research in this area makes assessing costs related to the illness difficult. In addition, gaps in the knowledge base and publications on the economic impact of eating disorders are potentially harmful, as they unintentionally minimize the severity of this mental health issue.

Although there is limited research on this topic, and the research that exists is dated, a snapshot of the financial implications of eating disorders can still be assessed indirectly. The secondary physical and psychiatric problems associated with eating disorders can point to the cost of the illness. Simon, Schmidt, and Pilling (2005) acknowledged comorbid psychiatric issues to consider, such as depression, anxiety, and suicidal tendencies. In addition, they pointed to the physical complications resulting from eating disorders, such as cardiovascular issues, electrolyte abnormalities, osteoporosis, and gastrointestinal issues, to name a few (Simon et al., 2005). Although there is no way to identify whether psychiatric and physical complications are a direct result of an eating disorder in cost-of-illness analyses, it is clear that eating disorders pose a far greater financial burden than one might assume.

Mond, Hay, Rodgers, and Owen (2009) compared women diagnosed with an eating disorder to a sample of overweight women to assess their relative health consequences. The study was performed on 5,255 Australian women ranging in age from 18 to the mid-40s. This population was representative of the female population of the country as a whole. The researchers utilized self-report questionnaires geared toward assessing behaviors associated with eating disorders, health-related quality of life, demographic information, and use of health services (Mond et al., 2009). Results of the study indicated that those who reported higher incidences of eating-disordered behavior also showed significant impairment in psychosocial functioning, whereas those with a high body mass index showed significant impairment in physical health (Mond et al., 2009). Finally, both groups reported more frequent visits to primary care doctors compared to overweight women and women without disordered eating patterns. This study demonstrates the impact of eating pathology on functioning, quality of life, and use of health services for psychological and physical health issues.

The research performed on this topic is somewhat dated. Studies from the 1990s point to the high financial impact of eating disorders on society. An Australian study performed in 1999 pointed to this impact in terms of the number of years lost due to death or disability (Mathers, Vos, & Stevenson, 1999). This study included a burden assessment ranking that quantified the burden associated with eating-disordered behavior, health factors, and socioeconomic disadvantage. The researchers found that eating-disordered behavior ranked 22nd on this burden assessment. For women between the ages of 15 and 24, the burden of disordered eating ranked 4th, indicating the severity of this mental health issue on quality of life and a possible construct of economic cost.

Another dated study examined the characteristics of bulimia nervosa in 275 patients with the diagnosis (Mitchell, Hatsukami, Eckert, & Pyle, 1985). Results of this study highlighted secondary impacts, such as those on social functioning. For example, the patients reported that their interpersonal/intimate relationships were negatively affected and that they had problems within the family, financial issues, and problems with employment. Although these studies point to the multifaceted nature and severity of disordered eating, additional up-to-date research is needed to provide the profession with an accurate understanding of the burden of this illness.

Studies show that when left untreated, eating disorders and eating pathology can negatively impact quality of life (Pohjolainen et al., 2010). Pohjolainen et al. (2010) found that when left untreated, women with a diagnosis of bulimia nervosa will improve their overall quality of life in approximately 10 years, whereas those women who seek out treatment will improve their overall quality of life to the same degree within a 6-month period. This study points to the benefits of treatment and prevention while also implying economic benefits for the patient and society with regard to the cost of illness.

Studies have proved that eating disorders have a significant impact on a range of areas for the patient and society, which points to the economic burden associated with this mental health issue. However, the true economic impact of eating disorders on society and the individual is difficult to assess. Research in this area is needed, and because of the indirect consequences of this mental health issue, exact causation of disordered eating could prove difficult to ascertain or measure.

Demographics

According to Seligman and Reichenberg (2012), anorexia nervosa typically manifests between the ages of 10 and 30; bulimia nervosa typically manifests later, succeeding anorexia nervosa in approximately 50% of cases; and BED typically manifests in early to middle adulthood. Although the stereotype is that these illnesses afflict only women, studies conducted over the past few decades have shown that approximately 10% to 15% of individuals diagnosed with an eating disorder are male (Peate, 2011; Yager et al., 2005). Chung and Bravender (2011) found that this percentage may be low because it takes into account only treatment-seeking individuals. A more accurate ratio may be 3:1, as men may be resistant to seeking treatment for a disorder thought of as affecting only females. Eating disorder symptomatology may look different in males than in females, with a "preoccupation with masculinity and athletic prowess" (Peate, 2011, p. 387). Chung and Bravender reported that the risk for an eating disorder increases for males if they are involved in sports with an emphasis on size or body shape, such as gymnastics, wrestling, bodybuilding, distance running, diving, rowing, or swimming. The research on whether sexual orientation puts men at an increased risk for eating disorders varies, with some articles stating that 80% of males reporting eating disorders are heterosexual (Peate, 2011) and others declaring that those afflicted are overwhelmingly gay and bisexual (Boisvert & Harrell, 2009; Chung & Bravender, 2011).

Talleyrand (2012) reported that the majority of eating disorders research has focused on Euro-American adolescent females. The focus of the assessment, diagnosis, and treatment of eating disorders is often a drive for thinness and an intense fear of gaining weight, commonly referred to as the *thin ideal*. Yet an emphasis on the thin ideal may be inappropriate when assessing, diagnosing, or treating ethnically diverse populations. Eating disorder behaviors and symptomatology may look different across cultures (Franko, Becker, Thomas, & Herzog, 2007; Talleyrand, 2012). Beauty standards are different across ethnic lines; however, in the majority of research studies the methods used to assess for disturbances in body image are largely centered on a Euro-American ideal. This focus on Western cultural critique sets may be distorting the outcomes in relation to diverse groups. Furthermore, in eating disorder research studies, ethnic women are often lumped together in a single comparison group, but African American, Asian, and Latina women are as diverse from one another as they are from their Euro-American counterparts (Talleyrand, 2012).

In the United States, the majority culture typically values "individualism, competition, rational thinking, economic displays of status and power, a patriarchal family structure, and a thin female physique" (Warren, Gleaves, Cepeda-Benito, del Carmen Fernandez, & Rodriguez-Ruiz, 2005, p. 241). Euro-American women are said to have internalized the thin ideal and see this type of body shape as attainable and necessary in order to be happy and successful (Gilbert, Crump, Madhere, & Schutz, 2009; Warren et al., 2005). It is typical and acceptable in Western cultures for women to have a moderate amount of body dissatisfaction. *Body dissatisfaction* involves negative perceptions, feelings, and/or thoughts about one's physical appearance (Pelegrini & Petroski, 2010; Warren et al., 2005). Body dissatisfaction and the internalization of the thin ideal are strongly correlated with an increased risk for eating disorders. Research suggests that ethnicity may be a protective factor against body image issues, as some cultures do not idolize the thin physique or put so much emphasis on physical appearance. Even though African American and Latina women do not focus on a drive for thinness, they are still vulnerable to eating disorder behaviors and risk factors (Talleyrand, 2012; Warren et al., 2005). When using the Contour Drawing Rating Scale, described in greater detail in "Assessment," African American and Latina women tend to choose a smaller silhouette, whereas Euro-American women choose larger silhouettes (Talleyrand, 2012).

Allegedly because of heavier body ideals in the African American culture, women of this ethnicity are "less likely to be concerned with their size and body shape, less likely to view themselves as overweight, and less reliant of dieting behaviors" (Talleyrand, 2012, p. 272). Perhaps because of this difference in body dissatisfaction, reported rates of anorexia nervosa are low for African American and Caribbean Blacks (0.14%); however, higher rates (1.9% and 2.36%, respectively) were reported for bulimia nervosa and BED (Talleyrand, 2012). According to Talleyrand (2010), obesity rates may be significantly higher for African American children than Euro-American children, and risk factors may not be the same across cultures; however, research on specific risk factors among African Americans is lacking. Gilbert et al. (2009) found that eating disorders may go undiagnosed in African American clients because of clinicians' cultural bias, even though the prevalence rate may be equal to that for Caucasian Americans and higher than that of any other ethnic minority group.

Research shows that Latina women are at an increased risk for BEDs and obesity, with lifetime prevalence rates as high as 5.61% (Franko, Jenkins, & Rodgers, 2012; Shea et al., 2012). Anorexia nervosa is less common in this population, with an extremely low lifetime prevalence rate of 0.8% (Marques et al., 2011; Talleyrand, 2012). Hispanic women tend to idealize a more full-figured, curvy body shape, and they tend not to place so much significance on physical appearance. Even though they do not strive for an ultrathin physique, Hispanic women are still vulnerable to risk factors that could lead to an eating disorder (Talleyrand, 2012).

Asian American women are predominantly underrepresented in the eating disorder research and literature. Some researchers suggest that Asian American and Euro-American women may adopt similar mainstream body image ideals (Grabe & Hyde, 2006; Shaw, Ramirez, Trost, Randall, & Stice, 2004), which accounts for the higher rates of body dissatisfaction within these two groups (Talleyrand,

2012). When assessing for an eating disorder or body dissatisfaction in Asian American women, counselors should look for unhappiness with specific body parts or facial features (Talleyrand, 2012). Research pertaining to the rate of eating disorders within this population is mixed, but it is generally accepted that eating disorders occur less often among Asian American women than Euro-American women (Cummins & Lehman, 2007).

Further research is needed on specific eating disorder symptoms in women of different cultures. Research is unclear as to how to define eating disorders within various ethnicities, but one thing that is clear is that Western-based criteria sets for defining eating disorders may lead to misdiagnosis in ethnically diverse populations. Specifically, assessing for the drive for thinness may not be appropriate among women of non-Western cultures, as these women may not idealize an ultrathin female body type or place such an emphasis on physical appearance as a measure of worth and social status. Talleyrand (2012) suggested that researchers focus on acculturation and ethnic identity in order to better understand potential risk factors for eating disorders and how they affect ethnically diverse females.

Etiology

The exact cause of eating disorders is unknown, but the consensus among researchers is that they are biopsychosocial diseases "involving different body systems and aspects related to the individual and their social relations" (Portela de Santana, da Costa Ribeiro Junior, Mora Giral, & Raich, 2012, p. 391; see also Keel & Forney, 2013; Polivy & Herman, 2002). Rather than continuing to treat the symptoms of eating disorders, such as starvation, body image, and perfectionism, researchers are investigating the etiology of the disorders in order to develop specific treatments aimed to treat the root cause.

To better understand individuals with anorexia nervosa and the brain's response to reward and loss, researchers are using magnetic resonance imaging to map the brain. The brain balances reward and aversion through the use of the limbic and executive systems. The limbic system is primarily responsible for emotion and responds with immediate gratification by sending positive feedback to the body in response to pleasure. The positive feedback tells the body to do more of what was pleasurable in the future. The executive system of the brain is in charge of long-term consequences, inhibition, and risk aversion for long-term survival. Patients with anorexia nervosa have an altered response to positive and negative feedback, such that the limbic and executive systems are not in balance. Dopamine is released in the brain during the act of eating or at the expectation of eating, but instead of experiencing pleasurable feelings those with anorexia nervosa experience a high level of anxiety, which leads to food restriction as a measure to decrease this anxiety (Friederich, Wu, Simon, & Herzog, 2013; Kaye, 2013). In one study on anorexia nervosa and dopamine levels, Kaye (2013) found that individuals in the control group (without anorexia) experienced euphoria with the release of dopamine, but those in the experimental group (with anorexia) experienced anxiety under similar conditions. These results are consistent with hypotheses that experiences that are commonly thought of as pleasurable can in fact be anxiety inducing for individuals with anorexia.

In a review of epidemiological, cross-cultural, and longitudinal studies, Keel and Forney (2013) highlighted four main risk factors for eating disorders: being an adolescent or young adult female, internalizing the thin ideal or weight phobia, having a negative self-evaluation and perfectionism, and being exposed to dieting. Although being a female may not seem as though it fits in a review of psychosocial risk factors, given that it is a biological factor, Keel and Forney proposed looking at how cultural factors, such as the idealization of thinness, influence men and women differently. Cross-cultural studies suggest that fear of gaining weight tends to manifest more readily in cultures in which the thin ideal is glorified. Keel and Forney were unable to find any case of bulimia in cultures without a Western influence. The question that remains is whether weight concerns and idealization of the thin ideal predate disordered eating or whether the patterns are strictly correlative. Personality traits, such as a negative self-evaluation, low self-esteem, and perfectionism, are psychological risk factors for eating disorders and may contribute to explaining why not all females exposed to Western influences become overly influenced by weight and shape and not all those with concerns about weight and shape develop eating disorders. The final risk factor highlighted in Keel and Forney's review was environmental. The findings suggest that higher levels of body dissatisfaction, use of maladaptive behaviors to control weight gain, and binge eating are significantly predicted in individuals who are exposed to friend dieting (Keel & Forney, 2013).

DIAGNOSIS

DSM–IV–TR

According to the *DSM–IV–TR* (APA, 2000), an individual diagnosed with anorexia nervosa refuses to maintain a weight that is considered minimally appropriate for his or her size and shape, has an intense fear of gaining weight despite being underweight, and has distorted perceptions of his or her body. Individuals who are diagnosed with bulimia nervosa engage in binge eating and, to counteract this excessive intake of food, engage in inappropriate compensatory behaviors. A *binge* is defined as out-of-control eating of a significantly large amount of food in a distinct amount of time. Bartholome, Raymond, Lee, Peterson, and Warren (2006) reported findings from various studies estimating that the average caloric intake during a binge episode range from 1,515 kilocalories to 2,963 kilocalories. Inappropriate compensatory measures, such as induced vomiting, laxatives, diuretics, enemas, and excessive exercise, are used in an effort to prevent weight gain. The final eating disorder diagnosis covered in the *DSM–IV–TR* is EDNOS. Individuals who have disturbances in eating but do not meet the full criteria for anorexia or bulimia are given this diagnosis. In the example that began this chapter, Sharon is restricting her food intake on a caloric level and not eating things that were previously enjoyable. Her issues with weight and her body image have an undue influence on her lifestyle, and she has recently lost a significant amount of weight. Although she exhibits symptoms characteristic of an individual suffering from anorexia nervosa, Sharon's weight is not less than 85% of what is expected for her height. Accordingly, she does not meet the diagnostic criteria for anorexia nervosa and is instead diagnosed with EDNOS.

According to the *DSM–IV–TR* (APA, 2000), binge eating is classified as an EDNOS. It is located under "Criteria Sets and Axes Provided for Further Study" in Appendix B. Many of the characteristics of BED are similar to those of bulimia nervosa, including the consumption of a large amount of food over a distinct amount of time and a feeling of lack of control over the amount of food one has ingested. However, the inappropriate compensatory behaviors characteristic of individuals with bulimia nervosa are not found in individuals suffering from BED. During a binge episode, an individual will experience three or more of the following: eating very quickly until overly and uncomfortably full; eating in the absence of hunger; eating alone because of feelings of shame associated with the amount of food being eaten; or feelings of depression, disgust, and guilt following a binge. According to Wonderlich, Gordon, Mitchell, Crosby, and Engel (2009), BED demonstrates validity in that its characteristics can be clearly distinguished from those of anorexia nervosa and bulimia nervosa. However, at the time of their study, the researchers found the boundary between obesity and BED to be unclear.

DSM–5

To create the fifth edition of the *DSM*, 12 individuals, viewed within the mental health community as experts in their field, made up the Eating Disorders Work Group. The group was tasked with reviewing the *DSM–IV–TR* (APA, 2000); analyzing the proposed new text for strengths and weaknesses; developing hypotheses for future directions in research, practice, and theory development; and conducting thorough literature reviews to analyze existing data (APA, 2013b). Based on their findings, the work group developed the *DSM–5* (APA, 2013a) diagnostic criteria for eating disorders, with some significant changes from the previous edition. Table 9.1 details the major differences between the *DSM–IV–TR* and *DSM–5* diagnostic criteria. Eating disorders has been reclassified as feeding and eating disorders in the *DSM–5* to signify the inclusion of feeding disorders of infancy and childhood with adult eating disorders. Two diagnoses not previously seen are avoidant/restrictive food intake disorder and other specified feeding and eating disorder. According to APA (2013a, p. 2), to minimize the use of the diagnosis other specified feeding and eating disorder, anorexia nervosa, bulimia nervosa, and BED have been defined in ways that accurately describe symptoms and behaviors often found in clinical settings. BED is now officially recognized as an eating disorder. Some researchers propose that binge eating is the most common eating disorder, estimating that perhaps 30% of all obese individuals seek treatment for binge eating (Bartholome et al., 2006).

Many of the new criteria for the diagnosis of anorexia nervosa are similar to those of the *DSM–IV–TR* (APA, 2000; e.g., a significantly low body weight, an intense fear of gaining weight, and a disturbance in the way in which the individual views his or her body). The *DSM–5* (APA, 2013a) revisions focus primarily on definitions of the criteria and the behaviors of the individual rather than his or her intentions, which are difficult to assess. A low body weight is measured in the context of the individual's age, sex, developmental trajectory, and physical health and is the result of a restricted food intake (APA, 2013a). Research has shown that not all individuals diagnosed with eating disorders have an intense fear of gaining weight or becoming fat (Talleyrand, 2012). Therefore, instead of focusing only on cognitive criteria, such as a drive for thinness, the *DSM–5* Eating Disorders Work Group also included a behavior-focused criterion that interferes with weight gain. The criterion of amenorrhea, or loss of the menstrual cycle, has been removed because a large number of women report no disruption in their

TABLE 9.1 DIAGNOSTIC CRITERIA FOR *DSM–IV* AND *DSM–5*

DSM–IV Diagnostic Criteria	*DSM–5* Diagnostic Criteria
Anorexia nervosa In postmenarcheal females, amenorrhea, such as, the absence of at least three consecutive menstrual cycles. (A woman is considered to have amenorrhea if her periods occur only following hormone, e.g., estrogen administration.)	Anorexia nervosa No requirement for amenorrhea.
Bulimia nervosa The binge eating and inappropriate compensatory behaviors both occur, on average, at least twice a week for 3 months.	Bulimia nervosa The binge eating and inappropriate compensatory behaviors both occur, on average, at least once a week for 3 months. Binge-eating disorder A. Recurrent episodes of binge eating. An episode of binge eating is characterized by both of the following: 1. eating, in a discrete period of time (e.g., within any 2-hour period), an amount of food that is definitely larger than most people would eat in a similar period of time under similar circumstances; 2. a sense of lack of control over eating during the episode (e.g., a feeling that one cannot stop eating or control what or how much one is eating). B. The binge-eating episodes are associated with three (or more) of the following: 1. eating much more rapidly than normal; 2. eating until feeling uncomfortably full; 3. eating large amounts of food when not feeling physically hungry; 4. eating alone because of being embarrassed by how much one is eating; 5. feeling disgusted with oneself, depressed, or very guilty after overeating. C. Marked distress regarding binge eating is present. D. The binge eating occurs, on average, at least once a week for 3 months. E. The binge eating is not associated with the recurrent use of inappropriate compensatory behaviors and does not occur exclusively during the course of bulimia nervosa or anorexia nervosa.
Eating disorder not otherwise specified The eating disorder not otherwise specified category is for disorders of eating that do not meet the criteria for any specific eating disorder.	Eating disorder not otherwise specified The eating disorder not elsewhere classified category is for disorders of eating that do not meet the criteria for any specific eating disorder.

Source. From *Diagnostic and Statistical Manual of Mental Disorders, Fourth Edition, Text Revision* (pp. 539–550), by American Psychiatric Association, 2000, Washington, DC: American Psychiatric Association. Copyright 2000 by the American Psychiatric Association. Also from *Diagnostic and Statistical Manual of Mental Disorders, Fifth Edition* (pp. 336–354), by American Psychiatric Association, 2013, Arlington, VA: American Psychiatric Association. Copyright 2013 by the American Psychiatric Association. Reprinted with permission. All rights reserved. *DSM = Diagnostic and Statistical Manual of Mental Disorders.*

menstrual cycle (Attia & Roberto, 2009). The subtypes restricting type and binge-eating/purging type used in the *DSM–IV–TR* remain in the *DSM–5*; however, the timeframe formerly classified as "current episode" is now specified as "the last 3 months" in an effort to improve continuity between practitioners. Two additional specifiers appear in the *DSM–5* to assist in diagnosis and continuity: level of remission and body mass index severity. Remission is specified as partial or full. According to the *DSM–5*, an individual in full remission, although previously meeting criteria for the disorder, has not, for a prolonged amount of time, met any criteria. An individual in partial remission has sustained an adequate body weight for a significant amount of time, but either an intense fear of gaining weight or behaviors that interfere with weight gain are still present, or disturbances in the way in which the individual perceives his or her body remain. The *DSM–5* uses body mass index ranges derived from the World Health Organization to classify this final specifier. The levels of severity extend from mild to extreme, with a mild being at or above 17 kg/m^2 and extreme less than 15 kg/m^2.

The criteria for a diagnosis of bulimia nervosa in the *DSM–5* (APA, 2013a) are similar to those in the *DSM–IV–TR* (APA, 2000), except with regard to frequency and type. According to the *DSM–5*, binge eating and inappropriate compensatory behaviors need to occur at least once per week for 3 months; this is in contrast to the higher frequency of twice per week over 3 months required by the *DSM–IV–TR*. The purging/nonpurging subtypes have been removed and levels of remission and severity subtypes included. According to the *DSM–5*, an individual in full remission for bulimia nervosa has gone a sustained amount of time meeting no criteria after previously meeting the full diagnostic criteria for the disorder; similarly, after previously meeting full criteria for the disorder, an individual in partial remission now meets some, but not all, criteria for a sustained amount of time. Levels of severity for bulimia nervosa range from mild (one to three episodes of inappropriate compensatory measures per week) to extreme (14 or more episodes on average per week).

The argument to formally include BED in the *DSM–5* (APA, 2013a) came from findings of a literature review conducted by the Eating Disorders Work Group. According to their findings, BED is clinically distinct from other eating disorder diagnoses (Wonderlich et al., 2009). It is estimated that a significant percentage of the population engages in binge eating. Community-based studies estimate that BED is present in 0.7% to 3% of the population (Berkman et al., 2006). The criteria for a diagnosis of BED include marked distress about recurrent binge-eating episodes, with the episodes occurring at least once per week over the course of 3 months. Unlike with bulimia nervosa, inappropriate compensatory measures are not associated with this disorder. According to the *DSM–5*, *bingeing* is defined as eating quicker than one normally would; eating until uncomfortably full; eating a lot even when not physically hungry; eating in isolation because of feelings of embarrassment and shame; or feeling disgusted, depressed, or guilty after eating. Like anorexia nervosa and bulimia nervosa, BED has levels of remission and severity specifiers. According to the *DSM–5*, full remission involves not meeting any criteria when previously full criteria had been met, and partial remission involves binge episodes occurring less than once per week for a sustained period of time. The severity specifiers range from mild (binges occurring one to three times per week) to extreme (an average of 14 or more binges per week).

Avoidant/restrictive food intake disorder is similar to anorexia nervosa in that food intake is restricted, leading to malnutrition and weight loss. However, in avoidant/restrictive food intake disorder there is no disturbance in the way in which one's weight and shape are perceived. In this disorder the avoidance of food is typically related to disinterest in eating or to a sensory characteristic of food. This disorder may remain into adulthood, but it typically manifests early in life (APA, 2013a).

Other specified feeding and eating disorder is similar to EDNOS (APA, 2000), but the clinician using this diagnosis chooses to specify the reason why the individual does not meet full diagnostic criteria for one of the disorders in the feeding and eating diagnostic class. For those clinicians who do not choose to specify the reason, the diagnosis of unspecified feeding and eating disorder is available. According to the *DSM–5* (APA, 2013a), individuals may be identified as having unspecified feeding and eating disorder when they do not meet all of the criteria for anorexia nervosa, binge eating, or another specific eating disorder. For example, a person may meet all of the criteria for anorexia nervosa but despite significant weight loss is within or above a normal weight range; the frequency of binge eating and inappropriate compensatory behaviors may be below that required for a diagnosis of bulimia or not sustained for the required 3 months; or the frequency and/or duration may be below that which is required for BED.

ASSESSMENT

A critical component of working with clients who struggle with an eating disorder is the use of assessments. Often assessments are the key to identifying specific eating pathology. Assessments can also help screen clients for an eating disorder prior to the beginning of treatment, for example when they are entering into some form of inpatient treatment. Assessments provide counselors with an additional dynamic piece for case conceptualization, treatment planning, and evidence-based outcomes.

An obstacle to finding adequate assessments for use with this population is the subjective versus objective understanding of characteristics of each diagnosis. Anderson, Lundgren, Shapiro, and Paulosky (2004) elaborated on this issue, pointing to the subjective understanding of a binge. For example, some clients believe that a binge involves eating until they are full, whereas *DSM–IV–TR* (APA, 2000) criteria for a binge delineate a specific amount of food to be eaten. This example highlights one symptom that can be interpreted many different ways. Many current assessments are based on the diagnostic criteria set forth in the *DSM–IV–TR*, which can be limiting.

Currently the majority of assessments used with children and adolescents originate from adult measures. Micali and House (2011) found that the reliability of assessments used with children and adolescents may increase with the use of self-report instruments that include parental report, especially with anorexia nervosa patients, who report fewer symptoms. Despite some of the limitations of eating disorder assessments, some assessments sufficiently measure eating pathology and eating disorders. The Eating Disorder Inventory–3, developed by Garner and Garfinkel, is a self-report assessment that measures characteristics commonly associated with anorexia nervosa and bulimia nervosa (Cumella,

2006). The Eating Disorder Inventory–3 was normed on 1,980 female patients who met criteria for anorexia nervosa (all types), bulimia nervosa, and EDNOS. The 91-item assessment measures a multitude of characteristics associated with the aforementioned diagnoses, such as drive for thinness, emotional dysregulation, and body dissatisfaction (Cumella, 2006). The Eating Disorder Inventory–3 also provides a symptom checklist, providing assessors with a list of symptoms identical to those outlined in the *DSM*. Finally, the Eating Disorder Inventory–3 includes response style indicators to protect against the significant levels of denial and feigning within this population (Cumella, 2006).

Garner also created the Eating Attitudes Test (EAT-26), a 26-item self-report questionnaire used to detect eating disorders in nonclinical settings. The EAT-26 is based on a previous 40-item questionnaire (the EAT-40). The items removed from the EAT-40 to make the EAT-26 were found to be redundant and without predictive significance, as the shorter assessment retained the robust correlations with clinical and psychometric variables (Garner, Olmsted, Bohr, & Garfinkel, 1982).

The Children's Eating Attitudes Test was created for use with younger children ages 8 to 13, as the original EAT was useful with adult and older adolescent populations but was not effective with younger children. However, the Children's Eating Attitudes Test is unsuitable for use in clinical settings because of its high likelihood of producing false positives and negatives and its inability to discriminate between anorexia nervosa and bulimia nervosa (Micali & House, 2011).

The Eating Disorder Examination (EDE) assesses eating pathology within the previous 4 weeks (Collins & Ricciardelli, 2005). The EDE maintains an interview format so that the assessor has the freedom to investigate eating behaviors in an effort to assess their frequency and severity. The four subscales of the EDE—Restraint, Eating Concern, Shape Concerns, and Weight Concerns—help with quantifying eating behaviors with regard to their frequency and severity (Collins & Ricciardelli, 2005). This assessment has strong internal consistency and reliability. The EDE is designed to discriminate between those with eating disorders and those with normal control and has strong construct validity (Collins & Ricciardelli, 2005). The Children's Eating Disorder Examination (ChEDE), a version of the EDE created for use with children and adolescents ages 8 to 14, is very similar to the original EDE. The ChEDE uses the same interview format, subscales, global score, and diagnostic system as the original assessment, but it differs in the way in which the questions are presented and how some are rated. Outcome findings for the ChEDE are mixed, with limitations found when assessing young people with anorexia nervosa symptomatology (Micali & House, 2011).

The Sociocultural Attitudes Towards Appearance Scale–3 (SATAQ-3) measures one's level of internalization of the thin ideal. This specific construct has been found to be a significant risk factor for eating disorders (Thompson, van den Berg, Roehrig, Guarda, & Heinberg, 2004). The SATAQ-3 measures not only internalization of the thin ideal but also awareness of and pressure related to the influence of media on body image (Thompson et al., 2004). In addition, the SATAQ-3 takes into account the influence of the media on body image related to athleticism and sports. The SATAQ-3 contains 21 items measuring awareness of the internalization of the thin ideal with a Likert-style response scale (Gilbert et al., 2009). Few assessments measure the influence of the media on body image as it relates to thinness and athleticism simultaneously, pointing to a significant benefit of the SATAQ-3.

The Contour Drawing Rating Scale is a body image assessment that uses visual stimuli in the form of silhouettes to assess one's experience of his of her body image (Wertheim, Paxton, & Tilgner, 2004). This scale contains nine portrayals of female and male body silhouettes. Test takers identify which silhouette best represents their own. The discrepancy between their current body size and the silhouette they identify as resembling their body size is purported to measure body dissatisfaction. The Contour Drawing Rating Scale has gone through significant validation and has firm test–retest reliability (.78; Gilbert et al., 2009).

Eating disorders are multidimensional and complex. A significant number of assessments aim to evaluate different facets of this mental health issue. Compulsive exercising is an example of one of these facets. The Exercise Dependence Scale–Revised and the Exercise Beliefs Questionnaire are two examples of assessments that assess levels of compulsive exercising. The Exercise Dependence Scale–Revised evaluates pathological levels of exercising based on *DSM–IV–TR* (APA, 2000) criteria of addiction (Albrecht, Kirschner, & Grusser, 2007; Hausenblas & Symons Downs, 2002) and categorizes athletes as nondependent, dependent, or at risk. It further categorizes the type of addiction as physiological or nonphysiological (Albrecht et al., 2007; Hausenblas & Symons Downs, 2002). The Exercise Beliefs Questionnaire is designed to evaluate general constructs of compulsive exercising across sporting activities, making it a dynamic instrument (Albrecht et al., 2007; Hausenblas & Symons Downs, 2002). As with any assessment, it is important to find an appropriate measure to use given the symptoms presented by the client while also taking into account other variables, such as the client's age, culture, and any extraneous but contributing symptoms.

A multitude of assessments aim to assess eating disorders, eating pathologies, body image perception, and other constructs related to eating disorders. The assessments outlined here are a snapshot of the different types of assessments in the field. Although no assessment is perfect, many assessments for this mental health issue can provide clinicians with a distinct understanding of the problem. It is highly encouraged that clinicians not use one assessment only but rather use a multitude of assessments combined with an extensive interview when assessing this construct.

TREATMENT MODELS AND APPROACHES

Treatment for eating disorders may vary depending on the type and severity of the disorder. Cognitive behavior therapy (CBT) is the most commonly used theoretical orientation for the treatment of eating disorders, especially bulimia, nervosa, and BEDs (Choate, 2010; Herpertz et al., 2011; Shea et al., 2012). However, research findings indicate that CBT is effective in only 50% of cases (Choate, 2010; Hill, Craighead, & Safer, 2011; Seligman & Reichenberg, 2012). Moreover, there has been a lack of research on the use of CBT with individuals suffering from anorexia nervosa, with outcomes producing only moderate effect sizes (Gowers, 2006). It is important to note that the majority of research pertaining to anorexia nervosa has been conducted with adolescent populations and therefore is not generalizable to clients outside of this particular demographic.

Clinicians must take into account the severity of the eating disorder and the type of treatment setting necessary to properly care for the client. Eating disorder treatment, much like treatment for other addictions, can take place in a variety of settings: outpatient, intensive outpatient, partial hospitalization, residential treatment, or inpatient hospitalization. The last setting is recommended for clients who are in need of medical stabilization, who suffer from a co-occurring psychiatric disorder requiring full-time supervision, who refuse oral intake, or who have additional stressors that may interfere with recovery (Yager et al., 2006). Clients are often referred to residential treatment centers when they are in need of structure and supervision, as these factors increase the client's likelihood of recovery. Outpatient treatment is the least intense setting available and is indicated for highly motivated, nonsuicidal clients whose weight is at or above 85% of their individually estimated healthy weight. Ongoing assessment is critical for clients struggling with eating disorders, as it is common for clients to experience fluctuations in the level of care needed (Berg et al., 2012).

Although CBT is the most recommended treatment approach, other modalities of treatment are becoming mainstream. Research indicates that interpersonal psychotherapy (IPT), dialectical behavior therapy (DBT), and family therapy (e.g., the Maudsley approach) are also viable treatment options for eating disorders (Choate, 2012). Fursland et al. (2012) postulated that treatment should focus on the diagnostic criteria of EDNOS, as more than half of individuals being treated for eating disorders do not meet the full criteria for anorexia nervosa or bulimia nervosa.

Enhanced CBT (CBT-E)

There are a number of variations in the way in which clinicians and researchers implement CBT in practice. The basic tenets of the theory especially effective with this population include self-monitoring; psychoeducation; behavioral change strategies, such as the establishment of regular food intake patterns and the elimination of inappropriate compensatory measures; cognitive restructuring; and relapse prevention (Fairburn, 2008; Fursland et al., 2012; Waller et al., 2011).

Fursland et al. (2012) created CBT-E to treat all eating disorders by focusing primarily on symptoms present in EDNOS. The CBT-E treatment model is designed for individual work with clients and consists of four distinct stages. CBT-E encourages therapists to work systemically with a treatment team consisting of at least a physician, as well as a dietician and psychiatrist, if necessary. For clients within a healthy weight range, treatment typically progresses from Stage 1 (modifying unhealthy behaviors) to Stage 4 (relapse prevention) in approximately 20 sessions; for clients whose weight is below their ideal, 40–50 sessions are often necessary.

Stage 1 of the CBT-E model focuses on providing psychoeducation and changing the client's maladaptive behaviors. During the psychoeducation component, clients are educated about the vicious cycle that maintains an eating disorder, health risks, and common myths associated with eating disorders. The CBT-E clinician and client work together to construct a map to illustrate the maladaptive thoughts, beliefs, and behaviors that maintain an eating disorder. The diagram assists the client in gaining a new perspective of the eating disorder in which change is more attainable and treatment can begin to focus on the establishment of healthy eating patterns. Clients self-monitor their eating patterns through the use of food logs that record food intake, thoughts, and feelings. Although low-weight clients are not expected to return to a healthy and medically desirable weight range at the completion of Stage 1, an improvement in regular eating and reduced maladaptive behaviors, such as binge eating and vomiting, should be seen (Fursland et al., 2012).

During Stage 2, the client and counselor take time to examine the overall treatment process. This stage is completed in just one session and is used to check on the client's progress in meeting goals set in Stage 1, reassess the client's level of involvement in therapy, and preview the course of therapy for the remainder of treatment (Fursland et al., 2012).

Stage 3 of the treatment takes approximately nine sessions to complete. The focus during this stage is addressing the components used to maintain the eating disorder, such as body checking, overvaluation of weight, and unhealthy dietary rules learned by the client. Studies report that many of these behaviors are outside of the client's conscious awareness. It is therefore the task of the clinician to educate clients about the manner in which their behavior perpetuates the eating disorder cycle (Fursland et al., 2012; Shafran, Fairburn, Robinson, & Lask, 2004).

In Stage 4 of CBT-E, the goal is to work on maintenance and relapse prevention. Clients are educated about the difference between a *lapse,* which is a recurrence of a symptom, and a *relapse,* which is a return to a full-blown eating disorder. Clients also work with their therapists to create a maintenance plan and schedule follow-up sessions (Fursland et al., 2012).

As CBT-E has only been tested in outpatient therapy, its efficacy is not generalizable to inpatient settings. Trials are being conducted to determine the effectiveness of the treatment for inpatient programs (Grave, 2010). The only published trial of CBT-E for the treatment of anorexia nervosa yielded results that were promising. In that trial, two thirds of participants who finished treatment reported an absence of symptoms; however, the high dropout rate in this population may have led to skewed results. In another controlled study in which participants met the diagnostic criteria for EDNOS, half of all participants reported an absence of binge and purge behaviors. At the 1-year follow-up, half of those participants also scored within the normal global range on an eating disorder assessment. Further studies are needed to determine the effectiveness of CBT-E for treating the full range of eating disorder diagnoses (Fursland et al., 2012).

IPT

IPT is an evidence-based practice for treating multiple psychological disorders, including bulimia. IPT has produced results comparable to those of CBT with regard to abstinence and recovery at 1-year follow-up in eating-disordered populations. IPT stems from the work of psychosocial theorists Harry Stack Sullivan and John Bowlby (Rafaeli & Markowitz, 2011). The focus of IPT is on exploring individuals' interpersonal relationships, identifying difficulties and life stressors, and incorporating new and effective ways of dealing with or eliminating problem areas. Interpersonal therapists such as Choate (2010) have found that individuals with bulimia learn to use inappropriate coping skills, such as bingeing and purging, as a way to escape from negative feelings and interpersonal relationship issues. Accordingly, issues related directly to food intake are not addressed in this model. Studies have shown the efficacy of IPT for use with both individuals and groups with bulimia nervosa and BED. IPT is less commonly used in treating anorexia nervosa because of the slow production of positive outcomes seen in this disorder (Carter et al., 2011; Choate, 2010).

IPT is used to identify problems within the areas of conflict avoidance, perfectionism, difficulties with role expectations, fear of rejection, deficits in social problem solving, and a lack of perceived social support. The IPT model calls for the development of individual insight, as this model hypothesizes that symptoms related to the eating disorder will diminish because of the connection between disordered eating behaviors and difficulties related to the client's interpersonal relationships (Choate, 2010). Because not everyone is capable of achieving insight, IPT may be unsuitable for some clients.

Interpersonal group psychotherapy (IPT-G) is an adaptation of IPT used to treat clients with bulimia nervosa (Choate, 2010). Choate (2010) reported that IPT-G should be conducted as a closed group, lasting approximately 20 sessions, with two group facilitators. Prior to the first group session, there should be an initial screening and a pregroup meeting to allow clients the opportunity to meet individually with facilitators. During the initial screening, the cofacilitators should attempt to find members who will be likely to benefit from as well as contribute to group discussions. This particular model excludes men, women with anorexia nervosa, people who are medically unstable, and individuals currently dealing with substance abuse. During the 90-minute individual meetings with group facilitators, members are informed about the structure of IPT-G and the advantages and disadvantages of group work in general. Benefits of group work include the learning and growth that can be attained from the feedback and experiences of other group members. One primary drawback and risk associated with group work is the inability to guarantee confidentiality.

During the initial stage of IPT-G (i.e., Sessions 1–5), facilitators focus on creating an environment in which the members feel safe enough to share their thoughts and feelings as well as assisting each member in linking their bulimic symptoms to current interpersonal problems. Fostering a safe and trusting environment can be particularly difficult when working with individuals with bulimia nervosa, because alienation, self-stigmatization, and shame are often related to the disorder (Choate, 2010). Group leaders must focus on normalizing individuals' discomfort and anxiety by emphasizing that these are common feelings experienced by members of a group, thereby cultivating group universality. In order to prepare group members for the working stage, facilitators take time during the fourth and fifth sessions to encourage feedback among members and guide individuals to focus more closely on their unique goals.

Throughout the working stage (i.e., Sessions 6–15), group members focus on their individual treatment goals and three broad group goals: learning communication skills, understanding the benefit of having the support of others, and learning to openly and directly express one's feelings within and outside of the group (Choate, 2010).

DBT

DBT, a cognitive–behavioral treatment, was originally created by Marsha Linehan as the result of her work with suicidal patients and later with clients with borderline personality disorder (Dimeff & Koerner, 2007). DBT uses cognitive–behavioral interventions such as psychoeducation, self-monitoring, cognitive restructuring, and skills training. DBT incorporates elements of behavioral science, mindfulness practices, and dialectical philosophy (Dimeff & Koerner, 2007).

DBT has been adapted for use with numerous Axis I disorders and across various treatment settings, including individual and group treatments as well as inpatient, outpatient, and residential treatment centers (Dimeff & Koerner, 2007; Federici, Wisniewski, & Ben-Porath, 2012; Linehan & Chen, 2005; Safer et al., 2009). Modified approaches of DBT have been successful in treating individuals with bulimia nervosa and BED. DBT is less successful for use with clients with anorexia nervosa or those whose eating disorders are assessed as being of higher risk (Federici et al., 2012).

There are many reasons why DBT is thought to work well with eating disorder treatment, including its focus on affect regulation, ambivalence, and collaboration (Federici et al., 2012; Wisniewski, Safer, & Chen, 2007). Affect regulation skills training is an important component of treating eating disorders because negative affect is the most common precursor to bingeing (Greeno, Wing, & Shiffman, 2000). Clients may also attempt to regulate or provide momentary relief to adverse emotions through binge episodes (Federici et al., 2012; Safer et al., 2009). Emotion identification and regulation are also difficult for clients with eating disorders (Harrison, Sullivan, Tchanturia, & Treasure, 2009). Proponents of this model emphasize affect regulation skills and specific interventions to assist clients in targeting maladaptive affect regulation behaviors. Wisniewski (2013) found DBT to be effective in addressing the ambivalence often found in clients with eating disorders. Through the use of motivational strategies to increase client commitment, the DBT model tries to balance acceptance and change (Wisniewski, 2013). There is evidence that collaboration is a necessary component in the treatment of eating disorders (Alexander & Treasure, 2012). Members of an effective treatment team must collaborate with one another as well as with the client and the family. In DBT clients are coached to manage the multitude of people that make up the treatment team, providing them with a sense of empowerment and self-efficacy (Wisniewski, 2013).

Safer et al. (2009) detailed a five-stage treatment model used with individuals and groups. The model begins with the pretreatment stage, during which the individual is assessed for eligibility. During the pretreatment interview the therapist begins forming the therapeutic relationship, conveying enthusiasm, educating the client about DBT, gaining a more thorough understanding of the client's disordered eating behaviors, assessing the client's level of commitment to therapy, reviewing the client's expectations, and providing an opportunity for the client to ask questions. Safer et al. noted that this part of the treatment process generally takes no more than two sessions.

During the second stage of treatment, the therapist works to teach the client mindfulness skills. Mindfulness is the act of being in the moment without judgment. Mindfulness is the underpinning of DBT. It is taught first and then revisited at the start of each stage (Safer et al., 2009). Binge eating is often associated with mindless eating, and therefore mindfulness is used to identify, in a nonjudgmental manner, feelings of emptiness and loneliness as well as hunger and fullness (Safer et al., 2009; Wisniewski, 2013). It is essential that the therapist reinforce mindfulness and thereby enhance emotion regulation and diminish binge eating.

The third stage of treatment introduces the topic of emotion regulation. During this stage, clients learn about emotion identification and functionality as well as ways to increase positive emotional experiences and decrease negative ones (Safer et al., 2009). The client is encouraged to be mindful of his or her emotions without labeling any particular emotions as good or bad. Individuals in treatment for bulimia nervosa and BED often amplify negative emotions by engaging in maladaptive behaviors such as binge eating and purging. To combat this tendency, clients are taught to reduce this suffering by effectively dealing with emotions. Clients are typically assigned a feelings log at this stage of treatment, which provides an outlet for the client to record feelings, precipitating events, judgments made, and actions taken. The logs are brought to therapy and discussed (Safer et al., 2009).

Clients typically want to work on issues related to improving their quality of life, such as relationship problems or issues related to finances and everyday life. According to Wisniewski (2013), issues in treatment should be addressed based on a four-tier hierarchy. Target 1 issues are addressed first in therapy and are related to suicide and the eating disorder. The focus is on keeping the client alive. Target 2 behaviors are focused on keeping the person in treatment. Behaviors such as not doing homework, failing to bring logs to the session, or showing up late are addressed at this second tier of the hierarchy. Target 3 behaviors are those related to quality of life, which are those the client most wants to work on. These often relate to interpersonal issues. Target 4 involves assessing current coping skills and assisting clients in developing effective skills to manage life problems (Wisniewski, 2013). The hierarchy in therapy is a tool to motivate clients to work in treatment and focus on quality-of-life issues after Target 1 and 2 behaviors are addressed.

Distress tolerance skills training takes place during the fourth stage of the Safer et al. (2009) model. Although it is difficult for anyone to experience pain, the researchers behind this model hypothesize that individuals with bulimia and BED experience more difficulty dealing with distress, therefore turning to behaviors that may increase their suffering (e.g., binge eating and purging). In this stage participants are taught survival skills for accepting reality and crises. DBT holds that by learning to accept, face, and tolerate the unpleasant experiences that occur throughout life, clients will increase their ability to cope effectively with their worlds. Clients are taught that it is okay to accept reality while at the same time not liking the situation. The crisis survival skills are effective coping mechanisms for use in overwhelming situations in which a break is needed. The client learns techniques such as distracting, self-soothing, improving the moment, and thinking of pros and cons. Being mindful and being able to identify and label emotions are important components highlighted in each stage of the model (Safer et al., 2009).

The final stage of the treatment model consists of wrapping up and enhancing relapse prevention. During this stage the client reviews the skills learned and works with the counselor to process emotions related to termination, and together they create a safety plan for the client to follow in the future (Safer et al., 2009).

To test for the efficacy of DBT treatment for BED and bulimia nervosa, Safer et al. (2009) conducted randomized studies using clients who met criteria for one of the eating disorders. Participants who were at less than 17.5% of their ideal body weight, currently psychotic or suicidal, abusing substances, in therapy or treatment, using psychotropic medications, or currently pregnant or breastfeeding were excluded from the studies. Participants were assessed at multiple points throughout treatment, including a baseline prior to the beginning of treatment and at 3-, 6-, and 12-month follow-ups. A variety of evidence-based assessments were used, including the EDE, Emotional Eating Scale, Rosenberg Self-Esteem Scale, and Beck Depression Inventory. Participants in these studies were randomly placed into DBT treatment groups or other controlled conditions, such as being waitlisted or placed in individual psychotherapy. Participants in the DBT for BED groups of multiple studies showed similar rates of improvement. Approximately 82% of the participants experienced significant improvements, evidenced by having no binge episodes within the 4 weeks prior to postassessment. Weight and shape changed in a positive direction, and there was a significant reduction in the desire to binge when upset. Participants in the DBT for bulimia nervosa study were compared with clients on a waitlist. At the end of the 20-week treatment the clients on the waitlist showed no improvement, whereas those in the study had an improvement rating of 28.6%. Improvement for this study was measured by an absence of binge and purging behaviors, with similar outcomes to those found in other CBT studies for bulimia nervosa. Providing evidence that emotion regulation is effective for this population, the participants indicated on the Emotional Eating Scale a reduced need to binge and purge when experiencing anger, anxiety, or depression (Safer et al., 2009). Wisniewski (2013) reported significant improvements in the areas of suicidal and nonsuicidal self-injury behaviors; eating disorder symptoms, such as restricting, bingeing, and purging; weight gain and nutritional balance; target behaviors found to interfere with treatment; staying in treatment; and collaboration throughout treatment.

Maudsley Family-Based Treatment (MFBT)

Much of the evidence-based research conducted in the field of eating disorders pertains to bulimia nervosa or BED. Gowers (2006) stated that there are minimal quality treatment trials on anorexia nervosa and that treatment is based mostly on clinical practice. Agras et al. (2004) outlined a number of reasons why research relevant to this disorder may be lacking: Only 0.6% of the population is diagnosed with the disorder, anorexia can present very differently across the population, and treatment is often long term and very costly. The nature of this disorder is complex, involving medical and psychiatric complications.

In the 1980s, Christopher Dare and colleagues created a family-based treatment for adolescents with anorexia nervosa at the Maudsley Hospital in London. MFBT integrates elements of strategic, structural, and narrative approaches. According to Hurst, Read, and Wallis (2012), MFBT is the most promising approach currently available for treating adolescents suffering from anorexia nervosa. In a large trial of 121 participants, MFBT was compared to adolescent-focused individual therapy. Adolescent-focused individual therapy aims to help clients tolerate emotions and to prevent the deprivation of food by focusing on ego deficits associated with anorexia (Hurst et al., 2012). The trial showed that both groups improved at the end of treatment, but those in the MFBT group showed a faster rate of improvement in physical health, measured by higher body mass indexes at follow-up. At the end of the treatment, full remission rates were 42% for MFBT and 23% for adolescent-focused individual therapy. In this study being in full remission was strictly defined as having a global EDE score within the normal range and a weight 95% of one's ideal body weight. Although there was no significant difference between the groups at the end of treatment, there was a significant difference at the 6- and 12-month follow-ups, such that those in the MFBT study had better outcomes (Hurst et al., 2012).

MFBT is generally conducted in three phases over 20–24 sessions and lasts, on average, 1 year (Hurst et al., 2012). In the first and longest phase of the treatment process, the focus is on changing maladaptive eating behaviors and returning the client to a near-normal weight. To accomplish this task, the adolescent's parents are charged with taking control of the anorexic behaviors by refeeding the adolescent. Lock and Le Grange (2013) reported the need to emphasize to the parents the seriousness of the illness, which they referred to as "orchestrating an intense scene" (p. 54). This is done in the first meeting and is a delicate process; the therapist must avoid "scapegoating the patient, blaming the parents, [or] exempting the siblings" (Lock & Le Grange, 2013, p. 60). The end result is that the parents will be in charge of restoring their adolescent to an appropriate weight. A core tenet of this approach is the idea that anorexia has taken control of the child. According to Hurst et al. (2012), the disorder stunts the child's development, preventing him or her from functioning at an appropriate developmental level and eating normally without the parents' help.

To assist in the refeeding process and to better understand the maladaptive patterns that the family engages in that contribute to the eating disorder pathology, the family typically engages in a family meal during the second session. Family meals will look very different across family systems because each family has its own rituals when it comes to mealtime. The therapist watches familial interactions across all subsystems and guides the parents in taking back control of the feeding and realigning the siblings. Often the parents will be encouraged to sit on either side of the patient and join together in filling his or her plate (Lock & Le Grange, 2013). The therapist then provides the parents with suggestions to improve refeeding and notes possible problem areas, such as improper or inadequate food choices, hostility, blaming, and avoidance (Hurst et al., 2012; Lock & Le Grange, 2005).

Research has shown that criticism of the patient with anorexia can have negative outcomes; therefore, the therapist works hard to modify and eliminate criticism through externalization. In line with narrative therapy, the family is encouraged to externalize the disorder from the adolescent and thereby join together as a team to beat the illness without blame or judgment (Hurst et al., 2012; Lock & Le Grange, 2005).

The family meets with the therapist approximately once a week during this first phase to discuss the client's weight, which is charted on a weight chart. The family analyzes the weight in terms of progress or regression, as well as interventions that worked over the previous week and possible improvements that could be made. The therapist uses a nondirective, collaborative approach, often looking to the family to discuss ideas for change among themselves. Families may become discouraged during this phase if weight gain is slow or nonexistent. Reasons for this will need to be explored by the family and therapist; possibilities include the parents not retaining enough control of the illness and the adolescent engaging in secretive maladaptive behaviors, such as exercising (Lock & Le Grange, 2005).

The second phase of treatment focuses on returning control of eating back to the adolescent and begins when the client is eating better and his or her weight has returned to a level that is near normal. This stage lasts approximately 2–3 months. During these months, the parents create trial periods during which the adolescent will be allowed to eat certain meals unsupervised or control meal portions. It is important that the parents, not the therapist, create these experimental situations, because intergenerational boundaries have been blurred during the illness and it is essential for the parents to take on the executive role in fighting the adolescent's disorder. Interventions commonly used in the first phase of treatment are highlighted in the second as well, such as continuing to emphasize the differences between the client's needs and those of the illness. This phase of treatment draws on aspects of structural family therapy (Lock & Le Grange, 2005, 2013).

If the client's weight continues to increase, treatment moves to the third and final phase, in which further issues surrounding the effects of anorexia nervosa on adolescence are explored. According to Lock and Le Grange (2013), because of the onset of anorexia the adolescent will typically be stunted in terms of adolescent development. As soon as possible the client is encouraged to return to social settings with peers; however, the adolescent may find himself or herself developmentally delayed. The therapist, parents, and adolescent explore possible areas of difficulty in relation to development and the illness, and problem-solving skills are worked on during this phase. This phase of treatment typically takes place over three or four sessions conducted over several months, during which issues such as sexuality, autonomy, and leaving home are discussed (Lock & Le Grange, 2013).

Although family therapy is commonly used in clinical practice for treating anorectics, there is very little research on its efficacy (Lock & Le Grange, 2005). Hurst et al. (2012) described the outcomes of five randomized control studies and other uncontrolled studies conducted using MFBT. Manualized practice of the treatment appeared to be useful in treating anorexia nervosa for 78% of patients and families. MFBT can be highly effective, but it is not without its challenges. It is a very intense, long-term treatment process, and family burnout is common; moreover, conducting MFBT with single-parent families is incrementally more difficult. Another challenge with this treatment approach is refeeding older adolescents who have already begun to individuate from the family. The parents and adolescent may find this stage of treatment particularly difficult as they renegotiate their roles to a greater degree than families with younger adolescents.

CONCLUSIONS

Eating disorder treatment can take place in a variety of settings and across various modalities. Clients' ability to afford treatment and their level of need will determine the level of care they are able to receive. Although CBT has been, and currently still is, the go-to treatment for eating disorders, DBT, IPT, and MFBT are also evidence-based treatments that have been proven effective with this population and that are gaining popularity in various treatment settings. Counselors deciding on a treatment method should consider the type of eating disorder, the level of motivation the client and his or her support structure have, their own theoretical beliefs, and the amount of time they and the client are looking to invest.

Although eating disorders were historically thought to afflict only Euro-American adolescent females, it is now understood that they do not discriminate based on age, culture, or gender. Although eating disorders may present differently in various subgroups, certain pathologies are similar, and researchers in the field are looking for effective ways to treat individuals of various cultures, ages, and sexes.

The field of eating disorders is evolving as research opens and closes doors in the areas of etiology, assessment, diagnosis, and treatment. This is evidenced by the inclusion of BED as a recognized eating disorder in the *DSM–5*; by research being conducted with brain mapping; and by the inclusion of newer treatment modalities that are now becoming mainstream in treatment centers, clinics, and private practice.

RESOURCES

Websites for Information and Support

Academy for Eating Disorders
www.aedweb.org/
Families Empowered & Supporting Treatment of Eating Disorders
www.feast-ed.org
Mayo Clinic, Eating Disorders
www.mayoclinic.org/diseases-conditions/eating-disorders/basics/definition/con-20033575
National Eating Disorders Association
www.nationaleatingdisorders.org/

University-Based Research and Treatment Sites

Columbia University Medical Center, Columbia Center for Eating Disorders
http://columbiaeatingdisorders.org/
Stanford University, Eating Disorders Research Program
http://edresearch.stanford.edu/
University of California, San Diego, Eating Disorders Center for Treatment and Research
http://eatingdisorders.ucsd.edu/

Books/Treatment Manuals

Astrachan-Fletcher, E., & Maslar, M. (2009). *The dialectical behavior therapy skills workbook for bulimia using DBT to break the cycle and regain control of your life.* Oakland, CA: New Harbinger.
Lock, J., & Le Grange, D. (2013). *Treatment manual for anorexia nervosa: A family-based approach* (2nd ed.). New York, NY: Guilford Press.
National Institute of Mental Health. (2011). *Eating disorders.* Bethesda, MD: Author.
Safer, D. L., Telch, C. F., & Chen, E. Y. (2009). *Dialectical behavior therapy for binge eating and bulimia.* New York, NY: Guilford Press.

Videos

Collins, L. (Producer). (2010). *Eating disorder research: Information for families* [Educational series]. (Available from Academy of Eating Disorders, 111 Deer Lake Road, Suite 100, Deerfield, IL 60015)

University of California, San Diego. (2010). *Is anorexia nervosa an "eating disorder"* [Educational series]. (Available from University of California, San Diego, 4510 Executive Drive, San Diego, CA 92121)
http://eatingdisorders.ucsd.edu/ed101/videos-eating-disorders.shtml

Online Screening

National Eating Disorders Association, Online Eating Disorder Screening
http://www.nationaleatingdisorders.org/online-eating-disorder-screening
Screening for Mental Health
http://mentalhealthscreening.org/

Referrals

Eating Disorders Resource Center, Treatment Centers
http://www.edrcsv.org/index.php/resources/treatment-professionals/treatment-centers.html
National Eating Disorders Association, Support Groups and Research Studies
http://www.nationaleatingdisorders.org/support-groups-research-studies

REFERENCES

Agras, W. S., Brandt, H. A., Bulik, C. M., Dolan-Sewell, R., Fairburn, C. G., Halmi, K. A., . . . Wilfley, D. E. (2004). Report of the National Institute of Health workshop on overcoming barriers to treatment research in anorexia nervosa. *International Journal of Eating Disorders, 354,* 509–521.

Albrecht, U., Kirschner, N. E., & Grusser, S. M. (2007). Diagnostic instruments for behavioral addiction: An overview. *Psychosocial Medicine, 4*(4), 1–11.

Alexander, J., & Treasure, J. (Eds.). (2012). *A collaborative approach to eating disorders.* New York, NY: Routledge.

American Psychiatric Association. (2000). *Diagnostic and statistical manual of mental disorders* (4th ed., text rev.). Washington, DC: Author.

American Psychiatric Association. (2013a). *Diagnostic and statistical manual of mental disorders* (5th ed.). Arlington, VA: Author.

American Psychiatric Association. (2013b). *Feeding and eating disorders.* Retrieved from http://www.psych.org/File%20Library/Practice/DSM/DSM-5/DSM-5-Eating-Disorders.pdf

Anderson, D. A., Lundgren, J. D., Shapiro, J. R., & Paulosky, C. A. (2004). Assessment of eating disorders: Review and recommendations for clinical use. *Behavior Modification, 28,* 763–782.

Attia, E., & Roberto, C. A. (2009). Should amenorrhea be a diagnostic criterion for anorexia nervosa? *International Journal of Eating Disorders, 42,* 581–589.

Bartholome, L. T., Raymond, N. C., Lee, S. S., Peterson, C. B., & Warren, C. S. (2006). Detailed analysis of binges in obese women with binge eating disorder: Comparison using multiple methods of data collection. *International Journal of Eating Disorders, 39,* 685–693.

Berg, K. C., Peterson, C. B., & Frazier, P. (2012). Assessment and diagnosis of eating disorders: A guide for professional counselors. *Journal of Counseling & Development, 90,* 262–269.

Berkman, N. D., Bulik, C. M., Brownley, K. A., Lohr, K. N., Sedway, J. A., Rooks, A., & Gartlehner, G. (2006, April). *Management of eating disorders* (Evidence Report/Technology Assessment No. 135, AHRQ Publication No. 06-E010). Rockville, MD: Agency for Healthcare Research and Quality.

Boisvert, J. A., & Harrell, W. A. (2009). Homosexuality as a risk factor for eating disorder symptomatology in men. *Journal of Men's Studies, 17*(3), 210–225.

Carter, J. D., Luty, S. E., McKenzie, J. M., Mulder, R. T., Frampton, C. M., & Joyce, P. R. (2011). Patient predictors of response to cognitive behaviour therapy and interpersonal psychotherapy in a randomised clinical trial for depression. *Journal of Affective Disorders, 128*(3), 252–261.

Choate, L. (2010). Interpersonal group therapy for women experiencing bulimia. *Journal for Specialists in Group Work, 35,* 349–364.

Choate, L. (2012). Assessment, prevention, and treatment of eating disorders: The role of professional counselors. *Journal of Counseling & Development, 90,* 259–261.

Chung, R. J., & Bravender, T. (2011, December). *Disordered eating in boys: Beyond the DSM–IV.* Retrieved from the Contemporary Pediatrics website: http://contemporarypediatrics.modernmedicine.com/news/disordered-eating-boys-beyond-dsm-iv

Collins, R. L., & Ricciardelli, L. A. (2005). Assessment of eating disorders and obesity. In D. M. Donovan & G. A. Marlatt (Eds.), *Assessment of addictive behaviors* (pp. 305–333). New York, NY: Guilford Press.

Cumella, E. J. (2006). Review of the Eating Disorder Inventory–3. *Journal of Personality Assessment, 87*(1), 116–117.

Cummins, L. H., & Lehman, J. (2007). Eating disorders and body image concerns in Asian American women: Assessment and treatment from a multicultural and feminist perspective. *Eating Disorders, 15,* 217–230.

Dimeff, L. A., & Koerner, K. (2007). *Dialectical behavior therapy in clinical practice: Applications across disorders and settings.* New York, NY: Guilford Press.

Fairburn, C. G. (2008). *Cognitive behavior therapy and eating disorders.* New York, NY: Guilford Press.

Federici, A., Wisniewski, L., & Ben-Porath, D. (2012). Description of an intensive dialectical behavior therapy program for multidiagnostic clients with eating disorders. *Journal of Counseling & Development, 90,* 330–338.

Franko, D. L., Becker, A. E., Thomas, J. J., & Herzog, D. B. (2007). Cross-ethnic differences in eating disorder symptoms and related distress. *International Journal of Eating Disorders, 40*(2), 156–164.

Franko, D. L., Jenkins, A., & Rodgers, R. F. (2012). Toward reducing risk for eating disorders and obesity in Latina college women. *Journal of Counseling & Development, 90,* 298–307.

Friederich, H., Wu, M., Simon, J. J., & Herzog, W. (2013). Neurocircuit function in eating disorders. *International Journal of Eating Disorders, 46,* 425–432.

Fursland, A., Byrne, S., Watson, H., La Puma, M., Allen, K., & Byrne, S. (2012). Enhanced cognitive behavior therapy: A single treatment for all eating disorders. *Journal of Counseling & Development, 90,* 319–329.

Garner, D. M., Olmsted, M. P., Bohr, Y., & Garfinkel, P. E. (1982). The Eating Attitudes Test: Psychometric features and clinical correlates. *Psychological Medicine, 12,* 871–878.

Gilbert, S. C., Crump, S., Madhere, S., & Schutz, W. (2009). Internalization of the thin ideal as a predictor of body dissatisfaction and disordered eating in African, African-American, and Afro-Caribbean female college students. *Journal of College Student Psychotherapy, 23,* 196–211.

Gowers, S. G. (2006). Evidence based research in CBT with adolescent eating disorders. *Child and Adolescent Mental Health, 11*(1), 9–12.

Grabe, S., & Hyde, J. S. (2006). Ethnicity and body dissatisfaction among women in the United States: A meta-analysis. *Psychological Bulletin, 132,* 622–640.

Grave, R. D. (2010). Inpatient cognitive behavior therapy for severe eating disorders. *Psychological Topics, 19*(2), 323–340.

Greeno, C. G., Wing, R. R., & Shiffman, S. (2000). Binge eating antecedents in obese women with and without binge eating disorder. *Journal of Consulting and Clinical Psychology, 68*(1), 95–102.

Harrison, A., Sullivan, S., Tchanturia, K., & Treasure, J. (2009). Emotional functioning in eating disorders: Attentional bias, emotion recognition and emotion regulation. *Psychological Medicine, 40,* 1887–1897.

Hausenblas, H. A., & Symons Downs, D. (2002). *Exercise Dependence Scale–21 manual.* Retrieved from http://www.personal.psu.edu/dsd11/EDS/EDS21Manual.pdf

Hay, P. J., & Mond, J. (2005). How to "count the cost" and measure burden? A review of the health-related quantity of life in people with eating disorders. *Journal of Mental Health, 14,* 539–552.

Herpertz, S., Hagenah, U., Vocks, S., von Wietersheim, J., Cuntz, U., & Zeeck, A. (2011). The diagnosis and treatment of eating disorders. *Deutsches Arzteblatt International, 108,* 678–685.

Hill, D. M., Craighead, L. W., & Safer, D. L. (2011). Appetite-focused dialectical behavior therapy for the treatment of binge eating with purging: A preliminary trial. *International Journal of Eating Disorders, 44*(3), 249–261.

Hurst, K., Read, S., & Wallis, A. (2012). Anorexia nervosa in adolescence and Maudsley family-based treatment. *Journal of Counseling & Development, 90,* 339–345.

Karim, R., & Chaudhri, P. (2012). Behavioral addictions: An overview. *Journal of Psychoactive Drugs, 44*(1), 5–17. doi:10.1080/02791072.2012.662859

Kaye, W. H. (2013). *When good traits go bad: Clues to more effective treatments for eating disorders.* Presentation at the University of California, San Diego, Eating Disorder Treatment Conference, San Diego, CA.

Keel, P. K., & Forney, K. J. (2013). Psychosocial risk factors for eating disorders. *International Journal of Eating Disorders, 46,* 433–439.

Linehan, M. M., & Chen, E. Y. (2005). Dialectical behavior therapy for eating disorders. In A. Freeman, S. H. Felgoise, A. M. Nezu, C. M. Nezu, & M. A. Reinecke (Eds.), *Encyclopedia of cognitive behavior therapy* (pp. 168–171). New York, NY: Springer.

Lock, J., & Le Grange, D. (2005). Family-based treatment of eating disorders. *International Journal of Eating Disorders, 37,* 64–67.

Lock, J., & Le Grange, D. (2013). *Treatment manual for anorexia nervosa: A family-based approach* (2nd ed.). New York, NY: Guilford Press.

Marques, L., Alegria, M., Becker, A. E., Chen, C., Fang, A., Chosak, A., & Diniz, J. B. (2011). Comparative prevalence, correlates of impairment, and service utilization for eating disorders across U.S. ethnic groups: Implications for reducing ethnic disparities in health care access for eating disorders. *International Journal of Eating Disorders, 44,* 412–420.

Mathers, C. D., Vos, E. T., & Stevenson, C. E. (1999). *The burden of disease and injury in Australia* (AIHW Cat. No. PHE 17). Canberra, Australia: Australian Institute of Health and Welfare.

Micali, N., & House, J. (2011). Assessment measures for child and adolescent eating disorders: A review. *Child and Adolescent Mental Health, 16*(2), 122–127.

Mitchell, J. E., Hatsukami, D., Eckert, E. D., & Pyle, R. L. (1985). Characteristics of 275 patients with bulimia. *American Journal of Psychiatry, 142,* 482–485.

Mond, J. M., Hay, P. J., Rodgers, B., & Owen, C. (2009). Comparing the health burden of eating-disordered behavior and overweight in women. *Journal of Women's Health, 18,* 1081–1089. doi:10.1089/jwh.2008.1174

National Association of Anorexia Nervosa and Associated Disorders. (2013). *Eating disorders statistics.* Retrieved from http://www.anad.org/get-information/about-eating-disorders/eating-disorders-statistics/

National Institute of Mental Health. (2012). *Eating disorders.* Retrieved from http://www.nimh.nih.gov/health/topics/eating-disorders/index.shtml

Peate, I. (2011). Dangerously misunderstood: Men and eating disorders. *British Journal of Healthcare Assistants, 5*(8), 383–387.

Pelegrini, A., & Petroski, E. L. (2010). The association between body dissatisfaction and nutritional status in adolescents. *Human Movement, 2*(1), 51–57.

Pohjolainen, V., Räsänen, P., Roine, R. P., Sintonen, H., Wahlbeck, K., & Karlsson, H. (2010). Cost-utility of treatment of bulimia nervosa. *Journal of Counseling & Development, 43,* 596–602.

Polivy, J., & Herman, C. P. (2002). Causes of eating disorders. *Annual Review of Psychology, 53,* 187–213.

Portela de Santana, M. L., da Costa Ribeiro Junior, H., Mora Giral, M., & Raich, R. M. (2012). La epidemiología y los factores de riesgo de los trastornos alimentarios en la adolescencia; una revisión [Epidemiology and risk factors of eating disorders in adolescence: A review]. *Nutrición Hospitalaria, 27,* 391–401.

Rafaeli, A. K., & Markowitz, J. C. (2011). Interpersonal psychotherapy (IPT) for PTSD: A case study. *American Journal of Psychotherapy, 65*(3), 205–223.

Ram, A., Stein, D., Sofer, S., & Kreitler, S. (2008). Bulimia nervosa and substance use disorder: Similarities and differences. *Eating Disorders, 16,* 224–240. doi:10.1080/10640260802016803

Root, T. L., Pinheiro, A. P., Thornton, S., Strober, M., Fernandez-Aranda, F., Brandt, H., . . . Bulik, C. M. (2010). Substance use disorders in women with anorexia nervosa. *International Journal of Eating Disorders, 43*(1), 14–21.

Safer, D. L., Telch, C. F., & Chen, E. Y. (2009). *Dialectical behavior therapy for binge eating and bulimia.* New York, NY: Guilford Press.

Seligman, L., & Reichenberg, L. W. (2012). *Selecting effective treatments: A comprehensive systematic guide to treating eating disorders* (4th ed.). Hoboken, NJ: Wiley.

Shafran, R., Fairburn, C. G., Robinson, P., & Lask, B. (2004). Body checking and its avoidance in eating disorders. *International Journal of Eating Disorders, 35*(1), 93–101.

Shaw, H., Ramirez, L., Trost, A., Randall, P., & Stice, E. (2004). Body image and eating disturbances across ethnic groups: More similarities than differences. *Psychology of Addictive Behaviors, 18,* 12–18.

Shea, M., Cachelin, F., Uribe, L., Striegel, R. H., Thompson, D., & Wilson, G. T. (2012). Cultural adaption of a cognitive behavior therapy guided self-help program for Mexican American women with binge eating disorders. *Journal of Counseling & Development, 90,* 308–318.

Simon, J., Schmidt, U., & Pilling, S. (2005). The health service use and cost of eating disorders. *Psychological Medicine, 35,* 1543–1551.

Smith, D. E. (2012). Editor's note: The process addictions and the new ASAM definition of addiction. *Journal of Psychoactive Drugs, 44*(1), 1–4. doi:10.1080/02791072.2012.662105

Stuhldreher, N., Konnopka, A., Wild, B., Herzog, W., Zipfel, S., Lowe, B., & Konig, H. (2012). Cost-of-illness studies and cost-effectiveness analyses in eating disorders: A systematic review. *International Journal of Eating Disorders, 45,* 476–491.

Talleyrand, R. M. (2010). Eating disorders in African American girls: Implications for counselors. *Journal of Counseling & Development, 88,* 319–324.

Talleyrand, R. M. (2012). Disordered eating in women of color: Some counseling considerations. *Journal of Counseling & Development, 90,* 271–280.

Thompson, J. K., van den Berg, P., Roehrig, M., Guarda, A. S., & Heinberg, L. J. (2004). The Sociocultural Attitudes Towards Appearance Scale–3 (SATAQ-3): Development and validation. *International Journal of Eating Disorders, 35*(3), 293–304.

Volkow, N. D., & Fowler, J. S. (2000). Addiction, a disease of compulsion and drive: Involvement of the orbitofrontal cortex. *Cerebral Cortex, 10*(3), 318–325. doi:10.1093/cercor/10.3.318

Waller, G., Cordery, H., Corstorphine, E., Hinrichsen, H., Lawson, R., Mountford, V., & Russell, K. (2011). *Cognitive behavior therapy for eating disorders: A comprehensive treatment guide.* New York, NY: Cambridge University Press.

Warren, C. S., Gleaves, D. H., Cepeda-Benito, A., del Carmen Fernandez, M., & Rodriguez-Ruiz, S. (2005). Ethnicity as a protective factor against internalization of a thin ideal and body dissatisfaction. *International Journal of Eating Disorders, 37*(3), 241–249.

Wertheim, E. H., Paxton, S. J., & Tilgner, L. (2004). Test–retest reliability and construct validity of Contour Drawing Rating Scale scores in a sample of early adolescent girls. *Body Image, 1*(2), 199–205.

Wisniewski, L. (2013). *Conceptual and practical DBT strategies in the treatment of complex eating disorder patients* [PowerPoint slides]. Cleveland Center for Eating Disorders, Cleveland, OH.

Wisniewski, L., Safer, D., & Chen, E. (2007). Dialectical behavior therapy and eating disorders. In L. A. Dimeff & K. Koerner (Eds.), *Dialectical behavior therapy in clinical practice: Applications across disorders and settings* (pp. 174–221). New York, NY: Guilford Press.

Wonderlich, S. A., Gordon, K. H., Mitchell, J. E., Crosby, R. D., & Engel, S. G. (2009). The validity and clinical utility of binge eating disorder. *International Journal of Eating Disorders, 42*, 687–705.

Yager, J., Devlin, M. J., Halmi, K. A., Herzog, D. B., Mitchell, J. E., Powers, P. S., & Zerbe, K. J. (2005). Eating disorders. *Focus, 3*, 503–510.

Yager, J., Devlin, M. J., Halmi, K. A., Herzog, D. B., Mitchell, J. E., Powers, P. S., & Zerbe, K. J. (2006). *Treatment of patients with eating disorders* (3rd ed.). Retrieved from http://psychiatryonline.org/pb/assets/raw/sitewide/practice_guidelines/guidelines/eatingdisorders-watch.pdf

CHAPTER 10

WORK ADDICTION
Summer M. Reiner

STUDENT LEARNING OUTCOMES

At the conclusion of this chapter students will

1. Describe the various types of work addiction/workaholism
2. List antecedents and consequences of work addiction/workaholism
3. Understand the assessment and diagnostic process related to work addiction
4. Identify current recommended treatments for work addiction

CASE AND CASE DISCUSSION

Michella is a 39-year-old Black woman. She was raised in the Caribbean with her mother until the age of 10, when she moved to the United States with her father. At the time of the transition, she did not speak English. She worked hard to learn the language and excel in school. She was unhappy in her teen years, as she grieved the loss of her mother and native home, struggled to make friends, and was constantly demeaned by her stepmother. When she was 16, her father died and her stepmother put her out on the street. Orphaned, but old enough to take care of herself, Michella took a job and focused even more intensely on her studies. She learned to juggle a busy life, achieved the goals she set, and received praise from her teachers and employers for her tenacity.

In college Michella continued to focus on her studies and managed a full-time job. She did not mind the long hours, as she felt productive and filled with pride. She earned an undergraduate degree and two master's degrees, all while working a full-time job. After graduating from college, she acquired a high-salary position. She worked long hours, ensuring that the work she submitted was meticulously error free. She enjoyed the praise she received for her excellent-quality work.

In just 2 years, Michella began to climb the leadership ranks. During her 5th year with the firm, she married and gave birth to a son. Michella felt on top of the world. She enjoyed her worker, wife, and mother roles and believed she was thriving in all three domains. Her dysfunctional and low-income past seemed to be behind her.

By her 10th year with the firm, she held the second highest position. Although she had a high-profile job and earned an outstanding salary, she was feeling tired, frustrated, and less fulfilled. In addition, she received constant complaints from her family about being physically and emotionally unavailable. Furthermore, her husband complained that she was not intimate with him often enough. She was appalled by her family's complaints. In her opinion, she was an active participant in the family: She cooked; cleaned; and drove her 6-year-old son to and from karate, swimming, piano, and violin. She also checked her son's homework each night; if she found mistakes, she instructed him to fix the answers. In terms of intimacy with her husband, she made time at least once a month to be with him.

Work was also less fulfilling. She had recently received feedback that her expectations of her coworkers were unreasonable and that she was often critical of their work. In her mind, most of the employees were lazy and incompetent; if they cared as much as she did, they would work as hard and as meticulously as her. She felt her life spiraling out of control but did not know how to reclaim the fulfillment she had previously enjoyed. Michella decided to seek counseling to deal with her frustrations at home and work.

OVERVIEW OF WORK ADDICTION

As the old saying goes, "Some work to live; some live to work." For some, work is a means to pay the bills; for others, work brings much meaning to life. In some cases, work goes beyond being meaningful in one's life to being compulsive and excessive, which Oates (1971) labeled *workaholism*. Over the past 40 years, several other researchers have further defined workaholism or work addiction and its features, antecedents, and outcomes. This chapter covers key aspects of work addiction, including (a) important definitions and antecedents related to work addiction, (b) types of work addiction, (c) consequences of work addiction, (d) diagnosis and assessment, and (e) treatment.

Many teasingly claim to be a workaholic as if it is a positive characteristic (Robinson, 1996). In fact, many have suggested that workaholism is a positive habit that benefits the worker and employer and that it is often rewarded in society with promotions, salary increases, and work stability (Brady, Vodanovich, & Rotunda, 2008; Burwell & Chen, 2002; Machlowitz, 1980; Robinson, 1996; Sussman, Lisha, & Griffiths, 2011). Researchers have acknowledged some positive outcomes associated with workaholism but claim that workaholism has serious consequences for workers, their families, and their employers (Andreassen, Hetland, Molde, & Pallesen, 2010; Brady et al., 2008; Burwell & Chen, 2002; Dungan, 2005; Gorgievski, Bakker, & Schaufeli, 2010; Machlowitz, 1985; Robinson, 1996; Schaufeli, Taris, & van Rhenen, 2008; Sussman et al., 2011; Taris, Geurts, Schaufeli, Blonk, & Lagerveld, 2008; van Beek, Hu, Schaufeli, Taris, & Schreurs, 2012; Van den Broeck et al., 2011).

Technology (e.g., smartphones, tablets) has contributed to the increasing adoption of workaholic tendencies (Aziz, Adkins, Walker, & Wuensch, 2010). Workers are able to remain connected to their work after hours, thus eroding the typical 40-hour workweek. Although the aforementioned external expectations are considered contributing factors to workaholism, most of the existing research has examined the internal factors of workaholism. Studies of workaholism have led to a variety of conceptions of the term.

Work Addiction

The terms *workaholism* and *work addiction* are interchangeable in the literature. The movement from *workaholism* in the 1970s to *work addiction* in the 1990s was an attempt to underscore the seriousness of the condition and to distance the meaning from trendy "I'm a workaholic" connotations (Robinson, 1996). The term *workaholism* was inspired by its symptomatology, which aligns closely with that of alcoholism (Oates, 1971): compulsion; an uncontrollable need; and a disturbance in one's health, relationships, and/or emotional well-being. Additional noted parallels between the two conditions concern salience, mood modifications, conflict, relapse (Aziz & Tronzo, 2011; Griffiths, 2005), tolerance, withdrawal symptoms (Aziz & Tronzo, 2011; Dungan, 2005; Griffiths, 2005; Robinson, 1996), self-deception, loss of willpower, and distortion of attention (Dungan, 2005). Some have stated that workaholism is a work–life imbalance (Seybold & Salomone, 1994), provides an escape (Aziz, Adkins, et al., 2010; Schaufeli, Taris, & van Rhenen, 2008; Seybold & Salomone, 1994), and is a means of avoiding intimacy with others (Robinson, 1996; Schaufeli, Taris, & van Rhenen, 2008; Seybold & Salomone, 1994).

Workaholics are believed to prolong their work and make more work for themselves (Aziz, Adkins, et al., 2010) and to work beyond the reasonable expectations (Schaufeli, Taris, & van Rhenen, 2008). They are addicted to the work, not the rewards (Robinson, 1996; Schaufeli, Taris, & van Rhenen, 2008). Like other addictions, workaholism has been described as a chronic, progressive disorder (Dungan, 2005; Robinson, 1996) starting with denial (Aziz, Adkins, et al., 2010; Burwell & Chen, 2002; Robinson, 1996), leading to an inability to manage one's life or work habits, and eventually ending with death (Dungan, 2005; Robinson, 1996). Some have suggested that workaholism becomes addictive because of the adrenaline highs from work binges, external recognition of accomplishments, and career advancements (Burwell & Chen, 2002; Johnstone & Johnston, 2005; Robinson, 1996; Sussman et al., 2011). When they are not working, workaholics are believed to experience withdrawal symptoms: depression, anxiety (Aziz, Adkins, et al., 2010; Robinson, 1996), irritability (Robinson, 1996), and preoccupation with work (Schaufeli, Taris, & van Rhenen, 2008).

Although many researchers have studied the existence of work addiction, it has not been officially recognized as a disorder in the *Diagnostic and Statistical Manual of Mental Disorders* (*DSM*; Dungan, 2005; Robinson, 2000b). Some have suggested that workaholism falls under obsessive-compulsive personality disorder (OCPD; Aziz, Uhrich, Wuensch, & Swords, 2013; Bonebright, Clay, & Ankenmann, 2000), thus not requiring recognition of its own in the *DSM*. More recently, however, authors have described workaholism as one of the many process addictions (e.g., addictions to gambling, the Internet, love, sex, exercise, compulsive spending; Griffiths, 2005; Sussman et al., 2011). Process addictions differ from substance addictions in that they introduce pleasure not via a product but rather via mood-altering events that become addictive in nature (Sussman et al., 2011). For example, workaholics can become addicted to the adrenaline rush they get from their work (Johnstone & Johnston, 2005; Robinson, 2001). Process addictions are interesting, as some are socially accepted and/or celebrated (e.g., addictions to exercise or work), whereas others are not. In fact, it has been suggested that work addiction is the most accepted and praised addiction the world has to offer (Bonebright et al., 2000; Burwell & Chen, 2002; Dungan, 2005; Machlowitz, 1985; Robinson, 1996; Spruell, 1987; Sussman et al., 2011).

Substance and process addictions serve similar functions and often co-occur (Sussman et al., 2011). Sussman et al. (2011) conducted a meta-analysis of 83 studies (studies with $N > 500$ were included in their analysis) and found that nearly 47% of the U.S. population experiences symptoms of an addictive disorder (i.e., addiction to tobacco, alcohol, illicit drugs, eating, gambling, the Internet, love, sex, exercise, work, shopping) over a 12-month period. They also estimated the prevalence of work addiction at 10%. Only the rates of addictions to cigarettes (15%) and alcohol (10%) met or exceeded that of work addiction. Work addiction was also estimated to have a co-occurrence rate of 20% with other substance or process addictions.

Dimensions of Work Addiction

Oates (1971) initially identified obsessive work thoughts and compulsive work behaviors as the key characteristics of workaholism. Over time, the dimensions were further conceptualized and studied by others. Spence and Robbins (1992) identified work involvement, drive, and work enjoyment as the main components of workaholism. Scott, Moore, and Miceli (1997) suggested similar dimensions: spending a great deal of time on work, being reluctant to stop working and preoccupied with work, and working beyond what is reasonably expected. According to Schaufeli, Taris, and Bakker (2008), workaholics spend a great deal of time on work; perceive increased job demands; and experience positive work outcomes, poor-quality social relationships, and health problems. The various aforementioned descriptions are complementary, but it should be noted that the majority of research conducted was on Spence and Robbins's conceptualization of workaholism.

Types of Work Addiction

Despite the growing body of research on workaholism/work addiction, there continues to be debate about whether workaholism is problematic in all cases. In fact, many have suggested that there are good and bad forms of workaholism (Andreassen, Ursin, & Eriksen, 2007; Aziz, Wuensch, & Brandon, 2010; Bonebright et al., 2000; Brady et al., 2008; Machlowitz, 1980; Oates, 1971; Robinson, 2000b; Schaufeli, Bakker, & Salanova, 2006; Schaufeli, Bakker, van der Heijden, & Prins, 2009; Schaufeli, Taris, & van Rhenen, 2008; Scott et al., 1997; Snir & Harpaz, 2009; Spence & Robbins, 1992; van Beek et al., 2012).

Heavy work investment is an element of work involvement. According to Snir and Harpaz (2009), time and effort are two core dimensions of heavy work investment. They argued that workaholism is a subtype of heavy work investment and that work devotion is the other subtype. They were not alone in their dichotomous conceptualization of positive and negative aspects of heavy work investment and workaholism. In the literature, positive workaholics have been labeled as fulfilled (Machlowitz, 1980), as hyperperformers (Scott et al., 1997), as happy hard workers (Buelens & Poelmans, 2004), as work engaged (Schaufeli, Salanova, González-Romá, & Bakker, 2002), and as having harmonious passion (Vallerand et al., 2003). In contrast, negative workaholics have been referred to as unfulfilled (Machlowitz, 1980) and as having obsessive passion (Vallerand et al., 2003).

Much of the literature depicting a dichotomous conception of workaholism seems to focus on similar constructs to Spence and Robbins's (1992) drive and work enjoyment. Some have suggested that the third dimension (i.e., work investment) is not valid and that it should be subsumed under the other two dimensions (Andreassen et al., 2007; Johnstone & Johnston, 2005; L. H. W. McMillan, O'Driscoll, & Brady, 2004). Research on the work enjoyment dimension has led to the emergence of the term *work engagement*, which reinforces more of the positive perspectives of workaholism. In fact, some authors have conceptualized work engagement as the antithesis of workaholism (Bakker, Schaufeli, Leiter, & Taris, 2008; Schaufeli et al., 2002; Schaufeli, Taris, & van Rhenen, 2008; van Beek et al., 2012) and suggested that it is a fulfilling state of mind that is characterized by vigor, dedication, and absorption (Schaufeli et al., 2002). Furthermore, engaged workers, unlike workaholics, maintain their social lives (Schaufeli, Taris, & van Rhenen, 2008). Qualitative evidence has revealed that work engagement is correlated with perceived good mental health (Schaufeli et al., as cited in Schaufeli, Taris, & van Rhenen, 2008).

The negative and positive concepts of workaholism are both supported and refuted in the literature. Some studies have found strong support for positive outcomes for different types of workaholics, thus justifying a distinction (Andreassen et al., 2007; Bonebright et al., 2000; Schaufeli, Taris, & van Rhenen, 2008). Supporters of positive and negative workaholism concepts have warned that further investigation not accounting for these differences would further confound the literature (Bonebright et al., 2000; Schaufeli, Taris, & van Rhenen, 2008). Others (Schaufeli, Shimazu, & Taris, 2009), however, found that good workaholism did not have positive outcomes, thus invalidating the notion of good workaholism. The negative and positive aspects of workaholism are often captured in the types of workaholism conceived by various researchers.

Oates (1971) described six types of workaholics: *dyed in the wool* (perfectionists), *overcommitted* (intolerant of others' incompetence), *situational* (driven by job security rather than intrinsic need), *pseudo* (motivated by advancement and power rather than productivity), *escapists* (would rather be at work than home), and *converted* (have set personal work limits because of past problems).

Naughton (1987) suggested that there are two types of workaholics and non-workaholics based on two dimensions: work involvement and obsession-compulsion. *Job-involved workaholics* are considered high in involvement and low in obsession-compulsion, whereas *compulsive workaholics* are high in both areas. *Non-workaholics* are low in both areas, and *compulsive non-workaholics* are low in involvement but high in obsession-compulsion in nonwork activities.

Fassel (1990) identified four types of workaholics. The *compulsive workaholic* works all the time, whereas the *binge workaholic* binges on work for days on end.

The *closet workaholic* conceals his or her excess work habits to prevent being discovered. Finally, the *anorexic workaholic* compulsively avoids work.

Spence and Robbins (1992) identified six types based on different combinations of their three identified dimensions of workaholism (i.e., investment, drive, enjoyment). *Workaholics* are high in work involvement and drive and low in enjoyment. *Work enthusiasts* are high in work involvement and enjoyment but low in drive. *Enthusiastic workaholics* are high in all three dimensions, whereas *disengaged workers* are low in all three dimensions. *Relaxed workers* are lower in engagement and drive but higher in work enjoyment. Finally, *disenchanted workers* are lower in work involvement and enjoyment but higher in drive.

Scott et al. (1997) believed that workaholic types should be identified by interactions of the following dimensions: job satisfaction, life satisfaction, job performance, job turnover rates, stress, physical and psychological problems, and interpersonal relationships. They described *obsessive-compulsive workaholics* as having high job and life satisfaction and job performance. *Perfectionist workaholics* were described as having high levels of stress, physical and psychological problems, and interpersonal problems and low levels of job satisfaction and performance and turnover. *Achievement-oriented workaholics* were characterized by high physical and psychological health, job and life satisfaction, and job performance and low interpersonal problems and turnover.

Finally, Robinson (2000a) suggested four types of workaholics based on anecdotal clinical observations. He suggested that work initiation and work completion were important factors in the characterization of workaholism. *Relentless workaholics* work all the time, including evenings, weekends, and holidays, and tend to get their work done ahead of schedule. *Bulimic workaholics* are overcommitted in work projects but procrastinate in accomplishing the work. They experience an adrenaline rush as a result of pushing up against a deadline. The *attention-deficit workaholic* also seeks adrenaline but is constantly looking for new and exciting or challenging work and has difficulty relaxing. *Savoring workaholics* are perfectionists who are methodical and intentional and often have difficulty finishing a task because it is never good enough.

Consequences of Work Addiction

Researchers have found a host of health, social, and work-related issues associated with workaholism. Some physical and mental health issues that have a relationship with workaholism are anger (Fassel, 1990; Oates, 1971; Robinson, 1998), anxiety (Fassel, 1990; Oates, 1971; Robinson, 1989, 2000a), burnout (Andreassen et al., 2007; Schaufeli, Bakker, et al., 2009; Schaufeli, Taris, & van Rhenen, 2008), depression (Fassel, 1990; Oates, 1971; Robinson, 1998, 2000a), health problems (e.g., heart disease; Andreassen, Hetland, Molde, et al., 2010; Aziz, Wuensch, & Brandon, 2010; Bonebright et al., 2000; Chamberlin & Zhang, 2009; Robinson, 2000a; Schaufeli, Taris, & van Rhenen, 2008; Shimazu, Schaufeli, & Taris, 2010; Spence & Robbins, 1992; Taris, van Beek, & Schaufeli, 2012), low leisure enjoyment (Bonebright et al., 2000; Bovornusvakool, Vodanovich, Ariyabuddhiphongs, & Ngamake, 2012; Brady et al., 2008; Snir & Zohar, 2008), low life satisfaction and purpose (Andreassen, Hetland, Molde, et al., 2010; Aziz, Wuensch, & Brandon, 2010; Bonebright et al., 2000; Bovornusvakool et al., 2012; Brady et al., 2008; Taris et al., 2012), stress (Andreassen et al., 2007; Aziz, Wuensch, & Brandon, 2010; Spence & Robbins, 1992), and suicide (Robinson, 2000a).

Some social issues related to workaholism are work–family conflict (Bonebright et al., 2000; Schaufeli, Bakker, et al., 2009; Taris et al., 2012), social conflict (Aziz, Wuensch, & Brandon, 2010; Schaufeli, Taris, & van Rhenen, 2008), loneliness (Bovornusvakool et al., 2012), and family problems (Robinson, 2000a; Robinson, Carroll, & Flowers, 2001; Robinson, Flowers, & Ng, 2006).

Work-related issues include difficulty with coworkers (Schaufeli, Bakker, et al., 2009; Shimazu et al., 2010), reduced efficacy and performance problems (Bonebright et al., 2000; Shimazu et al., 2010; van Beek et al., 2012), reduced flexibility (Bonebright et al., 2000; Gorgievski et al., 2010), and cynicism (Schaufeli, Taris, & van Rhenen, 2008; van Beek et al., 2012).

WORK ADDICTION AROUND THE WORLD

A number of studies of workaholism have been conducted around the world. Most of the findings suggested that workaholism has negative outcomes, but given certain motivations and coping responses, some outcomes were found to offset a number of the negative associations (Shimazu et al., 2010; Van den Broeck et al., 2011).

A study of 587 telecom managers in The Netherlands found that workaholism was related to health problems, poor-quality social relationships, increased job demands, and positive work outcomes (Schaufeli, Taris, & van Rhenen, 2008). Those workaholics with high drive, however, experienced increasingly more negative outcomes, such as negative social reactions outside of work, health complaints, and distress. Similarly, a Norwegian study of 661 cross-occupational employees from six different organizations revealed that workaholism had an impact on life satisfaction and health (Andreassen, Hetland, Molde, et al., 2010). Enjoyment of work was associated with increased work and life satisfaction but lower subjective health. Work involvement and drive were associated with job dissatisfaction and poor health. Drive had a negative correlation with life satisfaction.

A Belgian study of 370 white-collar workers revealed that those who worked compulsively for extrinsic rewards or out of fear of punishment experienced more exhaustion (Van den Broeck et al., 2011). Those who had autonomous motivation to work long hours were found to have vigor and appeared to be energized by work. Thus, the researchers concluded that the type of motivation accounted for the outcomes associated with workaholism. Other researchers, however, found that workaholics' coping style led to outcomes associated with the condition. In a Japanese construction machinery company ($N = 757$), workaholism was associated with active coping and emotional discharge (Shimazu et al., 2010). Active coping was conceptualized as thinking logically about work-related problems and finding solutions. Emotional discharge was described as openly sharing one's negative emotions in the workplace. Active coping was related to better health and performance, whereas emotional discharge was related to poor health. Those workaholics who used active coping tended to be slightly more productive than other employees.

A study of 477 Dutch self-employed workers found that outcomes associated with workaholism were mediated by the ability to detach from work (Taris et al., 2008). Those who could not detach from work experienced exhaustion, physical complaints, and lower levels of efficacy. In a study of 65 full-time workers recruited through two Israeli universities, workaholics preferred spending their time in work-related activities and during their leisure time preferred to think about work (Snir & Zohar, 2008). In fact, workaholics reported more positive affect during work than during leisure activity. Furthermore, they preferred to engage in leisure activity with people from work.

A study conducted in the United States examined work–life balance, workaholism, and cultural origin (Aziz, Adkins, et al., 2010). A convenience sample of 215 employees from a wide variety of professional fields participated in the study. The researchers found that cultural origin was not a significant factor in workaholism rates or in work–life balance. They did find, however, that workaholism was related to work–life imbalance. Another U.S. study of university employees ($N = 129$) and a human resource management group ($N = 103$) found that workaholism was related to greater work–family conflict and less gratification with leisure (Brady et al., 2008). Those with greater work enjoyment experienced less work–family conflict and greater work satisfaction.

IMPACT OF WORK ADDICTION

Impact on the Family

Researchers (Bonebright et al., 2000; Carroll & Robinson, 2000; Oates, 1971; Robinson, 1998; Robinson et al., 2001, 2006; Robinson & Post, 1995) have identified several negative outcomes for family members of workaholics. However, families are considered a protective factor for workaholics, as they act as stress buffers (L. H. W. McMillan et al., 2004).

Workaholism was found to be associated with marital conflict (Bonebright et al., 2000; Robinson & Post, 1995), dysfunction, family role confusion, lower general functioning, less effective problem solving (Robinson & Post, 1995), less communication, fewer affective responses, and less affective involvement. One spousal perception study (Robinson et al., 2006) found that workaholics tended to be overcontrolling and had impaired communications with their spouses, thus leading to a lack of marital affection. Another study (Robinson et al., 2001) found marital disaffection and less positive feelings toward the workaholic spouse.

Workaholics are also less involved in their children's development, are more demanding of their achievement, and expect perfection (Oates, 1971; Robinson, 1998). Children tend to resent their workaholic parent and become approval seekers to meet the exceptional expectations set by their parents. The negative outcomes of workaholism on children seem to continue even into their adulthood, as they were found to experience anxiety, depression, and parentification and developed an external locus of control (Robinson & Kelley, 1998).

Impact by Type

A number of researchers (Aziz, Wuensch, & Brandon, 2010; Bonebright et al., 2000; Spence & Robbins, 1992) have suggested that some of the aforementioned issues could be specifically associated with types of workaholism. Outcomes of workaholism by type have been researched by Spence and Robbins (1992). Upon reviewing these studies, one could argue that non-enthusiastic workaholics, enthusiastic workaholics, and disenchanted workers have the greatest potential for experiencing distress in the aforementioned life domains (i.e., health, social, work).

Burnout

Researchers have identified burnout as a potential consequence of workaholism (Bonebright et al., 2000; Porter, 1996; Schaufeli, Taris, & van Rhenen, 2008; Scott et al., 1997). According to Schaufeli, Taris, and van Rhenen (2008), *burnout* is a term that describes a "state of mental weariness" (p. 175). Burnout was conceived by Maslach (1993) as a three-dimensional construct involving exhaustion, cynicism, and lack of professional efficacy.

The work–life conflict workaholics experience, and their unwillingness to recharge their energy through leisure, places them at risk for burnout (Schaufeli, Bakker, et al., 2009; Schaufeli, Taris, & van Rhenen, 2008; Van den Broeck et al., 2011). Leisure is a time in which many engage in meaningful social relationships, rest, and renewal (Bonebright et al., 2000). In fact, much research has demonstrated relationships between workaholism, lack of leisure, and burnout (Andreassen et al., 2007; Schaufeli, Taris, & Bakker, 2008; Taris, Schaufeli, & Verhoeven, 2005). One study of 587 telecom managers in The Netherlands found that burnout was related not to the number of hours one spent on work but to poor social functioning, health-related and mental health–related concerns, job demands and poor outcomes, and a lack of resources (Schaufeli, Taris, & van Rhenen, 2008). Schaufeli, Bakker, et al. (2009) suggested that work engagement is the opposite of burnout but that both are related to workaholism, suggesting that workaholic types (Spence & Robbins, 1992) who are low in work engagement are at greater risk for burnout. Indeed, a Norwegian study of 235 bank employees (Andreassen et al., 2007) found that those with non-enthusiastic workaholic features were at the greatest risk for burnout. Burke and Matthiesen (2004) found that disenchanted workers were high in burnout.

Workers experiencing burnout have mentally distanced themselves from work (van Beek et al., 2012); are more cynical; and are more likely to be absent, to be planning to leave their job, and to underperform because of a lack of commitment (Maslach, Schaufeli, & Leiter, 2001).

ANTECEDENTS OF WORK ADDICTION

In a review of existing studies, personality traits (e.g., obsession-compulsion, an achievement orientation, perfectionism, and contentiousness), personal inducements (e.g., intrinsic work values and familial modeling/vicarious learning in the family), and organizational inducements (e.g., putting work before family, peer competition, vicarious learning in the workplace) were all found to be antecedents of workaholism (Liang & Chu, 2009).

Personality Traits

A number of personality traits can predispose workers to work addiction, including anxiousness (Robinson, 1996), an achievement orientation (J. H. McMillan & Hearn, 2008), high motivation (Andreassen et al., 2007), impatience (Andreassen et al., 2007), insecurity (Chamberlin & Zhang, 2009), low self-esteem (Burke & Fiksenbaum, 2009; Seybold & Salomone, 1994; van Beek et al., 2012), low self-worth (Chamberlin & Zhang, 2009; Seybold & Salomone, 1994; van Beek et al., 2012), narcissism (Andreassen, Ursin, Eriksen, & Pallesen, 2012), negative affect (Bovornusvakool et al., 2012;

Van Wijhe, Peeters, & Schaufeli, 2011), OCPD (Aziz et al., 2013; Bonebright et al., 2000), perfectionism (Bovornusvakool et al., 2012; Spence & Robbins, 1992; Taris et al., 2012), self-centeredness, a task orientation (Andreassen et al., 2007), and a Type A personality (Schaufeli, Shimazu, & Taris, 2009).

Perfectionism and negative affect were found in relation to workaholism in a sample of 226 U.S. undergraduate students (Bovornusvakool et al., 2012). Leisure boredom and loneliness were predicted by negative affect. Loneliness was also predicted by perfectionism. The researchers concluded that a negative mood state was an antecedent of workaholism, as the work may have alleviated the negative mood state. Similarly, in a study of 216 Americans from a variety of professions, negative affect was related to workaholism and positive affect was related to work engagement (Van Wijhe et al., 2011).

In a sample of Dutch medical residents (N = 2,115), having a Type A personality was related to workaholism (Schaufeli, Shimazu, & Taris, 2009). People with Type A personalities are characterized as being achievement oriented, impatient, and irritable. Although the researchers found that the workaholics perceived increased job demands and role conflict, they suggested that the workaholics with a Type A personality were more likely to hold these sorts of inaccurate negative perceptions (i.e., perceived and actual demands were not consistent). It is interesting to note that Machlowitz (1980) had previously hypothesized that Type A personality, OCPD, and workaholism were connected.

In addition to Type A personalities, those with narcissistic personalities were also found to be more likely to experience workaholism. In a study of 500 managers and their subordinates at a Norwegian bank, managers were found to have higher levels of narcissism, drive, enjoyment of work, and work engagement (Andreassen et al., 2012). The authors concluded that traits developed early in life, like narcissism, predisposed some individuals to workaholism later in life.

Relationships have also been found between workaholism and the five factors of personality: conscientiousness, extraversion, neuroticism, openness to experience, and agreeableness (Andreassen, Hetland, & Pallesen, 2010; Aziz & Tronzo, 2011). Some researchers (Andreassen et al., 2012; Aziz & Tronzo, 2011), in cross-industry studies, have examined relationships between the five factors of personality and work involvement, drive, and work enjoyment.

Personal Inducements

Personal inducements include intrinsic work values and familial modeling that are believed to promote workaholism. Values are influenced through a variety of sources, particularly family and one's culture. Institutions (e.g., educational, political, and religious institutions) can promote workaholism behaviors (e.g., competition, high standards; Fassel, 1990). A strong work ethic has existed in U.S. culture ever since the Puritans arrived. In the 20th century, a new value emerged: finding an occupation that matched one's personality, giving way to a value of enjoying one's work. Sayings such as "Enjoy your work and you'll never have to work another day in your life" permeate U.S. culture and convey the notion that work can be one's leisure. Thus, it is not surprising that researchers continue to find evidence that some workaholics report enjoyment and fulfillment through their work (Bonebright et al., 2000; Burke & Fiksenbaum, 2009) and feel justified working long hours.

In addition to culture, families can model workaholism and the valuing of work over other areas of one's life (Chamberlin & Zhang, 2009; Fassel, 1990; Machlowitz, 1980; Seybold & Salomone, 1994). Some have suggested that dysfunctional upbringings are responsible for the dispositions and traits that are associated with workaholism (Chamberlin & Zhang, 2009; Machlowitz, 1980; Robinson, 1996; Seybold & Salomone, 1994). According to Robinson and Post (1995), dysfunctional families typically experience boundary confusion, which leads to the development of a family hero who becomes responsible, controlling, and perfectionistic, all in an effort to compensate for poor self-worth and anxiety. Robinson (1990) argued that families with a workaholic are dysfunctional, thus creating a self-perpetuating cycle. Chamberlin and Zhang (2009) found evidence to support Robinson's (1990) claims. In their study of 347 college students, they found that those with higher perceptions of parental workaholism reported lower levels of psychological well-being and self-acceptance, more physical health complaints, and more workaholic tendencies. Previous research had revealed that children of workaholics believed that their parents had high expectations of them and that their parents' approval or love was dependent on their success (Machlowitz, 1980; Robinson, 1998). According to Robinson and Kelley (1998), children of workaholics experience similar emotional symptoms to those of alcoholics: anxiety, depression, and low self-esteem and self-acceptance.

Organizational Inducements

Work environments can be considered workaholic (Seybold & Salomone, 1994; Spruell, 1987). A high-pressure culture may encourage employees to work long hours to achieve success and rewards (Johnstone & Johnston, 2005). In fact, several studies have found that work overload and increased job demands were related to workaholism (Kanai & Wakabayashi, 2001; Taris et al., 2005). According to Spruell (1987), the worst case scenario is when workaholics become managers. Recent research found that managers' narcissism and workaholic tendencies could impact the organizational climate and culture (Andreassen et al., 2012). Indeed, they were found to influence work motivation, employee incentive, and workaholism. Given typical traits of workaholics (e.g., an inability to delegate tasks to others, an inefficient approach to work, criticism of others' efforts, expectations of perfection), workaholic managers may experience a great deal of conflict with their employees (Andreassen et al., 2012; Machlowitz, 1980). Furthermore, workaholic managers can create resentment, conflict, and low office morale (Klaft & Kleiner, 1988).

Stages of Workaholism Development

According to Garson (as cited in Robinson, 1996), workaholics experience a three-stage developmental process. Stage 1 involves being raised in a dysfunctional family with oppressive rules and unrealistic standards for achieving parental approval. In Stage 2, the young adult receives approval, appreciation, and promotions for his or her workaholic behaviors, thus feeding the addiction. Stage 3 occurs in middle adulthood and coincides with the midlife crisis. During this final stage, the negative outcomes of workaholism come to a head. If the addiction is not addressed it can lead to further deterioration or death from stress-related diseases or suicide.

DEFINITIONS, COSTS, AND DEMOGRAPHICS

Definitions

Burnout: A mental depletion or exhaustion coupled with cynicism and lack of professional efficacy.

Five factors of personality: Openness to experience, conscientiousness, extraversion, agreeableness, and neuroticism.

Obsessive-compulsive personality disorder (OCPD): According to the *Diagnostic and Statistical Manual of Mental Disorders, Fourth Edition, Text Revision (DSM–IV–TR;* American Psychiatric Association [APA], 2000), a minimum of four criteria must be met to diagnose OCPD 301.4. Five criteria of OCPD that closely align with the characteristics of workaholism are demonstrates perfectionism, excessively devoted to work and neglects leisure and friendships, overly conscientious, reluctance to delegate, and rigidity.

Type A personality: A temperament that is often characterized by an achievement orientation, impatience, irritability, and rigidity. Type A personalities are also considered competitive, controlling, and organized.

Work engagement: Considered a positive form of workaholism by which workers experience fulfillment through their hard work but not necessarily at the expense of social relationships. Work engagement is considered the opposite of burnout.

Workaholism/work addiction: There is no single definition for workaholism, but most definitions incorporate work thought obsessions and compulsive work behavior that impede other areas of one's life. Researchers are undecided about whether workaholism should be categorized as an OCPD or a process addiction.

Costs

The financial costs of workaholism have yet to be published in the literature. The research on workaholism typically focuses on the financial gains that people generate by overinvesting themselves in work. If one were to determine the financial costs, one would have to consider a variety of monetary losses. On an individual financial level, workaholics may incur a range of expenses associated with the progression of their condition (Holland, 2008). Early on, given the excessive hours they dedicate to work, workaholics may find that they are too busy to do their own house and yard work and need to hire someone else to do it. Given the infancy of their careers, one could speculate that these workaholics may experience financial hardship associated with paying domestic workers. Furthermore, workaholics may also have to depend on supplementary hours of child care, thus incurring additional child care costs. Later on in their work addiction, they may find themselves having mental health and/or medical problems or experiencing divorce (Holland, 2008). The costs associated with major medical and mental health conditions can be astounding, especially if one is hospitalized or placed in an inpatient facility. Divorce can also be expensive and may lead to absences from work. Workaholics and their families also have intangible costs due to the conflict and dysfunction within the family (e.g., missed bonding opportunities, resentment, legacy workaholism). The song *Cat's in the Cradle* by Sandy and Harry

Chapin may capture best some of the intangible losses and legacies of workaholism: The song describes how the father is too busy to spend time with his son, only to have his son grow up and be too busy to be with him.

Costs to employers can be tangible and intangible as well. Based on issues identified in the literature, one could speculate that employers could incur costs associated with reduced productivity due to perfectionism or burnout (Holland, 2008). Employers may also see more absenteeism and increased medical costs due to health issues and burnout. One could further surmise that there could be costs involved with losing other employees who feel challenged by the workaholic's critical, perfectionist standards and negative nature. In terms of intangible costs, the work environment, work culture, and relationships with customers could suffer.

Demographics

The rate of workaholism is not presently known, but in 1980 it was estimated at 5% of the U.S. population (Machlowitz, 1980), and by 2011 it was estimated at 10% (Sussman et al., 2011). The increase in workaholism appears to be related to 24/7 access to work via technology and increasing productivity expectations (Aziz, Adkins, et al., 2010). In terms of gender, a study with nationally representative samples of the adult populations of 20 countries ($N = 25,962$) found that men worked more hours than women in all countries studied. Spence and Robbins (1992), however, found that women scored higher than men on drive, work enjoyment, job stress, job involvement, and time commitment. Others have not found gender differences in workaholism rates (Burke, 1999; Doerfler & Kammer, 1986). Work devotion has been found to be more prevalent in the United States, Japan (Burke, 2007; Snir & Harpaz, 2009), the United Kingdom, France, Germany (Burke, 2007), Mexico, Portugal, and New Zealand (Snir & Harpaz, 2009).

Limited research has been conducted on workaholism by industry. A Dutch study ($N = 9,160$) revealed that workaholism was more prevalent in agricultural, construction, communication, consultancy, and commerce/trade sectors (Taris et al., 2012). Managers and other higher level professionals were also more likely than individuals in nonmanagerial positions to experience workaholism. Workaholism was lower in public administration, nursing, social work, and paramedic work. A study in New Zealand ($N = 146$) of business and social occupations revealed that those in the business field had higher levels of drive and lower levels of work enjoyment than those in social occupations (Johnstone & Johnston, 2005).

ASSESSMENT AND DIAGNOSIS

Assessment

Nearly half a dozen instruments are used to assess workaholism. The Workaholism Battery (Spence & Robbins, 1992) and the Work Addiction Risk Test (Robinson, 1989) have been researched more than other instruments (Schaufeli, Taris, & van Rhenen, 2008). The Workaholism Battery has been used in studies in the United States, Canada, Norway, Turkey, Japan, New Zealand, and Australia (Burke & Fiksenbaum, 2009). The Work Addiction Risk Test has been used in the United States and The Netherlands. Other work addiction assessments include the Work Attitudes and Behaviors Inventory (Haymon, as cited in Senholzi, 2005), the

Utrecht Work Engagement Scale (Schaufeli et al., 2002), and the Workaholism Analysis Questionnaire (Aziz et al., 2013). The benefits of each of the aforementioned instruments are that they can be self-administered, scored, and interpreted easily. Thus, work addiction is relatively easy to detect. However, given the close relationship that work addiction has with other conditions, professionals will also want to carefully assess behaviors as obsessive-compulsive before rendering a diagnosis. Brief details on a selection of instruments follow.

Work Addiction Risk Test (Robinson, 1989)

Responses on this 25-item instrument are made on a 4-point Likert-type scale (4 = *strongly agree* to 1 = *strongly disagree*). The items were compiled from a list of reported symptoms from practitioners working with families affected by work addiction. The Work Addiction Risk Test has five subscales: Compulsive Tendencies, Inability to Control Work Habits, Impaired Communication, Inability to Delegate, and Impaired Self-Worth (Flowers & Robinson, 2002). Scores range from 25 to 100. A score of 70 or higher indicates highly work addicted and at risk for burnout, and scores between 55 and 69 indicate mildly work addicted. Robinson (1996) reported α = .85 and a test–retest reliability of .83.

Workaholism Battery (Spence & Robbins, 1992)

The Workaholism Battery has three subscales: Work Involvement, Drive, and Enjoyment. Responses to items are made on a 5-point Likert-type scale (1 = *strongly disagree* to 5 = *strongly agree*). Work Involvement has seven items, Drive has seven items, and Enjoyment has nine items. Reported coefficient alphas across the three scales range from .67 to .86. Aziz, Wuensch, and Brandon (2010) reported Cronbach's alphas of .72 for Work Involvement, .82 for Drive, and .88 for Enjoyment in their research.

Work Attitudes and Behaviors Inventory (Haymon, as cited in Senholzi, 2005)

The Work Attitudes and Behaviors Inventory is a 72-item checklist with Likert-type agreement responses. Five factors emerged in a statistical analysis of this test: anxiety, obsessive-compulsive behavior, mania, intolerance, and self-doubt. Cronbach's alphas for the various scales range from .61 to .83 (Senholzi, 2005). However, Senholzi (2005), in her validation of the Work Attitudes and Behaviors Inventory, found that only 58 items loaded on the same five factors with a range of .69 to .82: anxiety (α = .82), obsessive-compulsive behavior (α = .79), mania (α = .69), intolerance (α = .78), and self-doubt (α = .75).

Utrecht Work Engagement Scale (Schaufeli et al., 2002)

The Utrecht Work Engagement Scale is a 17-item instrument with a 7-point scale ranging from 0 (*never in the last year*) to 6 (*daily*). The instrument has three subscales—Vigor (six items, αs = .68–.80), Dedication (five items, α = .91), and Absorption (six items, αs = .73–.75)—for a total α = .84–.89 across all 17 items in two sets of samples. A high score indicates a high level of work engagement and thus low risk for burnout. Andreassen et al. (2012), however, reported alphas of .87 for Vigor, .91 for Dedication, and .87 for Absorption, for a total of .95 across all 17 items. The Utrecht Work Engagement Scale was later shortened to a nine-item questionnaire with a total reliability coefficient of .85 and .92 (median = .92) across 10 countries (Schaufeli et al., 2006).

Workaholism Analysis Questionnaire (Aziz et al., 2013)
The Workaholism Analysis Questionnaire is a 29-item questionnaire scored on a 5-point Likert scale ranging from 1 (*strongly disagree*) to 5 (*strongly agree*), with higher scores indicating higher levels of workaholism. Cronbach's alpha was .934 in the original study (Aziz et al., 2013).

Limitations of Work Addiction Instruments
The Workaholism Battery and the Work Attitudes and Behaviors Inventory have been called into question regarding their validity and reliability across populations (Robinson, 1996). The Workaholism Battery and the Work Addiction Risk Test have been questioned on their factor structures and psychometric properties (Aziz et al., 2013). The Workaholism Analysis Questionnaire used snowball sampling, thus bringing into question its generalizability. Finally, the Utrecht Work Engagement Scale has been criticized for a lack of confirmation of factorial group invariance (Seppala et al., 2009).

OCPD
Some work addiction studies have examined the relationship between workaholism and OCPD. One instrument used for this purpose is the Schedule for Nonadaptive and Adaptive Personality (Clark, 1993). This is a 375-item true/false measure of personality disorders and related trait pathology (Aziz et al., 2013). The 25-item OCPD scale of the Schedule for Nonadaptive and Adaptive Personality measures the diagnostic criteria from the *DSM–IV–TR* (American Psychiatric Association, 2000).

Personality
Narcissism and neuroticism are among the personality traits related to workaholism. Work addiction researchers (Andreassen et al., 2012) have used the Narcissistic Personality Inventory (Raskin & Terry, 1988) to determine the relationship between narcissism and workaholism. High scores on the 40-item Narcissistic Personality Inventory represent dominance, extraversion, aggression, impulsivity, self-centeredness, self-indulgence, and nonconformance.

Some researchers (Andreassen, Hetland, & Pallesen, 2010; Aziz & Tronzo, 2011) have looked at the relationship between the five factors of personality and workaholism. The NEO-Five Factor Inventory (Costa & McCrae, 1992) has 60 items answered on a 5-point Likert-type scale ranging from 0 (*strongly disagree*) to 4 (*strongly agree*). It measures the five basic factors of personality: neuroticism, extraversion, openness to experience, agreeableness, and conscientiousness.

A sample of other assessments that have been used in relationship to work addiction research includes the Maslach Burnout Inventory (Maslach, Jackson, & Leiter, 1996), Work Interference With Family Scales (Gutek, Searle, & Klepa, 1991), Satisfaction With Life Scale (Diener, Emmons, Larsen, & Griffin, 1985), Purpose in Life Test (Crumbaugh & Maholick, 1964), Self-Acceptance Scale (Phillips, 1951), Leisure Boredom Scale (Iso-Ahola & Weissinger, 1990), Free Time Boredom Scale (Ragheb & Merydith, 2001), Work-Family Conflict Scale (Carlson, Kacmar, & Williams, 2000), and Work–Life Imbalance Scale (Fisher, Bulger, & Smith, 2009).

Diagnosis

According to Robinson (1996), an addiction to work is distinct from healthy work behavior when work interferes with health, happiness, social relationships, and romantic relationships. However, Dungan (2005) suggested that detecting workaholism is challenging, especially in the early stages. Indeed, Burwell and Chen (2002) argued that workaholism is often rationalized and denied. Authors have offered a variety of factors necessary to identify workaholism. Dungan identified four signs of work addiction: obsessions, negative consequences, loss of control, and denial. Bonebright et al. (2000) suggested that work should be considered an addiction if it meets the same criteria as substance dependence in the *DSM*. Similarly, Griffiths (2005) stated that individuals must meet six criteria to be considered workaholics: salience (work is the most important activity), mood modification, tolerance, withdrawal, conflict, and relapse. Robinson (2000a) offered the most complex set of cues (i.e., 10 items) for identifying work addiction: staying busy, needing control, perfectionism, social conflict, work binges, leisure boredom, memory brownouts, impatience and irritability, self-inadequacy, and self-neglect. Sussman et al. (2011), however, cautioned against labeling individuals as workaholics unless they are at risk for serious conditions or outcomes.

Like other process/behavioral addictions, work addiction is not described in the *DSM*. Some have argued that work addiction should be considered a form of OCPD. Given the ongoing ambiguity, the clinician, when suspecting workaholism, should assess for OCPD and workaholism. Using clinical judgment, the clinician should determine whether the client has OCPD, OCPD with workaholism, or workaholism alone.

TREATMENT

Despite the mounting research on workaholism, little information has been published on research-based treatments for the condition. Several workaholism treatment recommendations have been presented, but none have been empirically tested. Clearly, there is a significant need for empirical studies on the treatment of workaholism. There is also a need for specialized treatment programs.

Inpatient

Inpatient care provides the most intense form of treatment, literally ensuring that the workaholic takes a break from work. Individuals may require inpatient care if they are unable to comply with treatment during a 24-hour period, live in an environment that is not conducive to recovery, have physical or mental complications, or lack judgment and require 24-hour supervision (New York State Office of Alcoholism and Substance Abuse Services, n.d.). Inpatient care typically lasts 30 to 90 days and is expensive. Inpatient facilities can cost between $20,000 and $32,000 (Hazelden, 2013), with luxury facilities costing even more; these costs do not include costs incurred by time off from work. Unfortunately, it is unlikely that most insurance companies will pay for treatment for workaholism or other process addictions. Insurance companies are more likely to pay for coexisting substance addiction or mental health conditions (e.g., depression, anxiety, and suicide).

At the time of this writing, a search of the Internet revealed only two inpatient facilities that listed a specialization in work addiction. There are, however, a number of facilities that specialize in process addictions. Individuals with coexisting addictions or mental health concerns will need to look for facilities that can address their coexisting issues.

Inpatient care ensures that the individual cannot access work and is forced to spend a great deal of leisure time with himself or herself and other patients. The time spent at the facility will likely bring out the leisure boredom that many workaholics experience. Treatment should ideally focus on addressing the underlying emotions associated with the workaholic behavior (Burwell & Chen, 2002; Seybold & Salomone, 1994); reestablishing healthy relationships with family and friends (Brady et al., 2008; Burwell & Chen, 2002; Dungan, 2005; Robinson, 1996, 2000b; Seybold & Salomone, 1994; Shifron & Reysen, 2011); addressing leisure development (Seybold & Salomone, 1994); and constructing a plan for a balanced life (Bonebright et al., 2000; Robinson, 1996; Seybold & Salomone, 1994), including creating a transition plan and identifying a sponsor (Dungan, 2005).

Outpatient

Outpatient care is a far more affordable treatment option in general. Most individuals seeking treatment for their work addiction will likely benefit from outpatient treatment, as only the most severe cases will need to consider inpatient treatment. Agencies, hospitals, or private counselors can provide outpatient care. As previously stated, insurance is unlikely to cover a process addiction, such as work addiction, but will likely cover some of the other conditions associated with workaholism (e.g., depression, anxiety). Individuals may also be able to work with an employee assistance program to engage in therapy (Schaufeli, Bakker, et al., 2009). Employee assistance program services are typically free to the worker and his or her immediate family members.

Unlike substance dependence treatment protocols that require abstinence, some process addictions (e.g., workaholism) require that one learn moderation of the addictive behavior (Dungan, 2005; Robinson, 1996, 2000a; Shimazu et al., 2010). It would be impractical or unhealthy to eliminate work from most people's lives. In fact, Dungan (2005) suggested that workaholics would simply acquire a new form of work addiction (e.g., volunteerism). Instead, many experts have recommended that workaholics develop a self-care plan (Robinson, 1996, 2000a) that focuses on life balance (Bonebright et al., 2000; Robinson, 1996; Seybold & Salomone, 1994). In order to arrive at a reasonable and meaningful self-care plan, workaholics are encouraged to begin their treatment by examining their feelings associated with their family of origin (Chamberlin & Zhang, 2009; Robinson, 1996; Shifron & Reysen, 2011).

According to Robinson (1996), understanding the unresolved feelings associated with growing up in a dysfunctional family is essential in the treatment of workaholism. He suggested that genograms, inner child work, and family systems work can help reveal the generational origins of addiction and the wounding and unresolved depression, anxiety, and/or anger associated with the dysfunction. He also believed that it was critical to deal with low self-esteem, intimacy issues, perfectionism, and obsessive control patterns to achieve recovery from workaholism. Others have also suggested that treatment focus on the underlying issues of self-esteem (Burwell & Chen, 2002) and life purpose (Bonebright et al., 2000).

In addition to addressing underlying issues, some have suggested that workaholics be encouraged to explore the consequences (related to health, social relationships, or work) of their work addiction (Chamberlin & Zhang, 2009). Furthermore, therapy should focus on stress management (Bonebright et al., 2000). Workaholics are encouraged to investigate leisure activities that bring pleasure (Burwell &

Chen, 2002; Chamberlin & Zhang, 2009; Robinson, 1996; Seybold & Salomone, 1994), especially enjoyable family activities (Seybold & Salomone, 1994). The adopted leisure activities should be placed in the self-care plan. Dungan (2005) suggested that workaholics have a sponsor to help them to keep on track with their self-care or recovery plan.

MODELS AND APPROACHES

Work addiction researchers have speculated that workaholics could benefit from individual, group (Seybold & Salomone, 1994), and family (Brady et al., 2008; Chamberlin & Zhang, 2009; Robinson, 1996; Seybold & Salomone, 1994; Shifron & Reysen, 2011) counseling. Some have suggested that clients' counseling goals should match the type of workaholism with which they have presented (Naughton, 1987; Robinson, 2000a). Furthermore, clients with OCPD and Type A personality concerns should be treated by a therapist trained to address those issues (Seybold & Salomone, 1994).

Group Counseling

Group counseling is believed to be effective in treating work addiction because it has been evidenced to work with other addictions (Seybold & Salomone, 1994) and with conditions often experienced by the workaholic (e.g., depression, self-esteem, anger). Groups are believed to benefit the workaholic in setting realistic, obtainable goals for change. Furthermore, the group provides a safe space for self-reflection and accountability.

Family Counseling

Family counseling is considered a necessary aspect of treatment. As previously mentioned, some individuals engage in workaholic behaviors as a result of a dysfunctional family environment (Seybold & Salomone, 1994). Furthermore, the family often experiences resentment toward the workaholic. Allowing all family members to understand how the workaholism and family dysfunction impact each member of the family is an essential part of the recovery process. Dungan (2005) suggested that family members acknowledge the benefits they receive from the excessive work and make a choice to select a relationship with the workaholic over material goods. Failure to do this, in his opinion, will keep the family in denial. Working on communication within the family is also considered essential (Seybold & Salomone, 1994). In a similar vein, communicating the self-care plan (developed in individual counseling) with the family can help set realistic expectations for time spent with the family. Furthermore, sharing the plan can set the stage for family members to support the workaholic while keeping him or her accountable.

Theoretical Approaches

Rational emotive behavioral therapy (Ellis, 1995) and Adlerian individual psychology have been identified as approaches with potential for effectively addressing workaholism (Burwell & Chen, 2002; Shifron & Reysen, 2011). According to Burwell and Chen (2002), rational emotive behavioral therapy can help to address the core issues of low self-esteem that fuel workaholic behaviors. Shifron and Reysen (2011), however, suggested that therapists help the workaholic, through an Adlerian framework, to examine his or her family constellation and lifestyle. They suggested that the goals of therapy are to acknowledge that work should not dominate one's life, establish effective family roles and boundaries, and teach family members to acknowledge change efforts made by the workaholic. They proposed a two-stage approach to addressing workaholism. The first stage involves an analysis of lifestyle to uncover hidden goals and to engage in couples therapy. In the second stage, the focus is on identifying and developing tools to reach goals while also engaging in family therapy.

EVIDENCE-BASED APPROACHES

There is an absence of literature on evidence-based treatment for workaholism (Van Wijhe, Schaufeli, & Peeters, 2010). Thus, Van Wijhe et al. (2010) suggested that treatments should address the reinforcing behavior, focus on maladaptive beliefs, address the work and family environments, and address the behavioral and compulsive components of workaholism. Models and theoretical orientations that may have promise as treatments for work addiction include motivational interviewing (Miller & Rollnick, 1991), family counseling, behavioral counseling, cognitive therapy, and cognitive behavior therapy because of the evidence of their success with other related conditions (Van Wijhe et al., 2010). Burke (2005), however, cautioned against retrofitting treatments for work addiction. He argued that the empirical evidence of work addiction as true condition, as well as the evidence of different types of work addiction, might have some consequences if the wrong treatment approach is selected.

Support groups (Dungan, 2005; Robinson, 1996) have been recommended for those in recovery from work addiction. Others have further suggested that employers be encouraged to support the workaholic in the work environment (Chamberlin & Zhang, 2009; Shimazu et al., 2010).

Workaholics Anonymous (n.d.) is an international fellowship for those interested in no longer working compulsively. They currently hold meetings in 31 states and the District of Columbia and in 14 countries. In addition, they offer a 24-hour hotline and Internet and telephone group-support meetings. They encourage newcomers to learn about the recovery process, to attend meetings and conferences, and to partner with a sponsor. Their website boasts a variety of resources available for download. In addition, they offer support to friends and family of those with a work addiction.

Workaholics Anonymous operates with 12 steps and 12 traditions that were adapted from Alcoholics Anonymous. According to Robinson (1996), Workaholics Anonymous has a high success rate helping individuals through their recovery of workaholism.

Some researchers have asserted that the employer serves a critical role in supporting a workaholic's recovery (Chamberlin & Zhang, 2009; Shimazu et al., 2010). Authors have suggested that employers be educated on the potential losses associated with a culture of workaholism and the benefits of encouraging workers to detach and recover from their work (Chamberlin & Zhang, 2009; Shimazu et al., 2010). Shimazu et al. (2010) suggested that employers offer training programs to help their employees work smarter, not harder. They suggested programs on time management, problem solving, and assertiveness. Chamberlin and Zhang

(2009) encouraged counselors to connect with employers to provide the sort of education suggested. If an employer is unwilling to help address the problem (e.g., changing demands), the workaholic may find it beneficial or necessary to find an environment that values a work–life balance over workaholism.

CONCLUSIONS

Work and discussions around a work ethic have been evident throughout history. The terms *workaholic* and *burnout* have also been widely discussed in the literature. More recently, greater attention has been given to the effects of work-related behavior on an individual's health and well-being, as well as on one's family and quality of life. As a result, work carried to the extreme has often been viewed as an addiction, particularly when consequences are evident.

Diagnosing and assessing when work becomes an addiction is complex. A number of instruments are available to help clinicians assess whether work is approaching an addiction. However, very few of these measures have been adequately researched and validated in large part because of the difficulty of identifying work as an addiction.

The *Diagnostic and Statistical Manual of Mental Disorders, Fifth Edition* (APA, 2013) provides a brief discussion of addictions and includes gambling as a behavior disorder or process addiction. The template used to identify gambling as a disorder can perhaps, with adaptations, serve as a guide in determining when work could be considered an addiction.

RESOURCES

Websites

American Counseling Association
 http://www.counseling.org/
Association for Specialists in Group Work
 http://www.asgw.org/
International Association of Addictions & Offender Counselors
 http://www.iaaoc.org/
International Association of Marriage and Family Counselors
 http://www.iamfconline.org/
National Career Development Association
 http://ncda.org/
Personal website of Bryan E. Robinson
 http://www.bryanrobinsononline.com/about/
Personal website of Wilmar Schaufeli
 http://www.wilmarschaufeli.nl/
Workaholics Anonymous
 http://www.workaholics-anonymous.org/page.php?page=home
Workaholics Anonymous, Audio Archives of Conference Proceedings
 http://www.workaholics-anonymous.org/page.php?page=audioarchive

Videos

Core Concepts of Motivational Interviewing by Cathy Cole
 http://www.psychotherapy.net/video/motivational-interviewing-concepts

Couples Therapy for Addictions: A Cognitive-Behavioral Approach by Barbara S. McCrady
   http://www.psychotherapy.net/video/couples-therapy-addictions
Harm Reduction Therapy for Addictions by G. Alan Marlatt
   http://www.psychotherapy.net/video/marlatt-harm-reduction
Integrating Therapy With 12-Step Programs by Joan Ellen Zweben
   http://www.psychotherapy.net/video/12-step-addiction-therapy

REFERENCES

American Psychiatric Association. (2000). *Diagnostic and statistical manual of mental disorders* (4th ed., text rev.). Washington, DC: Author.

American Psychiatric Association. (2013). *Diagnostic and statistical manual of mental disorders* (5th ed.). Arlington, VA: Author.

Andreassen, C. S., Hetland, J., Molde, H., & Pallesen, S. (2010). "Workaholism" and potential outcomes in well-being and health in a cross-occupational sample. *Stress & Health*, 27(3), e209–e214. doi:10.1002/smi.1366

Andreassen, C. S., Hetland, J., & Pallesen, S. (2010). The relationship between "workaholism," basic needs satisfaction at work and personality. *European Journal of Personality*, 24(1), 3–17. doi:10.1002/per.737

Andreassen, C. S., Ursin, H., & Eriksen, H. R. (2007). The relationship between strong motivation to work, "workaholism," and health. *Psychology & Health*, 22, 615–629. doi:10.1080/14768320600941814

Andreassen, C. S., Ursin, H., Eriksen, H. R., & Pallesen, S. (2012). The relationship of narcissism with workaholism, work engagement, and professional position. *Social Behavior & Personality*, 40, 881–890.

Aziz, S., Adkins, C. T., Walker, A. G., & Wuensch, K. L. (2010). Workaholism and work–life imbalance: Does cultural origin influence the relationship? *International Journal of Psychology*, 45(1), 72–79. doi:10.1080/00207590902913442

Aziz, S., & Tronzo, C. L. (2011). Exploring the relationship between workaholism facets and personality traits: A replication in American workers. *Psychological Record*, 61(2), 269–285.

Aziz, S., Uhrich, B., Wuensch, K. L., & Swords, B. (2013). The Workaholism Analysis Questionnaire: Emphasizing work–life imbalance and addiction in the measurement of workaholism. *Journal of Behavioral & Applied Management*, 14(2), 71–86.

Aziz, S., Wuensch, K. L., & Brandon, H. R. (2010). A comparison among worker types using a composites approach and median splits. *Psychological Record*, 60, 627–641.

Bakker, A. B., Schaufeli, W. B., Leiter, M. P., & Taris, T. W. (2008). Work engagement: An emerging concept in occupational health psychology. *Work & Stress*, 22(3), 187–200. doi:10.1080/02678370802393649

Bonebright, C. A., Clay, D. L., & Ankenmann, R. D. (2000). The relationship of workaholism with work–life conflict, life satisfaction, and purpose in life. *Journal of Counseling Psychology*, 47, 469–477.

Bovornusvakool, W., Vodanovich, S. J., Ariyabuddhiphongs, K., & Ngamake, S. T. (2012). Examining the antecedents and consequences of workaholism. *The Psychologist-Manager Journal*, 15(1), 56–70. doi:10.1080/10887156.2012.649994

Brady, B. R., Vodanovich, S. J., & Rotunda, R. (2008). The impact of workaholism on work–family conflict, job satisfaction, and perception of leisure activities. *The Psychologist-Manager Journal*, 11(2), 241–263. doi:10.1080/10887150802371781

Buelens, M., & Poelmans, S. A. Y. (2004). Enriching the Spence and Robbins' typology of workaholism: Demographic, motivational and organizational correlates. *Organizational Change Management*, 17, 440–458.

Burke, R. J. (1999). Workaholism in organizations: The role of organizational values. *Personnel Review, 30,* 637–645.

Burke, R. J. (2005). Workaholism in organizations: Work and well-being consequences. In A. G. Antoniou & C. L. Cooper (Eds.), *Research companion to organizational health psychology* (pp. 366–381). Cheltenham, England: Edward Elgar.

Burke, R. J. (2007). *Research companion to working time and work addiction.* Cheltenham, England: Edward Elgar.

Burke, R. J., & Fiksenbaum, L. (2009). Work motivations, satisfactions, and health among managers: Passion versus addiction. *Cross-Cultural Research, 43*(4), 349–365.

Burke, R. J., & Matthiesen, S. (2004). Workaholism among Norwegian journalists: Antecedents and consequences. *Stress & Health, 20,* 301–308.

Burwell, R., & Chen, C. P. (2002). Applying REBT to workaholic clients. *Counselling Psychology Quarterly, 15*(3), 219–228. doi:10.1080/09515070210143507

Carlson, D. S., Kacmar, K. M., & Williams, L. J. (2000). Construction and initial validation of a multidimensional measure of work–family conflict. *Journal of Vocational Behavior, 56,* 249–276.

Carroll, J. J., & Robinson, B. E. (2000). Depression and parentification among adults as related to parental workaholism and alcoholism. *The Family Journal, 8*(4), 360–367.

Chamberlin, C. M., & Zhang, N. (2009). Workaholism, health, and self-acceptance. *Journal of Counseling & Development, 87,* 159–169.

Clark, L. A. (1993). *Schedule for Nonadaptive and Adaptive Personality (SNAP).* Minneapolis: University of Minnesota Press.

Costa, P. T., Jr., & McCrae, R. R. (1992). Reply to Ben-Porath and Waller. *Psychological Assessment, 4*(1), 20–22.

Crumbaugh, J. C., & Maholick, L. T. (1964). An experimental study in existentialism: The psychometric approach to Frankl's concept of noogenic neurosis. *Journal of Clinical Psychology, 20,* 200–207.

Diener, E., Emmons, R. A., Larsen, R. J., & Griffin, S. (1985). The Satisfaction With Life Scales. *Journal of Personality Assessment, 49,* 71–75.

Doerfler, M. C., & Kammer, P. P. (1986). Workaholism: Sex and sex role stereotyping among female professionals. *Sex Roles, 14,* 551–560.

Dungan, F. A. (2005). Work addiction: Cunning, baffling, and powerful. *American Journal of Pastoral Counseling, 8*(1), 35–45. doi:10.1300/J062v08n01.04

Ellis, A. (1995). Changing rational-emotive therapy (RET) to rational emotive behavior therapy (REBT). *Journal of Rational-Emotive and Cognitive-Behavior Therapy, 13,* 85–90.

Fassel, D. (1990). *Working ourselves to death: The high cost of workaholism, the rewards of recovery.* San Francisco, CA: HarperCollins.

Fisher, G. G., Bulger, C. A., & Smith, C. S. (2009). Beyond work and family: A measure of work/nonwork interference and enhancement. *Journal of Occupational Health Psychology, 14,* 441–456.

Flowers, C. P., & Robinson, B. (2002). A structural and discriminant analysis of the Work Addiction Risk Test. *Educational and Psychological Measurement, 62,* 517–526.

Gorgievski, M. J., Bakker, A. B., & Schaufeli, W. B. (2010). Work engagement and workaholism: Comparing the self-employed and salaried employees. *Journal of Positive Psychology, 5*(1), 83–96. doi:10.1080/17439760903509606

Griffiths, M. (2005, April). Workaholism is still a useful construct. *Addiction Research & Theory,* pp. 97–100.

Gutek, B. A., Searle, S., & Klepa, L. (1991). Rational versus gender role explanations for work–family conflict. *Journal of Applied Psychology, 76,* 560–568.

Hazelden. (2013). *Top 5 most frequently asked questions.* Retrieved from http://www.hazelden.org/web/public/top5questions.page

Holland, D. W. (2008). Work addiction: Costs and solutions for individuals, relationships and organizations. *Journal of Workplace Behavioral Health, 22*, 1–15. doi:10.1080/15555240802156934

Iso-Ahola, S. E., & Weissinger, E. (1990). Perceptions of boredom in leisure: Conceptualization, reliability, and validity of the Leisure Boredom Scale. *Journal of Leisure Research, 22*, 1–17.

Johnstone, A., & Johnston, L. (2005). The relationship between organizational climate, occupational type and workaholism. *New Zealand Journal of Psychology, 34*(3), 181–188.

Kanai, A., & Wakabayashi, M. (2001). Workaholism among Japanese blue-collar employees. *International Journal of Stress management, 8*, 129–203.

Klaft, R. P., & Kleiner, B. H. (1988). Understanding workaholics. *Business, 38*, 37–40.

Liang, Y. W., & Chu, C. M. (2009). Personality traits and personal and organizational inducements: Antecedents of workaholism. *Social Behavior & Personality, 37*, 645–660.

Machlowitz, M. (1980). *Workaholics: Living with them, working with them.* Reading, MA: Addison-Wesley.

Machlowitz, M. (1985). *Whiz kids: Success at an early age.* New York, NY: Arbor House.

Maslach, C. (1993). Burnout: A multidimensional perspective. In W. B. Schaufeli, C. Maslach, & T. Marek (Eds.), *Professional burnout: Recent developments in theory and research* (pp. 19–32). Washington, DC: Taylor & Francis.

Maslach, C., Jackson, S. E., & Leiter, M. P. (1996). *Maslach Burnout Inventory manual* (3rd ed.). Palo Alto, CA: Consulting Psychologists Press.

Maslach, C., Schaufeli, W. B., & Leiter, M. P. (2001). Job burnout. *Annual Review of Psychology, 52*, 397–422.

McMillan, J. H., & Hearn, J. (2008). Student self-assessment: The key to stronger student motivation and higher achievement. *Educational Horizons, 87*(1), 40–49.

McMillan, L. H. W., O'Driscoll, M. P., & Brady, E. C. (2004). The impact of workaholism on personal relationships. *British Journal of Guidance & Counselling, 32*(2), 171–186. doi: 10.1080/03069880410001697729

Miller, W. R., & Rollnick, S. (1991). *Motivational interviewing.* New York, NY: Guilford Press.

Naughton, T. J. (1987). A conceptual review of workaholism and implications for career counseling and research. *The Career Development Quarterly, 35*, 180–187.

New York State Office of Alcoholism and Substance Abuse Services. (n.d.). *Criteria for admission.* Retrieved from http://www.oasas.ny.gov/atc/admission.cfm

Oates, W. (1971). *Confessions of a workaholic.* New York, NY: World.

Phillips, E. L. (1951). Attitudes towards self and others: A brief questionnaire report. *Journal of Consulting Psychology, 15*, 79–81.

Porter, G. (1996). Organizational impact of workaholism: Suggestions for researching the negative outcomes of excessive work. *Journal of Occupational Health Psychology, 1*, 70–84.

Ragheb, M. G., & Merydith, S. P. (2001). Development and validation of a multidimensional scale measuring free time boredom. *Leisure Studies, 20*, 41–59.

Raskin, R. N., & Terry, H. (1988). A principal components analysis of the Narcissistic Personality Inventory and further evidence of its construct validity. *Journal of Personality and Social Psychology, 54*, 890–902.

Robinson, B. E. (1989). *Work addiction.* Deerfield Beach, FL: Health Communications.

Robinson, B. E. (1990). Workaholic kids. *Adolescent Counselor, 2*, 44–47.

Robinson, B. E. (1996). The psychosocial and familial dimensions of work addiction: Preliminary perspectives and hypotheses. *Journal of Counseling & Development, 74*, 447–452.

Robinson, B. E. (1998). The workaholic family: A clinical perspective. *American Journal of Family Therapy, 26*(1), 65–75.

Robinson, B. E. (2000a). A typology of workaholics with implications for counselors. *Journal of Addictions & Offender Counseling, 21*, 34–48.

Robinson, B. E. (2000b). Workaholism: Bridging the gap between workplace, sociocultural, and family research. *Journal of Employment Counseling, 37*, 31–47.

Robinson, B. E. (2001). Workaholism and family functioning: A profile of familial relationships, psychological outcomes, and research considerations. *Contemporary Family Therapy, 23*(1), 123–135.

Robinson, B. E., Carroll, J. J., & Flowers, C. (2001). Marital estrangement, positive affect, and locus of control among spouses of workaholics and spouses of nonworkaholics: A national study. *American Journal of Family Therapy, 29*, 397–410.

Robinson, B. E., Flowers, C., & Ng, K-M. (2006). The relationship between workaholism and marital disaffection: Husbands' perspective. *The Family Journal, 14*, 213–220. doi:10.1177/1066480706287269

Robinson, B. E., & Kelley, L. (1998). Adult children of workaholics: Self-concept, anxiety, depression, and locus of control. *American Journal of Family Therapy, 26*(3), 223–238.

Robinson, B. E., & Post, P. (1995). Work addiction as a function of family of origin and its influence on current family functioning. *The Family Journal, 3*, 200–206.

Schaufeli, W. B., Bakker, A. B., & Salanova, M. (2006). The measurement of work engagement with a short questionnaire: A cross-national study. *Educational and Psychological Measurement, 66*, 701–716.

Schaufeli, W. B., Bakker, A. B., van der Heijden, F. M. M. A., & Prins, J. T. (2009). Workaholism, burnout and well-being among junior doctors: The mediating role of role conflict. *Work & Stress, 23*(2), 155–172. doi:10.1080/02678370902834021

Schaufeli, W. B., Salanova, M., González-Romá, V., & Bakker, A. B. (2002). The measurement of engagement and burnout: A two sample confirmatory factor analytic approach. *Journal of Happiness Studies, 3*(1), 71–92.

Schaufeli, W. B., Shimazu, A., & Taris, T. W. (2009). Being driven to work excessively hard: The evaluation of a two-factor measure of workaholism in The Netherlands and Japan. *Cross-Cultural Research, 43*(4), 320–348.

Schaufeli, W. B., Taris, T. W., & Bakker, A. B. (2008). It takes two to tango: Workaholism is working excessively and working compulsively. In R. J. Burke & C. L. Cooper (Eds.), *The long work hours culture: Causes, consequences and choices* (pp. 203–226). Bingley, England: Emerald.

Schaufeli, W. B., Taris, T. W., & van Rhenen, W. (2008). Workaholism, burnout, and work engagement: Three of a kind or three different kinds of employee well-being? *Applied Psychology, 57*(2), 173–203. doi:10.1111/j.1464-0597.2007.00285.x

Scott, K. S., Moore, K. S., & Miceli, M. P. (1997). An exploration of the meaning and consequences of workaholism. *Human Relations, 50*, 287–314.

Senholzi, M. A. (2005). *The validation and generalization of the Work Attitudes and Behaviors Inventory (WABI)*. Retrieved from http://diginole.lib.fsu.edu/cgi/viewcontent.cgi?article=4506&context=etd

Seppala, P., Mauno, S., Feldt, T., Hakanen, J., Kinnunen, U., Tolvanen, A., & Schaufeli, W. (2009). The construct validity of the Utrecht Work Engagement Scale: Multisample and longitudinal evidence. *Journal of Happiness, 10*, 459–481. doi:10.1007/s10902-008-9100-y

Seybold, K. C., & Salomone, P. R. (1994). Understanding workaholism: A review of causes and counseling approaches. *Journal of Counseling & Development, 73*, 4–9.

Shifron, R., & Reysen, R. R. (2011). Workaholism: Addiction to work. *Journal of Individual Psychology, 67*(2), 136–146.

Shimazu, A., Schaufeli, W. B., & Taris, T. W. (2010). How does workaholism affect worker health and performance? The mediating role of coping. *International Journal of Behavioral Medicine, 17*(2), 154–160. doi:10.1007/s12529-010-9077-x

Snir, R., & Harpaz, I. (2009). Cross-cultural differences concerning heavy work investment. *Cross-Cultural Research, 43*(4), 309–319.

Snir, R., & Zohar, D. (2008). Workaholism as discretionary time investment at work: An experience-sampling study. *Applied Psychology, 57*(1),109–127. doi:10.1111/j.1464-0597.2006.00270.x

Spence, J. T., & Robbins, A. S. (1992). Workaholism: Definition, measurement, and preliminary results. *Journal of Personality Assessment, 58*, 160–178.

Spruell, G. (1987). Work fever. *Training and Development Journal, 41*, 41–45.

Sussman, S., Lisha, N., & Griffiths, M. (2011). Prevalence of the addictions: A problem of the majority or the minority? *Evaluation & the Health Professions, 34*(1), 3–56. doi:10.1177/0163278710380124

Taris, T. W., Geurts, S. A. E., Schaufeli, W. B., Blonk, R. W. B., & Lagerveld, S. E. (2008). All day and all of the night: The relative contribution of two dimensions of workaholism to well-being in self-employed workers. *Work & Stress, 22*(2), 153–165. doi:10.1080/02678370701758074

Taris, T. W., Schaufeli, W. B., & Verhoeven, L. C. (2005). Internal and external validation of the Dutch Work Addiction Risk Test: Implications for jobs and non-work conflict. *Journal of Applied Psychology, 54*, 37–60.

Taris, T. W., van Beek, I., & Schaufeli, W. B. (2012). Demographic and occupational correlates of workaholism. *Psychological Reports, 110*, 547–554. doi:10.2466/03.09.17.PR0.110.2.547-554

Vallerand, R. J., Blanchard, C., Mageau, G. A., Koestner, R., Ratelle, C., Léonard, M., . . . Marsolais, J. (2003). Les passions de l'ame: On obsessive and harmonious passion. *Journal of Personality and Social Psychology, 85*, 756–767.

van Beek, I., Hu, Q., Schaufeli, W. B., Taris, T. W., & Schreurs, B. H. J. (2012). For fun, love, or money: What drives workaholic, engaged, and burned-out employees at work? *Applied Psychology, 61*(1), 30–55. doi:10.1111/j.1464-0597.2011.00454.x

Van den Broeck, A., Schreurs, B., De Witte, H., Vansteenkiste, M., Germeys, F., & Schaufeli, W. (2011). Understanding workaholics' motivations: A self-determination perspective. *Applied Psychology, 60*, 600–621. doi:10.1111/j.1464-0597.2011.00449.x

Van Wijhe, C., Peeters, M., & Schaufeli, W. (2011). To stop or not to stop, that's the question: About persistence and mood of workaholics and work engaged employees. *International Journal of Behavioral Medicine, 18*(4), 361–372. doi:10.1007/s12529-011-9143-z

Van Wijhe, C. I., Schaufeli, W. B., & Peeters, M. C. W. (2010). Understanding and treating workaholism: Setting the stage for successful interventions. In C. Cooper & R. Burke (Eds.), *Psychological and behavioral risks at work* (pp. 107–134). Farnham, England: Ashgate.

Workaholics Anonymous. (n.d.). *Welcome to Workaholics Anonymous.* Retrieved from http://www.workaholics-anonymous.org/page.php?page=home

CHAPTER 11

EXERCISE ADDICTION

Michele Kerulis

STUDENT LEARNING OUTCOMES

At the conclusion of this chapter students will

1. Understand the American College of Sports Medicine's exercise guidelines
2. Explain the relationship between the increased use of multimedia technology and the decrease in physical activity
3. Define the seven components of exercise dependence
4. Define muscle dysmorphia
5. Explain the relationship between eating disorders and exercise dependence

CASES AND CASE DISCUSSION

Mary is a first-generation 23-year-old Chinese American woman. While in college, Mary participated in intramural sports with her friends in order to stay active but never engaged in regular exercise. Once she graduated from college, Mary moved to a new town and joined a health club. Mary began attending beginner aerobics classes as a way to meet new people and improve her health. At first Mary enjoyed the classes and the health benefits, such as increased stamina, weight loss, and a healthier appearance. She also noticed that she felt an energetic buzz after she engaged in strenuous exercise. She began to attend classes multiple times per week in order to maintain these newfound benefits, and within several months Mary was attending several classes every day. She justified this increased exercising by attending classes that focused on different parts of the body. Not long after she started exercising every day, Mary injured her knee during a class. Her doctor recommended that she stay off her knee and refrain from exercising for several weeks while she healed. Mary followed this advice for several days but found that she was becoming irritable and depressed and that she felt guilty that she was letting her body go by not exercising. Mary went back to the gym against her doctor's advice with the intention of reducing the number of classes she would attend. At her first class Mary tore her anterior cruciate ligament and had to have surgery to repair her damaged knee.

As an adolescent, Andrew was small in stature and was bullied for his appearance. As he matured, Andrew began to lift weights as a way to build muscle mass and to improve his appearance. By the time he was in college, Andrew had grown taller than most of his peers. At this time, he began to go to the gym on a daily basis, spending 3 to 4 hours at a time on his workouts. He also spent hours developing a workout plan as well as a detailed nutritional plan in order to maintain his now healthy and muscular body. To his friends and peers, Andrew appeared strong, lean, and healthy; however, Andrew felt that he was too small, and he often compared himself to professional athletes he saw on television. He often wore baggy sweat suits instead of well-fitted clothing that accentuated his physique. If Andrew missed too much gym time, he felt intense guilt and would spend more time there on his next visit. Andrew's friends noticed that he started to cancel dates and would not hang out anymore because he was always at the gym. They began to get worried for him and asked him to see a counselor. Andrew refused and isolated himself even more. He eventually began to use performance-enhancing steroids to pump up his appearance.

OVERVIEW OF EXERCISE ADDICTION

The positive effects of physical activity have been well documented and include decreased risk of disease and illness, increased cardiovascular health, and increased positive mood states (Gletsu & Tovin, 2010). It was not until the 1990s, however, that the benefits of exercise were formally recognized by the medical profession. In 1992, the American Heart Association compared a lack of physical activity to smoking and hypertension and recommended regular exercise as part of a healthy lifestyle (Fletcher et al., 1992). Wilmore, Costill, and Kenney (2008) provided a summary of additional important announcements related to exercise, including the Centers for Disease Control and Prevention's work with the American College of Sports Medicine (ACSM) in 1994 in which they announced physical activity as a public health initiative, the National Institutes of Health's advocacy of exercise as a benefit to cardiovascular health in 1996, and the Surgeon General's report about the benefits of exercise (U.S. Department of Health and Human Services, 1996).

The importance of exercise and physical movement was further publicized; for example, the Exercise Is Medicine program, a collaborative effort between the ACSM and the American Medical Association, was launched on November 5, 2007, and aimed to increase awareness of physical activity and exercise in health settings ("Exercise Is Medicine," n.d.). The program provides information for medical professionals, fitness professionals, the media, the general public, and policymakers and is focused on improving health and decreasing health care costs. The program has been successful in the United States, and additional campaigns have been launched in other areas of North America, Africa, Australia, Europe, and Asia.

Another noteworthy campaign was launched on February 9, 2010, by First Lady Michelle Obama. The Let's Move! campaign (http://www.letsmove.gov/)

is dedicated to teaching people about fitness with a particular focus on helping children live a healthy and active lifestyle. According to the campaign, childhood obesity has tripled in the past few decades, and now approximately 40% of children are overweight or obese. This shift is attributed to larger portion sizes; cuts in school programming, including physical education classes; decreased participation in physical activities, such as walking to school and playing outside; and increased time spent using electronic entertainment. In fact, researchers from the Let's Move! campaign reported that children ages 8–17 spend an average of 7.5 hours a day using media (television, cell phones, video games, and computers), and only one third of high school students engage in the recommended amount of exercise. As technology use continues to grow, health and fitness campaigns must continue to address the need to engage in physical activity.

The ACSM's (2011) position stand on the quantity and quality of exercise resulted in four guidelines for exercise that can be modified for people with chronic illness and physical limitations. The first guideline instructs people to engage in cardiorespiratory training (activities that increase heart rate and respiration) 5 days a week for at least 30 minutes per day. Examples include brisk walking and jogging. Numerous health benefits are linked with cardiorespiratory training, such as decreased disease and increased cognitive ability. Cardiorespiratory training (heart rate training) can be tracked by using a wristwatch and chest strap coded to monitor heartbeats per minute and calories burned.

The second guideline recommends that exercisers engage in resistance training (weight training) that targets each muscle group two or three times a week (ACSM, 2011). Examples include lifting weights, using resistance bands, or engaging in weight-bearing exercises like pushups. Resistance training has been associated with stronger and leaner muscles, which result in an increase in metabolic activity. In other words, muscles require energy, and stored energy in the body is utilized during and after workouts to restore the muscles used during exercise. The body continues to burn stored energy (calories) long after workouts—another major benefit of regular exercise.

ACSM's (2011) third guideline encourages exercisers to engage in flexibility or stretching that targets each muscle group 2 or 3 days a week. Flexibility refers to a joint's ability to move through a full range of motion and helps correct muscle imbalances and posture. Benefits of increased flexibility include decreased risk of injury and increased enjoyment of physical activities. Stretches should be held for approximately 20 seconds or more.

ACSM's (2011) final guideline is to engage in neuromotor training (functional fitness) for 30 minutes 2 or 3 days a week. Functional fitness includes tai chi, yoga, and balancing exercises. Functional training is especially important in older adults to prevent falls and increase confidence in exercise participation. In fact, older adults who participated in tai chi exercises significantly decreased their fear of falling (Sattin, Easley, Wolf, Chen, & Kutner, 2005).

Exercise guidelines are put in place to help people incorporate a healthy dose of physical activity into their lives. Food consumption also comes into play when examining exercise behaviors. Tips to help curb food cravings (Kerulis, 2013) can be beneficial for people who want to gain a sense of control over their eating. However, sometimes people overuse exercise (or food) to compensate for other areas of discomfort in their lives, which can result in exercise addiction. According to Freimuth, Moniz, and Kim (2011), approximately 3% of the population suffers from exercise addiction, and Grave, Calugi, and Marchesini (2008) reported that 45.4% of people who had eating disorders also had issues related to exercise compulsion. Clinicians can familiarize themselves with diagnostic criteria, treatment modalities, and assessments that aid in the identification of exercise dependence and addictions. This chapter covers (a) definitions and diagnostic criteria relevant to exercise addiction and dependence, (b) relationships between exercise addiction and eating disorders, (c) treatment models, and (d) assessments.

EXERCISE ADDICTION AND EXERCISE DEPENDENCE

Exercise Addiction

In today's world, people are told that exercise should be included as part of a healthy lifestyle. Television shows like *The Biggest Loser* depict overweight individuals exercising for hours at a time in order to lose weight and improve their lives. In this manner, exercise is associated with health and well-being; but what happens when exercise becomes excessive? What constitutes excessive exercise? Are the reality show contestants engaging in excessive exercise? What about elite athletes who must practice several hours every day? At what point does excessive exercise become exercise addiction or dependence?

Defining exercise addiction is difficult because the word *addiction* brings to mind stereotypes that are commonly associated with addiction to substances such as alcohol, cannabis, and other illicit drugs. Exercise is not typically thought to be negative, but in fact dependence on exercise can turn what once was a positive activity into a negative experience.

Erickson (2007) believed that *addiction* is too broad of a term and is often misunderstood and that *dependence* is a more accurate term from a scientific perspective. Dependence best reflects the maladaptive pattern of cognitive, behavioral, and physiological symptoms as defined in the *Diagnostic and Statistical Manual of Mental Disorders, Fifth Edition* (*DSM–5*; American Psychiatric Association [APA], 2013).

Exercise Dependence

Currently there is no standard definition of *exercise dependence*; however, Hausenblas and Downs (2002) recommended that exercise dependence be operationalized based on the *DSM* criteria for substance dependence. It was suggested that exercise dependence is a "multidimensional maladaptive pattern of exercise, leading to clinically significant impairment or distress" (p. 113). Three or more of the following seven criteria must be present in order to diagnose exercise dependence (Hausenblas & Downs, 2002):

- *Tolerance.* The person needs to increase the amount of exercise to achieve the desired effects.
- *Withdrawal.* The person experiences exercise withdrawal symptoms, such as anxiety or fatigue, or the same exercise is done to avoid withdrawal symptoms.
- *Intention effects.* The person exercises more often or for longer than intended.
- *Loss of control.* There is ongoing desire or unsuccessful attempts to stop the behavior.

- *Time.* An inordinate amount of time is spent in the activity.
- *Conflict.* Social, occupational, and recreational activities occur less frequently or are stopped altogether because of exercise.
- *Continuance.* Exercise is continued despite physical and psychological injury due to exercise.

According to de Coverley Veale (1987), exercise dependence can be classified as either primary or secondary. Primary exercise dependence describes a pattern of behavior that exists on its own, without any co-occurring disorder such as an eating disorder (de Coverley Veale, 1987). de Coverley Veale emphasized that an individual with primary exercise dependence is likely to exercise strictly for the benefits of exercise, such as improved performance, rather than for weight loss alone. In contrast, secondary exercise dependence manifests as a way to control and change the body's composition (Hausenblas & Downs, 2002).

The key difference between these two classifications is whether an eating disorder such as anorexia nervosa or bulimia nervosa can be excluded (de Coverley Veale, 1987). A characteristic shared by both anorexia nervosa and bulimia nervosa is a distorted perception of body shape and weight (APA, 2000). In order to control this distortion, the individual with the eating disorder may engage in excessive exercise in addition to bingeing and purging or other weight loss methods (APA, 2000). Diagnosing primary exercise dependence versus secondary exercise dependence comes down to determining the goal of the exercise (de Coverley Veale, 1987). Is improving performance a goal, or is the individual engaging in excessive exercise in addition to maladaptive eating habits as a way to control his or her perception of the body (de Coverley Veale, 1987)?

EXERCISE AND DISORDERED EATING

Anorexia Nervosa and Bulimia Nervosa

Anorexia nervosa is characterized by a refusal to maintain a minimally normal body weight, fear of gaining weight, a significant disturbance in one's perception of the shape and size of the body, and amenorrhea (APA, 2000). Individuals with anorexia nervosa may utilize excessive exercise as a method of weight loss in addition to extreme calorie and food restrictions. There are two subtypes of anorexia nervosa: restricting type and purging type. Someone with anorexia nervosa, restricting type, restricts the intake of food through dieting, fasting, or excessive exercise, whereas an individual with anorexia nervosa, purging type, "engages in binge eating or purging (or both)" (APA, 2000, p. 585).

Bulimia nervosa is characterized by recurrent episodes of binge eating; engagement in compensatory behavior to prevent weight gain, such as excessive exercise; and maladaptive patterns of self-evaluation (APA, 2000). As with anorexia nervosa, two subtypes of bulimia nervosa exist: purging type and nonpurging type. Bulimia nervosa, purging type, describes the behavior of "self-induced vomiting or the misuse of laxatives, diuretics, or enemas" to compensate for a binge-eating episode (APA, 2000, p. 591). Bulimia nervosa, nonpurging type, is characterized by the use of maladaptive compensatory behaviors such as fasting or excessive exercise rather than vomiting or misuse of laxatives, diuretics, or enemas (APA, 2000, p. 591).

Although individuals with either anorexia nervosa or bulimia nervosa may engage in excessive exercise to lose weight, researchers have found significant differences between the exercise habits of individuals with anorexia nervosa and bulimia nervosa and healthy individuals. The negative emotionality associated with excessive exercise is different in subtypes of these disorders (Mond & Calogero, 2009). Obligatory exercise is seen when an individual feels compelled to exercise despite injury or damage to social and professional relationships. This type of exercise is seen more often in individuals with anorexia nervosa, purging type, than bulimia nervosa, restricting type (Mond & Calogero, 2009). In addition, individuals with anorexia nervosa, purging type, and bulimia nervosa, purging type, are more likely to exercise for "weight control and physical attractiveness, and less for enjoyment" than those with anorexia nervosa, restricting type (Mond & Calogero, 2009, p. 232).

Individuals with eating disorders who engage in excessive exercise often feel extreme guilt when exercise is missed or when exercise is engaged in for reasons having to do with weight or body shape (Mond & Calogero, 2009). These individuals are also likely to engage in excessive exercise that interferes with daily social and familial functioning (Mond & Calogero, 2009). Those with eating disorders often report that there is little or no enjoyment in the pursuit of excessive exercise (Mond & Calogero, 2009).

It is important to distinguish between individuals who engage in excessive exercise in a compulsive and pathological manner and those who exercise frequently and do not exhibit pathology (Freimuth et al., 2011). Elite athletes who engage in frequent exercise may be viewed as having an exercise addiction, but this is an inaccurate characterization. Elite athletes likely fit several of the criteria for exercise dependence as defined by Hausenblas and Downs (2002): an increased amount of time is spent on the physical activity, other activities are reduced, and withdrawal is evident when exercise is cut back (Freimuth et al., 2011). However, despite meeting these three criteria, elite athletes are not necessarily dependent on exercise (Freimuth et al., 2011), as their physical participation in movement is a function of their careers.

Freimuth et al. (2011) proposed a four-phase model that may be used as a guideline to distinguish healthy exercise from maladaptive exercise. This model may provide a clearer diagnostic picture for clinicians working with athletes.

- Phase 1 describes exercise as recreational and healthy. The individual is motivated by healthy reasons, and the activity adds to the quality of life.
- Phase 2 describes at-risk exercise. The individual begins to feel motivated less by the intrinsic rewards of exercise and more by the means to reduce anxiety and other mood states.
- Phase 3 describes exercise that begins to be problematic. In this phase, the individual is organizing his or her day around exercise. Negative consequences are more prominent, such as relationship issues.
- Phase 4 is defined as exercise addiction. The individual's life revolves around exercise despite injuries and the inability to complete daily life functions.

Muscle Dysmorphia

Body dysmorphic disorder is a disorder in which an individual has a preoccupation with an imagined defect in appearance (APA, 2000). A subgroup of body dysmorphic disorder, muscle dysmorphia, is a condition in which the individual has a pathological concern with muscle size and overall leanness of the body (Rohman, 2009). An individual with muscle dysmorphia appears to have an obsession with attaining a perceived ideal body image (Baghurst & Kissinger, 2009). Engaging in excessive exercise is one way in which the individual may attempt to modify the body and to satisfy the perceived unhappiness with body image (Baghurst & Kissinger, 2009). This obsession may impair psychological, physical, and social functioning at a clinical level. It should be noted that although both men and women are susceptible to muscle dysmorphia, it is typically found in men (Pope, Gruber, Choi, Olivardia, & Phillips, 1997).

An individual with muscle dysmorphia shows many behavioral, emotional, cognitive, and perceptual disturbances (Rohman, 2009). Specifically, the individual may have feelings of guilt if diet or workouts are neglected, wear layers of clothing to create an appearance of being larger (despite the already muscular appearance), and have thoughts that his or her appearance is not good enough (Rohman, 2009).

Muscle dysmorphia has been classified under several different clinical areas. Some consider it to fall in the somatoform disorders with body dysmorphic disorder (Pope et al., 1997), whereas others place it on the obsessive-compulsive disorder continuum (Maida & Armstrong, 2005). Regardless of where muscle dysmorphia is placed clinically, it is an area of concern for treatment providers, as those with the disorder are at increasing risk for turning to addictive behaviors to achieve their goals. Exercise dependence, eating disorders, and the use of performance-enhancing drugs such as anabolic steroids are concerns for those with muscle dysmorphia (Rohman, 2009). Although muscle dysmorphia was not included in the *Diagnostic and Statistical Manual of Mental Disorders, Fourth Edition, Text Revision* (*DSM–IV–TR;* APA, 2000), Pope et al. (1997) proposed diagnostic criteria that can be used to assist a treatment provider when working with an individual with muscle dysmorphia. In addition, the *DSM–5* includes information on muscle dysmorphia as a form of body dysmorphia (APA, 2013).

A number of studies have focused on exercise dependence and applied treatment programs. Exercise dependence was initially utilized to depict cases of overcommitment to exercising among individuals who continued to run despite their injuries and other complications (Little, 1969). Many individuals still experience these dependent behaviors, and diagnosis and treatment is imperative in the rehabilitation process. Exercise dependence was also primarily defined as a positive addiction because it was thought to produce psychological and physiological benefits (Glasser, 1976). The positive perception of exercise dependence in the past may have contributed to the patterns of those behaviors today. Exercise dependence is presently characterized as an obsessive and unhealthy preoccupation with exercise or sport (Hamer & Karageorghis, 2007). With media influence and the current trend involving excessive physical activity, individuals have begun to magnify these behaviors.

Participating in physical activity regularly can reduce the risk of heart disease, diabetes, and cancer while increasing energy levels and improving the ability to cope with stressors (Gletsu & Tovin, 2010). Physical activity is in fact an important component of weight management and disease prevention. Even knowing the immense number of positive benefits of physical activity, individuals continually decide to abandon physical activities. But while some people abandon physical activity, many do the exact opposite by abusing it.

Bamber, Cockerill, Rodgers, and Carroll (2003) interviewed 56 female exercisers about their exercise behaviors and attitudes. Their diagnostic criteria for exercise dependence included four areas of impaired functioning: psychological, social and occupational, physical, and behavioral. Impairment in a minimum of two areas was considered imperative for a proper diagnosis. The absence or presence of an eating disorder was used to distinguish between primary and secondary exercise dependence (Bamber et al., 2003). Diagnosis of exercise dependence also includes neuroadaptation, including tolerance and withdrawal; adverse consequences, including conflict and reduction in other activities; and preoccupation with the chosen exercise (Allegre, Souville, Therme, & Griffiths, 2006). Compulsive exercise has been empirically linked to eating pathology in terms of both cognitions and behaviors (Taranis & Meyer, 2011). These compulsive exercise patterns are a common feature among individuals who have been diagnosed with eating disorders. Exercise dependence is present in 46%–55% of individuals treated for eating disorders (Grave et al., 2008). In a compelling study by Taranis and Meyer (2011), 498 women were examined and completed self-report measures, including the Eating Disorder Examination Questionnaire (Mond, Hay, Rodgers, Owen, & Beumont, 2004b) and the Compulsive Exercise Test (Taranis, Touyz, & Meyer, 2011). Specific results indicated that elements of compulsive exercise were associated with levels of eating-disordered cognitions and an increased frequency of eating-disordered behaviors (Taranis & Meyer, 2011).

A study carried out in the Australian Capital Territory examined relationships between exercise behavior, eating-disordered behavior, and quality of life. Self-report measures of frequency of exercise, eating disorder psychopathology, and quality of life were completed by 169 women ages 18 through 45 who engaged in exercise activities regularly. The questionnaires included an analysis of eating-disordered behavior, exercise commitment, exercise reasoning, exercise frequency, weight, height, quality of life, and demographic information. The study mainly reviewed how exercise becomes excessive. Results indicated that exercising to improve physical appearance or body tone and feeling guilty following exercise appear to be the variables most strongly associated with higher levels of eating disorder psychopathology and reduced quality of life (Mond, Hay, Rodgers, Owen, & Beumont, 2004a). Therefore, the findings suggested that exercise is excessive when it is associated with feelings of guilt or when it is undertaken primarily to change one's physical appearance (Mond et al., 2004a).

INPATIENT AND OUTPATIENT TREATMENT SETTINGS

The American Society of Addiction Medicine (2014) defines *treatment* as a planned, intentional intervention in the health and behavior of a dependent individual that is designed to assist that individual to achieve sobriety, physical and mental health, and a maximum functional ability. Although this definition is aimed at individuals with substance dependence, it is reasonable to apply it to those with exercise dependence. Many different types of treatment protocols exist, including inpatient and outpatient options. Outpatient treatment can be looked at as on-the-job training: The individual is learning new life skills while still immersed in his or her own life, and the new skills can be applied in the moment. Inpatient treatment can be likened to going away to college: The individual is embedded in the treatment program with controlled access to the world outside the treatment facility. Regardless of the type of treatment that is pursued, receiving treatment offers an individual the opportunity to achieve improved physical and mental health as well as improved functioning in life.

Both inpatient and outpatient treatment programs are beneficial for patients with eating disorders and exercise dependence. Treatment is based on the severity of the condition. Other determinants for choosing the proper program include time and finances. The amount of time and money a patient can spend for treatment will affect the type of intervention that is chosen as well. Inpatient treatment includes more intense supervision, whereas outpatient programs are directed more liberally (J. Mrozack & J. Pagone, personal communication, February 15, 2013).

The cost of treatment can vary by center. One midwestern program charges $845 per day for inpatient treatment and $335 per day for outpatient care. Cost also depends on the location of the treatment center, the services rendered, and the duration of treatment.

Several eating disorder units at treatment centers utilize inpatient and outpatient programs. These programs incorporate cognitive behavior therapy as well as self-regulation models. The goal of the treatment is for patients to identify and utilize coping skills to interrupt unhealthy eating and exercise patterns. Both group sessions and individual sessions assist patients in developing coping mechanisms. On admission, patients are given a self-assessment. As the treatment is implemented, meals are monitored calorically. Each patient works with a case manager, a therapist, and a dietician. During the process of therapy, families of the patients are included in the decision-making process, especially if the patients are adolescents. The average duration of the therapeutic process is 14–21 days (D. Smith, personal communication, February 15, 2013). Records of several facilities have shown a minimum of 5 days and a maximum of 7 months of treatment per diagnosis (D. Smith, personal communication, February 15, 2013).

Other eating disorder units consist of two different programs that utilize a structural process model and emotion regulation. One program uses a cognitive dialectical model in conjunction with the structural process model and emotion regulation. The second program utilizes a structured day-to-day therapeutic approach involving body image awareness, expressive therapy, and equine-assisted psychotherapy. One unique experience is the practice of using horses to help patients achieve emotional growth. Patients are able to use feelings, behaviors, and patterns to understand the horses and, in return, themselves. They interact with the horses to attach meaning to their lives and gain a better understanding of rules and family dynamics. The patients do not ride the horses but observe their motions and interactions among one another (J. Mrozack & J. Pagone, personal communication, February 15, 2013). This interesting approach has also been used with individuals experiencing eating disorders and exercise dependence. By observing the horses and their purpose, patients can develop empathy for their own situation.

EVIDENCE-BASED MODELS AND ASSESSMENTS

Models for treating exercise addiction are quite subjective. The appropriate approach will depend on various aspects of the diagnosis and the person's unique situation. Dialectical behavior therapy and cognitive behavior therapy are the models most often utilized. In addition to a thorough intake and assessment of dependent and addictive behaviors, clinicians can use a number of instruments to assess additional exercise-related attitudes and behaviors.

Dialectical behavior therapy was designed by Marsha Linehan at the University of Washington as a psychotherapeutic treatment that teaches adaptive skills to enhance emotion regulation capabilities (Linehan et al., 1999). Several treatment programs have successfully used dialectical behavior therapy as a treatment approach (Lenz, Taylor, Fleming, & Serman, 2014). Another effective treatment modality is cognitive behavior therapy, "which helps people problem solve, become behaviorally activated, and identify, evaluate, and respond to their negative thoughts" (Beck, 2011, p. 6). Cognitive behavior therapy is also effective at the symptomatic level in improving self-esteem (Gowers, 2006). Treatment plans can be directed toward individuals with eating disorders that are comorbid with exercise dependence. Patients who experience these symptoms benefit from inpatient and outpatient programs depending on the severity of issues (D. Smith, personal communication, February 15, 2013). Another way to examine treatment is to consider the behavioral addictions criteria in the *DSM–5* (APA, 2013). With this in mind it is necessary to distinguish exercise addiction from compulsions and impulses. Hausenblas and Downs (2002) identified exercise addiction based on modifications of the *DSM–IV–TR* (APA, 2000) criteria for substance dependence. Tolerance, withdrawal, lack of control, intention effects, time, reduction in other activities, and continuance are all defined as criteria for a behavioral addiction. This diagnosis is more accessible with the use of the *DSM–5* (APA, 2013).

An assessment of exercise dependence is vital in the implementation of proper treatment plans. Several diagnostic instruments have been used to assess exercise addiction and dependence, or at least measure commitment to or involvement with exercise in general. One such measure, the Commitment to Running Scale (Glasser, 1976), indicates that compulsive exercise is a positive addiction; however, it is difficult to determine whether an individual is addicted to running. The Exercise Beliefs Questionnaire (Loumidis & Wells, 1998) focuses on four factors in an attempt to provide a measure of one's assumptions about exercise. These factors are (a) social desirability, (b) physical appearance, (c) mental and emotional functioning, and (d) vulnerability to disease and aging. This measure produces information about one's thought processes related to exercise that may provide insight into whether exercise is an addiction.

The Exercise Dependence Questionnaire (Ogden, Veale, & Summers, 1997) is considered by its developers to be a valid and reliable instrument. It is a measure of compulsivity related to exercise, typically sporting events, and includes eight scales: interference with social/family/work life, positive reward, withdrawal symptoms, exercise for weight control, insight into problem, exercise for social reasons, exercise for health reasons, and stereotyped behavior.

Bodybuilders as a group are more likely than non-bodybuilders to be dependent on exercise and to experience exercise as an addiction. The Bodybuilding Dependency Scale (Smith, Hale, & Collins, 1998) focuses on the exercise dependence of bodybuilders by assessing compulsive behaviors and thinking in the areas of social dependence in a weightlifting environment, training dependence or the compulsion to lift weights, and mastery dependence or the need to control one's training schedule.

The Exercise Dependence Interview (Bamber, Cockerill, & Carroll, 2000) is unique in that it provides a measure of compulsive exercising and compulsive eating. The Exercise Dependence Interview has not been evaluated in terms of validity and reliability. The Commitment to Exercise Scale (Davis, Brewer, & Ratusny, 1993) provides a measure of pathology related to the continuation of physical activities despite injuries and compulsive thinking about the need to exercise. The Exercise Dependence Scale (Hausenblas & Downs, 2002) applies the criteria for substance dependence from the *DSM–IV–TR* (APA, 2000) to compulsive exercise. The scale attempts to examine physiological and nonphysiological aspects of addiction and uses the categories of at risk, dependent, and nondependent.

The Exercise Addiction Inventory (Terry, Szabo, & Griffiths, 2004) is described as a brief screening tool for identifying individuals at risk for exercise addiction. It assesses the components of behavioral addictions proposed by Griffiths (1996), which include salience, mood modification, tolerance, withdrawal symptoms, social conflict, and relapse. The Exercise Addiction Inventory is touted as having very good internal reliability, content validity, concurrent validity, and construct validity (Terry et al., 2004).

The Exercise Orientation Questionnaire (Yates, Edman, Crago, Crowell, & Zimmerman, 1999) measures attitudes toward exercise by focusing on self-control, orientation to exercise, self-loathing, weight reduction, competition, and identity.

The Exercise Dependence Scale–21 (Symons Downs, Hausenblas, & Nigg, 2004) operationalizes exercise dependence according to the *DSM–IV–TR* (APA, 2000) criteria for substance dependence. The Exercise Dependence Scale–21 differentiates among people who are at risk for exercise dependence, nondependent–symptomatic, and nondependent–asymptomatic and specifies whether individuals show evidence of physiological dependence or not in terms of tolerance, withdrawal, intention effect, lack of control, time, reduction in other activities, and continuance.

Not all of the instruments described here have been validated, so clinicians must collect additional data when examining clients for exercise addiction or dependence. It is recommended that the instruments described in this chapter be used alongside observations, self-reports, and other assessments in order to gain a comprehensive understanding of exercise as an addiction. A number of measures are available that examine exercise addiction, compulsion, or dependence. For an extensive list of sport and exercise assessments, see Ostrow's (2002) *Directory of Psychological Tests in the Sport and Exercise Sciences.*

CONCLUSIONS

Exercise, when carried to the extreme, is an addiction. Concepts associated with exercise addiction are the same as those associated with substance addictions or other process addictions, such as addictions to gambling, food, or sex. Choice is present in all addictions, coinciding with anticipatory thoughts. For a person with an exercise addiction, the result of participating in an exercise activity can be experienced as a high. Craving is present with an exercise addiction. In order to feel good, the exerciser needs to do something physical, such as run, lift weights, swim, or ride a bicycle. Building up a tolerance, in relation to an exercise addiction, could mean that one has to run longer, faster, or at a higher altitude in order to achieve the same eventual reward, pleasure, or heightened feeling. A dependent exerciser might find it necessary to continually change or adapt his or her routine in order to receive the same pleasurable effect. Control, often present with an exercise addiction, involves a feeling of having to exercise, as if choosing to do so is out of one's control. Finally, consequences of an exercise addiction are observable, physically, psychologically, and interpersonally. A long-term addiction to exercise will break down one's body structurally, such as in the back, knees, hips, and neck, as well as organ systems. Finally, the time committed to an exercise addiction interferes with family, work, and most aspects of life. Outside of exercise, this addiction leaves minimal time for anything or anyone else in the person's life. It is important to differentiate between a person who is training extra-long hours for a specific event, such as a professional athlete or fitness competitor, and a person who has developed a dependence on or addiction to exercise. An extensive intake can guide clinicians in making this determination.

Research has provided valuable information on chemical and structural changes that take place in the brain with both substance and process addictions. A person addicted to exercise experiences a sense of euphoria as demonstrated by brain scans and related technology. Exercise can result in the release in the brain of rewarding chemicals, including dopamine, serotonin, and endorphins. People who suffer from exercise addiction or dependence may long for the relief of this chemical release and therefore engage in overexercising behaviors. Further research is needed to assist behavioral specialists in understanding and treating this process addiction.

RESOURCES

Websites

10 Tips on Combatting Food Cravings From the Adler School's Dr. Michele Kerulis
   http://theadlerschool.wordpress.com/2013/04/21/10-tips-on-combatting-food-cravings-from-the-adler-schools-dr-michele-kerulis/
Exercise Is Medicine
   http://www.exerciseismedicine.org/
Exercise Is Medicine Fact Sheet
   http://www.jcdh.org/misc/ViewBLOB.aspx?BLOBId=389
Let's Move!
   http://www.letsmove.gov/

Videos

Let's Move!, Videos and Photos
   http://www.letsmove.gov/videos-and-photos

REFERENCES

Allegre, B., Souville, M., Therme, P., & Griffiths, M. (2006). Definitions and measures of exercise dependence. *Addiction Research and Theory, 14,* 631–646.
American College of Sports Medicine. (2011). Quantity and quality of exercise for developing and maintaining cardiorespiratory, musculoskeletal, and neuromotor fitness in apparently healthy adults: Guidance for prescribing exercise. *Medicine and Science in Sports & Exercise, 43,* 1334–1359. doi:10.1249/MSS.0b013e318213fefb. Retrieved from http://journals.lww.com/acsm-msse/Fulltext/2011/07000/Quantity_and_Quality_of_Exercise_for_Developing.26.aspx

American Psychiatric Association. (2000). *Diagnostic and statistical manual of mental disorders* (4th ed., text rev.). Washington, DC: Author.

American Psychiatric Association. (2013). *Diagnostic and statistical manual of mental disorders* (5th ed.). Arlington, VA: Author.

American Society of Addiction Medicine. (2014). *Research and treatment.* Retrieved from http://www.asam.org/research-treatment/treatment

Baghurst, T., & Kissinger, D. B. (2009). Perspectives on muscle dysmorphia. *International Journal of Men's Health, 8*(1), 82–89.

Bamber, D., Cockerill, I. M., & Carroll, D. B. J. (2000). The pathological status of exercise dependence. *British Journal of Sports Medicine, 34*(2), 125–132.

Bamber, D. J., Cockerill, I. M., Rodgers, S., & Carroll, D. (2003). Diagnostic criteria for exercise dependence in women. *British Journal of Sports Medicine, 37,* 393–400.

Beck, J. S. (2011). *Cognitive behavioral therapy: Basics and beyond* (2nd ed.). New York, NY: Guilford Press.

Davis, C., Brewer, H., & Ratusny, D. J. (1993). Behavioral frequency and psychological commitment: Necessary concepts in the study of excessive exercising. *Journal of Behavioral Medicine, 16,* 611–628.

de Coverley Veale, D. M. (1987). Exercise dependence. *British Journal of Addiction, 82,* 735–740.

Erickson, C. K. (2007). *The science of addiction.* New York, NY: Norton.

Exercise Is Medicine. (n.d.). Retrieved from http://exerciseismedicine.org/

Fletcher, G. F., Blair, S. N., Blumenthal, J., Caspersen, C., Chaitman, C., Epstein, S., . . . Pina, L. (1992). Statement on exercise: Benefits and recommendations for physical activity programs for all Americans. *Circulation, 86,* 340–344.

Freimuth, M., Moniz, S., & Kim, S. R. (2011). Clarifying exercise addiction: Differential diagnosis, co-occurring disorders, and phases of addiction. *International Journal of Environmental Research and Public Health, 8,* 4069–4081. doi:10.3390/ijerph8104069

Glasser, W. (1976). *Positive addiction.* New York, NY: Harper & Row.

Gletsu, M., & Tovin, M. (2010). African American women and physical activity. *Physical Therapy Review, 15,* 405–409.

Gowers, S. G. (2006). Evidence based research in CBT with adolescent eating disorders. *Child & Adolescent Mental Health, 11*(1), 9–12.

Grave, R. D., Calugi, S., & Marchesini, G. (2008). Compulsive exercise to control shape or weight in eating disorders: Prevalence, associated features, and treatment outcome. *Comprehensive Psychiatry, 49,* 346–352.

Griffiths, M. D. (1996). Behavioural addiction: An issue for everybody? *Journal of Workplace Learning, 8*(3), 19–25.

Hamer, M., & Karageorghis, C. I. (2007). Psychobiological mechanisms of exercise dependence. *Sports Medicine, 37,* 477–484.

Hausenblas, H. A., & Downs, D. S. (2002). Exercise dependence: A systematic review. *Psychology of Sport and Exercise, 3,* 89–213.

Kerulis, M. (2013, April 21). *10 tips on combatting food cravings from the Adler School's Dr. Michele Kerulis.* Retrieved from http://theadlerschool.wordpress.com/2013/04/21/10-tips-on-combatting-food-cravings-from-the-adler-schools-dr-michele-kerulis/

Lenz, A. S., Taylor, R., Fleming, M., & Serman, N. (2014). Effectiveness of dialectical behavior therapy for treating eating disorders. *Journal of Counseling & Development, 92,* 26–35. doi:10.1002/j.1556-6676.2014.00127.x

Linehan, M. M., Schmidt, H., Dimeff, L. A., Kanter, J. W., Craft, J. C., Comtois, K. A., & Recknor, K. L. (1999). Dialectical behavior therapy for patients with borderline personality disorder and drug-dependence. *American Journal on Addictions, 8,* 279–292.

Little, J. C. (1969). The athlete's neurosis: A deprivation crisis. *Acta Psychiatrica Scandinavica, 45,* 187–197.

Loumidis, K. S., & Wells, A. (1998). Assessment of beliefs in exercise dependence: The development and preliminary validation of the Exercise Beliefs Questionnaire. *Personality & Individual Differences, 25*, 553–567.

Maida, D. M., & Armstrong, S. L. (2005). The classification of muscle dysmorphia. *International Journal of Men's Health, 4*, 73–91.

Mond, J. M., & Calogero, R. M. (2009). Excessive exercise in eating disorder patients and in healthy women. *Australian and New Zealand Journal of Psychiatry, 43*, 227–234.

Mond, J. M., Hay, P. J., Rodgers, B., Owen, C., & Beumont, P. J. V. (2004a). Relationships between exercise behavior, eating-disordered behavior and quality of life in a community sample of women: When is exercise 'excessive'? *European Eating Disorders Review, 12*, 265–272.

Mond, J. M., Hay, P. J., Rodgers, B., Owen, C., & Beumont, P. J. V. (2004b). Validity of the Eating Disorder Questionnaire (EDE-Q) in screening for eating disorders in community samples. *Behaviour Research and Therapy, 42*, 551–567.

National Institutes of Health, Consensus Development Panel on Physical Activity and Cardiovascular Health. (1996). Physical activity and cardiovascular health. *Journal of the American Medical Association, 276*, 241–246.

Ogden, J., Veale, D., & Summers, Z. (1997). Development and validation of the Exercise Dependence Questionnaire. *Addiction Research, 5*, 343–356.

Ostrow, A. C. (2002). *Directory of psychological tests in the sport and exercise sciences.* Morgantown, WV: Fitness Information Technology.

Pope, H. G., Gruber, A. J., Choi, P., Olivardia, R., & Phillips, K. A. (1997). Muscle dysmorphia: An underrecognized form of body dysmorphic disorder. *Psychosomatics, 38*, 548–557.

Rohman, L. (2009). The relationship between anabolic androgenic steroids and muscle dysmorphia: A review. *Eating Disorders, 17*, 187–199.

Sattin, R. W., Easley, K. A., Wolf, S. L., Chen, Y., & Kutner, M. H. (2005). Reduction in fear of falling through intense tai chi exercise training in older, transitionally frail adults. *Journal of the American Geriatrics Society, 53*, 1168–1178.

Smith, D. K., Hale, B. D., & Collins, D. J. (1998). Measurement of exercise dependence in bodybuilders. *Journal of Sports Medicine and Physical Fitness, 38*(1), 66–74.

Symons Downs, D., Hausenblas, H. A., & Nigg, C. A. (2004). Factorial validity and psychometric examination of the Exercise Dependence Scale–Revised. *Measurement in Physical Education and Exercise Science, 8*, 183–201.

Taranis, L., & Meyer, C. (2011). Associations between specific components of compulsive exercise and eating-disordered cognitions and behaviors among young women. *International Journal of Eating Disorders, 44*, 452–458.

Taranis, L., Touyz, S., & Meyer, C. (2011). Disordered eating and exercise: Development and primary validation of the Compulsive Exercise Test (CET). *European Eating Disorders Review, 19*(3), 256–268. doi:10.1002/erv.1108

Terry, A., Szabo, A., & Griffiths, M. (2004). The Exercise Addiction Inventory: A new brief screening tool. *Addiction Research and Theory, 12*, 489–499. doi:10.1080/16066350310001637363

U.S. Department of Health and Human Services. (1996). *Physical activity and health: A report of the Surgeon General.* Atlanta, GA: National Center for Chronic Disease Prevention and Health Promotion.

Wilmore, J. H., Costill, D. L., & Kenney, W. L. (2008). *Physiology of sport and exercise* (4th ed.). Champaign, IL: Human Kinetics.

Yates, A., Edman, J., Crago, M., Crowell, D., & Zimmerman, R. (1999). Measurement of exercise orientation in normal subjects: Gender and age differences. *Personality & Individual Differences, 27*, 199–220.

CHAPTER 12

COMPULSIVE BUYING/ SHOPPING ADDICTION

Kimberly Frazier

STUDENT LEARNING OUTCOMES

At the conclusion of this chapter students will

1. Identify key terms and definitions related to compulsive buying disorder/ shopping addictions
2. Comprehend the costs and demographics associated with compulsive buying disorder/shopping addictions
3. Comprehend major screening, assessment, diagnosis, and treatment procedures related to buying/shopping addictions
4. Understand the literature and identify resources available for professionals working with compulsive buying disorder/shopping addictions

CASE AND CASE DISCUSSION

Teigan is a 24-year-old woman who has come to counseling to discuss a drastic change in her life: moving back home with her mother and younger sister. When asked "What brings you to counseling?" Teigan states that she had to drop out of college because she was unable to pay her tuition and soon afterward had to move in with her mother because she was not able to consistently pay her rent and other bills. Teigan discloses that she has been at home for less than 6 months and is constantly fighting with her mother regarding how she spends her money. Teigan is furious that her mother does not treat her like an adult and feels angry that she is forced to be back home, which limits her independence. Teigan emphatically states that she feels singled out by her family and friends as having a problem with money because she owes her mother, little sister, aunt, best friend, and boyfriend money. Teigan states that she only borrows money to pay her bills because the money she earns from her part-time job is mostly spent on clothes and shoes. She explains that because her purchases are always made at thrift stores and store sales, it is really not a lot of money.

Teigan tells the counselor that shopping is the only thing that has made her feel better since being forced to move in with her mother. When asked how often she goes shopping, Teigan says she shops only twice a week (Monday and Thursday) because that is when the stores get new merchandise. She says she feels euphoric just thinking about the things she plans to buy this week and the stores she plans to go to see the new merchandise. Teigan says that it is her money, so why should her mother and friends care how she spends it? She does state that she feels bad about owing her friends and family money, but there is always new merchandise she has to see. Teigan says that she becomes critical of herself when she buys something new and she still has not paid her mother or friends back. Her solution is to get a job that pays more so she can pay people back but continue shopping, as she cannot imagine not going to her favorite stores every week.

As you read Teigan's case, think about the main issues present for this client. Think too about how these issues should be addressed in the counseling relationship and how you might build a relationship with Teigan in order to effectively deal with these issues. Also think about how the presenting issues have affected her relationship with her mother, sister, other family members, boyfriend, and friends. Finally, what treatments and interventions would best treat the issues that Teigan has presented? Your treatments should include any possible assessments that work well with shopping addiction/compulsive buying, such as the Compulsive Buying Scale.

OVERVIEW OF COMPULSIVE BUYING/SHOPPING ADDICTION

German psychiatrist Emil Kraepelin was the first to describe a disorder referred to as *oniomania* and categorize his patients affected by this disorder as "buying maniacs." Shopping addiction has been referred to in the literature as *compulsive shopping, compulsive buying, addictive buying, compulsive consumption, excessive buying, uncontrolled buying,* and *spendaholisim* (Dell'Osso, Allen, Altamura, Buoli, & Hollander, 2008). *Compulsive buying disorder* is defined as an impulse-control disorder that is characterized by impulsive drives and compulsive behaviors to buy unneeded things that cause personal distress, impair social and job functioning, and cause financial issues (Dell'Osso et al., 2008; Hartston & Koran, 2002).

This disorder is not recognized in the *Diagnostic and Statistical Manual of Mental Disorders, Fourth Edition, Text Revision* (*DSM–IV–TR*; American Psychiatric Association [APA], 2000) or the *Diagnostic and Statistical Manual of Mental Disorders, Fifth Edition* (*DSM–5*; APA, 2013); hence, those meeting the criteria for compulsive buying disorder are frequently diagnosed with an impulse-control disorder not elsewhere classified. There has been much debate about the inclusion of compulsive buying disorder in the *DSM*; those arguing against the inclusion state that the disorder is not a medical problem but rather a moral problem. They also argue that to include this and similar addictions (e.g., addictions to gambling, the Internet, and sex) only serves to create additional avenues for the prescription of pharmaceutical drugs (Hollander, 2006; Lee & Mysyk, 2004). In addition, the inclusion of shopping addiction in the *DSM* would call for a change in the definition of the behaviors that lead to the addiction. It is further believed that there is not currently a clear number or specific variety of behaviors that can be classified as addictive and leading to compulsive shopping (Hartston, 2012).

Supporters of the inclusion of shopping addiction in the *DSM* argue for a need for a broader definition of behaviors that can become addictive. Research focused on the brain and addictions has found similarities in neurobiological responses for impulse-control disorders and substance addictions (Holden, 2001; Karim & Chaudhri, 2012; Martin & Petry, 2005). Some suggest that the disorder should be categorized into a new autonomous subgroup of disorders. Another argument favors categorizing compulsive buying into the group of behavioral and substance addictions that focus on impulse, reward sensitivity, and frontostriatal circuit impairment. Regardless of whether it is included in the *DSM*, the literature supports the view that compulsive buying disorder is serious for those who have been impaired by the disorder (Dell'Osso et al., 2008; Hartston, 2012; Karim & Chaudhri, 2012).

Definitions

Compulsive buying: Part of the broader category of compulsive consumption behaviors, defined as chronic, repetitive activity that becomes the primary response to negative events or feelings (Faber & O'Guinn, 1992; Workman & Paper, 2010).

Compulsive buying behavior: A chronic tendency to spend beyond one's needs and means (Palan, Morrow, Trapp, & Blackburn, 2011).

Hyperstimulation: Addictive behaviors that create changes in the brain and cause a drug-like high, such as sex, gaming, and shopping (Dell'Osso, Altamura, Allen, Marazziti, & Hollander, 2006).

Impulse buying: The making of unplanned and/or spontaneous purchases (Rook & Fisher, 1995).

Impulse-control disorders: Psychological disorders that are characterized by an inability to refrain from performing a specific action that is harmful to either oneself or others (APA, 2000).

Obsessive-compulsive disorder: A disorder in which obsessions or compulsions serve as significant sources of distress and interfere with an individual's ability to function. The obsessions are persistent and feature reoccurring ideas and impulses that cannot be ignored or repressed (APA, 2013; Workman & Paper, 2010).

Cost and Demographics

All around the world, shopping is seen as a leisure activity used to ease the stress of a bad day or garner confidence through the purchase of, say, a new outfit for a job interview. Compounding the view of shopping as a leisure activity is the increased accessibility of shopping around the clock online. The role of culture in compulsive buying should not be overlooked. The availability of limitless buying opportunities as well as globalization has increased the number of compulsive buyers around the world. The current culture is one that equates goods and materialism with achieving happiness and success (e.g., buying the right perfume or clothing will make one irresistible and successful; Benson & Eisenach, 2013).

For those who are addicted, shopping is more than just a leisure activity; it is a part of their lifestyle and everyday routine. People addicted to shopping engage in the act of shopping repeatedly, and this act influences their self-esteem and personal mood. Compulsive buying or shopping addiction is estimated to impact about 6% of the general U.S. population, approximately 17 million people (Benson & Eisenach, 2013; Hartston, 2012; Williams, 2012). The activity of shopping becomes a source of praise, accomplishment, and excitement. Discovering a sale or searching for clothes becomes an avenue for validation and identity for the addicted shopper. Shopping aids the addict in building self-confidence and satisfaction (Hartston, 2012). Early studies of shopping addiction identified females suffering from the addiction at higher rates than males, with the age of onset being in the early 20s. However, research has since shown that both men and women suffer in equal numbers, with few gender differences (Black, 2001; McElroy, Keck, Pope, Smith, & Strakowski, 1994). The only gender difference manifests in what is purchased: Women often purchase makeup, jewelry, clothing, and shoes, whereas men purchase automotive and electronic items (Black, 2001, 2007). Faber and O'Guinn (1992) studied compulsive buying in the United States and found that younger people with incomes less than $50,000 often made up the largest portion of the population of compulsive buyers.

Shopping addiction or compulsive buying creates consequences associated with the shopping behavior, such as distress, marital and social conflict, and financial debt, and has a negative impact on the quality of work and life functioning. One buying episode can cost between $92 and $110 dollars, and the most commonly purchased items include jewelry, cosmetics, clothing, shoes, and household items (Williams, 2012). Once shopping has become addictive and compulsive, hyperstimulation can occur as the buyer ascribes an exaggerated sense of importance to the items purchased. Feelings that shopping addicts commonly exhibit during purchasing episodes range from euphoria to relief, leading many researchers to believe that compulsive buying is a reaction to stress (Miltenberger et al., 2003; Müller, Arikian, de Zwaan, & Mitchell, 2013; O'Guinn & Faber, 1989).

Shopping addicts can become dependent on the elevation of mood that buying can bring, thus leading to addiction. The addiction can be further reinforced when addicts begin linking elevation of mood with higher self-esteem and life satisfaction (Clark & Calleja, 2008; Dittmar, 2005; Hartston, 2012). In contrast, the negative feelings associated with compulsive buying include depression, anxiety, and self-criticism. The cyclic nature of the positive feelings (elevated mood, euphoria, etc.) and the negative feelings (depression, self-criticism, etc) aids in reinforcing the behaviors and allows the addiction to continue (Miltenberger et al., 2003; Palan et al., 2011). Studies investigating the consequences resulting from compulsive shopping concluded that 53% of compulsive shoppers had large financial debts, 41% of compulsive shoppers were unable to pay their debts, 8% suffered legal issues due to their addiction, 8% had criminal issues associated with their addiction, and 45% developed feelings of guilt associated with the addiction and the consequences of the addiction (Christenson et al., 1994; Dell'Osso et al., 2008; Williams, 2012).

ASSESSMENT AND DIAGNOSIS

Some research investigations have focused on dividing compulsive shopping into subtypes in order to better understand triggers and types of consumption. Four types of consumers have been proposed: (a) the emotionally reactive consumer, who places importance on what the item purchased symbolizes and links the motivation to buy with compensatory emotion; (b) the impulsive consumer, who is overcome with a sudden desire to buy and often has psychological ambivalence about and is in a state of constant struggle over reining in the addiction; (c) the fanatical consumer, who is motivated by an intense devotion to one specific product; and (d) the uncontrolled consumer, who seeks to reduce psychological distress and anxiety through the act of buying (Mueller, Claes, et al., 2010; Valence, d'Astous, & Fortier, 1988). Woodruffe (1996) proposed viewing the act of buying on a continuum. In this continuum model, consumers are divided into apathetic shoppers and compulsive buyers. This belief stems from the distinction between compulsive buying and regular leisure buying (Mueller, Mitchell, et al., 2010).

Assessment

Shopping addiction is assessed using questionnaires that measure behavioral aspects associated with compulsive buying. To assess whether someone can be diagnosed with shopping addiction, one must assess the strength of the person's compulsive buying tendencies. One of the first assessments focused on helping clinicians diagnose compulsive buying was the Compulsive Buying Measurement Scale created by Valence et al. (1988). This assessment focused on the four dimensions of excessive buying: tendency to spend, feeling an urge to buy or shop, postpurchase guilt, and family environment. Benefits of the scale are that it focuses not only on the loss of financial control but also on the psychological aspects of compulsive buying. The Compulsive Buying Measurement Scale showed reliability and validity; however, high scores on the scale corresponded to heightened anxiety levels. High scores on the scale also show frequent comorbidity with disorders such as alcoholism and depression within the family (Albrecht, Kirschner, & Grüsser, 2007). The *Hohenheimer Kaufsuchttest* (Hohenheim Shopping Addiction Test) is a German modified version of the Compulsive Buying Measurement Scale that also seeks to differentiate between normal and compulsive buying. The German scale has high reliability and construct validity (Albrecht et al., 2007).

In 2005 the *Erhenbung von kompensatorischem und suchtigem Kaufverhalten* (Survey on Compensatory and Addictive Shopping Behavior) was introduced. This self-report assessment focuses on risk for compulsive shopping and the tendency to compulsively shop. The creators based this assessment on the theory that compulsive buying is an extreme form of compensatory buying. The instrument has 16 items and has been found to have high reliability and construct validity. The 16 items are based on a continuum and range from inconspicuous buying behaviors to compulsive buying behaviors (Albrecht et al., 2007).

Another scale, the Compulsive Buying Scale created by Faber and O'Guinn (1989, 1992), is used to assess compulsive buying tendencies. The self-report Compulsive Buying Scale consists of seven items on an interval scale (*strongly agree* to *strongly disagree, very often* to *never*). An example question is "If I have any money left at the end of the pay period I just have to spend it." This scale was created based on previous research and reports on compulsive buyers and addicted shoppers. The Compulsive Buying Scale focuses on loss of financial control and is used to obtain knowledge about specific feelings, motivations, and behaviors associated with compulsive buying. Researchers have found the scale to be an adequately valid and reliable measure. Lower self-reported scores on this scale indicate greater levels of compulsive buying (Albrecht et al., 2007; Palan et al., 2011).

The Minnesota Impulsive Disorder Interview was created to assess several impulse-control disorders, such as compulsive explosive disorder, pathological gambling, and compulsive buying. The compulsive buying screen of this test includes four questions with five subsections. The buying screen is considered positive for compulsive buying if all questions related to compulsive buying are answered affirmatively. If a person tests positive for compulsive buying, it is recommended that another 82 items be administered to gain a more accurate diagnosis. To date there are no published data regarding the validity and reliability of the Minnesota Impulsive Disorder Interview (Albrecht et al., 2007).

Another assessment for compulsive buying is the Yale-Brown Obsessive Compulsive Scale–Shopping, a modified version of the Yale-Brown Obsessive Compulsive Scale. This instrument is designed to measure severity and change. The Yale-Brown Obsessive Compulsive Scale–Shopping consists of 10 items and rates time spent on buying, distress experienced, and degree of control over cognitions and behaviors. The instrument has high internal consistency and good interrater reliability (Albrecht et al., 2007).

Diagnosis

Comorbidity

Compulsive buying is not classified as a disorder in the *DSM–5* (APA, 2013) or the *International Statistical Classification of Diseases* (World Health Organization, 2007) because of the lack of conclusive research concerning this behavior (APA, 2013; Mueller, Mitchell, et al., 2010). The *DSM–5* includes unspecified obsessive-compulsive and related disorder, which is used for clients who do not meet the full criteria outlined for a diagnosis of obsessive-compulsive and related disorder but have traits of the full disorder. In addition, a task force for the *DSM–5* conceded that some conditions require further study in terms of clear empirical evidence focused on diagnosis, diagnostic reliability and validity, clinical need, and potential of research advancement before they can be included in the *DSM* (APA, 2013).

As written in the *DSM–IV–TR* (APA, 2000), some mental health professionals classify compulsive buying as an impulse-control disorder not elsewhere classified, which includes also nonparaphilic sexual compulsion and skin picking. Other mental health professionals using the *DSM–IV–TR* believed that compulsive buying should be looked at as a metacategory of obsessive-compulsive spectrum disorder, which would include impulse-control disorders, somatoform disorders, eating disorders, and a few neurological disorders. Some research suggests a neurobiological link between behavioral addictions and substance disorders; hence, a category that includes behavioral addictions and substance disorders along with compulsive buying would mirror this research (Mueller, Mitchell, et al., 2010).

Previous research has suggested that shopping addiction could be related to elevated rates of Axis I disorders. Shopping addicts often meet the *DSM–IV–TR* criteria for Axis I or Axis II disorders and can sometimes meet the criteria of both Axis I and Axis II disorders (Mueller, Mitchell, et al., 2010; Williams, 2012). Mueller, Mitchell, et al. (2010) found that subjects with compulsive buying disorder had a significantly higher prevalence of affective, anxiety, obsessive-compulsive, and eating disorders compared to a control group. Researchers believe that there is a link between mood disorders and compulsive shopping. Shopping addicts tend to score low on scales of self-esteem compared to nonaddicted shoppers, leading researchers to believe the feelings of low self-esteem found in compulsive shoppers could also be linked with major depressive disorder (Faber & O'Guinn, 1992). Research has also shown a strong link between obsessive-compulsive disorder and shopping compulsion: Shopping addicts have intrusive thoughts about buying that cause anxiety, which incites the cycle of having to buy something in order to alleviate the anxiety. The relationship between shopping addiction and other Axis I and Axis II disorders needs continued investigation to better aid clinicians in the diagnosis and treatment of those affected (Mueller, Mitchell, et al., 2010; Ridgway, Kukar-Kinney, & Monroe, 2008).

Taking into account previous studies on comorbidity and compulsive shopping, Mueller, Mitchell, et al. (2010) sought to look at psychiatric comorbidity in a sample of compulsive buyers to identify specific clusters based on the severity of compulsive buying and to examine whether more severe compulsive buying is associated with greater psychiatric comorbidity. The researchers found support for earlier findings, in that nearly 90% of the participants with compulsive buying reported a history of Axis I disorders, 51% met the criteria for a current Axis I disorder, and 21% presented with a history of impulse-control disorders other than compulsive buying (Mueller, Mitchell, et al., 2010).

Differential Diagnosis
A diagnosis of shopping addiction compared to another disorder depends on the client's buying behaviors and feelings of arousal and elevated mood when in the act of buying. In addition, compulsive buying is often associated with the addict decreasing anxiety or increasing self-esteem, whereas other disorders are characterized by a compulsion to buy in the manic phase or hypomanic episodes of the disorders (Williams, 2012). Clinicians can also differentiate compulsive shopping from other affective disorders by investigating the level of insight a client has when buying. Studies have shown that shopping addicts have greater insight into their impulsivity compared to clients who are in manic and hypomanic episodes. In addition, compulsive buyers often report that before a buying episode there are negative emotions and after a buying episode there are positive emotions. The fact that negative emotions trigger a buying episode, but a feeling of relief and positive emotions follows the buying episode, leads clinicians to believe that buying serves as a maladaptive means of alleviating negative emotions (Williams, 2012).

Williams (2012) investigated whether compulsive buyers regulate negative emotions through their purchasing behaviors. Her study included a pathological gambling group, a compulsive buying group, and a healthy control group. The results showed that compared to the other two groups, compulsive buyers reported a greater urge to acquire items, purchase merchandise, and spend more money. However, Williams was unable to support the theory that compulsive buyers regulate negative emotions through purchasing behaviors. Although descriptive studies suggest a relationship between regulating negative behaviors through buying behaviors, more empirical and descriptive research is needed (Williams, 2012).

Clinical Symptoms

Clients with shopping addiction often report being preoccupied with buying and are bombarded with uncontrollable impulses to buy things. They describe their thoughts for buying items as intrusive and irresistible. This often causes distress and impaired social functioning for shopping addicts. Compulsive buying is often chronic but can follow brief periods of remission. Shopping often happens alone; however, addicts do not limit their buying to themselves and often shop to improve not only their self-image but family and friends' image of them (Dell'Osso et al., 2008).

McElroy et al. (1994) developed diagnostic criteria for compulsive buying disorder. The criteria include the following: (a) frequent preoccupation with shopping or intrusive, irresistible, "senseless" buying impulses; (b) clearly buying more than is needed or can be afforded; (c) distress related to buying behavior; and (d) significant interference with work or social functioning.

Black (2007) listed four stages for compulsive buying/shopping: (a) anticipation, (b) preparation, (c) shopping, and (d) spending. In the first phase, the person has thoughts and/or preoccupations with having a certain item or shopping in general. The second phase can involve selecting the store to shop in or selecting the clothes to wear during the shopping trip. The third phase involves going out and shopping for the specific item or shopping in general. The fourth state involves purchasing the item(s). After the person purchases the item(s), feelings of shame and embarrassment often overwhelm him or her. In addition, many shopping addicts describe having a feeling of exhilaration in the third and fourth phases while shopping and making purchases (Black, 2001, 2007).

THE BRAIN AND COMPULSIVE BUYING/SHOPPING ADDICTION

One feature of compulsive buying is increasing tolerance, which is marked by a need to spend more money in order to get the same fulfillment from each shopping episode. Because increased tolerance is also a common trait of addiction, researchers reason that addiction and compulsive buying affect the same parts of the brain (Karim & Chaudhri, 2012). Long-standing addictions alter how reward physiology is processed in the brain and change the actual cortical connections in the brain. This altering of the brain impairs an individual's ability to self-regulate behaviors and makes it harder to overcome the addiction (Hartston, 2012). In behavioral addictions, the circuitry of the brain is altered, turning the basic drives (i.e., natural rewards) into craving/repetitive behaviors. In response to the repeated behavior, the part of the brain associated with reward, emotion, and decision making eventually changes to create behavioral reinforcement and habit formation. Because the parts of the brain affected by addiction are crucial in decision making, reward prediction, and driving cravings, ultimately emotions are also regulated (Hartston, 2012; Karim & Chaudhri, 2012).

Raab, Elger, Neuner, and Weber (2011) investigated whether there were differences in brain activity between compulsive buyers and noncompulsive buyers in the decision-making parts of the brain. Researchers scanned the brains of 26 noncompulsive buyers and 23 compulsive buyers while the participants conducted the Saving Holdings or Purchase task. For 100 products, participants were first shown the product and then the product with its price. Then they had to decide whether they would purchase the product. Participants fixated on a cross-hair between the presentation of each item. Overall, results indicated significant differences in brain activity between compulsive buyers and noncompulsive buyers. Compulsive buyers had more activity in the part of the brain that regulates arousal; however, there was no evidence to support differences in brain activity in the decision-making part of the brain (Raab et al., 2011).

TREATMENT APPROACHES

Current treatment strategies for shopping addiction include pharmacology, individual therapy, couples therapy, counseling geared toward compulsive buying (Debtors Anonymous, Simplicity Circles), and group therapy. A consensus on effective treatment strategies for shopping addiction has yet to be reached; however, current research shows promise for psychotherapy and pharmacology. Because compulsive buying has high comorbidity, more than one type of treatment is ideal (Benson & Eisenach, 2013).

Pharmacology

Antidepressant drugs and other mood stabilizers are often used to treat clients suffering from shopping addiction. Research suggests that there is promise for using these types of drugs to treat the disorder as well as previous success using them with other compulsive disorders (Benson & Eisenach, 2013). In a 12-week study with 24 subjects, the effectiveness of 60 mg of citalopram each day was investigated. Researchers found that 17 participants reported being much improved or very much improved on the Clinical Global Impression–Improvement Scale. These same participants had follow-up interviews at the 3-month and 12-month mark, and during a 6-month check participants still taking citalopram were found to be less likely to relapse than those who had completely discontinued the drug. Though the results are promising, a limitation of the study is that it did not exclude those participants suffering from other depressive mood disorders, which could have clouded results. Additional studies need to be conducted to conclusively link the benefits of specific antidepressants to the treatment of shopping addiction (Dell'Osso et al., 2008; Koran, Bullock, Hartston, Elliott, & D'Andrea, 2002).

Grant, Odlaug, Mooney, O'Brien, and Kim (2012) investigated the effectiveness of memantine for treating compulsive buying. Nine participants were selected who met the following criteria: (a) preoccupation with buying or buying more than one can afford; (b) buying unneeded items or shopping for longer durations of time than originally intended; and (c) preoccupation with buying results in marked distress, interferes with social or occupational functioning, and causes financial problems. Results of the study showed that participants' compulsive buying symptoms improved significantly with the use of memantine (Grant et al., 2012).

Psychotherapy

Often psychotherapy is used to allow clients to tell their stories and to achieve a deeper understanding of their symptoms. Those suffering from compulsive buying might select psychotherapy as a treatment if they are high functioning and do not have other addictive disorders. This type of high-functioning compulsive buyer with no other addictive disorders is very rare, as often compulsive buying co-occurs with another disorder (Benson & Eisenach, 2013). More targeted therapy that focuses on ways to break the compulsive buying cycle while creating a financial situation that will enhance the client's life is also being used as a treatment for compulsive buying. Couples therapy is another treatment used for compulsive buying, primarily because of the financial consequences of the disorder and its impact on marriage. In couples therapy the focus is on rebuilding the aspects of the marriage that have been damaged because of the compulsion and allowing both partners to heal. Overall there is a lack of empirical evidence regarding the effectiveness of psychotherapy with compulsive buying; hence, future research needs to focus on empirical evidence rather than anecdotal data (Benson & Eisenach, 2013).

Cognitive Behavior Therapy

Kellett and Bolton (2009) proposed a cognitive–behavioral model for treating compulsive buying. This model consists of four phases: (a) antecedent factors that encompass the early life experiences of the client; (b) internal emotional and external triggers; (c) the act of buying; and (d) postpurchase emotional, behavioral, and financial factors. In this cognitive–behavioral model the behaviors are cyclical in nature; hence, the final stage triggers the beginning of the first stage all over again.

- *Stage 1: Antecedent factors.* Research has suggested that specific childhood environments could be linked to compulsive shopping/buying later in life. Compared to individuals in a control group, addicted clients disclosed that in their childhoods their parents had used money and gifts as a form of positive reinforcement for wanted behaviors (Kellett & Bolton, 2009). This specific brand of parenting leads to the child forming a strong attachment to possessions. Those suffering from shopping addiction tend to harbor a belief in the importance and worship of material goods. Theorists believe that in childhood possessions create a way for shopping addicts to define themselves.

   Specific cognitions for compulsive shopping include the following: (a) thinking that buying will compensate for and alleviate negative feelings, (b) thinking that things bought will create emotional security and attachment, (c) believing that every item is unique and that if it is not purchased a special opportunity will be lost, and (d) having a sense of personal responsibility for each item purchased (Kyrios, Frost, & Steketee, 2004).
- *Stage 2: Triggers.* Triggers that push the client to purchase items are divided into internal cognitive triggers and external environmental triggers. Internal triggers include tension and anxiety before the act of shopping takes place. It is only when the act of shopping takes place that these internal feelings (i.e., tension, anxiety, etc.) subside. External environmental triggers focus on the environment to which shopping addicts subject themselves during the buying experience. Retail stimuli include the color tones, textures, sounds, and smells of the shopping environment and the purchased item(s). The shopping environment is psychologically designed to be pleasing and to motivate shoppers to purchase; hence, the entire experience aids in enticing shopping addicts to buy (Kellett & Bolton, 2009).

- *Stage 3: The act of buying.* This stage focuses on the feelings that occur during the act of purchasing items. Research indicates that shopping addicts are totally unaware of what is going on around them during the act of shopping. Because they are so absorbed in the process of shopping, their shopping behavior is reinforced, because they are experiencing mood-altering and euphoric feelings as they shop (Kellett & Bolton, 2009).
- *Stage 4: Postpurchase.* Cognitively speaking, shopping addicts become aware of their reality once their purchases have been made and they have left the shopping environment. After the purchase is made, the euphoria and positive feelings associated with buying things begin to fade and addicts become aware of the possible negative consequences (low self-esteem, impending financial debt, etc.). At this point addicts experience feelings of guilt, shame, and regret. This also triggers feelings of negativity toward the self. Afterward addicts commonly conceal the purchases made, shroud the purchases in secrecy, and fear being discovered (Kellett & Bolton, 2009).

Group Therapy

Group therapy has the most consistent evidence of effectiveness for treating compulsive buying. Researchers suggest that group therapy is effective for several reasons: (a) Group settings help diminish feelings of being alone and increase the feeling of being understood; (b) because group members receive feedback from other members, distorted thoughts and maladaptive behaviors are able to be addressed immediately in the group; (c) group members know how compulsive buyers think, feel, and behave, so members are less able to be in denial about destructive behaviors and more able to take personal responsibility; and (d) the group setting allows members to see the different stages of recovery and support one another throughout the process (Benson & Eisenach, 2013).

Compulsive buyers groups seek to provide group members with a deeper understanding of the reality of their buying behavior (i.e., the extent of the behavior, the context in which it occurs, the internal and external triggers). Group therapy also teaches members skills and strategies that focus on engaging in nonbuying activities, planning purchases in advance, and carrying a limited amount of cash and debit cards. Some of the group strategies include relaxation techniques, experiential experiences, and visualizations. Journal writing is used during group treatment to ensure that group members are able to write about their feelings before, during, and after buying or resisting. Group therapy helps members to create a spending plan and to use a buddy system and allows individual members to share their experiences as they move through the stages of recovery. Treatment programs such as Debtors Anonymous are often used in conjunction with groups to aid in recovery. Debtors Anonymous is modeled after the Alcoholics Anonymous program. It is a 12-step program that focuses on creating abstinence from any new debt, ultimately working toward curing debt through solvency. Simplicity Circles provide a place for compulsive buyers to gather and discuss their personal journey and meet the needs that were once fulfilled through shopping (Benson & Eisenach, 2013).

Müller et al. (2013) looked at the effectiveness of cognitive behavior group therapy versus guided self-help for aiding in diminishing compulsive buying.

Their study included 56 participants who were assessed for their level of compulsive buying symptoms using the Compulsive Buying Scale and for comorbidity using the Structured Clinical Interview for DSM–IV Axis I Disorders. Researchers assessed the participants for compulsive buying and psychiatric comorbidity at the onset of the study, after the intervention, and at a 6-month follow-up. They found that the cognitive behavior group therapy was more effective at reducing compulsive buying symptoms; the study did not support the assumption that guided self-help was effective at reducing compulsive buying symptomatology (Müller et al., 2013).

CONCLUSIONS

A limited amount of research on shopping addiction/compulsive buying specifically investigates the tipping point at which acceptable levels of shopping morph into a full-blown addiction. The lack of conclusive research and indecision in the mental health community further hinder having compulsive buying listed in the *DSM–5* (APA, 2013; Mueller, Mitchell, et al., 2010). A growing body of literature supports the idea that compulsive buying causes significant personal, social, and financial problems for those affected.

Future research needs to focus on the role of the brain and genetics in shopping addiction, and possible identifiers that predispose some individuals to becoming compulsive buyers need to be explored. Research studies should examine which personality traits, if any, are linked to compulsive buying. More rigorous research investigating the role of neurobiological mechanisms in compulsive buying disorder is needed (Karim & Chaudhri, 2012; Palan et al., 2011).

Future research on shopping addiction should focus on different types of shopping environments, including how the environment affects the addicted individual (Saraneva & Saaksjarvi, 2008; Workman & Paper, 2010). Research in the future also needs to investigate the comorbidity of compulsive buying/shopping addiction as well as how compulsive buying is related to other compulsive disorders (Workman & Paper, 2010). Finally, future research needs to focus on links between personality traits as well as links between materialistic values and the overall impact of compulsive buying.

RESOURCES

Websites

The Control Center: The Beverly Hills Center for Self Control & Lifestyle Addictions
  http://www.thecontrolcenter.com
Debtors Anonymous
  http://debtorsanonymous.org
Encyclopedia of Children's Health
  http://www.healthofchildren.com
Encyclopedia of Mental Disorders
  http://www.minddisorders.com
Illinois Institute for Addiction Recovery
  http://www.addictionrecov.org
Intervention Support
  http://www.interventionsupport.com

PsychCentral
  http://psychcentral.com
Shopaholics Anonymous
  http://www.shopaholicsanonymous.org
Shopping Addicts Support (an online group for people with shopping addiction)
  https://groups.yahoo.com/group/shopping_addicts/
Stopping Overshopping
  http://www.shopaholicnomore.com

Treatment Centers

The Control Center: The Beverly Hills Center for Self Control & Lifestyle Addictions
  http://www.thecontrolcenter.com/
Foundations Recovery Network
  http://www.foundationsrecoverynetwork.com/
Illinois Institute for Addiction Recovery
  http://www.addictionrecov.org/
The Shulman Center for Compulsive Theft, Spending and Hoarding
  http://www.theshulmancenter.com/

Videos

Shop 'Til You Drop: The Crisis of Consumerism
  http://www.mediaed.org/cgi-bin/commerce.cgi?preadd=action&key=148

REFERENCES

Albrecht, U., Kirschner, N. E., & Grüsser, S. M. (2007). Diagnostic instruments for behavioural addiction: An overview. *GMS Psycho-Social Medicine, 4*, Doc 11. Retrieved from http://www.egms.de/static/en/journals/psm/2007-4/psm000043.shtml

American Psychiatric Association. (2000). *Diagnostic and statistical manual of mental disorders* (4th ed., text rev.). Washington, DC: Author.

American Psychiatric Association. (2013). *Diagnostic and statistical manual of mental disorders* (5th ed.). Arlington, VA: Author.

Benson, A. L., & Eisenach, D. A. (2013). Stopping overshopping: An approach to the treatment of compulsive-buying disorder. *Journal of Groups in Addiction & Recovery, 8*(1), 3–24. doi:10.1080/1556035X.2013.727724

Black, D. W. (2001). Compulsive buying disorder: Definition, assessment, epidemiology and clinical management. *CNS Drugs, 15*(1), 17–27.

Black, D. W. (2007). A review of compulsive buying disorder. *World Psychiatry, 6*(1), 14–18.

Christenson, G. A., Faber, J. R., de Zwann, M., Raymond, N. C., Specker, S. M., Eckern, M. D., . . . Mitchell, J. E. (1994). Compulsive buying: Description characteristics and psychiatric comorbidity. *Journal of Clinical Psychiatry, 55*, 5–11.

Clark, M., & Calleja, K. (2008). Shopping addiction: A preliminary investigation among Maltese university students. *Addiction Research and Theory, 16*, 633–649.

Dell'Osso, B., Allen, A. A., Altamura, C., Buoli, M., & Hollander, E. (2008). Impulsive-compulsive buying disorder: Clinical overview. *Australian and New Zealand Journal of Psychiatry, 42*, 259–266.

Dell'Osso, B., Altamura, A. C., Allen, A., Marazziti, D., & Hollander, E. (2006). Epidemiologic and clinical updates on impulse control disorders: A critical review. *European Archives of Psychiatry & Clinical Neuroscience, 256*, 464–475.

Dittmar, H. (2005). A new look at "compulsive buying": Self-discrepancies and material-istic values as predictors of compulsive buying tendency. *Journal of Social and Clinical Psychology, 24*, 832–859.

Faber, R. J., & O'Guinn, T. C. (1989). Classifying compulsive consumers: Advances in the development of a diagnostic tool. *Advances in Consumer Research, 16*, 738–744.

Faber, R. J., & O'Guinn, T. C. (1992). A clinical screener for compulsive buying. *Journal of Consumer Research, 19*, 459–469.

Grant, J., Odlaug, B., Mooney, M., O'Brien, R., & Kim, S. W. (2012). Open-label pilot study of memantine in treatment of compulsive buying. *Annals of Clinical Psychiatry, 24*(2), 119–126.

Hartston, H. (2012). The case for compulsive shopping as an addiction. *Journal of Psychoactive Drugs, 44*(1), 64–67.

Hartston, H. J., & Koran, L. M. (2002). Impulsive behavior in a consumer culture. *International Journal of Psychiatry in Clinical Practice, 6*, 65–68.

Holden, C. (2001, November 2). "Behavioral" addictions: Do they exist? *Science, 294*, 980–982.

Hollander, E. (2006). Is compulsive buying a real disorder, and is it really compulsive? *American Journal of Psychiatry, 163*, 1670–1672.

Karim, R., & Chaudhri, P. (2012). Behavioral addictions: An overview. *Journal of Psychoactive Drugs, 44*(1), 5–17.

Kellett, S., & Bolton, J. (2009). Compulsive buying: A cognitive–behavioral model. *Clinical Psychology and Psychotherapy, 16*, 99–209.

Koran, L. M., Bullock, K. D., Hartston, H. J., Elliott, M. A., & D'Andrea, V. (2002). Citalopram treatment of compulsive shopping: An open-label study. *Journal of Clinical Psychiatry, 63*, 704–708.

Kyrios, M., Frost, R. O., & Steketee, G. (2004). Cognitions in compulsive buying and acquisition. *Cognitive Therapy and Research, 28*(2), 241–258.

Lee, S., & Mysyk, A. (2004). The medicalization of compulsive buying. *Social Science & Medicine, 58*, 1709–1719.

Martin, P. R., & Petry, N. M. (2005). Are non-substance-related addictions really addictions? *American Journal on Addictions, 14*, 1–7.

McElroy, S. L., Keck, P. E., Pope, H. G., Jr., Smith, J. M. R., & Strakowski, S. M. (1994). Compulsive buying: A report of 20 cases. *Journal of Clinical Psychiatry, 55*(6), 242–248.

Miltenberger, R. G., Redlin, J., Crosby, R., Stickney, M., Mitchell, J., Wonderlich, S., . . . Smyth, J. (2003). Direct and retrospective assessment of factors contributing to compulsive buying. *Journal of Behavior Therapy, 34*, 1–9.

Mueller, A., Claes, L., Mitchell, J. E., Wonderlich, S. A., Crosby, R. D., & de Zwaan, M. (2010). Personality prototypes in individuals with compulsive buying based on the Big Five model. *Behaviour Research and Therapy, 48*, 930–935.

Mueller, A., Mitchell, J. E., Black, D. W., Crosby, R. D., Berg, K., & de Zwaan, M. (2010). Latent profile analysis and comorbidity in a sample of individuals with compulsive buying disorder. *Psychiatry Research, 178*, 348–353.

Müller, A., Arikian, A., de Zwaan, M., & Mitchell, J. E. (2013). Cognitive–behavioural group therapy versus guided self-help for compulsive buying disorder: A preliminary study. *Clinical Psychology and Psychotherapy, 20*, 28–35.

O'Guinn, T. C., & Faber, R. J. (1989). Compulsive buying: A phenomenological exploration. *Journal of Consumer Research, 16*(2), 147–157.

Palan, K., Morrow, P., Trapp, A., & Blackburn, V. (2011). Compulsive buying behavior in college students: The mediating role of credit card misuse. *Journal of Marketing Theory and Practice, 19*(1), 81–96.

Raab, G., Elger, C., Neuner, M., & Weber, B. (2011). A neurological study of compulsive buying behaviour. *Journal of Consumer Policy, 34*, 401–413.

Ridgway, N. M., Kukar-Kinney, M., & Monroe, K. B. (2008). An expanded conceptualization and a new measure of compulsive buying. *Journal of Consumer Research, 35*, 622–639.

Rook, D., & Fisher, R. J. (1995). Trait and normative aspects of impulsive buying behavior. *Journal of Consumer Research, 22*(3), 305–313.

Saraneva, A., & Saaksjarvi, M. (2008). Young compulsive buyers and the emotional roller-coaster in shopping. *Young Consumers, 9*(2), 75–89.

Valence, G., d'Astous, A., & Fortier, L. (1988). Compulsive buying: Concept and measurement. *Journal of Consumer Policy, 11*, 419–433.

Williams, A. (2012). Evaluation of the mood repair hypothesis of compulsive buying. *Open Journal of Psychiatry, 2*, 83–90.

Woodruffe, H. (1996). Methodological issues in consumer research: Towards a feminist perspective. *Marketing Intelligence and Planning, 14*(2), 13–18.

Workman, L., & Paper, D. (2010). Compulsive buying: A theoretical framework. *Journal of Business Inquiry, 9*(1), 89–126.

World Health Organization (2007). *International statistical classification of diseases and related health problems, 10th revision*. Geneva, Switzerland: Author.

CHAPTER 13

INTERNET ADDICTION

Joshua C. Watson

STUDENT LEARNING OUTCOMES

At the conclusion of this chapter students will

1. Define Internet addiction
2. Recognize the various subtypes of Internet addiction
3. Describe the diagnostic criteria used to assess for Internet addiction
4. Identify various techniques and instruments that can be used to assess for Internet addiction
5. Apply evidence-based practices for addressing and treating Internet addiction across various clinical settings
6. Locate additional resources to assist them and their clients in dealing with an Internet addiction

CASE AND CASE DISCUSSION

Michael is a 20-year-old college sophomore who lives alone in a small apartment located close to the campus. Although he is cordial with many of his classmates, he reports not having any close friendships. Michael attributes his lack of friends to his low self-esteem. For as long as Michael can remember, he has dealt with self-esteem issues, believing that he was never good enough and that others saw him as a loser. As a result, he began to isolate himself more and more and became quite introverted through the years. Despite not having any friends from the college, Michael reports having numerous friends online. He notes that he enjoys meeting new people in online chat rooms and that he has an extensive online social network of friends all over the world. Although they have never met in person, he considers them close friends for whom he would do anything if asked. The Internet provides Michael with the ideal place to meet and interact with other people without fear of rejection.

According to Michael, a typical day includes spending 10–12 hours online and in chat rooms. He reports spending most of his time in class thinking about being back at home and chatting with his online friends. As soon as his classes end and he arrives back at his apartment, he immediately turns on his computer and logs into the chat rooms. While online, time seems to pass by without his knowing. He reports several occasions when he would look at his clock and see that he had spent the entire night awake and online. His time online has escalated at the expense not only of his health but also of his schoolwork. Because of the amount of time he spends online, Michael has begun having difficulty completing assignments on time. Although he tries to get his work done, he is drawn to the computer to see what his friends are up to. Claiming that he is only going to "check in and see what is going on," he ends up engrossed in conversation for hours. As a result, he was placed on academic probation this past semester and is in danger of being dismissed from school should his grades not improve. When questioned by his instructors, Michael routinely makes up excuses as to why he is unable to complete an assignment, never mentioning his time spent online.

Although he is often tired from a lack of sleep, Michael contends that being online is a rush for him and that he has never felt as alive as he does when he is online. According to Michael, "My online friends all care about the real me; I can be who I am and say what I feel and not get hurt by anyone." Despite the concerns expressed by his instructors and his family, Michael does not see how his actions are harming anyone. He believes others should just stay out of his business, stating, "If chatting with friends makes me happy, that is all that really matters." Michael has been told that in order to remain enrolled in college, he needs to speak to a counselor. Reluctantly, he has decided to do so and is appearing for his first session at the campus counseling center.

OVERVIEW OF INTERNET ADDICTION

In 1962, a researcher at the Massachusetts Institute of Technology by the name of J. C. R. Licklider authored a number of memos that described his ideas for creating a globally interconnected set of computers known as an "intergalactic computer network" (Leiner et al., 2012). As Licklider envisioned it, this network would allow virtually any user to quickly access data and information from any location. From this early idea the Internet was born. Today the Internet is a widespread information infrastructure consisting of millions of private, public, academic, commercial, corporate, and government networks. Among the more popular components of the Internet are the World Wide Web and electronic mail. According to the latest statistics, the Internet is accessed by more than 2.4 billion people, approximately one third of the world's population (Miniwatts Marketing Group, 2012). In the United States alone, nearly 71% of the population has regular access to the Internet (Busko, 2008). Despite its popularity and countless benefits, the Internet has become a source of problematic behavior for a growing number of people. The scope of this problem is such that for the first time ever Internet addiction has been included as a disorder in need of further study in the *Diagnostic and Statistical Manual of Mental Disorders, Fifth Edition* (*DSM–5*; American Psychiatric Association [APA], 2011). In this chapter I examine the emerging construct of Internet addiction, how it is conceptualized in the current diagnostic nomenclature, and how it can be addressed and processed in the counseling relationship.

Definitions

Although not yet officially codified within any existing diagnostic framework, Internet addiction is growing in prevalence, and both therapeutic professionals and the general public are beginning to recognize the widespread effects of this potentially problematic condition. Ironically, the mention of Internet addiction actually began as a joke. In 1996 Dr. Ivan Goldberg, a psychiatrist in New York, was satirically commenting on APA's *Diagnostic and Statistical Manual of Mental Disorders, Fourth Edition* (APA, 1994). To parody the complexity and rigidity of the manual, he created a fictional disorder known as "Internet addiction disorder" and posted its symptoms on a professional message board. Much to his surprise he received several replies to his post from colleagues stating that they in fact met criteria for the disorder themselves or knew clients who seemed to fit this profile. The "disorder" caught on, and others began exploring the viability of its existence in clients.

One of the first mentions of Internet addiction as a legitimate clinical condition can be found in a 1996 paper presented by Dr. Kimberly Young at the annual convention of the American Psychological Association. In her paper, Young defined Internet addiction as an impulse-control disorder that did not involve an intoxicant. She believed that prolonged exposure to the Internet could produce detrimental effects in a person's life that may even require treatment to address. Using a modified version of the existing *DSM* diagnostic criteria for pathological gambling, Young defined Internet addiction as having five or more of the following symptoms: preoccupation with the Internet, a need to spend more time online to get the same satisfaction, unsuccessful attempts to decrease use, a feeling of restlessness or irritability when attempting to cut back, an online presence much longer than intended, secretive behavior/lying about online pursuits, distress or dysfunction as a result of this behavior, or use of the Internet to self-medicate. Based on these selection criteria, Young found a significant number of heavy Internet users who met the criteria for addiction.

The initial response to Young's (1996) work was mixed. Some clinicians and academicians frowned on it and did not see the term *addiction* as being applicable to cases involving overuse of the Internet because addictions usually involved the ingesting of a drug or foreign substance (Rachlin, 1990). Others (e.g., Levey, 1996) pointed to the fact that unlike other addictive substances, the Internet in fact provided some benefit to society. Those who supported Young's conceptualization of a new condition related to excessive and problematic Internet usage pointed to the existence of other process addictions (e.g., gambling, overeating, and exercise) that already were being addressed in counseling sessions. Although a consensus as to the validity of her work could not be reached, what was important was the fact that her research laid the foundation for others to build on in developing this emerging construct.

Since Young's (1996) pioneering study, additional research has been conducted to further the profession's understanding of this emerging problem. A review of the professional literature shows that the terminology used to describe the condition of pathological and obsessive Internet usage has varied across studies, most likely related to the relative newness of this phenomenon and the ambiguity surrounding the proper way to assess how much is too much when it comes to a person's Internet usage. Terms that have been used in the professional literature to refer to this condition of problematic Internet usage include *Internet addiction, Internet use disorder, cyberspace addiction, Internet addiction disorder, online addiction, Net addiction, Internet addicted disorder, high Internet dependency,* and *problematic Internet usage* (Byun et al., 2009; Widyanto & Griffiths, 2006). To date there has yet to be a conclusive or uniform definition proposed to describe this emerging condition. This lack of agreed-on terminology makes studying the topic of pathological Internet usage difficult. However, for the purposes of this chapter, the term *Internet addiction* is used to refer to the collective phenomena associated with both problematic and pathological Internet usage.

Clinically speaking, Internet addiction appears to share many features in common with impulse-control, substance abuse, and obsessive-compulsive disorders (Aboujaoude, Koran, Gamel, Large, & Serpe, 2006). It is similar to impulse-control disorders in that people experience a surge in anxiety and an urge to perform an act that is deemed pleasurable in the moment but ultimately results in long-term distress and dysfunction. Individuals may find that the Internet provides them with a release from their problems in that they can forget about their everyday worries and immerse themselves in a virtual world where they can be who they want to be and act how they want to act. This release, however, is only temporary and masks the true problems that will continue to persist in their everyday lives if left unaddressed. Internet addiction also is like a substance abuse disorder in that individuals develop a tolerance to the stimulus, which leads to the need for increased exposure to achieve previous states of elevated mood. In other words, people who become addicted to the Internet often find that they need to keep increasing the amount of time they spend online to experience the same euphoric feeling they have in the past. With tolerance come withdrawal symptoms. Should a person who has become addicted to the Internet attempt to decrease or even cease usage, he or she will experience a variety of unpleasant symptoms. Finally, Aboujaoude et al. (2006) posited that Internet addiction shares similarities with obsessive-compulsive disorders in that ritualized and structured behaviors may develop. A person addicted to the Internet may feel compelled to check his or her e-mail account every 10 minutes or believe that he or she needs to be logged into a chat room at the same time every day. However, unlike in obsessive-compulsive disorders, these ritualized behaviors bring pleasure to the individual and do not result in personal distress.

Subtypes

According to Young (1996), an addiction to the Internet can take many different forms. Each individual may feel drawn to or compelled to engage in a distinct activity or aspect of the Internet. In this section I look at the five primary subtypes of Internet addiction commonly mentioned in the professional literature. Although they are distinct subtypes, it is entirely possible for the Internet-addicted person to be compelled to use the Internet for more than one of these reasons. Users of each subtype often experience excessive usage; withdrawal phenomena; tolerance; and negative familial, social, academic, and career repercussions (Block, 2008).

Cybersex Addiction

It is estimated that one in five Internet addicts is engaged in some form of online sexual activity (Delmonico & Griffin, 2011). This includes viewing pornography (pictures or videos) or engaging in a cybersexual relationship. The rise in the number of people using the Internet for sexual activities can be traced back to three factors: access, affordability, and anonymity. Pornographic content is readily available on the Internet. Ropelato (2012) noted that more than 4 million sites on the Internet feature pornographic content; this number represents 12% of all Internet domains. In addition, 35% of all Internet downloads and 25% of all search engine queries are for online pornography (Gobry & Saint, 2011). Online pornography has become so omnipresent that it actually becomes a challenge not to come across it when surfing the Web or looking up information on Internet search engines. Not only is the information readily available, it is also quite affordable. In many cases, images and streaming content are viewable free of charge. In other cases, viewers are able to gain access to huge libraries of content by purchasing memberships to sites. Perhaps most important is the anonymity online pornography provides. Individuals can search for material that meets their sexual needs without fear or judgment or embarrassment. When treating individuals with a cybersex addiction, clinicians must discuss the underlying factors that may have led the individual to this type of behavior (e.g., intimacy issues, grief and loss, spirituality, depression, anxiety; Delmonico & Griffin, 2011).

Cyber-Affair/Relational Addiction

A growing number of people are participating in online affairs. These include relationships that develop through social networking sites and chat rooms. According to Young (2012), online affairs represent the most frequently treated problem at the Center for Internet Addiction. The problem with online affairs is that individuals engaged in these affairs do not perceive themselves as doing anything wrong. The relationship did not get physical and there was no real intimacy. However, Maheu and Subotnik (2001) defined infidelity as occurring whether sexual or emotional stimulation is derived from either the virtual world or the real world. Online affairs do create the same type of emotional bond that brings married couples together, and the effects of an online affair can be just as devastating as those of a physical affair. Individuals who engage in online affairs often become more secretive in their computer usage. They may move computers to secluded rooms, set passwords to restrict access, delete their viewing history, or access the Internet when their partner is either asleep or not at home.

Online Gambling

Online gambling is a category that encompasses many activities. Purchasing land-based lottery tickets, playing interactive online lotteries, playing online bongo, playing in online casinos, placing online bets with sports or race books, and competing against others in games of chance in which money changes hands are all considered forms of online gambling (Wood & Williams, 2009). In 2010 online gambling revenues topped $29 billion, representing a 150% increase in revenue since 2005 (Conrad, 2012). As gambling sites become more popular, the number of people who develop problems related to pathological gambling will increase. It is estimated now that one in five users of online gambling sites probably meets the diagnostic criteria for pathological gambling disorder. Like with Internet pornography, the increased availability and anonymity afforded the user have led to the growing number of websites that offer gambling options.

Online Gaming

Online gaming addiction is defined by Young (2009) as an addiction to online video games, role-playing games, or any interactive gaming environment available through the Internet. With progresses in technology and the Internet, online gaming is becoming more popular every day. According to an article by McGonigal (2011), more than 500 million people worldwide play online games at least 1 hour per day, including a staggering 183 million in the United States alone. McGonigal also noted that more than 5 million people report playing online games for more than 40 hours per week, the equivalent of a full-time job. Young attributed the popularity of online games to the ability to provide gamers with a social connection they may lack in their everyday lives and the positive feelings associated with collaborating with or competing against other players.

Information Overload

The wealth of information available on the Internet makes it quite appealing. In this subtype, the addicted person is compelled to surf the Internet. Sometimes this surfing is for specific content, but mainly it is not designed for a specific purpose. As information catches the surfer's eye, he or she is drawn to new sites. This pattern of aimless wandering can lead to hours of online surfing. Sites that contain viral content, such as videos, pictures, and top stories, can captivate audiences. Other times the surfing is more structured. Viewers may surf the Web to check out the latest sports scores, local weather, stock performance, celebrity gossip, or even national headlines. This behavior, in and of itself not bad, becomes problematic when the amount of time spent online becomes greater than what the individual had originally intended and the effort needed to stop surfing becomes greater.

Prevalence

Because Internet addiction is not an official classification in any diagnostic system, gathering evidence as to the prevalence of this disorder is challenging. In 1999, Greenfield and ABCNews.com jointly surveyed Internet users nationwide. Data were collected from more than 17,000 participants, and an estimated 6% of those participants met criteria for Internet addiction. Despite being one of the largest psychological studies conducted solely on the Internet, the self-report nature of the study and the use of online surveying methodologies temper these estimates. A similar study was conducted in 2006 by a team of researchers at Stanford University Medical Center. Using a random-digit dialing telephone approach, the team surveyed 2,513 adults in all 50 states. They found that one in eight Americans suffer from one or more signs of Internet addiction (Aboujaoude et al., 2006). Additional findings included the following:

- 4% said they were preoccupied with the Internet when they were offline
- 6% had personal relationships that suffered as a direct consequence of their inappropriate Internet usage
- 6% regularly went online to escape from depression or negative moods
- 9% were secretive and felt they had to hide their Internet activities from friends and family
- 11% regularly stayed online for longer periods of time than they intended
- 14% had a very hard time staying offline for more than 4 days in a row

Overall, Young (2011b) estimated that 6% to 15% of the general population exhibit signs of Internet addiction that might warrant clinical attention. Although the estimates vary, what is agreed on is the fact that the rapid and unfettered increase in the number of people accessing a relatively unrestricted Internet substantially increases the likelihood that a number of those users will be at risk for developing an addiction to the Internet (Christakis, 2010).

Prevalence rates appear to be slightly higher among college students than the general population. Numerous studies using student samples from a variety of institutions suggest that the prevalence rate among this population might range from 10% to 20% (Chak & Leung, 2004; Morahan-Martin & Schumacher, 1999; Niemz, Griffiths, & Banyard, 2005; Scherer, 1997). The increased prevalence can most likely be attributed to a number of factors. First, the Internet has been a constant presence in the lives of many younger adults. They have grown up with the technology, and it has become a pervasive source of information and entertainment in their lives. Second, college and university campuses house some of the largest collections of computers, and a large number of Internet users—and abusers—reside on college campuses (Chou, Condron, & Belland, 2005).

As you evaluate these statistics, keep in mind that they were formulated based on a loose description of Internet addiction. As additional research is conducted and a more formalized conceptualization of this disorder is developed, these numbers are sure to vary. In the following section I examine how Internet addiction is currently diagnosed and assessed in individuals.

ASSESSMENT AND DIAGNOSIS

Diagnostic Criteria

A challenge in diagnosing Internet addiction is that the disorder does not appear in any known diagnostic system and there are no widely accepted diagnostic criteria for it (Weinstein & Lejoyeux, 2010). In addition, Block (2008) argued that diagnosing individuals with an Internet addiction is complicated by the fact that a large number of individuals who meet criteria for addiction also exhibit other diagnosable mental health disorders. In other words, it is difficult to tell whether a person's dependence on the Internet is itself a separate problem or merely a way to self-medicate against other problems.

Despite these challenges, there is movement to objectively define the construct of Internet addiction. Seen by many as a compulsive-impulsive spectrum disorder, Internet gaming disorder is included in the *DSM–5* (APA, 2011, 2013) as a disorder in need of further study. Although not an official disorder, its inclusion in the appendixes of the *DSM–5* highlights the growing realization that problematic Internet usage has the potential to become a pathological and additive problem that cannot and should not be ignored. Although there are no formal diagnostic criteria for Internet addiction, four components are widely seen as being essential to such a diagnosis (Block, 2008):

1. Excessive Internet use, often associated with a loss of sense of time or a neglect of basic drives
2. Withdrawal, including feelings of anger, tension, and/or depression when the computer is inaccessible or Internet access is restricted
3. Tolerance, including the need for better computer equipment, more software, a faster Internet connection, or more hours of use
4. Adverse consequences, including arguments, lying, poor school or work performance, social isolation, diminished personal hygiene, and fatigue

Assessment

Assessment for Internet addiction is accomplished through client self-report. As Young (1999) noted, the symptoms of Internet addiction may not always be revealed in an initial clinical interview. Counselors must routinely assess for clues to determine the extent of their client's current Internet usage and assess whether that usage has become problematic. Although there is no structured clinical interview protocol to follow, counselors might find it helpful to use one of the available assessment instruments developed in recent years. One of the first such instruments was the Internet Addiction Diagnostic Questionnaire (IADQ) developed by Young (1998). A description of this early instrument and other promising instruments follows, and additional sources of information or instruments to use are provided at the end of this chapter in the "Resources" section.

IADQ

One measure that can be used to assess for Internet addiction is the IADQ (Young, 1998). Developed based on the diagnostic criteria for pathological gambling, the IADQ is a quick screening tool that consists of eight questions to which clients respond with either a positive (yes) or negative (no) response. Five positive responses establish that the individual may in fact be engaging in compulsive Internet usage. In her description of the IADQ, Young (1998) recommended that all client responses be considered contextually. For example, excessive Internet usage that may legitimately be required for academic activities (searching for resources to use in a term paper or writing a dissertation) or career-related activities (e-mailing prospective clients or researching applicable zoning laws for a planned housing development project) would be excluded.

In 2001 further modifications were made to the scoring system of the IADQ by Beard and Wolf. They noted that each of the first five criteria must be present for a diagnosis of Internet addiction. Their rationale for the change was that each of these criteria could be met without causing much impairment in an individual's daily functioning. Their presence alone would not necessarily classify someone as having an uncontrollable problem. They further noted that *at least* one of the remaining three items (Items 6–8) also had to be met for a diagnosis of Internet addiction to be made. Although additional researchers (Dowling & Quirk, 2009) have found that using five criteria as the cutoff for diagnosing addiction may in fact be too robust, this is the scoring system that remains in place for the IADQ. Salient example questions from the IADQ include "Have you repeatedly made unsuccessful efforts to control, cut back, or stop Internet use?" "Do you feel restless, moody, depressed, or irritable when attempting to cut down or stop Internet use?" "Do you stay online longer than originally intended?" and "Have you jeopardized or risked the loss of a significant relationship, job, or educational or career opportunity because of the Internet?"

Generalized Problematic Internet Use Scale–2
Based on the theoretical concept of "generalized problematic Internet use" posited by Davis (2001, p. 187), the Generalized Problematic Internet Use Scale–2 (Caplan, 2010) is one of the few theory-driven instruments designed to measure problematic Internet use. This scale consists of 15 items and utilizes an 8-point response set with values ranging from 1 (*definitely disagree*) to 8 (*definitely agree*). The higher an individual scores on the instrument, the more problematic the Internet use. In addition to a total score, the measure also provides scores along five subscales. These five subscales are defined as (a) Preference for Online Social Interaction, (b) Mood Regulation, (c) Cognitive Preoccupation, (d) Compulsive Internet Use, and (e) Negative Outcomes. According to Caplan (2010), either the overall composite index of the Generalized Problematic Internet Use Scale–2 or the separate subscales can be used to diagnose problematic Internet usage in clients. An internal consistency reliability alpha of .89 was found for the instrument and has been replicated in follow-up studies (Caplan, 2010; Tutgun, Deniz, & Moon, 2011).

Internet-Related Addictive Behavior Inventory
The Internet-Related Addictive Behavior Inventory (Brenner, 1997) can be used to estimate excessive Internet use based on the *DSM–IV* (APA, 1994) criteria for assessing substance-related diseases. This inventory is a 32-item questionnaire to which respondents select either a true or false response. The items were devised to assess Internet use behaviors and experiences similar to those experienced by chemical substance abusers. Although specific criteria for determining whether an individual is addicted to the Internet was not included in Brenner's (1997) instrument, a general rule is that the more "true" responses a person indicates, the more likely it is that he or she is addicted to the Internet. Example items include "I have spent at least three hours on the Internet at least twice," "More than once I have gotten less than four hours sleep at night because I was using the Internet," "I know most of my friends from the Internet," and "If it weren't for my computer, I wouldn't have any fun at all."

Nonstandardized Assessment
In addition to using formal assessment tools, counselors can assess for the presence of Internet addiction through unstructured interviews. One of the first topics that should be discussed with clients is triggers. Triggers are stimuli in a client's life that create the urge to use the Internet. They can be behavioral, social, emotional, or cognitive. Identifying the precipitants that drive a person to the Internet will be helpful in structuring a treatment plan to lessen dependence on the Internet. Young (1999) noted that four types of triggers that lead to excessive Internet usage should be assessed: (a) applications, (b) feelings, (c) cognitions, and (d) life events.

When individuals become overly involved with the Internet, it typically is the case that their usage is confined to one or two primary applications, the first trigger. These applications become triggers for excessive usage (Young, 1996). Counselors working with these clients should engage in conversations to determine which applications (e.g., chat rooms, social media sites, video-viewing sites, role-playing games) they are most likely to turn to when they log on. Relevant questions that should be asked of clients include the following: What are the applications you use when on the Internet? How many hours per week do you spend using each application? How would you rank order each application from most to least important? What do you like best about each application? Although some clients may struggle initially to answer these questions, the skilled counselor should persist and help clients see that honest responses will help both counselor and client better understand the scope of the problem and begin working on a solution.

The second trigger that should be assessed is feelings or emotions. For many individuals dealing with addiction, their usage of a particular substance or engagement in a specific behavior produces a feeling or sensation that cannot be obtained through other means. For those addicted to the Internet, their online activity provides that rush or sense of euphoria that they are missing in their life when they are offline. As they engage in their online activities, any previous feelings of stress, depression, anxiety, or self-doubt are eased. When assessing for feeling triggers, counselors would be best served by focusing on contrasting the feelings a person experiences when online and offline. In addition, the counselor could assess how long it takes clients to begin feeling a sense of relief and pleasure once they first log on to the Internet. The less time it takes, the stronger their addiction has become.

A third trigger is cognitions or thoughts. In her research, Young (1996) noted that addictive Internet usage may provide a psychological escape for people that allows them to avoid real or perceived problems. What initially may have begun as a stress reliever or coping device may have turned into an uncontrollable aspect of their lives to the point where their thoughts are centered on being online and finding time to log on and engage in their various cyber-activities. As mentioned earlier, many people turn to the Internet because it provides them with an avenue to live the life they feel they cannot live in the everyday world. Online they can be who they want, engender whatever characteristics they want, and engage in activities that normally may be out of their comfort zone. Assessing for this trigger, counselors should question clients as to the reasons why they log on to the Internet and how it contributes to their sense of self. Examining people's core beliefs about who they are and what their worth is will help determine whether their addictive Internet usage is triggered by faulty cognitions.

A final trigger to assess when diagnosing and treating an Internet disorder is life events. In some cases, individuals may experience a traumatic or stressful life event that exceeds their coping skills. In these cases, the individual may turn to the Internet as a safe haven or refuge where they can find relief from the pain they are experiencing in the real world. Most of the time this relief is only temporary, necessitating that individuals log on more frequently and stay connected to the Internet for longer periods of time. For example, a high school student is being bullied at school and feels that he is a social outcast. Once at home, he can log on to the computer and engage in chat rooms where he can be whoever he wants to be and find the companionship and social networking that he lacks. Another example would be a spouse who begins having an online affair or engaging in cybersex to help deal with the pain of a troubled marriage. Counselors can assess for this trigger by asking clients to recount any particularly distressing events in their lives recently or any continual stressors they find themselves struggling to deal with more and more on a daily basis.

Neuroimaging

One of the latest advances in assessing Internet addiction involves the use of neuroimaging. Several researchers are reporting findings that indicate significant changes in brain function and structure associated with Internet addiction. Examining 17 Chinese adolescents who met criteria for Internet addiction, Lin et al. (2012) reported evidence of significant white matter abnormalities in areas of the brain associated with emotional processing and decision making in these teens (see Figure 13.1). In addition, they found decreased white matter integrity in the parts of the brain traditionally associated with addictions. In Figure 13.1, the image on the right corresponds to those individuals who were diagnosed as being Internet addicted.

In another study, Hong et al. (2013) compared magnetic resonance images of a group of adolescents diagnosed with Internet addiction and a healthy comparison group. They found that the adolescents who were addicted to the Internet showed significantly reduced functional connectivity spanning a distributed network that included the cortico-subcortical brain region, an area of the brain already known to play a critical role in the pathology of addiction. As additional studies are conducted, researchers' understanding of the effect excessive Internet usage has on the topography and functionality of the brain will increase, allowing for the development of more accurate methods of assessing the presence of Internet addiction.

TREATMENT

Models and Approaches

At present, a paucity of quality research identifies effective treatments for Internet addiction. Previous authors have suggested opportunities to apply cognitive behavior therapy (CBT; Orzack & Orzack, 1999), motivational enhancement therapy (Orzack & Orzack, 1999; Stern, 1997), and family therapy (Young, 1999). Although these represent a start, further clinical trials are needed to definitively state whether these approaches are clinically efficacious in treating Internet addiction.

Cognitive Behavior Therapy–Internet Addiction (CBT-IA)

One approach that recently has been developed specifically for treating this phenomenon is CBT-IA (Young, 2011a). Combining elements of CBT and harm reduction therapy (HRT), this approach addresses the unique challenges associated with assessing and treating this problem behavior. At its core, CBT-IA relies heavily on principles of CBT. Helping individuals identify the thoughts that trigger their emotions is fundamental to understanding the nature and purpose of their pathological Internet usage. However, Internet addiction produces additional chal-

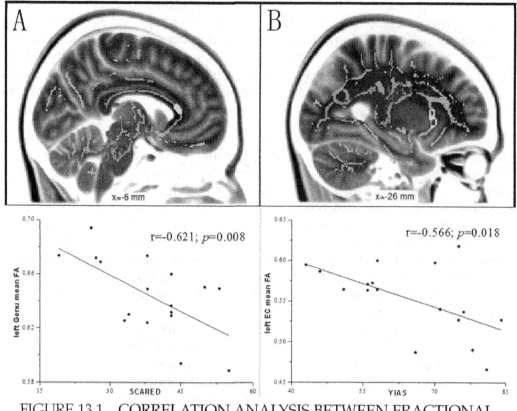

FIGURE 13.1   CORRELATION ANALYSIS BETWEEN FRACTIONAL
ANISOTROPY AND BEHAVIORAL MEASURES WITHIN
THE INTERNET ADDICTION DISORDER GROUP

Note. The image on the left shows the negative correlation between fractional anisotropy (FA) values in the left genus of the corpus callosum and the Screen for Child Anxiety Related Emotional Disorders, and the image on the right shows the negative correlation between FA values in the left external capsule and Young's Internet Addiction Scale for the 22 participants in this study. These results suggest that individuals with Internet addiction demonstrated significant widespread reductions of FA in major white matter pathways and that this deficit might be linked to behavioral impairment.

Source. From "Abnormal White Matter Integrity in Adolescents With Internet Addiction Disorder: A Tract-Based Spatial Statistics Study," by F. Lin, Y. Zhou, Y. Du, L. Qin, Z. Zhao, J. Xu, and H. Lei, 2012, *PLoS One, 7,* e30253. In the public domain.

lenges that are not found when treating other addictions using CBT. The Internet has become a salient and ever-present component of our daily lives. It is used in business, commerce, recreation, and much more. Because complete abstinence from the Internet is impractical, Young (2011a) incorporated elements of HRT into her new approach. The result is a three-phase model that can be applied to "reduce symptoms, improve impulse control, challenge cognitive distortions, and address personal and situational factors specifically associated with compulsive use of the internet" (Young, 2011a, p. 305). The following sections provide an overview of the three phases of the CBT-IA model.

Phase 1: Behavioral modification. During this initial phase, the counselor and client work collaboratively to identify the scope of the problem and then establish a set of goals designed to help modify the client's current pattern of Internet usage and produce a healthier pattern of usage. To determine the scope of the problem, the counselor asks clients to keep a journal of their Internet usage over a period of time (typically 1–2 weeks) to establish an understanding of what their typical usage patterns are. In keeping this journal, clients should note all times that they access the Internet, the precipitating event that led to them accessing the Internet, the amount of time they spent online, and the consequences of their online activities.

Clients are encouraged to be as specific as possible when completing their daily Internet log. Precipitating events should include any emotional, behavioral, or cognitive triggers. For example, a client may seek solace in the Internet when he or she feels depressed or has received difficult news. In other instances, clients may turn to the Internet when they simply feel bored. The identification of precipitating events will be important later in helping to mitigate potential triggers that repeatedly lead to compulsive Internet usage. Once the precipitating event is recorded, the client should list the actual online activity that followed. The Internet is an ever-expansive source of information and stimuli. Online activities could include time spent surfing the Web, checking and sending e-mail, logging into social networking sites (e.g., Facebook, LinkedIn), participating in chat rooms, accessing online pornography, and gaming or role playing. Next, clients are asked to record the duration of their Internet usage in terms of the number of minutes, or in some cases hours, spent online. There are many reported cases of individuals completely losing track of time when online, with several hours passing without them realizing what they have missed. Finally, the consequences of the Internet usage should be noted. These may be positive, negative, or in some cases both positive and negative. Consequences should include a listing of any and all activities accomplished online, any emotional needs met or unmet, and any daily activities that may have been interrupted or neglected as a result of time spent online (Young, 2011a).

Once a baseline of client usage has been recorded, the client and counselor should begin working to remove all evidence of problematic online behavior (Young, 2011a). By restructuring their computer usage, clients can begin to grab hold of their problematic usage patterns and begin establishing new healthy ways of accessing the Internet. There are several ways in which a client can restructure his or her computer usage. The first is to remove any easy access points or reminders of problematic Internet activities. This includes removing all bookmarks, cached files, and links to sites that cause clients to lose control. Clients also may be asked to suspend their online accounts to chat rooms or social networking sites so that the temptation to access is not as great. In cases in which the desire to access problematic content is beyond the control of the client, it may be necessary to use filtering software that physically restricts access to certain components of the Internet. Examples of popular filtering software products include Net Nanny, Cyber Patrol, Safe Eyes, Pure Sight PC, and Surf Control. Clients can enlist the assistance of a supportive ally (friend or family member) to set the restrictions for them. Yet another way that computer usage can be restructured is by limiting the amount of time allowed to be online (either at a given time or in a given day). Timers can be set to provide a sensory cue to the client that it is time to end activities. In time, the use of timed Internet sessions will help clients focus more on necessary online activities than problematic ones. A final way that computer usage can be restructured is by adding in natural break times to deter prolonged Internet access. Clients are encouraged to get up and leave their computer for a period of time so that they can regain perspective on what may need to be accomplished and how that task is being neglected as a result of their Internet usage.

Phase 2: Cognitive restructuring. In this phase the maladaptive cognitions or perceptual distortions used by clients to make their behavior appear more acceptable are addressed. Those who turn to the Internet may do so because they believe that it is the only place where they can find happiness or that no one in the real world could ever love or respect them. These thoughts allow them to justify their usage. Counselors combat these distorted perceptions by challenging their validity. Clients are asked to prove that their beliefs ("I only matter online") are as absolute as they make them out to be. Absent this evidence, progress is made to try and change clients' perspectives and see that they can find what they are looking for without having to turn to the Internet.

As counselors work through Phase 2 with their clients, three primary goals are established. The first is to help clients deal with their denial and see that they are indeed addicted to the Internet. Self-recognition of the problem will be a critical step. Accepting the scope of the problem will help alleviate some of the ambivalence toward treatment and allow the client to fully participate in his or her recovery (Young, 2011a). The second goal is for clients to recognize the cognitive distortions they use. This may require the counselor educating the client as to how people often find ways to make their reality more palatable by distorting the way they view the world. Once cognitive distortions are identified and clients become aware of their attempts to skew the reality of their situation, the third goal can be addressed. This third goal deals with helping clients see that change is possible. Many times clients believe that their problems are so great that any attempts to try and correct maladaptive behavior would be unsuccessful. Keeping clients positive and focused as they work through their issues step by step will be helpful to the overall success of the therapy.

Phase 3: HRT. In this phase HRT is used to identify and address any coexisting factors associated with the development of Internet addiction. Although compulsive Internet usage is the expressed problem, often several underlying issues are associated with it. These might include any number of social, occupational, relational, personal, or situational stressors. When these stressors begin to exceed the coping capabilities of an individual, the Internet may be seen as a release or a safe haven in which problems can be avoided, at least temporarily. Escaping into the Internet lets individuals be who they want to be and seek the affirmation and respect that may be lacking in the real world. As Young (2004) noted, Internet addicts frequently become dependent on the Internet because it provides them with an instant and permissible means of avoiding life problems. When this is the case, simply stopping an individual from accessing the Internet will not solve the issue. The root cause of their problems is still left unresolved. In these situations, HRT becomes an important way for the addict to identify the underlying issues contributing to the addiction as part of recovery (Marlatt, Blume, & Parks, 2001).

During this phase clients and counselors work to achieve two primary goals. First, they collaboratively identify the underlying problems that led to compulsive Internet usage in the first place. Because the addictive behavior is viewed as a faulty coping mechanism, the focus should be on identifying the issue that the client is struggling to cope with in his or her life. Once these issues are identified, the client and counselor work to implement new coping strategies that are healthier and more productive. For example, a client may engage in online gaming to help compensate for feelings of low self-esteem. In the virtual world, the client is able to achieve great successes, and these victories lead to a sense of accomplishment. The client feels important and relevant. As a result, the client gradually begins to interact more with others in the virtual world than in reality because the virtual world meets a need that is unfulfilled in everyday life. The counselor, using HRT, would work with this client to find ways to increase his self-esteem in reality. As the client learns new ways to feel better about himself in his everyday life using these new coping strategies, the Internet becomes less of an option for coping with feelings of inadequacy and low self-worth. Over time, the underlying issue is addressed therapeutically and the harmful pattern of addiction (in this case the excessive amount of time spent in online gaming forums) is reduced. You should note that in this phase the emphasis is not on instantly removing Internet access for the client. Instead, a decrease in problematic Internet usage comes about when alternatives are created that in time become more favorable to the client.

Techniques and Interventions

In addition to theoretical models designed to comprehensively address the full scope of an Internet addiction, researchers have suggested several additional techniques and interventions that could be applied in the counseling relationship with clients afflicted with this addiction. Because complete abstinence from the Internet may not be feasible (Orzack & Orzack, 1999), the following techniques and interventions are all designed to help curb or structure the online experiences of addicted individuals. Young (1997, 1999) suggested the majority of these techniques based on her clinical experiences with Internet-addicted clients.

1. *Practice the opposite.* Rather than allowing clients free reign to access the Internet whenever they want, counselors should work with clients to establish a schedule that constricts and limits clients' amount of time online. If possible, online activity should be restricted to only those activities that are necessary (i.e., academic or career-related activities).
2. *Establish external stoppers.* Set external cues that can be used as timers or reminders that it is time to get offline. For example, having to pick up the kids from school at 3 p.m. means that the client would need to log off no later than 2:30 p.m.
3. *Set realistic goals.* To prevent withdrawal symptoms, goals should be jointly constructed to gradually decrease Internet usage. Rather than abstaining from the Internet altogether right away, individuals should be encouraged to gradually reduce their time online each week.
4. *Create reminder cards.* These visual cues should be created to help clients see what they risk losing should they continue with this unwanted behavior. Index cards can be created that list the potential losses the client faces. These can include family, friends, employment, money, and many other things. The key is to be specific to the client.

5. *Develop a personal inventory.* Have clients make a list of all of the activities or obligations they have neglected as a result of their online activities. Sometimes seeing these losses in writing, especially in an accumulated list, drives home the point that usage has become uncontrollable and has overwhelmed the client. Once the list is created, steps can be taken to begin fulfilling one of those obligations or crossing one missed opportunity off the list.

6. *Seek out social support.* Rather than try to beat the addiction alone, Internet addicts are encouraged to participate in support groups with others who share a similar affliction. Having the support of others who can truly understand where they are coming from and relate to the feeling of helplessness they feel toward the Internet can be comforting.

7. *Participate in family therapy.* Because excessive Internet usage inevitable takes time away from friends and family, group therapy with those who have been marginalized is often a good therapeutic idea to help rebuild fractured relationships. In addition, the family members of the addicted individual can learn ways that they can become more supportive and assist the person in recovering from the addiction rather than enabling him or her to remain addicted.

CONCLUSIONS

The diagnosis of individuals with Internet addiction will continue to be challenging until further research is undertaken to objectively define this emerging disorder and the criteria used to diagnosis it. In the meantime, counselors should recognize that the number of individuals who are developing unhealthy and problematic addictions to the Internet is increasing, and as access to online applications increases, the likelihood that a counselor will encounter an individual dealing with this issue also will increase. Counselors therefore should be assessing for the signs that a client may have a problematic relationship with the Internet and should begin working to address this dependency in the counseling relationship. The resources that follow are provided to assist you in your work with clients. Included are websites and resources that provide counselors with additional training in treating Internet addictions; referral sources for clients to receive specialized treatment in both inpatient and outpatient settings; and access to the latest research on Internet addiction, including strategies for assessing and treating this emerging problem.

RESOURCES

Center for Internet Addiction
   http://www.netaddiction.com
The Center for Internet and Technology Addiction
   http://www.virtual-addiction.com/
MentalHelp.net, Internet Addiction and Media Issues Introduction
   http://www.mentalhelp.net/poc/center_index.php?id=66restart
   http://www.netaddictionrecovery.com/

REFERENCES

Aboujaoude, E., Koran, L. M., Gamel, N., Large, M. D., & Serpe, R. T. (2006). Potential markers for problematic Internet use: A telephone survey of 2,513 adults. *CNS Spectrums, 11,* 750–755.

American Psychiatric Association. (1994). *Diagnostic and statistical manual of mental disorders* (4th ed.). Washington, DC: Author.

American Psychiatric Association. (2011). *DSM–5 development.* Retrieved from http://www.dsm5.org

American Psychiatric Association. (2013). *Diagnostic and statistical manual of mental disorders* (5th ed.). Arlington, VA: Author.

Beard, K. W., & Wolf, E. M. (2001). Modification in the proposed diagnostic criteria for Internet addiction. *Cyberpsychology & Behavior, 4,* 377–383. doi:10.1089/109493101300210286

Block, J. J. (2008). Issues for *DSM–5* Internet addiction. *American Journal of Psychiatry, 165,* 306–307. doi:10.1176/appi.ajp.2007.07101556

Brenner, V. (1997). Psychology of computer use: XLVII. Parameters of Internet use, abuse, and addiction: The first 90 days of the Internet usage survey. *Psychological Reports, 80,* 879–882. doi:10.2466/pr0.1997.80.3.879

Busko, M. (2008). *Internet addiction: Fact or fiction?* Retrieved from http://forum.psychlinks.ca/internet-behavior/11468-internet-addiction-fact-or-fiction.html

Byun, S., Ruffini, C., Millis, J. E., Douglas, A. C., Niang, M., Stepchenkova, S., . . . Blanton, M. (2009). Internet addiction: Metasynthesis of 1996–2006 quantitative research. *Cyberpsychology & Behavior, 12,* 203–207. doi:10.1089/cpb.2008.0102

Caplan, S. E. (2010). Theory and measurement of generalized problematic Internet use: A two-step approach. *Computers in Human Behavior, 26,* 1089–1097.

Chak, K., & Leung, L. (2004). Shyness and locus of control as predictors of Internet addiction and Internet use. *Cyberpsychology & Behavior, 7,* 559–570. doi:10.1089/cpb.2004.7.559

Chou, C., Condron, L., & Belland, J. C. (2005). A review of the research on Internet addiction. *Educational Psychology Review, 17*(4), 363–388. doi:10.1007/s10648-005-8138-1

Christakis, D. A. (2010). Internet addiction: A 21st century epidemic? *BMC Medicine, 8,* 61.

Conrad, B. (2012). *Online gambling statistics and facts.* Retrieved from http://www.techaddiction.ca/online-gambling-statistics.html

Davis, R. A. (2001). A cognitive–behavioral model of pathological Internet use. *Computers in Human Behavior, 17*(2), 187–195.

Delmonico, D. L., & Griffin, E. J. (2011). Cybersex addiction and compulsivity. In K. S. Young & C. N. de Abreu (Eds.), *Internet addiction: A handbook and guide to evaluation and treatment* (pp. 113–131) New York, NY: Wiley.

Dowling, N. A., & Quirk, K. L. (2009). Screening for Internet dependence: Do the proposed diagnostic criteria differentiate normal from dependent Internet use? *Cyberpsychology & Behavior, 12,* 21–27. doi:10.1089/cpb.2008.0162

Gobry, P. E., & Saint, N. (2011). *15 things you need to know about Internet porn.* Retrieved from http://www.businessinsider.com/15-things-you-need-to-know-about-internet-porn-2011-8?op=1

Greenfield, D. N. (1999). Psychological characteristics of compulsive Internet use: A preliminary analysis. *Cyberpsychology & Behavior, 2,* 403–412. doi:10.1089/cpb.1999.2.403

Hong, S-B., Zalesky, A., Cocchi, L., Fornito, A., Choi, E-J., Kim, H-H., . . . Yi, S-H. (2013). Decreased functional brain connectivity in adolescents with Internet addiction. *PLoS One, 8,* e57831.

Leiner, B. M., Cerf, V. G., Clark, D. D., Kahn, R. E., Kleinrock, L., Lynch, D. C., . . . Wolff, S. (2012). *Brief history of the Internet.* Retrieved from http://www.internetsociety.org/internet/what-internet/history-internet/brief-history-internet

Levey, S. (1996, December). Breathing is also addictive. *Newsweek,* pp. 52–53.

Lin, F., Zhou, Y., Du, Y., Qin, L., Zhao, Z., Xu, J., & Lei, H. (2012). Abnormal white matter integrity in adolescents with Internet addiction disorder: A tract-based spatial statistics study. *PLoS One, 7,* e30253.

Maheu, M., & Subotnik, R. (2001). *Infidelity on the Internet: Virtual relationships and real betrayal.* Naperville, IL: Sourcebooks.

Marlatt, G. A., Blume, A. W., & Parks, G. A. (2001). Integrating harm reduction therapy and traditional substance abuse treatment. *Journal of Psychoactive Drugs, 33,* 13–21. doi: 10.1080/02791072.2001.10400463

McGonigal, J. (2011). *Video games: An hour a day is key to success in life.* Retrieved from http://www.huffingtonpost.com/jane-mcgonigal/video-games_b_823208.html

Miniwatts Marketing Group. (2012). *Internet users in the world: Distribution by world regions, 2013 Q4.* Retrieved from http://www.internetworldstats.com/stats.htm

Morahan-Martin, J., & Schumacher, P. (1999). Incidence and correlates of pathological Internet use among college students. *Computers in Human Behavior, 16,* 1–17. doi:10.1016/S0747-5632(99)00049-7

Niemz, K., Griffiths, M., & Banyard, P. (2005). Prevalence of pathological Internet use among university students and correlations with self-esteem, the General Health Questionnaire (GHQ), and disinhibition. *Cyberpsychology & Behavior, 8,* 562–570. doi:10.1089/cpb.2005.8.562

Orzack, M. H., & Orzack, D. S. (1999). Treatment of computer addicts with complex comorbid psychiatric disorders. *Cyberpsychology & Behavior, 2,* 465–473.

Rachlin, H. (1990). Why do people gamble and keep gambling despite heavy losses? *Psychological Science, 1,* 294–297. doi:10.1111/j.1467-9280.1990.tb00220.x

Ropelato, J. (2012). *Internet pornography statistics.* Retrieved from http://internet-filter-review.toptenreviews.com/internet-pornography-statistics.html

Scherer, K. (1997). College life online: Healthy and unhealthy Internet use. *Journal of College Student Development, 38,* 655–665.

Stern, D. J. (1997). Internet addiction, Internet psychotherapy. *American Journal of Psychiatry, 154,* 890.

Tutgun, A., Deniz, L., & Moon, M. K. (2011). A comparative study of problematic Internet use and loneliness among Turkish and Korean prospective teachers. *Turkish Online Journal of Educational Technology, 10*(4), 14–30.

Weinstein, A., & Lejoyeux, M. (2010). Internet addiction or obsessive Internet use. *American Journal of Drug and Alcohol Abuse, 36,* 277–283.

Widyanto, L., & Griffiths, M. D. (2006). Internet addiction: A critical review. *International Journal of Mental Health and Addiction, 4,* 31–51. doi:10.1007/s11469-006-9009-9

Wood, R. T., & Williams, R. J. (2009). *Internet gambling: Prevalence, patterns, problems, and policy options.* Retrieved from http://hdl.handle.net/10133/693

Young, K. S. (1996, August). *Internet addiction: The emergence of a new clinical disorder.* Poster presented at the 104th Annual Convention of the American Psychological Association, Toronto, Ontario, Canada.

Young, K. S. (1997, August). *What makes the Internet addictive: Potential explanations for pathological Internet use.* Paper presented at the 105th Annual Convention of the American Psychological Association, Chicago, IL.

Young, K. S. (1998). Internet addiction: The emergence of a new clinical disorder. *Cyberpsychology & Behavior, 1,* 237–244. doi:10.1089/cpb.1998.1.237

Young, K. S. (1999). Internet addiction: Symptoms, evaluation and treatment. In L. VandeCreek & T. Jackson (Eds.), *Innovations in clinical practice: A source book* (Vol. 17, pp. 19–31). Sarasota, FL: Professional Resource Press.

Young, K. S. (2004). Internet addiction: A new clinical phenomenon and its consequences. *American Behavioral Scientist, 48,* 402–415.

Young, K. S. (2009). *Video games and gaming addiction.* Retrieved from http://netaddiction.com/online-gaming/

Young, K. S. (2011a). CBT-IA: The first treatment model for Internet addiction. *Journal of Cognitive Psychotherapy, 25*(4), 304–312. doi:10.1891/0889-8391.25.4.304

Young, K. S. (2011b). Clinical assessment of Internet-addicted clients. In K. S. Young & C. N. de Abreu (Eds.), *Internet addiction: A handbook and guide to evaluation and treatment* (pp. 19–34) New York, NY: Wiley.

Young, K. S. (2012). *Internet infidelity.* Retrieved from http://netaddiction.com/

CHAPTER 14

ADDICTIONS: STATUS, RESEARCH, AND FUTURE

Robert L. Smith

STUDENT LEARNING OUTCOMES

At the conclusion of this chapter students will

1. Identify common features and components of the assessment and treatment of substance use and addictive disorders
2. Discuss current issues in the field of addictions treatment
3. Discuss evidence-based practices and research in addictions treatment and assess the future of addictions research and treatment methods

CASES AND CASE DISCUSSION

Tony started smoking at 14 or 15 years of age. At 58, he says it seems like yesterday that he lit up his first cigarette. For the past 40 years he has smoked off and on, mainly on. For a time he was up to two packs of cigarettes a day. He has attempted to quit on several occasions. The usual result is a reduction in smoking rather than complete cessation.

Tony says his dad was a chain smoker for most of his life. Other than a cough now and then, his dad had never experienced consequences of his smoking habit. Tony's dad died in a car accident at the age of 95 with a cigarette in his mouth. Tony feels his dad led a productive and long life, and he plans to do the same. Tony has regular physical checkups. His doctor would like him to quit but assesses Tony's health as good. Tony does not plan on quitting and currently smokes less than a pack of cigarettes per day.

Cary was depressed as a child. She did not participate in social events while in high school. She experimented with marijuana at the age of 14. Marijuana soon became a crutch throughout high school to help her relax and chill out. After graduating and turning 21, Cary started drinking. She has enjoyed drinking and smoking weed for the past 15 years. During this time Cary has gone from job to job. Most of her jobs have involved working as a waitress and last for only a year or two. Cary has little interest in college. She has experienced blackouts from drinking recently. Cary lacks motivation.

Bill works for a construction company. He handles most of the indoor painting and cabinet work. His job exposes him to paint and other inhalants on a daily basis. After work Bill feels anxious and is irritated easily. For several years he turned to alcohol to calm his nerves. However, recently he has stopped drinking. Instead, when Bill comes home he will often use inhalants and finds himself passing out for the evening.

A South Korean man collapsed of exhaustion and died of heart failure. This occurred after a 50-hour StarCraft session that included three all-nighters in a row. During the marathon role-playing video game session, he only stopped to use the washroom or to sleep for a short period of time. Similar cases in China have been recorded (Lam, 2010).

 A 13-year-old from China jumped off a tall building after playing World of Warcraft, another popular role-playing video game, for 36 hours. He left a suicide note indicating that he wanted "to join the heroes of the game he worshipped." His parents sued the Chinese distributors of the game (Lam, 2010).

These five cases include many of the characteristics of addictive behavior. For an accurate assessment of each case, clinicians should refer to the *Diagnostic and Statistical Manual of Mental Disorders, Fifth Edition (DSM–5)*, Substance Related and Addictive Disorders (American Psychiatric Association, 2013, p. 481). Clinicians should specifically review the criteria for alcohol use disorder, cannabis use disorder, and inhalant-related disorders for Cases 1, 2, and 3. However, for Cases 4 and 5 involving Internet use and gaming, no standardized criteria are available. Standardized criteria are also lacking for six of the 10 most common process addictions: addictions to food, video games, sex, shopping, exercise, and work (Moos, 2003). Gambling is the only process addiction included in the *DSM–5* (American Psychiatric Association, 2013).

Whereas Chapter 1 addressed problems of defining process addictions and the increased complexity of these conditions, the major focus of this chapter is on treatment and interventions currently applied to substance and process addictions. The content is unique, as it attempts to provide an in-depth examination of the major process addictions treatment models. Evidence-based approaches for treating process and substance addictions are emphasized. Researchers have identified that changes in the brain occur with repeated behaviors, similar to long-term drug use. The behavior patterns of individuals with process addictions mimic those of persons who abuse substances, an interesting finding that demonstrates the similarities between substance and process addictions. It is therefore not surprising that many of the treatment approaches currently used with substance addictions are also recommended for addressing process addictions.

This chapter focuses on four areas in particular: (a) common features and components of the assessment and treatment of substance use and addictive disorders, (b) current issues in the field of addictions treatment, (c) evidence-based practice and research in addictions treatment, and (d) future considerations and recommendations. Findings reported in this book indicate that some features and components are common to all substance use or addictive disorders. These findings represent the current status of and future prospects for addictions treatment.

COMMON FEATURES AND COMPONENTS OF ASSESSMENT AND TREATMENT

The authors of chapters in this book conducted independent literature reviews of the prevalence, demographics, etiology, diagnosis, assessment, and treatment of a wide range of addictions. It is noteworthy that there is considerable overlap in both the assessment and treatment of most addictions. These common features afford direction regarding the current treatment of addictions and suggest opportunities for future research. The use of a comprehensive integrated treatment package is recommended when working with substance and process addictions.

Substance and process addictions have a number of features in common. First, neuroscience research has demonstrated changes in brain circuitry due to substance and behavioral addictions. These occurrences in the underlying neurological substrate of people with addictive disorders are perhaps the reason why psychotropic medications have been used effectively in treating both process and substance addictions. Such medications as naltrexone and selective serotonin reuptake inhibitors have been recommended to reduce cravings or urges, whether they be for a substance or behavior, as well as reduce the risk of having an early relapse or dropping out of treatment. Second, comorbidity is a common feature associated with addictions, with depression found to be prominent in the histories of addicts. Third, the disease model, including the progression of the disease, has served as a guide when working with addictions. Both substance and process addictions seem to follow the same progression, which concludes with severe consequences in both cases.

Diagnosis and treatment planning are standard components of a comprehensive integrated treatment package for working with addictions. Clinicians also need to take into account co-occurring substance-related disorders, other addictive disorders, mental disorders, and physical disorders. They also need to consider the accumulation of consequences over time, such as family and occupational issues.

Instruments and checklists are regularly used during diagnosis. Chapters in this text have provided descriptions of a number of instruments considered useful in problem specification, treatment planning, process monitoring, and outcome evaluation. The therapeutic alliance and motivation toward treatment need to be emphasized throughout the treatment process. Motivational interviewing and motivational enhancement therapy models are recommended at the beginning of treatment in order to establish a strong therapeutic alliance and encourage recovery based on one's current stage of change. Similarly, harm reduction and other avoidance strategies derived from public health models should be enlisted to mitigate the harmful consequences of an addictive lifestyle. Comprehensive case management is also suggested during the early stages of a comprehensive integrative treatment model.

A treatment component often introduced in recovery is the 12-step facilitation model. The 12-step or recovery model emphasizes self-help and group work, which can potentially result in remission of symptoms without prolonged or intensive professional treatment. However, most individuals benefit from an integrated approach that includes recovery group participation as one part of treatment.

Cognitive behavior therapy (CBT) continues to be the most frequently identified evidence-based treatment component of most comprehensive models. CBT techniques are evidence based and target particular distortions or errors in thinking that maintain or exacerbate the addictive process. Some of the particular distortions that maintain an addiction can be assessed through specialized testing associated with the addictive disorder. CBT is frequently conducted in group sessions, which seems to be a very effective treatment modality because group therapy reduces shame and encourages beneficial treatment expectancies. Specific CBT approaches, such as Seeking Safety, a package providing concurrent treatment of addictions and posttraumatic stress disorder (Najavits, 2002), use a treatment manual consisting of homework exercises for participants. Therapeutic homework bridges the gap from one session to the next, affording structure and continuity during the middle sessions of treatment.

Because addiction has consequences for family and social systems, family therapy, community interventions, and occupational support are needed to maintain treatment gains in the recovery process. Careful transition planning is needed in any comprehensive treatment model in order to reduce the risk of relapse as clients reenter their home, work, or school. Family members may also need support as well as opportunities to participate in their own therapy and recovery.

Each individual and his or her family present unique treatment needs. The common components of treatment provide a menu of potential services for building integrative treatment packages. It is professionally responsible to incorporate empirically supported treatment techniques whenever possible. A comprehensive integrative treatment program should also incorporate gender-specific interventions, including restrictions or boundaries for group work and residential treatment if needed. In addition, the evolution or course of addiction appears to be closely tied to recovery from life trauma. Individually tailored integrative treatment packages should include concurrent treatment for posttraumatic stress disorder, other anxiety disorders, depression or mood disorders, and other comorbid mental disorders.

Although differences in mental health disorders between men and women and among individuals from various ethnic backgrounds and cultures may be decreasing, the selection of treatment components should take into consideration their suitability for multicultural application. Clinical trials of evidence-based techniques may not include many members of minority groups. Therefore, the evidence-based treatment program may reflect the biases of a dominant Caucasian culture or fail to recognize the cultural strengths of others. Assimilation could account for declining differences among those in recovery; however, differences in socioeconomic status, race or ethnicity, nationality, and other demographics should be recognized and respected.

Several of the chapters in this book refer to emerging and promising treatment techniques. Integrative treatment involves the selection of common treatment components according to individual, family, and cultural needs. Integrative treatment planning should consider promising new techniques in addictions treatment, including dialectical behavior therapy, eye-movement desensitization and reprocessing, mindfulness, yoga, and other interventions derived from non-

Western cultures. Recovery from addictive disorders is intrinsically a spiritual growth process involving compassionate shame reduction and a balancing of one's lifestyle. The future of addictions treatment will involve new spiritual approaches, alternative medical care, wellness, and positive psychology. Instillation of hope, encouragement of well-being, and rebalancing of lifestyles will help clients and their families realize the promises of recovery and achieve health.

ISSUES RELATED TO ADDICTIONS

Defining Addictions

Assessing when and at what point an excessive behavior such as shopping, using the Internet, or exercising reaches the threshold of an addiction is an issue that demands further study. Despite attempts to define addiction, a general consensus on the operationalization of this concept has not been formalized. Partly for this reason, the term *addiction* has been excluded from contemporary diagnostic manuals (e.g., the *DSM–5*). The lack of a clear definition of addiction, coupled with the lack of evidence-based criteria for many process addictions, hinders clinicians' efforts to diagnose and treat these disorders. Also, the lack of operational clarity makes it difficult for researchers to determine prevalence rates, costs to society, and relapse rates and recommend evidence-based treatments.

Treating Addictions in Context

The context of addiction is often severely underemphasized. This issue, discussed by Moos (2002), is as relevant today as it was 15 years ago. It is within context, or one's everyday setting, that extratherapeutic factors come into play that can facilitate change or instigate a relapse. Someone with an addiction should ideally have a network of supportive individuals, access to helpful agencies, opportunities to work, and hope for being self-sufficient. Family members of those addicted to alcohol and other drugs are most helpful when they are able to provide a supportive climate while attempting to understand the circumstances of individuals who are suffering from stress; lacking in self-esteem; losing hope; carrying a financial burden; unemployed; and separated from social systems, including family and friends.

Support systems, including monetary resources, are necessary if family and social networks are to be able to help individuals struggling to maintain a productive lifestyle. This issue emphasizes the need for treatment that focuses on the individual and his or her relationship to work, family, friends, finances, social networks, spirituality, hobbies, entertainment, hope, future perspectives, food and drink intake, physical maintenance, and healthy activities that are rewarding and pleasurable. It is essential that treatment extend beyond the clinician's office, hospital setting, or group room into the global environment of the individual (White, Kelly, & Roth, 2012).

The Clinician–Client Relationship

The importance of clients establishing a meaningful relationship with professionals who are in a position to help is recognized by every professional group, including physicians, attorneys, psychiatrists, social workers, professional counselors, family therapists, and so on. Licensed and certified professional counselors and others trained in the behavioral sciences have long recognized the importance of this relationship. Essential conditions of an effective relationship are supported by research and have been identified as necessary components in order for change to take place (Norcross & Wampold, 2011). The necessary and essential ingredients for change were first identified in a seminal article by Rogers (1957). Essential factors include accurate empathy, unconditional positive regard, and genuineness. These factors—subsequently labeled *core conditions* or *core dimensions*—were further researched, with findings demonstrating their significance in counseling, family therapy, and psychotherapy (Carkhuff, 1969a, 1969b; Hubble, Duncan, & Miller, 1999; Lambert & Bergin, 1986; Lutz, Martinovich, Lyons, Leon, & Stiles, 2007).

The core conditions provide the foundation of the therapeutic alliance (Norcross & Wampold, 2011) and are essential in work with substance and process addictions. Conversely, confrontational approaches often lead to ineffective outcomes compared with supportive approaches such as person-centered therapy and motivational interviewing (Miller & Rollnick, 2012).

Duration and Continuity of Care

Duration of care has been identified as a significant factor related to treatment outcome in both mental health and substance abuse care. In a sample of more than 20,000 Veterans Affairs patients, Moos (2002) found that individuals who had more mental health care reported better risk-adjusted substance use, more positive family relations, and fewer legal issues compared to those who were treated for a brief period of time. Humphreys and Tucker (2002) have stated that research findings on duration of care support the need for a shift in resources from intensive to more long-term care.

Findings on duration of care with substance abuse clients support the viewpoint that addiction treatment has the best chance of success if it is long term, consistent, and contextual in nature (White et al., 2012). Unfortunately, a large number of clients fail to initiate treatment, and a significant number leave treatment programs after a brief period of time.

Motivation to Change

It has been the practice in some settings to view individuals with substance or process addictions as unmotivated or resistant to change. Speculation concerning lack of motivation includes fear, denial, and anxiety. Recent brain research provides support for the dopamine hypothesis—addiction to the pleasure obtained from a dopamine rush as a contributing factor in the lack of motivation among addicted individuals (Melis, Spiga, & Diana, 2005).

Miller, Forcehimes, and Zweben's (2011) research on motivational interviewing is at the forefront in examining commitment to change. Findings from their work are displayed in Table 14.1. By carefully listening to the words used by clients, perhaps clinicians can better recognize and assess motivation to change. Applied research studies of this nature are needed to help clinicians accurately assess clients' level of motivation. Destructive thoughts and self-defeating behavior patterns can be modified once they are identified.

TABLE 14.1   COMMITMENT:
DEGREE OF MOTIVATIONAL CHANGE

Stronger Commitment			Weaker Commitment	
5	4	3	2	1
I guarantee	I am devoted to	I look forward to	I favor	I mean to
I will	I pledge to	I consent to	I endorse	I foresee
I promise	I agree to	I plan to	I believe	I envisage
I vow	I am prepared to	I resolve to	I accept	I assume
I give my word	I intend to	I expect to	I volunteer	I bet
I assure	I am ready to	I concede to	I aim	I hope to
I dedicate myself			I aspire	I will risk
I know I will			I propose	I will try
			I am predisposed	I think I will
			I anticipate	I suppose I will
			I predict	I imagine I will
			I presume	I suspect I will
				I contemplate
				I guess I will
				I wager
				I will see (about)

Source. Adapted from *Treating Addiction: A Guide for Professionals* (p. 161), by W. R. Miller, A. A. Forcehimes, and A. Zweben, 2011, New York, NY: Guilford Press. Copyright 2011 by The Guilford Press. Reprinted with permission.

Prochaska, DiClemente, and Norcross (1992) provided clinicians with a framework for working with substance and process addictions. Their stages of change model has been used extensively as part of comprehensive substance abuse treatment programs. Table 14.2 expands on this model by including motivational strategies suggested for use during treatment. Adapted from the Center for Substance Abuse Treatment (1999), the motivational strategies in Table 14.2 include practical suggestions to help change the misuse of substances and behavior patterns that lead to addiction.

The Medical Model: Addiction as a Disease of the Brain

A prevailing issue in treatment is the designation of addiction "as a chronic disease of the brain that involves relapse, progressive development, and the potential for fatality if not treated" (Smith, 2012, p. 1). Government agencies as well as much of the medical community consider addiction to be a brain disease (Volkow, 2009). Although this definition remains controversial, particularly in regard to process addictions, research demonstrates impaired brain functioning in pathological gamblers that parallels that in substance abusers (Petry, 2007). Classification of addiction as a disease affects treatment and its availability. This disease classification also leads to substance and process addictions becoming a political issue involving costs, benefits, and patient care.

Imaging studies of the brains of deceased drug-addicted individuals and drug-induced research on animals support the classification of addiction as a brain disease. Brain scans reveal physical changes in areas of the brain that are

TABLE 14.2   MOTIVATIONAL STRATEGIES BASED
ON STAGES OF CHANGE

Client's Stage of Change	Appropriate Motivational Strategies for the Clinician
Precontemplation The client is not yet considering change or is unwilling or unable to change.	Establish rapport, ask permission, and build trust. Raise doubts or concerns in the client about substance-using patterns by • Exploring the meaning of events that brought the client to treatment. • Eliciting the client's perceptions of the problem. • Offering factual information about the risks of substance use. • Providing personalized feedback about assessment findings. • Exploring the pros and cons of substance abuse. • Helping a significant other intervene. Express concerns and keep the door open.
Contemplation The client acknowledges concerns and is considering the possibility of change but is ambivalent and uncertain.	Normalize ambivalence. Help the client tip the decisional balance scales toward change by • Eliciting and weighing the pros and cons of substance use and change. • Examining the client's personal values in relation to change. • Emphasizing the client's free choice, responsibility, and self-efficacy for change. Elicit self-motivational statements of intent and commitment from the client. Elicit ideas regarding the client's perceived self-efficacy and expectations regarding treatment.
Preparation The client is committed to and planning to make a change in the near future but is still considering what to do.	Clarify the client's own goals and strategies for change. Offer a menu of options for change or treatment. Negotiate a change or treatment plan and behavior contract. Consider and address barriers to change. Help the client enlist social support. Elicit from the client what has worked in the past either for him or her or for others he or she knows. Assist the client to negotiate finances, child care, work, transportation, or other potential barriers. Have the client publicly announce plans to change.
Action The client is actively taking steps to change but has not yet reached a stable state.	Engage the client in treatment and reinforce the importance of remaining in recovery. Support a realistic view of change through small steps. Acknowledge difficulties for the client in early stages of change. Help the client identify high-risk situations through a functional analysis and develop appropriate coping strategies to overcome these. Assist the client in finding new reinforcers of positive change. Help the client assess whether he or she has strong family and social support.

(Continued)

TABLE 14.2   MOTIVATIONAL STRATEGIES BASED
ON STAGES OF CHANGE (Continued)

Client's Stage of Change	Appropriate Motivational Strategies for the Clinician
Maintenance The client has achieved initial goals, such as abstinence, and is now working to maintain gains.	Help the client identify and sample drug-free sources of pleasure (i.e., new reinforcers). Affirm the client's resolve and self-efficacy. Help the client practice and use new coping strategies to avoid a return to use. Maintain supportive contact (e.g., explain to the client that you are available to talk between sessions). Develop a "fire escape" plan if the client resumes substance use. Review long-term goals with the client.
Recurrence The client has experienced a recurrence of symptoms and must now cope with the consequences and decide what to do next.	Help the client reenter the change cycle, and commend any willingness to reconsider positive change. Reframe the recurrence as a learning opportunity. Assist the client in finding alternative coping strategies. Maintain supportive contact.

Source. Adapted from *Enhancing Motivation for Change in Substance Abuse Treatment* (Treatment Improvement Protocol Series No. 35), by Center for Substance Abuse Treatment, 1999, Rockville, MD: Substance Abuse and Mental Health Services Administration. Copyright 1999 by the Substance Abuse and Mental Health Services Administration. In public domain.

critical for judgment, decision making, learning, memory, and behavior control (Petry, 2007; Thayer & Hutchison, 2013; Volkow, 2009). One such change occurs in the dopamine system, altering it so that only the substance of choice—or the excitement of a particular behavior pattern—is capable of triggering the release of dopamine and the production of pleasure (Smith, 2012).

Yet critics of the brain disease theory state that it does not explain the spontaneous recovery experienced by some drug users. Spontaneous recovery is supported by the fact that many individuals who are addicted get better without treatment (White et al., 2012) or by attending 12-step meetings. Evidence shows that individuals with traditional diseases such as cancer, heart problems, and diabetes rarely experience spontaneous recovery. Dialogue regarding spontaneous recovery will continue to prompt changes in the definition of disease as well as modifications in the treatment of individuals suffering from addictions.

RESEARCH AND EVIDENCE-BASED TREATMENT

The most widely accepted evidence-based treatment for working with process as well as substance disorders is CBT (Straussner, 2012). Additional approaches, such as motivational interviewing, motivational enhancement therapy, contingency management, dialectical behavior therapy, and family therapy, have also been cited as evidence-based treatments and are covered in this book.

In order to be considered evidence based, treatments are evaluated according to one or more models, including the evidence-based medicine model (Guyatt & Rennie, 2002) and the stage model for behavior therapy research (Onken, Blaine,

Genser, & Horton, 1997). To reach the standard of evidence-based practice, treatments such as CBT follow the stage model for behavior therapy research. The stage model includes a sequence that starts with an idea for treatment and works its way to its validation, when eventually the treatment is considered effective (McGovern & Carroll, 2003).

CBT has been extensively researched as a treatment for addictions with successful outcomes (Morgenstern, Naqvi, Debellis, & Breiter, 2013). However, CBT and other evidence-based models used to treat addictions need to undergo further research, particularly with diverse cultures. Additional studies are needed that identify under what conditions a treatment is most effective (e.g., inpatient vs. outpatient settings; confrontational vs. supportive environments; clinicians with low-, medium-, or high-level relationship skills; client's stage of addiction; and available support systems).

Applied research can perhaps demonstrate methods of changing cognitions prior to a disorder becoming an addiction, as CBT posits that cognitions play a major role in the development of disorders such as gambling and alcohol abuse (Petry, 2007). Common cognitions associated with these disorders that should be targeted include the following:

Gambling disorder cognitions
- When gambling I feel important.
- Gambling provides the excitement I need.
- I make the money, I'll spend it how I want.
- I deserve to have a good time.
- There is nothing like the rush of going to the casino and playing for a big return.

Alcohol use disorder cognitions
- I have to drink to feel good and relax.
- I feel empty without a bottle.
- I can't stop drinking, so why should I try?
- Others drink, so what's wrong with a drink now and then?
- Other people get addicted, not me. I can stop any time.
- I have more fun when I am drinking.
- I doubt if drinking will affect me.
- One has to have some vice in this life.

These examples of process and substance addictions require research that will assist clinicians in identifying the most effective methods of applying CBT under specified conditions. In addition to CBT, other evidence-based interventions requiring further applied research include motivational interviewing, motivational enhancement therapy, contingency management, dialectical behavior therapy, and family therapy.

A final recommendation is that future research needs to focus on how individuals change. If we as experts can identify how change occurs, then we can perhaps alleviate the pain and suffering of many individuals experiencing substance and process addictions. The underlying premise of this approach is a belief that it is not the drug (substance) or the activity (process) per se that is the addiction but rather the thinking and behaviors that lead to the addiction.

Following are some fundamental thoughts on how individuals change, adapted from *Why and How People Change Health Behaviors* (Leutzinger & Harris, 2005):

- Be aware of all factors related to the change you are attempting.
- Be aware of current thoughts and behaviors related to your planned change.
- Get yourself ready: Go forward with energy, a positive outlook, and confidence.
- Use goal-setting principles: Set small and large goals that can be measured.
- Follow through and be committed: Keep to a schedule and refer to your goals.
- Stay in the present and plan for the future: Observe small change and expect long-term change.
- Be prepared for setbacks: View any barrier or setback as a challenge.
- Be aware of your environment: Create a change environment with supportive friends and family and helpful resources.
- Utilize available resources: Family members, peers, coworkers, church groups, support groups, and counselors are available to assist during the change process.
- Realize that compliments from others are motivating and energizing.
- Build on and celebrate successes: Small changes create larger change; however, recognize and celebrate progress.

Suggestions such as these can be very helpful during the change process. Clients should work with well-trained professional counselors to change thinking and behavior patterns in order to have the best chance for successful treatment of substance and process addictions.

THE FUTURE

Alcohol treatment studies from the past several decades indicate that "common treatments lead to 12-month abstinence rates of about 25%" (Thayer & Hutchison, 2013, p. 543). This mediocre outcome has led to an increase in research focusing on understanding the underlying mechanisms of behavioral change and on developing interventions to increase the effectiveness of addictions treatment. As a result, there has been an upsurge in the use of cognitive neuroscience to study the effectiveness of psychotherapy (Morgenstern et al., 2013).

Although a neuropsychological approach will clearly be an area of emphasis, it is only one of several research streams concerning addictions that should be considered. White et al. (2012) pointed out that the area of addiction treatment focusing on alcohol and other drugs is shifting from long-standing pathology and intervention paradigms toward a solution-focused recovery paradigm (pp. 297–298).

TREATMENT IN CONTEXT

Applied studies that focus on the relevance and impact of the current environmental factors of individuals who are addicted are necessary. The individual needs to be considered and treated within the context of his or her living conditions (White et al., 2012). In one experiment, rats neglected food and drink, instead choosing to press levers that provided them with morphine. Some rats' self-administration resulted in fatality, exemplifying a loss of control over behavior to an addictive substance (White et al., 2012).

Stafford (2013), however, reported contradictory evidence to the rat study, citing the results of lesser known experiments conducted by Canadian psychologist Bruce Alexander at Simon Fraser University in British Columbia. Alexander built an enclosure measuring 95 ft² (8.8 m²) for a colony of rats of both sexes. This "Rat Park" was 200 times the area of standard rodent cages and had decorated walls, running wheels, and a nesting area. Inhabitants lived together and had access to a plentiful supply of food (Stafford, 2013).

The Rat Park was an enriched, nondeprived environment as opposed to an environment of isolated rats in small cages. Alexander found that rats raised alone in cages drank as much as 20 times more morphine than rats living at the Rat Park. The Rat Park inhabitants only drank more morphine if it was combined with sugar. These findings suggest that sugar allowed the rats to ignore the bitter taste of the morphine long enough to become addicted. When naloxone, which blocks the effects of morphine, was added to a morphine/sugar mix, the rats' consumption increased, suggesting that they were actively trying to avoid the effects of morphine but would tolerate it in order to taste the sugar (Stafford, 2013). The results of this study highlight the importance of examining and building on previous research findings. The vast diversity in study populations and treatment philosophies makes it clear that there is no single approach to the treatment of addictions (Straussner, 2012). In Alexander's experiment, when the rats were provided with a social environment with several available activities, drinking morphine was not as enticing as playing with friends and exploring the surroundings (Alexander, Beyerstein, & Hadaway, 1981). These findings seem to support the need for understanding the importance of the immediate environment in the plight of addicted individuals.

ADDITIONAL ISSUES

Services Provided and Training

An alarming finding is that only about one in 10 individuals who are addicted to alcohol or drugs gets treatment, and treatment often fails because it does not utilize proven methods for addressing the underlying factors of addiction, leading to relapse (Brody, 2013). A report by the National Center on Addiction and Substance Abuse at Columbia University (2012) concluded that "the vast majority of people in need of addiction treatment do not receive anything that approximates evidence-based care" (p. i), adding that "only a small fraction of individuals receive interventions or treatment consistent with scientific knowledge about what works" (p. 13).

This report also stated that most addiction treatment providers are not medical professionals and are not equipped with the knowledge, skills, or credentials needed to provide the full range of evidence-based services, including medication and counseling (Brody, 2013). Trends in addiction treatment indicate that "a growing harm reduction ideology is becoming evident, as is a shift to what is termed the 'recovery movement,' and greater use of evidence-based practices" (Straussner,

2012, p. 128). Along with needing to learn and apply evidence-based practices, counselors should understand the facets of process addictions. Wilson and Johnson (2013) raised a concern about whether counselors and other clinicians are being trained in recognizing, diagnosing, and treating process addictions. Training programs should address these issues by emphasizing the use of evidence-based interventions with both process and substance addictions. A focus on training clinicians in applying these practices using effective relationship-building skills that motivate and empower clients should also be emphasized.

Emphasis should also be placed on counseling as a necessary part of the treatment of addictions. It is widely recognized that the combination of medication and counseling has the best chance of successfully treating individuals with addictions (Straussner, 2012). Consequently, counseling modalities such as CBT should be a mainstay of training. Additional evidence-based modalities, such as motivational interviewing, contingency management, dialectical behavior therapy, and family therapy, should be included in clinician training programs. Internships should emphasize mastery of skills in the application of evidence-based practices.

The Patient Protection and Affordable Care Act:

Implementation of the Patient Protection and Affordable Care Act (2010) will impact funding for the treatment of addictions, particularly substance use disorders. The number of individuals insured will increase, as will the number of those covered by Medicaid (NCADD New Jersey, n.d.). The potential for a doubling of beneficiaries who have behavioral health disorders and addiction exists. Yet substance abuse services may only represent about 2% of the overall health care system (Enos, 2011). Some researchers predict that the increase in federal Medicaid dollars (in 2014) will lower the burden on states and localities. Medicaid will begin covering more people, including childless adults, at or below 133% of the federal poverty level (NCADD New Jersey, n.d.). Clinicians treating addictions may need to assume a greater role in helping their clients become eligible for Medicaid. Yet it has been estimated that 10% to 25% of individuals with substance use disorders will remain uninsured, even after mandates associated with the health reform law take effect.

CONCLUSIONS

This chapter has synthesized much of the material presented earlier in this book, focusing on the commonalities of addictions, etiology, assessment strategies, and viable treatments. Although there are some specific interventions for particular disorders, there are also core treatment models, such as the biopsychosocial or medical model, the recovery or disease model, CBT, and the transtheoretical stages of change model. Motivational interviewing is used early in treatment, whereas relapse prevention is common at the close of the treatment. Integrative treatment combines the aforementioned general strategies with specific interventions. Research findings will strengthen the foundation supporting evidence-based treatment. The future of treating addictions will include medical advances, the use of psychotropic medications, and the use of innovative approaches such as mindfulness and yoga. Addictions and mental health professionals will also need to continue the dialogue regarding what constitutes an addiction, and further training will be necessary if the field is to prepare the next generation of clinicians to effectively work with substance and process addictions.

REFERENCES

Alexander, B. K., Beyerstein, B. L., & Hadaway, P. F. (1981). Effect of early and later colony housing on oral ingestion of morphine in rats. *Pharmacology, Biochemistry, Behavior, 15*, 571–576.

American Psychiatric Association. (2013). *Diagnostic and statistical manual of mental disorders* (5th ed.). Arlington, VA: Author.

Brody, J. E. (2013). *Effective addiction treatment. The New York Times.* Retrieved from http://well.blogs.nytimes.com/2013/02/04/effective-addiction-treatment/?_r=0

Carkhuff, R. R. (1969a). *Helping and human relations: A primer for lay and professional helpers. Vol. I. Selection and training.* New York, NY: Holt, Rinehart & Wilson.

Carkhuff, R. R. (1969b). *Helping and human relations: A primer for lay and professional helpers. Vol. II. Practice and research.* New York, NY: Holt, Rinehart & Wilson.

Center for Substance Abuse Treatment. (1999). *Enhancing motivation for change in substance abuse treatment* (Treatment Improvement Protocol Series No. 35). Rockville, MD: Substance Abuse and Mental Health Services Administration.

Enos, G. (2011). *Future of addiction treatment: New patients, new funders, new partners.* Retrieved from http://www.addictionpro.com/article/future-addiction-treatment-new-patients-new-funders-new-partners

Guyatt, G., & Rennie, D. (Eds.). (2002). *Users' guides to the medical literature: A manual for evidence-based clinical practice.* Chicago, IL: American Medical Association.

Hubble, M. A., Duncan, B. L., & Miller, S. D. (Eds.). (1999). *The heart and soul of change.* Washington, DC: American Psychological Association.

Humphreys, K., & Tucker, J. A. (2002). Toward more responsive and effective intervention systems for alcohol-related problems. *Addiction, 97*, 126–132. doi:10.1046/j.1360-0443.2002.00004.x

Lam, R. (2010). *Top 10 cases of extreme game addiction.* Retrieved from http://listverse.com/2010/11/07/top-10-cases-of-extreme-game-addiction/

Lambert, M. J., & Bergin, A. E. (1986). The effectiveness of psychotherapy. In A. E. Bergin & S. L. Garfield (Eds.), *Handbook of psychotherapy and behavior change* (3rd ed., pp. 157–211). New York, NY: Wiley.

Leutzinger, J., & Harris, J. (2005). *Why and how people change health behaviors.* Omaha, NE: Health Improvement Solutions.

Lutz, W., Martinovich, Z., Lyons, J. S., Leon, S. C., & Stiles, W. B. (2007). Therapist effects in outpatient psychotherapy: A three-level growth curve approach. *Journal of Counseling Psychology, 54*, 32–39.

McGovern, M. P., & Carroll, K. M. (2003). Evidence-based practices for substance use disorders. *Psychiatric Clinics of North America, 26*, 991–1010.

Melis, M., Spiga, S., & Diana, M. (2005). The dopamine hypothesis of drug addiction: Hypodopaminergic state. *International Review of Neurobiology, 63*, 101–154.

Miller, W. R., Forcehimes, A. A., & Zweben, A. (2011). *Treating addiction: A guide for professionals.* New York, NY: Guilford Press.

Miller, W. R., & Rollnick, S. (2012). *Motivational interviewing: Preparing people for change.* New York, NY: Guilford Press.

Moos, R. (2002). The mystery of human context and coping: An unraveling of clues. *American Journal of Community Psychology, 30*, 67–88.

Moos, R. H. (2003). Addictive disorders in context: Principles and puzzles of effective treatment and recovery. *Psychology of Addictive Disorders, 17*, 3–12.

Morgenstern, J., Naqvi, N. H., Debellis, R., & Breiter, H. C. (2013). The contributions of cognitive neuroscience and neuroimaging to understanding mechanisms of behavior change in addiction. *Psychology of Addictive Behaviors, 27,* 336–350. doi:10.1037/a0032435

Najavits, L. M. (2002). *Seeking safety: A treatment manual for PTSD and substance abuse.* New York, NY: Guilford Press.

National Center on Addiction and Substance Abuse at Columbia University. (2012). *Addiction medicine: Closing the gap between science and practice.* Retrieved from http://www.casacolumbia.org/upload/2012/20120626addictionmed.pdf

NCADD New Jersey. (n.d.). *The future of addiction care in NJ.* Retrieved from http://ncaddnj.org/page/The-Future-Of-Addiction-care-In-NJ.aspx

Norcross, J. C., & Wampold, B. E. (2011). Evidence-based therapy relationships: Research conclusions and clinical practices. *Psychotherapy, 48,* 98–102. doi:10.1037/a0022161

Onken, L. S., Blaine, J. D., Genser, S., & Horton, A. M. (Eds.). (1997). *Treatment of drug-dependent individuals with comorbid mental disorders* (NIDA Research Monograph No. 172). Rockville, MD: National Institute on Drug Abuse.

Patient Protection and Affordable Care Act, Pub. L. No. 111-148 & Pub. L. No. 111-152, 111th Congress, 2nd Session (2010).

Petry, N. M. (2007). Gambling and substance use disorders: Current status and future directions. *American Journal on Addictions, 16,* 1–9. doi:10.1080/1055490601077668

Prochaska, J. O., DiClemente, C. C., & Norcross, J. C. (1992). In search of how people change: Applications to addictive behaviors. *American Psychologist, 47,* 1102–1114.

Rogers, C. R. (1957). The necessary and sufficient conditions of therapeutic personality change. *Journal of Consulting Psychology, 21,* 95–103.

Smith, D. E. (2012). Editor's note: The process addictions and the new ASAM definition of addiction. *Journal of Psychoactive Drugs, 44,* 1–4. doi:10.1080/02791072.2012.662105

Stafford, T. (2013). *Drug addiction: The complex truth.* Retrieved from http://www.bbc.com/future/story/20130910-drug-addiction-the-complex-truth/2

Straussner, S. L. A. (2012). Clinical treatment of substance abusers: Past, present and future. *Clinical Social Work Journal, 40,* 127–133. doi:10.1007/s10615-012-0387-0

Thayer, R. E., & Hutchison, K. E. (2013). Neuroimaging in clinical studies of craving: Importance of reward and control networks. *Psychology of Addictive Behaviors, 27,* 543–546. doi:10.1037/a0030275

Volkow, N. D. (2009). *Suiting treatment to the nature of the disease.* Retrieved from http://www.drugabuse.gov/news-events/nida-notes/2009/10/suiting-treatment-to-nature-disease

White, W. L., Kelly, J. F., & Roth, J. D. (2012). New addiction-recovery support institutions: Mobilizing support beyond professional treatment and recovery mutual aid. *Journal of Groups in Addiction & Recovery, 7,* 297–317. doi:10.1080/1556035X.2012.705719

Wilson, A. D., & Johnson, P. (2013). Counselors understanding of process addictions: A blind spot in the counseling field. *The Professional Counselor, 3,* 16–22. Retrieved from http://tpcjournal.nbcc.org/counselors-understanding-of-process-addiction-a-blind-spot-in-the-counseling-field/

INDEX

Exhibits, figures, and tables are indicated by "e," "f," and "t" respectively.

(Continued)

(Continued)

D

O

Q

R